TARK

Also by Terry Pluto

48 Minutes: A Night in the Life of the NBA with Bob Ryan

A Baseball Winter: The Off-Season Life of the Summer Game
 with Jeff Neuman

Weaver on Strategy with Earl Weaver

Sixty-One: The Story of the 1961 Yankees with Tony Kubek

You Can Argue but You'd Be Wrong with Pete Franklin

TARK

College Basketball's Winningest Coach

by Jerry Tarkanian and Terry Pluto

McGraw-Hill Publishing Company
New York   St. Louis   San Francisco   Bogotá   Hamburg
Madrid   Mexico   Milan   Montreal   Panama
Paris   São Paulo   Tokyo   Toronto

1 2 3 4 5 6 7 8 9 DOC DOC 8 9 2 1 0 9 8

ISBN 0-07-062802-5

Library of Congress Cataloging-in-Publication Data

Tarkanian, Jerry, 1930–
    TARK : college basketball's winningest coach.

    1. Tarkanian, Jerry, 1930–   . 2. Basketball—
United States—Coaches—Biography. 3. University of
Nevada, Las Vegas—Basketball. I. Pluto, Terry,
1955–   . II. Title.
GV884.T37A3   1988   796.32'3'0924 [B]   88-23041
ISBN 0-07-062802-5

Book design by Sheree Goodman

For all the players, coaches, friends, and
family who have contributed to my career
—Jerry Tarkanian

For my father, Tom Pluto
—Terry Pluto

ACKNOWLEDGMENTS

The authors would like to thank the following people for their help in this project: Sidney Green, Reggie Theus, Lynn Archibald, Dale Brown, Eddie Sutton, Kevin Mackey, Al Menendez, Pete Newell, Mark Warkentien, Tim Grgurich, Abe Lemons, Gene Keady, Dick Versace, Jim Valvano, Bud Presley, Ralph Readout, Dr. Jerry L. Crawford, Dr. Ann Mayo, Dr. Richard Lapchick, Chris Karamanous, Irwin Molasky, Winston Karim, Jackie Robinson, Sam Robinson, Gary Wright, Glenn McDonald, Bob Rule, Loel Schader, Pat McCubbin, Roberta Pluto, Faith Hornby and McGraw-Hill's Tom Miller.

Contents

vii

1

First Person: Introduction

All I've ever wanted to do was coach basketball. I'm still like a kid when it comes to the game. It's in my brain and in my blood and is with me every minute of every day.

The sport has filled my entire life. I love the kids I work with, and my association with them has been the highlight of my career. I find most of their families extraordinary. Outside of my own family, one of the things I enjoy most is going over X's and O's with coaching friends, picking each other's brains, rehashing old stories, laughing at new jokes.

I thank God each day that I'm in a profession that I enjoy so much, and that is so fulfilling for me.

The job stays with me twenty-four hours a day. When I go to sleep at night, I'm thinking, "I could or should have done this in practice." It's the first thing I think about in the morning, and it's total misery awakening the morning after we've lost a game. Before my mind even clears, I feel something like a kick in the stomach, and then, as I focus my thoughts, I remember we lost the night before and I torture myself by thinking of what I should have done differently.

I'm never away from it, day or night. Other coaches go through the same ordeal, but we're doing something we love; and putting in all those hours and living with it night and day takes nothing away from our enjoyment of it.

Besides my family, basketball is nearly all I think or talk about. I don't have any hobbies. I don't play golf; I don't play tennis. We live

1

only thirty minutes from Lake Mead, which is a great fishing and boating spot. I've been there three times in fifteen years. I've tried to go boating. Everyone kept telling me how much fun I would have and said that I was missing a lot by not going out in a boat. So I went out with some of our boosters and I was in the middle of the lake and I was thinking, "I don't get it. What's fun about this?"

I admit that I'd rather watch a basketball game than do about anything else. I'm invited to dozens of golf tournaments each year and I go because they want me there and the tournaments are for good causes, but I don't play. I just ride around in a golf cart thinking basketball. When I go to the beach, I end up sitting in the sand, drawing X's and O's. When I go to the movies, I can't follow the plot or keep the characters straight. I don't know who is who or what's going on because I'm not concentrating on the movie; I'm thinking about my team. My mind keeps wandering, so I have to lean over and ask Lois, my wife, what's happening. Then she gets mad at me, and says I'm ruining the movie for her because while she's explaining to me, something else is happening. Now she'll only go to the movies with me once a year, on Christmas Eve, when the entire family goes together.

As for other hobbies, such as yard work—forget it. I hate yard work. Lois likes to mess around outside, planting flowers and everything. I don't get it and I don't like anything about it. When we were a young married couple, she was always after me to mow the lawn. We probably had more arguments about yard work during our early married life than about anything else.

So when I started working at basketball clinics and getting paid for speaking engagements, I took the money I made from that and gave it to her so she could hire someone to mow the lawn and do whatever else was needed. I told her that she could assume that every Saturday when I'm sitting around the house watching games, I'm really cutting the grass and pulling weeds because I'm the guy paying to have it done.

I always knew that some day I would coach. When I was a player at Fresno State, I took notes on all our opposing teams and I spent hour after hour just following coaches around to listen to them and watch them and learn from them.

But there was a time early in my career when I had serious doubts that I could ever be a good coach. I was still in college and dating Lois.

I remember telling her, "They must be right. They all say the same thing about coaching, but I can't coach the way they tell you to."

At first she didn't know what I was talking about. "Of course you can coach," she said. "Who are 'they'?"

2

I explained to her that "they" were the professors I had in coaching theory classes. According to all the coaching courses and textbooks of the 1950s, if I went into coaching, I would just be asking for trouble. They all believed and taught that coaches were supposed to keep a distance from their players. They were not to become close. The coach was the general; the players were the troops.

The professors and textbooks took the human element out of the game. They kept telling us to stay away from the players on a personal basis. "If you spend too much time with the kids, they won't respect you. If they don't respect you, they won't listen to you. If you become their friend, they'll take advantage of that friendship. They'll run all over you, and you won't be able to have a good player-coach relationship." Keep your distance was what they preached.

I felt deep within me that a good coach should be involved in the lives of his players. A good coach should do more than teach players a zone defense or how to shoot a jumper. He has kids over to his house for Sunday dinner, or they just hang around his office, talking about life and school and girlfriends. If a kid has a personal problem, it's the coach's problem. At least that's how I thought it should be. I knew that if I ever became a coach, that's how it would be between me and my players.

Those thoughts from professors and books about a "general and his troops" and "distancing" from players seem so out of date now. But I remember that day very clearly, talking with Lois. It was my whole life, and how could I, not even a college graduate, be right and all those other, more knowledgeable individuals be wrong?

Since then, I've learned that there is no one way of coaching that can be used by everyone. It depends on the individual. Each coach has to choose what to do or what not to do.

The biggest mistake coaches make, I feel, is in trying to emulate someone else, in trying to be something they are not just because they heard it at a clinic or read it in a book. A coach must be his own person in determining how he's going to react. Some coaches work best through motivation, some through intricate strategies, and some through fear. There are various ways to go. Not every coach can use the same methods as a Bobby Knight, a Gene Keady, a Jim Valvano, or any other coach. Every coach should do it the way that best fits his own personality, the way he feels most comfortable.

Even if we have more talent, I go into games thinking the other team is better and I'm scared we're going to lose. But I never talk to the players about winning and losing. Before a game I'll go over what the other team likes to do. If the other team is not very good, I'll talk them up so that our kids will play hard. If the other team is better than we are, I'll pump up our confidence so our players can believe that we can beat them.

But I don't talk about winning and losing. I talk about effort. I talk about playing hard and I talk about loyalty. At the beginning of a season we never set any goals as to the number of wins we want or how far our team will go. Instead, we talk about preparing ourselves physically, mentally, and emotionally to play the best we are capable of playing. That is the only thing I ask of the players.

We also talk about pride in ourselves, in our family, in our team, in the university and community. If our players do everything they can, physically, emotionally, and mentally, and they go out and are not successful in winning a game, then they really didn't lose anything. They can still have a feeling of pride. If they lose because they are not prepared, because they took shortcuts, then they not only lost a game, they also lost their pride. They didn't do everything within their power to do what was needed.

I'm not underestimating the value of winning. I want to win as much as any coach in the country. I'd rather be coaching at a small high school and winning, than coaching on the college level and getting hammered on the court every week. When I lose, I feel as if I'm dying. But what I'm emphasizing is that by doing your best—mentally, physically, and emotionally—each game, you can always have pride in yourself, and you will always win far more than you lose, because there are many other teams not willing to make the sacrifices you're making.

We prepare our players to work hard for a full forty minutes, to have constant intensity and complete concentration for the entire game. We know that if they do that, most other teams will crack at some point because they have not made the sacrifices that enable them to go that hard for that long.

From the same standpoint, the basis of a team's being successful is that each person on the team is willing to sacrifice his personal goals for team goals. That is a lot easier to say than to do. Everyone has inner selfish desires. We talk with our kids and try to get them to turn this around—to be unselfish, to be willing to make inner sacrifices. This is our basic approach to the game.

I believe the key to a relationship between a coach and players is loyalty. I know that kids will mess up at times. I know that on occasion they will do stupid things. When I was a kid, I messed up sometimes and I didn't always make the wisest decisions. But if a kid is loyal to me and to his teammates and to the program and the school, he'll always get a second chance and a third and fourth. I'd rather

4

take a kid who was a thief than a kid who is disloyal. You can teach a kid not to steal, show him why he was wrong, but it's difficult to develop loyalty in someone who has never shown it before. I always feel that if he is a loyal person, he will eventually straighten out. I never run off a kid who is playing poorly or has been injured. If I gave him a four-year scholarship commitment, I'll stick by him even if he can't help us on the court. Loyalty is really a two-way street. Lots of people demand loyalty but are not willing to give it back.

That's one reason why I don't believe in offering players cash or a car to recruit them. I am convinced that you can't buy loyalty.

Until recently, we haven't been able to recruit to UNLV the kind of blue-chip high school players who go to schools such as Kentucky, North Carolina, and Louisville. We've had only four McDonald's high school All-Americans during the fifteen years I've been at Las Vegas.

People may laugh when I say that some of our kids weren't even all-neighborhood or that this kid didn't even start for his high school team, but it's true. If you look at our 1987 Final Four team, the only highly recruited high school player was Freddie Banks, and we were able to sign Freddie because he grew up in Las Vegas.

Armon Gilliam developed into a great player and was the second pick in the 1987 National Basketball Association draft, but Armon said that he didn't play organized basketball until he was a high school junior, and he jokes that five white kids played in front of him. In Pittsburgh, Armon's hometown, the Dapper Dan Tournament is held at the end of each season. All-star high school players are brought from throughout the United States to play Pennsylvania's all-stars. The Dapper Dan committee likes to have Pittsburgh kids in the game for local interest. Not only was Armon not selected for that game, he wasn't even picked for the preliminary game which features top Pennsylvania county players against top Pittsburgh city players. Sonny Vaccaro, the developer of the tournament, says that one of the greatest sports miracles of all time was that a Pittsburgh kid not even picked as a substitute for any of the games was eventually selected number two in the pro draft. Armon, he says, was one of the few players who didn't make any of those teams but went on to play college ball, let alone lead his team to the Final Four.

Gerald Paddio was a good, but not an elite, junior college player. Mark Wade and Jarvis Basnight were also junior college transfers. Wade, who eventually broke the NCAA assist record, went to Oklahoma before coming to the University of Nevada at Las Vegas, and played so little at Oklahoma that he left. Basnight did not even make all conference in junior college, and his team finished last in its league.

5

Our 1983 team, which was ranked number one in the country for two weeks, had only one consensus high school All-American—Sidney Green. He was the only member of the team to make the NBA. As for the other players, the roster looked like this:

- Eric Booker was a transfer from the University of San Francisco, where he was better known as a tennis player.

- Paul Brozovich was a transfer from Pittsburgh, where he played for my assistant coach, Tim Grgurich. After Tim left Pittsburgh, the new Pitt coach didn't want Brozovich. He did not renew Paul's scholarship, so Paul transferred to UNLV.

- Jeff Collins ran into the same problem at Arizona. A new coach came in and said that he didn't want Jeff, so Jeff transferred to UNLV.

- Larry Anderson was a big scorer for us. He was recognized as a good high school player but was not recruited heavily by many colleges. The school we beat out to sign Larry was North Carolina-Charlotte.

- My son, Danny, was the point guard.

- Eldridge Hudson had been a very talented player, but was returning after severe knee surgery.

I was particularly proud of the 1983 team. It was probably the most efficient group our school ever had. It set the school field-goal percentage record even though we were not a great shooting team, and it averaged only 11 turnovers a game. This team suffered our most heartbreaking loss ever in a tournament game against North Carolina State in 1983, the year N.C. State went on to win the NCAA championship. The game was won by a last-second tip-in by Thurl Bai. Many times, in public and private, N.C. State coach Jimmy Valvano has stated that he, his staff, and his players all regarded UNLV as the toughest team they played that year.

That 1983 team was picked to finish third in our conference. Their record was 28–3, and they beat a lot of teams with more talent. To my knowledge, they may be the only team ever to go from being entirely left off of every preseason poll to eventually being number one for part of the season. Our kids won because they were hungry, because

6

they knew how to play hard, and because they weren't spoiled. That team typified what every coach wants. They had a great work ethic and great character, were unselfish, and loved each other. We had an excellent point guard, a shooting wing guard, one superstar, and a group of role players. Everyone accepted his role and worked hard at it. This was the type of team that you knew played to its full potential. The players gave everything they had and reached tremendous levels. It was a team of overachievers and I don't know of anything more satisfying for a coach than feeling his team has reached its highest level.

The good teams we've had at UNLV have all had this in common: they are loyal, they play hard, and they get a kick out of proving their critics wrong. Most of my players didn't have to worry about illegal offers because they weren't in a position to get any. One of my favorite lines is that I like transfers because their cars and clothes are already paid for. It usually gets a laugh, but there's truth in it. And what also is true is that they come to UNLV because they want to. For some, it's their last chance at college ball.

The differences I've had with the NCAA usually came from the extra benefit rule, which can be made to sound terrible but really means that a player can't receive anything that doesn't also go to any other student. The way the rule is written, it makes it extremely difficult for a coach to have a really solid helping relationship with a kid except on the basketball court. Yet I feel a coach should be able to develop a close, special relationship with his players just as any other good college instructor is able to have with any of his students.

Suppose a student shows up at his music professor's home and the kid is upset because he just got a message that his father is seriously ill and he needs to get home right away. And suppose the kid is poor and doesn't have enough money for a plane ticket. The professor sits the kid down and the professor's wife gives the kid something to eat. The wife then hands the kid a phone and tells him to call his mother at the hospital. The professor agrees, even though he knows it's long-distance. Then the professor tells the kid to make plans to go back home and he'll cover the ticket or loan the money.

What would you think of this professor?

I'd like him to educate my kid, that's what. Many professors do things like that for students and we never hear about it.

According to the NCAA rules, I couldn't take care of one of my basketball players the same way. I couldn't even let him make that long-distance call. That's because the player supposedly would be getting an "extra benefit" not available to other students.

7

The music professor is supposed to teach his kids more than how to play the violin. If a student has a personal problem and asks the professor to help, the professor is free to step in and do what he can.

A basketball coach should be able to do more than teach defense and offense. Every college kid has personal problems, and basketball players are no exception. Most are black. A number have only one parent in the home, and few of these kids have any money. I have to laugh when I hear some people talk about not needing to provide transportation money for an athlete returning to school each year because the athlete had all summer to work and save for the day he needs to purchase the ticket back to college. That athlete may work all summer, but the hands in his pocket are many and usually belong to members of his family who need financial help fast—for food on the table, to pay for a baby, or rent, or a broken car, or similar urgent needs. Soon after each summer payday, that money is gone.

A big reason I got into coaching was to work with kids. I love the game, but I also like having the kids around my office, and my wife likes working with them on their studies. That's also why I make a point of spending so much time with my players—I just like them. Sure, they cause me grief and pain at times. But often, particularly years later, the results of your efforts are like gold at your feet.

If that kid whose father was ill had shown up at your door, what would you have done? The same thing any of us would and should do—show him the telephone. If you do otherwise, it takes the human decency out of coaching. I'm not talking about buying a kid fancy clothes or giving him large sums of money. But suppose a player's car breaks down and he needs to go someplace and you give him that ride. That could be a violation. And if so, when it came out in the media, it would come out as giving "extra benefits" to players.

I've heard some critics say, "Well, he wouldn't do it for the kid if he couldn't dunk or shoot baskets," but that's not true, you see, and no one ever bothered to find out if it were true. If they did, they'd find dozens of kids and adults that we've helped in similar ways over the years who've never played a single day of organized basketball.

My wife once worked with several of our players who were taking a course in English literature. They watched plays by Shakespeare, Chekhov, Shaw, and others. She wanted to have the players come to our house right after practice and have dinner together while she reviewed with them background information on the play to be seen that evening. Lois thought that would help them focus on the main points of each play.

She called Bill Hunt of the NCAA enforcement division and was told that if she served them food more than three or four times a year it would be a violation of the NCAA code. Since the plays were to be shown over several weeks, that gave her the choice of not giving the players the extra help they needed, expecting them to come over right after practice with little chance to eat, or breaking an NCAA regulation.

It is legal for a coach to have a kid come over to his house for tutoring, but if the coach's wife offers that kid a free sandwich and some milk, the extra benefits rule could be invoked. The athletic director at Nevada-Reno told me that he wanted to invite his daughter's boyfriend to Christmas dinner. The boyfriend also was a football player at Reno. The NCAA said that if he fed the player, he had to bill the kid for the meal. I'm not joking.

I'm not saying the NCAA is a bad organization. It is involved in many worthwhile activities. I feel we need such a ruling body for intercollegiate sports. I believe that those in charge, however, should be realistic and humanitarian and that how the enforcement staff operates should be reevaluated. If a coach recruits a kid from out of town, he should be allowed to let that kid occasionally use his telephone to call home. If the kid is homesick, the coach should be able to have that kid over for dinner. When the kid's parents come to town to see their son play, why shouldn't the coach be allowed to take the parents to dinner? If the kid has some brothers and sisters, why not let the coach give him some college T-shirts for his family? What harm does that do? It makes the kid and his family feel that the university cares about their son, and what kid has ever been bought by a T-shirt? I just don't see how that can be called cheating.

So many of the kids in college basketball are from economically deprived backgrounds. A coach has to assume the role of watching out for the kid's personal welfare. When a kid has a problem, he should know that the coach is the guy he needs to see. The coach shouldn't give the kid large sums of money, but he should say, "This is my kid, and I'm gonna get involved and help out."

Louisiana State University coach Dale Brown says we should look at what college basketball has done financially for the NCAA itself, for many universities, and for the lifestyle of coaches. Then look at the players, the individuals who are the ones who bring in the money. Often you are prevented from treating them with dignity. Sometimes, a college athlete has fewer rights than other students.

Coaches should be obligated to take visiting parents home for dinner. It should be part of their job instead of a violation. When they

9

come to see their son play in front of thousands of people, the coach should be able to help them get a room or provide a meal. It hurts me at our senior game activities when I see some families couldn't make it because of the expenses involved. I think we forget sometimes how difficult it is for many families to afford the money to travel to see their sons play and then also pay hotel and meal expenses. Let these families share in the pride developed by the athletic program and their kids.

If you are going to drive that player hard on the basketball court, make him sweat every day in practice and face the pressure that comes when you play Division I competition, you should also be receptive to that kid's needs.

I never said I was a rebel or a reformer. My goal in life was not to take the NCAA to court or to be labeled controversial, a maverick, or whatever. When I was a young coach, I was all for the police, the government, apple pie, the flag, and John Wayne. If I saw someone get arrested on the television news, I figured he should be sent right to jail, skip the trial. The guy had to be guilty or he wouldn't have been arrested.

Now, I've changed. I've learned life is not as simple as that. There are no clear-cut good guys or bad guys. Everything is far more complex. I can see now what happened during my interactions with the NCAA. I may not feel some of the things were fair, but I can see how they happened. A few times all the hurt will boil up in me and burst out, but most of the time I can look at it as a part of learning about life.

The NCAA scares just about every coach to death because coaches know that the NCAA can find a violation on every campus thanks to the extra benefit rule. We're all vulnerable, because any humanitarian act can be called a violation. It may not be something a coach did for a kid. It could be a former player, a booster, or almost anyone, because almost anyone can be called a "representative of the athletic department's interest." We were told during the UNLV investigation that if any individual tells a kid that he thinks UNLV is the best school for that kid to attend, at that moment that individual could be labeled a "representative" of a school's athletic interests.

When it comes to the extra benefit rule, a coach's guilt or innocence depends on how the NCAA chooses to interpret it. They may choose to interpret broadly for one school and very restrictively for another. For example, during the UNLV hearing, a question came up about something done for athletes. The school presented written information showing that the privilege was available for other students. Bill Hunt of the NCAA stated the privilege was an extra benefit because the form stated "other," not "all other," students. We looked up the word "other" in the dictionary and found one of its meanings is "*all* the rest," but that did not matter.

Almost all our UNLV players come from solid backgrounds with good parents. They are kids like Armon Gilliam, whose father is a minister, or Gary Graham and his closely knit family, or Freddie Banks, a local kid whose family is one of the closest I've ever known. Paul Brozovich's mother worked hard to help him with school needs and lived long enough with cancer to see her son graduate. I could go on and on. Most of our players and their parents aren't rich, but they are wonderful people with great character, the kind of people you want to have in any program. They deserve recognition for the positive manner in which they live their lives.

Once in a while we have taken kids that some other colleges would not. For a long time, I was one of the few coaches taking junior college players, and we were ripped for that. But it seems that junior college players are considered legitimate now that Bobby Knight signed Keith Smart and Dean Garrett and won a national championship with them at Indiana.

The vast majority of our players, even the ones with tough backgrounds, have done extremely well for us. Occasionally, a kid doesn't work out and that's often the only thing you'll hear about.

I think you can have a player who has had some problems, put him in the right setting, surround him with solid people, and he'll respond. That's what we do at UNLV, and our success rate has been tremendous. It isn't just what we've done for the kids, but more what they have done for themselves when they are placed in the right environment and given the chance.

It also says a lot about how our players have helped each other. But you have to do a lot of one-on-one work and show a lot of understanding with this type of student. It comes down to communication and trust. To me that's fine. I love that part of coaching.

I don't understand the kind of coach who expects every student athlete to be perfect and then, the first time a player steps out of line, jumps all over him and holds that incident against the kid. That same coach may have gone out and raised some hell as a kid or even as an adult. That's all right with me. I don't mind raising a little hell either, but you should judge your players the way you'd like to be judged. I can understand jumping on the kid, and I agree you have to discipline

11

him, but I also feel the coach needs to be forgiving and understanding, because what the player did may be similar to something the coach himself did when he was a kid.

I also know that these young men need attention and when they get it, they usually straighten out. That's the human side of basketball, and that was the case with me. As a kid, I always knew where to find the next party. My father died when I was 11, and my mother was left with three children to raise. I remember many nights I came home late and she chased me with a broom.

At Fresno State I lived with eight guys and we've all turned out to be pretty successful, but all through college we were involved in numerous activities considered pretty rowdy at the time. If we had been caught doing some of that stuff and someone said, "Hey, those guys have no business being in college," then none of us would have made it.

I just know my own background has caused me to be nonjudgmental when it comes to students with problems. And that's why, if he can meet the rules of university enrollment, I will always give any kid a chance.

Maybe that's the reason I take certain players. It took me six years to get through college, and I never would have made it if my mother hadn't been patient with me. She could have said, "Hey, you've been in school for four years already. Get out of the house and get a job." Instead she stuck with me. So I remember how I was when I was young, and when I see my players pulling some similar stunts, I remind myself of those days and try to give the kids room to mature. To me that's a significant part of what coaching is about.

2

Early Life

Jerry Tarkanian was just like some of his players when he came out of
high school. He didn't have a clear focus on what he wanted to do
with his life. He wanted to go to college. He talked about getting a
degree, a good job, a bank account, and a nice car. He wanted the
American Dream. But he didn't really understand what it took to get
it.

While the discipline for sports was always there, he was not motivated to put the same amount of time and effort into other aspects of
his life. He'd cut classes to go to a game or a party. He enjoyed fool-
ing around with his pals far too much to be a serious student.

One afternoon, he and his buddies decided they would go see close
friend Lee Walls play baseball. Walls, 19, was in the major leagues.
He had just been sent by Pittsburgh to a farm team in Waco, Texas.
His Pasadena buddies thought it would cheer him up if they came to
watch him play. The distance didn't matter. They dropped everything
else and within four hours were on their way. When they got to Am-
arillo, however, they found that Lee had been recalled by Pittsburgh.
What the heck, they decided, we're already in Texas, why not go on
to Pittsburgh? They spent ten days traveling and two with Lee, who
was totally shocked to see them at the stadium. "It was one of the
best times in my life," says Tarkanian. "We slept in parks, saw a lot
of the country and had a great time just being with each other. Going
out to see Lee was no big deal. We were a close group, and he was

our friend. To this day several of us who hung around together still meet once each year in Pasadena.''

That same group at one time was the scourge of the beaches. They caused havoc with guys wearing white buck shoes, a sign of the well-dressed man of the times. Jerry and his friends, most of whom couldn't afford much more than tennis shoes, would toss all the white bucks they could find into the bonfires. A guy would take off his shoes to walk in the sand with his date and come back to find scorched leather. There were fights and scrambles and pretty girls, all of which made each summer a memorable event.

Some of Jerry's buddies weren't exactly the kind who went on to Harvard or Stanford. Instead of counting on a spot in dear old dad's law firm, the only place at the bar waiting for them was a stool at Jimmy's Playroom in Pasadena. Tarkanian knew that the rich were indeed different from him and his friends. The rich had expectations and certainties; Jerry and his buddies had big dreams and little understanding of how to make them a reality.

Tarkanian: ''No one in my family had graduated from college. And most of the guys who knew me in Pasadena never believed that I'd make it through college. When I left for Fresno State, they laughed and told me they'd give 2,000-to-1 odds that I'd never make it through.

''That's why I know exactly what a kid means when he says he really wants to get a degree, even though anybody can see that the kid doesn't even know where to begin. In the abstract, a degree sounds great. It did to me, and I know it did to my mom. She probably didn't understand either what it took or that I'd fooled around so much that a solid foundation wasn't there for college. She just wanted the best for me. She wanted me to graduate and have that diploma to hang on the wall.''

Tarkanian's family was greatly influenced by its Armenian roots. Much of what Tarkanian has done—and much of his world view—was shaped by his Armenian relatives. That's why to understand Jerry Tarkanian is to understand Armenians.

For centuries they have suffered persecution and discrimination. Recognized as the first country to accept Christianity, the nation often was attacked and occupied by outsiders. In 1894, the Turks began a campaign to wipe out the Armenians. By 1918, they had slaughtered almost two million. Many of the survivors emigrated to America, clinging to their language, customs, and each other. A people with great pride in their culture, they have fought tenaciously for almost seventy

14

years within national and international courts and congresses to expose the magnitude of the slayings and to have the Turkish government formally admit responsibility for the first genocide attempt of the twentieth century.

If you were to draw a comparison of cultures, Armenians are similar to Jews. They both have deep, rich historical roots and an ability to survive. To adapt to the adverse conditions of their life, Armenians have developed certain cultural characteristics: perseverance, strong family ties, firm religious beliefs, and almost fanatical loyalty.

All of these characteristics are found in Tarkanian.

Often when you see him coaching on television or see his picture in the paper, your immediate response is, "There is one very sad man. He looks as if his best friend just died."

If you were to wander through Tarkanian's home in Las Vegas and examine the pictures on the walls, you'd see that same expression in the faces of his relatives. Most Armenians still are scarred by the Turkish massacre. Tarkanian's relatives were among the victims. Memories of those who died were kept alive by those who survived. Jerry's mother barely escaped, and she often vividly described to her son what had happened.

Jerry's maternal grandfather was Mickael Effendi Tarkhanian, a respected government official in Malatya, Armenia. His high office is noted in the title "Effendi." He had two sons and four daughters, one of whom, Haigouhie (Rose), would eventually become Jerry's mother. The oldest son, Mehran, studied medicine at an Armenian university. From the pictures they've seen of Mehran, Jerry and Lois believe their son Danny resembles him.

In Armenian families, there is a special bond between the father and his first son. That fact was not lost on the Turkish militia when they imprisoned both Mickael and Mehran. They beheaded Mehran, making Mickael watch. Then Mickael was decapitated.

Not realizing what had happened, Jerry's grandmother sent her youngest son, Levon, to the prison with food for Mickael and Mehran. When the young boy approached the gates, the guard told him they were gone. When Levon persisted, the guard said they did not need food. Then, finally, the guard turned the plate upside down, signifying they were dead.

Levon ran home, yelling and weeping. Haigouhie begged her mother to take all the children and flee the village. Her mother feared for their lives, particularly that of her remaining son, but did not feel they all could leave. She quickly sewed a few gold coins into Haigouhie's slip and sent her and Levon on horseback to safety.

Not far from town, on a hillside, the children turned and saw the soldiers herding a group of women and children into a church. Huge wooden bars were dropped to lock the doors, and the building was set on fire. Jerry's mother would never forget the screams she heard that day.

A sympathetic Turkish family sheltered the children for a few weeks and then guided them to Syria. From there they went to Beirut, Lebanon, where they found refuge with a friendly family. Jerry's father, George Tarkanian, was related to that family, and on one of his trips from America to Lebanon, he met Rose. They eventually married. Her one condition for returning to America with him was that Levon would join them as soon as immigration legalities could be completed.

The Tarkanians established a home in Euclid, Ohio, a suburb very near Cleveland on the shores of Lake Erie. Their first child died shortly after birth. In 1927, a daughter, Alice, was born. And in 1930 they had their first son, Jerry. Father and first son soon developed that special bond, and ten years later another son, Myron, was born.

Jerry received his name in a most unusual way. His mother intended for him to be named Gregory, after Saint Gregory of the Armenian Orthodox Church, but impatient hospital officials could not understand her Armenian-English pronunciation and Jerry became the name on the birth certificate. It was not Gerald or anything else, just Jerry with no middle name.

Armenians who had fled their homeland maintained close ties in America. Dick Kilimian drove Jerry and his parents home from the hospital because the Tarkanians had only a covered truck which they used in their business. It was Herespema Gogjian, a close friend from the old country, who helped the new mother.

The Tarkanians ran a small grocery store during the Great Depression of the 1930s. Jerry's father worked hard for his family, holding a second job at a factory and a third delivering ice.

Jerry's favorite memory is of his father waking him early each morning and taking him around in his truck as he went from merchant to merchant, buying food for the store. When Jerry was 11, his father became critically ill and died of tuberculosis. It was a difficult and painful death. Along with the memories of those wonderful rides they'd shared, Jerry also remembers well how much his father suffered.

In 1946, Rose married Vahan Davidian, and the family—stepfather, mother, older sister, younger brother, and Jerry—moved to Pasadena, California.

The family quickly developed friendships within the Armenian community. Aroosiag Jamgochian, an Armenian friend, recalled young Jerry and his interest in sports.

16

Aroosiag Jamgochian: "All through Jerry's school years, he would spend every spare moment at the gym, on the field, playing, watching, learning, and always with the greatest enthusiasm. His stepdad often discussed Jerry's absorption with sports with his mom. 'Dughan gamats, gamats, bedg eh vor joogh mu undreh yev jamanaguh anor tartsneh, ches khorheer?' ... or, 'Little by little the boy ought to start thinking about a career and turn his interest and his time towards that direction, don't you think so?' As Jerry grew older, his mother heard the question more often, and always her reply ran something like this, 'Let us leave the boy alone. He does his schoolwork, and we always know where he is. There is nothing better than for him to be involved in something he likes so well. He enjoys sports so much, he puts heart and soul into whatever he does. Just watch and see, someday he'll make us all proud and happy that we didn't ask him to turn away from playing ball.'"

His mother's faith in him was reciprocated by a deep love from Jerry. Lois remembers that early in their married life she had a deep concern about any harm coming to his mother, because she did not know if Jerry could handle it. "He absolutely idolized her," says Lois. "She was a wonderful woman who lived her life for her children."

While in Ohio, Jerry had always had an almost encyclopedic knowledge of sports. He could rattle off game and player statistics like a teletype machine. It was in Pasadena, however, that he began to focus on basketball. There was something about the game that became a passion for him from almost the first time he touched a ball.

In Pasadena, the junior high went from the seventh grade to the tenth grade, then the high school went from the eleventh to the fourteenth. So the high school also was a junior college. It was in junior college that Jerry started going to Jimmy's Playroom.

Tarkanian: "My friends and I would just sit around, talk sports, tell jokes. There was a local assistant football coach and counselor at Pasadena City College, Art Dittbenner, and he'd tell me that I could go to college, come back, and still see the same guys doing the same things in the same way at Jimmy's Playroom. This made a real impression on me. I thought about it and realized that I could end up just like some of those older guys, hanging around the bar, drinking beer, and never getting out of Pasadena, never doing much of anything but being another guy on a barstool."

Thanks to basketball, Jerry did get a chance to break away from Pasadena. Pasadena High had a great athletic tradition overall. Lee

Walls, Dick Williams, and Bob Lillis all played baseball there around the time of Jerry's enrollment. All eventually had pro careers as players and coaches. Classmate Dick Davis became the U.S. Amateur golf champ. Harry Hugasian was a football All-American at Stanford and later became a running back with the Chicago Bears. Hugh Stewart was a world-class tennis player.

Pasadena's athletic reputation helped Tarkanian attract the attention of Fresno State.

Tarkanian: "Fresno State invited five guys from our group for a visit: myself, my closest friend, Dale Arambel, and three football players. They offered each of us scholarships, and we jumped at the chance to all go to the same school. To me it was tremendous. I had a shot at getting out of Pasadena and doing something with my life. Back then, you had to work to keep your athletic scholarship. There was no such thing as a full ride—tuition, room, and board all paid in exchange for playing ball. And there certainly was nothing like a Pell Grant, where the government gives cash payments to kids who can prove financial need. Hell, they would have had to pay about every kid I knew if there had been. At Fresno I worked for $50 a month. I was assigned to the football office, and that turned out to be one of the biggest breaks I got in college.

"Most of my friends were football players, so it was no problem working for head football coach Clark Van Galder. He was a tremendous individual, a super coach, and a great man. By far he was the one single person who had the most influence on my life as a coach. He was an extraordinarily intense individual, and he demanded equal intensity from his players. How he got it was by becoming close with them, by forging an emotional bond. He would take me and my roommate Fred Bistrick, Fresno's quarterback, to the high school games with him. We'd also go see his sons play. We spent a lot of time with his family.

"I was his personal aide, his gofer or whatever. I was there to follow him around and do whatever errands he wanted taken care of. I watched films with him, ate with him, listened to him in staff meetings. Van Galder was completely different from the other coaches I knew. Courses like "The Theory of Coaching" would emphasize a coach's being like a general to his troops, and Van Galder would show it worked the other way—being a friend as well as a coach to your players.

"He knew we had no money, so he'd bring a turkey to our house for Thanksgiving. If he knew we had something wrong in our families, he'd give us a few bucks for gas so we could go see our parents.

"Van Galder knew that I also wanted to be a coach, and we had long talks about it. He said that a coach shouldn't change his personality, because the kids can spot a phony in about two seconds. He was an emotional man, and on game days his face would turn scarlet. The man was on fire; his veins seemed to be about ready to pop right out of his forehead. He thought that a coach should inspire his players, and that the way to win wasn't only to concentrate on X's and O's, but to have his team play hard and with the most heart. He wanted to get his kids to play with more intensity than the other team. He talked a lot about 'playing over your head.' If I've been successful at all, I owe it to Van. I loved that man.

"I never learned those lessons about coaching in the classroom. Van Galder wasn't thrilled with the guys who wrote the coaching texts. He used to say, 'Show me a coach with a Ph.D. and I'll show you a coach with too much time on his hands.' We'd both laugh and feel it was true. He used to say that the books were wrong, that they wanted to make coaches all act the same, when imitating was the worst thing a coach could do. He thought the guys writing the books had spent too much time in ivory towers and not enough in the locker room.

"After all my years in coaching, I feel more strongly than ever that he was right. The books have changed a lot since then and there are a few great coaches with Ph.D.s, such as Tom Davis of Iowa, but the rest remains the same.

"Believe me, Van Galder got involved. If a kid had a problem, he wanted to know about it and he tried to help. The players knew he cared about them, and they would have done anything for him. His influence on me was so great, not so much in terms of what he did on the field, since he was primarily a football coach, but mainly in what he did with his kids."

In addition to getting to know coach Van Galder, Fresno State also was the place Jerry found his wife.

Tarkanian says, "Probably the only people who ever figured I'd marry Lois were Lois and me."

Lois Huter and Jerry Tarkanian were indeed Fresno State's odd couple. Lois's father was in the Navy, and her family moved back and forth between the East and West coasts, depending upon where he was stationed. For much of her early life, Lois lived in rural areas where she worked on farms while attending school. It was picking cotton and grapes in California, strawberries and tobacco in Connecticut, where she also graduated from high school.

19

After high school, Lois's father was called into active duty because of the Korean War, and her family moved from Connecticut to Fresno, where they bought a small vineyard. Fresno was just a big farm town in the early 1950s; although it did have a college, Fresno State. Like Jerry, Lois was the first member of her family to go to college, but there the similarity ended. When they met, Lois had just turned 19, yet she was on her way to finishing college in three years and was already teaching. She was a top student, worked on the school newspaper, and was president of both the journalism honor society and Tokalon, Fresno State's women's honorary academic society. Lois knew nothing about sports, and was a fanatical reader. She was receiving high grades and was first finalist for campus queen. During her senior year, she was already a full-time teacher. Tarkanian is still impressed by that fact.

Tarkanian: "I'm not talking about student teaching. It was a full-time, paying position. Lois didn't make much, but it at least was something. At the time, Fresno had such a shortage of teachers that they hired a few kids still in college and put them in front of a class."

Lois has always liked the underdog. She avoided joining a sorority despite the fact that it was considered a social necessity in the 1950s. Lois and her close friend, Bobbi Sisk, were determined to show that a person could become important on campus and a school officer without being in a sorority.

That was Lois Huter: a smart, talented, independent woman.

So what was she doing with Jerry Tarkanian?

He was 24 and working hard at hardly working when it came to school. He did just enough to stay eligible so he would be able to play basketball.

Lois had been dating the editor of the school paper, Pete Lang. Her friends were serious, dedicated students who liked to talk about politics and philosophy. Jerry was a member of a group known as the Fun Guys, for obvious reasons. They were jocks, and they talked about sports and beer. Lois wanted to write and teach. Jerry wanted to play basketball for as long as he could, and when that was over, he wanted to coach. He couldn't imagine a life without basketball. Like Lois, he read everything he got his hands on—as long as it was a sports page or a sports magazine.

Tarkanian: "I loved everything about college. Eight of us athletes lived in a four-bedroom house during my first year at Fresno. The next year, it was seven of us in a two-bedroom house. That was all we could afford. We slept on the sofa, in chairs, on the floor. No one much cared. Only one guy in the house had any money, and that was Sid Goldberg.

His parents would send him stuff to eat in the mail, packages of cookies and such, and we'd have a party with it. Of course, any excuse was good enough for us to have a party. But we didn't have money. I remember that one of our guys drove a meat delivery wagon. One time the freezer broke, so his boss said to get rid of the meat because it was starting to spoil. He brought it home and we ate it. There were other times when we ate horse meat because it was cheap. I remember going into Chrisman's diner with one of my friends, Harry Gaykian, and we'd ask for a cup of hot water because it was free. Then we'd take the catsup bottle, pour the catsup into the hot water, and call it tomato soup. They always had stacks of crackers at diners, so we had that to eat with our soup.

"We'd spend a lot of time at places that didn't cost much, like Fresno's swim park. We had great volleyball games there with Max Shuster, Pat Smith, and Fritz Lauritzen.

"By today's standards, our parties were very tame stuff...singing, dancing, guys doing a little yelling. But back then in Fresno, it was considered pretty wild. While we never got in any real trouble, it's safe to say that the police knew where we lived, because they stopped by once or twice to tell us to shut up. The saddest day of the year was when we all had to pack up and go home for the summer."

Tarkanian's roommates remember him for his persistence in keeping their house clean, which was no easy matter since the number of beds and closets never equaled the number of bodies. Jerry especially hated smoking, and to this day proudly tells his players he has never touched a cigarette. Goldberg was the only smoker in their house, so Jerry was always on him to quit smoking and to clean up his ashes. One day Jerry told Goldberg that if he found ashes in the living room again, he would put them in Goldberg's bed. Well, Jerry found them, and Goldberg found ashes on his sheets that evening. Though he protested that they weren't his, Jerry said that since Goldberg was the smoker, he was responsible for any ashes found in the house.

If Jerry and his friends hadn't tried to raise the college prank to an art form, he probably never would have met his wife.

Tarkanian: "Fresno State had a square dance club, and they were supposed to supply the entertainment for the school one afternoon. Some of the guys from our house heard about it and thought we should get into the act. When the club put on its square dance records, we would sneak in and pull the plug. Then we'd laugh and make jokes about it. Okay, it doesn't sound like much now, but it was a big deal at Fresno State. We wrecked the dance, and everyone was all upset and wanted to throw us out of school. This was during my first year at

21

Fresno. We were brought before the student court, which had a lot of power at the school. Let's put it like this: the student court had enough clout to get us suspended, and that was not something I wanted my mother to hear about."

Lois was on the student court. She said she never had seen or heard of Jerry before because she didn't follow sports. Of course, that first year at Fresno State you had to be one very serious basketball fan to know Jerry Tarkanian, because he averaged about 2 points, shot about 40 percent, and spent a lot of time getting well acquainted with the benches in the old California Collegiate Athletic Association, a forerunner to the Pacific Coast Athletic Conference, UNLV's league.

Tarkanian says, "A lot of guys said that I asked Lois out because I wanted her to go easy on me. She was on the student court and could make my life miserable. But I don't know—I guess I just sort of liked her. She was very pretty and obviously smart, and I suppose it wouldn't have hurt if she did decide I wasn't the worst guy in the world. I asked my roommate, Sid Goldberg, to help me meet Lois. He got a big kick out of it, because Lois and I were total opposites, and he tried to help match us up."

Lois: "One day after a student court session, I was walking down the hallway and I heard someone running after me. I turned around and it was Jerry, and the first thing he did was say hello, and then he was asking me out. I immediately assumed he was doing it so I would help get him out of trouble. I asked him if that was the reason, and naturally he said that the student court had nothing to do with it. And, naturally, I didn't believe it, so I told him to forget it. No date.

"When the student court met to decide what to do with Jerry and his buddies, three members—a majority of the court—thought there was no need for punishment. They saw it as a childish prank. But I said that those guys deserved something...they had wrecked the dance. A lot of people had worked hard to put on the event, and Jerry and his friends ruined it. What message would we be giving the student body if we let them get by? We had a discussion about it, and I finally talked the other members into giving Jerry and his friends a specific campus responsibility, putting up and taking down the voting booths for the student elections. I thought that for once those guys should do something positive on campus. Did I push for punishment because Jerry had asked me out? Was he trying to soften me up? I have no idea. But it is safe to say that I didn't think much of our first conversation.

"The crazy thing was that Jerry kept after me, even after his case was settled before the student court. He asked me out several times,

22

and I kept turning him down. I was in a class with Darryl Rogers, the school's football star who now coaches the Detroit Lions, and all of a sudden Darryl started talking to me, telling me what a great guy this Jerry Tarkanian was. Jerry had other friends come up to me and give these testimonials about him and his character. Now I can look back and see that this was his first recruiting job.

"I was breaking up with my steady boyfriend at the time, but I still had absolutely no interest in Jerry. Since Jerry seemed so interested in me, however, I finally agreed to go out with him. I admit it: he wore me down. All I can remember from that first date is that we went to the movies, and he had no money. None. He was really poor. Afterwards, we stopped at a restaurant for coffee. I didn't drink coffee then and I don't today. I ordered a hot chocolate, and Jerry had coffee. That may not seem to matter, but back then coffee was a nickel and hot chocolate was 20 cents. That was how we ended all of our dates, with hot chocolate and coffee. It would drive him nuts, but he never let on about it until after we were married. Then he told me how I tried to bankrupt him."

Tarkanian: "I still remember that hot chocolate, and it irritated the hell out of me. Everyone else in college was drinking coffee—why not Lois? And why couldn't she get something cheaper than hot chocolate? But I kept my mouth shut and just dug a little deeper into my pockets. Lois did pay me back, because she worked at a movie theater, and once a week she'd let me and some of the guys in for free. It was our one big night out."

Tarkanian's family worried about Jerry at college. They knew he was broke, and they knew that being away from home and broke was no bargain. Jerry's 12-year-old brother, Myron, used to send Jerry a few dollars he saved from his paper route each month.

Tarkanian: "My mother bought me an old Hudson. I mean a real old Hudson. Well, it looked a lot better than it ran, because it barely ran at all. The thing just never wanted to start. I had to park it on top of a hill near our house, or else I could forget about driving the next day. With the Hudson on the hill, I could give it a little push, get inside, and start it while it rolled down the hill. That was the only way it would kick over. It didn't help that the Hudson never had a full tank of gas. I used to pull into a station and put a half-dollar's worth in the tank. That was all I could afford, but it was enough to get me to Lois's house. That old Hudson and Goldberg's newer car were the only means of transportation we had among all of us.

23

"The guys in our house could get very creative in stretching our money. For example, television was just starting to become popular, but there was no way we could ever buy a set. Yet the World Series was on TV, college football games were on, and a lot of other stuff we liked to watch. So what we did was this: When a big game was being broadcast, we'd go to an appliance store which had a five-day free trial on a television set. We'd have the TV at our house for a week and then take it back. When another game was on, we'd find another store with a free-trial deal and do the same thing."

Meanwhile, the guys at Jerry's house were astounded that he was dating Lois Huter. At first, Fred Bistrick, Duke Snider, Jim Nash, Bill Wells, and "the Rock" Malleck thought it was pretty funny that Lois even agreed to be seen with Jerry. Other friends, Max Shuester and Pat Smith, thought they were a good couple.

"Then the guys started to get mad," says Jerry, "because I spent more time during my senior year with Lois than I did with them. They'd get really angry over our long phone conversations. One night I was talking on the telephone to her, and suddenly everything went dead. The guys had grabbed a pair of scissors and cut the wire."

So Jerry was broke, he had a car that could only start on top of a hill, and he had a girlfriend who was trying to drink him into the poorhouse with her hot chocolate. His friends thought he was crazy or that Lois had suddenly gone insane, or maybe they both were just plain nuts to be seeing each other. But Jerry was happy. He had a girl he considered the smartest and prettiest on campus. With Lois's help, he was doing better in school. On the basketball court, he got a chance to start as a senior.

As a junior, he was a practice player, a kid who specialized in blood, guts, and defense. Most players like to shoot; Tarkanian was a floor leader—he wanted to get right into a scorer's face and dare him to shoot. He liked to try to stop someone else's dribble as much as he liked to dribble the ball up the floor, even if he lacked the speed of most players he guarded.

Tarkanian's close friend, Fred Bistrick, used to call Jerry "the Little Old Man," because Jerry looked sad and because he worried all the time. The other players used to call Jerry slow. Tarkanian was the opposite of the athletes he would later recruit. When you can't move and you can't jump, and you end up guarding guys who do, that makes an impression. Often, coaches who, as players, moved up and down the court as if they had Dumbo the Elephant on their backs make a point to find players who can outrun a greyhound. In Tarkanian's se-

24

nior season, his determination and ability to endure were the reasons why he was named team captain.

Lois started going to the Fresno State games, and here is how she remembers Jerry: "He was never a great player—not at all—but he tried so hard."

What does Tarkanian think of those words? "Sounds like a pretty good scouting report to me."

But what friends back then wanted to know was not what Lois thought of Jerry Tarkanian the point guard, but what she thought of Jerry Tarkanian the Fun Guy. Just why did she keep going out with him?

Lois: "It seemed that everyone I knew told me not to date Jerry. My friends thought I had completely lost my mind. And there were many who did not think I should date an Armenian. There was still a lot of prejudice at that time in Fresno—I think the first time one of the top sororities admitted an Armenian girl was in my last year in college. I had broken up with my boyfriend, and there was an empty spot in my life. There was no other boy who really caught my interest. And Jerry came along. He was very sweet and persistent. I found that the image of Jerry did not match the real Jerry, and one of my closest friends, Sally O'Neal, told me she knew some of the Fun Guys and they were really quite nice, and she particularly liked Jerry as a person. Sally and I were both strong Catholics with similar standards, and what she said meant a lot to me.

"At times Jerry was almost like a lost puppy, and I guess he brought out the mothering instincts in me. I enjoyed being with him, and we fell in love. He was sincere, and that's what won me over—at least, I think that's what won me over. I've tried to analyze it and I think it's also because I'm always taking up causes. I have a lot of sympathy for people who have been stepped on by the world.

"But we do have several important things in common. I think we are both extremely loyal individuals. We are both family-oriented and both quite religious, although few people know this about Jerry. People would look at Jerry and me and see me as the one who got the grades and did what you're supposed to do. They saw me as the establishment person. I guess I look establishment and he doesn't. But I was always fighting the establishment, and maybe marrying Jerry was part of that.

"In fact, I don't even remember how or when Jerry asked me to marry him. One day we just decided to get married. It was something that we both knew was coming and we both knew would be right. We spent so much time together that getting married was a given. It wasn't a matter of if, but when. One day he said, 'Let's get married.' That was it and we did.''

Before Lois and Jerry were married, he had saved enough money to buy a television set. Jerry finally had his degree and was teaching and coaching at San Joaquin Memorial, a Catholic high school.

Tarkanian: ''I also was still living in a house with five guys. I didn't know how to tell them that I was getting married. We were all sitting around watching a football game, and I just came out with it: 'Hey guys, I'm getting married.' It was unbelievable. No one said anything. They were all watching the game. I could have told them the house was burning down and they wouldn't have moved.''

But what did get their attention was that after he married Lois, Jerry moved out and took the television set with him.

If Jerry Tarkanian had it to do all over again, he'd still marry Lois Huter, but he has some second thoughts about what happened after the wedding.

Tarkanian: ''Our wedding was nice. I got a new suit, the first real suit I ever owned. In college it was mostly T-shirts, blue jeans hanging at the waist, and basketball shoes. My mom bought me my first pair of dress shoes for the wedding. You know, I've kept those black shoes all these years. My family came up from Pasadena, and so did my good friends Bob Mallis, Roy McMillan, Bob Miller, Ernie Johanson, and Donald Albeck.

''I was teaching at San Joaquin Memorial, and along with being the basketball coach, I also was an assistant football coach and taught math, English, and history. We were married in the afternoon at St. Therese Church. That evening, our wedding night, I took Lois to the Idaho State–Fresno State football game. That made her madder than hell, and she still is mad about it. Whenever we get into an argument, she brings up that football game on our wedding night. Now that I think about it, I guess it was a dumb idea. But I was living at that house with guys starting on the Fresno football team, and it seemed like everyone I knew was either playing or going to the game, so I dragged Lois along. Where else could you go with only a couple of days available?''

That first year of their marriage was special. Both Lois and Jerry were teaching and being paid. Two people living together with two paychecks.

''I felt like the richest guy in the world,'' says Jerry. ''I didn't know anything about big business or money. All I knew was that we had a television set, we ate decently, and I had more than I ever dreamed of having. I earned $3,850 at San Joaquin High and I was getting paid on a 10-month schedule, meaning each check was $385. I couldn't imagine how you could even spend $385 in a month, and Lois was making about that much, or maybe more. At that time it seemed nobody could be better off than two schoolteachers.''

Tarkanian likes to say it took him about six years to get through college, and he insists that he still would be trying to earn his bachelor's if he hadn't met Lois.

Lois: "I always told Jerry that he wasn't a dumb person, not at all. Some of the guys he hung around with weren't good students, but once he began dating me, he changed. I guess I was setting a higher standard and he began to follow it. I nagged him a little and I tried to encourage him a lot. His whole life all Jerry ever wanted was to be a basketball coach—not a big-name coach, just a high school basketball coach. I remember reading in one of his yearbooks that he used to go to sleep with a basketball. I have no doubt that was true, but I had nothing against his basketball. To me, his being a basketball coach was part of his being a teacher.

"I felt honored and blessed just to go to college. Neither of my parents even finished high school, because they both had to help their families financially. Jerry's family was thrilled to see him graduate and become a high school teacher. They thought what he did was magnificent. We had no idea our life would become what it is today. Our horizons and dreams were very limited. Jerry came from a small school, and he wasn't a star player. He had no big-name coaching mentor. Clark Van Galder was the man who had the greatest influence on Jerry, but Clark was a football coach. Furthermore, Fresno was a somewhat isolated place. It was a big deal to take a trip to Los Angeles or the Bay area. The world seemed to pass Fresno by, and when we got married, we were just two small-town kids happy to have jobs.''

Tarkanian: "Lois is right. I thought high school would be it, too. I know I loved high school coaching. In fact, during my last year in college, the new Fresno State basketball coach, Bill Vandenberg, offered me a paid position as freshman coach at the college. Vandenberg had done a lot to help me as a player, making me team captain my senior year. He also had a strong influence on my coaching career. I was honored to be offered the position, but I turned it down to work extra hours for no pay at Edison High School.

"During my last year in college, I did my student teaching at Edison High, a school in Fresno with a predominantly black enrollment. Right before the season, the basketball coach had a nervous breakdown and the assistant football coach, Ellis Carasco, was told he also had to coach basketball. He told me he knew virtually nothing about basketball, and I was excited to help him. I got a real break because he let me do most of the tactical and strategic part of coaching. Ellis took care of the discipline and the pregame and halftime talks. It was tremendous, because this man was gutsy enough to let me, a guy who hadn't even graduated from college, do a lot of coaching. Most coaches won't let an assistant do as much.

"I remember one incident about that team very clearly. We had won the city and county championships and were to play Taft High School for the valley championship. But before we bussed to Taft, we were told our players could not eat their pregame meal in any restaurant in Taft, and our Edison High administration told the student body, primarily blacks, not to attend the game because of possible violence. So we ended up eating in Bakersfield and just walking around a park before bussing the last miles to Taft, and we didn't have a single Edison student in the stands cheering for us. Can you believe that? I was absolutely furious. Then, during the game, people in the crowd made racist remarks and threw pennies, wads of paper, and other objects at our players. We lost that game by a point. It was my first experience in sports with that kind of full-blown bigotry. I read a few years ago in the *Los Angeles Times* about some football players at Taft Junior College who were leaving and told about the prejudice shown them. I guess in some places things never change."

Ellis Carasco was named the Fresno High School basketball coach of the year.

The Edison experience, along with recommendations from Clark Van Galder and Ellis Carasco, helped Jerry secure his first full-time job at San Joaquin Memorial. In those days you just didn't walk out of college and into a head high school coaching job. Edison had offered Jerry a chance to stay as a junior varsity coach, but Jerry really wanted to be a varsity coach. He had applied for a job at Selma, a rural high school outside of Fresno. It came down to a choice between Jerry and a coach from Indiana for the Selma opening.

"The superintendent took the guy from Indiana," says Tarkanian. "And he told me it was because they played better basketball in Indiana."

*   *   *

The experience at Edison High was exactly what Jerry needed to convince himself that he could be a coach. He continually dreamed of coaching. But until he was on the bench deciding who should go into the game and who should come out, and until he was down on his hands and knees in a huddle with 3 seconds on the clock, the score tied, and the kids all looking at him, expecting him to draw up a play so his team could get the ball in bounds and get off a shot, he didn't know what it meant to be a coach. Until he stood helplessly by and watched a kid miss a foul shot that cost him a game, he hadn't been a coach. At Edison, Jerry Tarkanian found out he could indeed be Coach Tarkanian.

Tarkanian: "Basketball has always been my love. At Fresno State, I kept a file on every team we played. In that file, I put all the information down on index cards—their defense, their offense, the tendencies, strengths, and weaknesses of some of the individual players. The reason I was named team captain during my senior year certainly wasn't because of my natural talent, but because I could analyze the game. I was still a player, but I looked at the game as a coach. I knew that there was more to basketball than running around, shooting, and dribbling. I think I could grasp the team concept better than most players, and that was because I took the time to look at what really happened on the floor. In the classroom, I found that my concentration would sometimes fade. On the court, it never did.

"A lot of great athletes don't understand the game. They just play and their physical gifts carry them. In fact, when some of them try to think, they freeze. They lose that natural talent, that instinctive creativeness that is a part of so many great players' games. That is why you ask some kids what they did on this move or that move, and they can't really tell you. They just jumped and invented something while in the air. I never had the talent to play like that. I had to think about every move I made before I took the first step."

There was one other player on the Fresno team who looked at basketball the same way. That was Rolland Todd, who coached at UNLV in the late 1960s and with the Portland Trail Blazers during their early years in the NBA. After games, he and Jerry got together and reviewed everything. They broke the game down, almost play by play. Even in Jerry's first year as a high school coach, he would meet with Rolland to discuss the games.

Tarkanian says, "My goal was to coach basketball, not to make a lot of money or be on television. If I had to say what my biggest dream was at the moment I walked out of college, it would be to get a job as a high school coach in the Pasadena area so I could be near my family and friends. I wanted to go back to Jim's Playroom, drink beer with the guys, and talk about our next high school game.''

When Jerry did get his first full-time job at San Joaquin, he was confident that he was prepared. And after coaching at San Joaquin, Jerry discovered he liked the Catholic school setting. The kids were driven and gutsy, there was tremendous school spirit, and the priests were very supportive.

As for the talent, that was a little different story.

The player who saved Tarkanian was Tom Cleary, who was 6-foot-7. Jerry thanked God that he had at least one kid with size, because his next-best player was 5-foot-5 Pete Lango. Then there were the Armenian twins, Larry and Terry Hanoian, who were perhaps 5-foot-3.

Tarkanian: ''I did have a 6-foot-3 kid, Billy Schuh, who played quite a bit, and my sixth man was a 5-foot-5 redhead, Bill Laubacher. We had the strangest-looking team you've ever seen. I mean, if you put all those kids together and started guessing what they were, all of them would be collecting their Social Security checks before you figured out that they were a basketball team.''

San Joaquin was the surprise of its league, finishing with a 13–7 record. Lois helped Jerry with the team by keeping statistics at the games and taking an active role with the kids.

The highlight of the season was the upset of Tarkanian's old team, Edison. The final score was 32–31, so obviously Jerry didn't want to run-and-gun with his former players. San Joaquin was at least a 30-point underdog in the game, because Edison was a city school with a lot of good, experienced athletes. They were everything San Joaquin wasn't—big, fast, and established winners. Edison was clearly the best team in the Fresno area, and San Joaquin was much smaller, not just on the court but in terms of enrollment.

Tarkanian: ''I knew that the only way to beat Edison was to take the air out of the ball and slow it down. Boy, did we slow it down. We walked the ball up the court, and we passed it around a million times. We showed great patience. That was the San Joaquin team's one great talent—intelligence and the ability to respond to coaching. The kids played so damn hard and did everything I asked of them. I remember how excited Don Leiss was when he scored the winning basket. Beating Edison was a miracle, and I still love to sit back and think about that game.''

In Tarkanian's second year at San Joaquin, he had an 18–4 record. His first child, Pamela Rose, was born that year. The baby came early, and Jerry was very surprised to get the call to rush home and take Lois to the hospital. He had just invested in what a school booster had told him was the "car of the future," a Goliath. While Lois was in labor pains, the Goliath, never a smooth runner, chugged its way to the hospital. The forward-and-backward jerking of the car made the pains even worse, and by the time the couple reached the maternity ward, Lois was ready to kill Jerry.

It was at this time that Jerry discovered that his salary of $3,850 a year—their sole income—didn't exactly make the Tarkanians a threat to the Rockefellers. Lois and Jerry wanted to have more children and raise a family, and that took money. Jerry did get a $200 raise after his first year, but Catholic high schools seldom can afford to pay their teachers high salaries. Jerry started looking around at other openings. Edison still had an interest in Tarkanian, but it was as an assistant coach. Jerry was promised that he would eventually be the head coach, but he didn't want to wait. Besides, after two good years at San Joaquin, he saw no reason to take a step backward.

Bullard, a new high school in Fresno, looked like a good opportunity. Athletic director Jerry Jury was doing the hiring of coaches. A good friend of Jerry's from Fresno State, Bob Bennett, was applying to be the baseball coach. Bennett and Tarkanian both were interviewed. It was obvious that along with being the athletic director, Jerry Jury was going to coach something, and that something would be either baseball or basketball. He decided to hire Bob Bennett as the baseball coach and to take the basketball job himself, which made Jerry the odd man out. Jerry was crushed. Bullard seemed like a chance for him to build a high school basketball program in his own fashion. A new school would have been perfect for a young coach, and Jerry was a coach with a lot of ideas and energy who needed a place to work.

Tarkanian: "In the end, I had three other high school offers, and I took Antelope Valley High in southern California. Looking back on it, I'm not sure why. I guess I thought it was a big school—2,400 students—and there should be a lot of basketball players out there somewhere. But Antelope was a football school. I don't mean just that it had a good football program, but that all it wanted to have was a football program. When I took the job, they had a 13-game basketball schedule. The doors to the gym were locked on weekends. The athletic director had been the football coach, and he didn't want the basketball program to grow."

The Tarkanians lasted one very long year at Antelope Valley High. Jerry had an 11–14 record, the only losing season of his career.

How bad was it?

Tarkanian: "It may have been the most difficult time in our marriage. I'd come home from practice and not say a word to Lois. It was like she wasn't there. I just came into the house, walked past her, and went right to bed. I didn't eat, I didn't talk, and I was in bed by 7 o'clock every night. It wasn't anything Lois did. It had nothing to do with Lois. My team was so bad, I was getting beat and I hated it. I never believed that a school with 2,400 students could be so bad. I practiced the kids so hard.

"When that season was over, I was determined that a losing record would never happen to us again. I went to the recreation department and got the gym open on the weekends, and I manned it. I did the same thing during the week. I remember taking our little Pam piggyback on my shoulders each day to work. She spent more time in a gym that year than most athletes. We had the kids playing every day, and I was manning the gym sixty hours a week. My brother, Myron, spent the summer with us to help me. We built a good foundation for Antelope Valley's basketball program in the future, and they began to win some games down the line. Within three years, products of the youth program we started helped their team to the finals of the California Interscholastic playoffs."

At this point, the now famous towel entered Tarkanian's life.

Tarkanian: "My big break came when the Redlands High position opened up. Redlands is between Pasadena and Palm Springs. I wrote Redlands inquiring about the job, and then heard that they planned to give it to someone within the school system. Then Lois and I wrote them back, just to thank them for considering me, and that was it. Or at least, I thought that was it for Redlands. But the person decided not to take the job, and Redlands remembered our thank-you letter and called me. I'm convinced that if it weren't for that second letter, I never would have gotten the job."

Redlands paid its basketball coach $7,000, and the Tarkanians were very grateful for the raise. Like Antelope Valley, Redlands had a strong football tradition. But Redlands also wanted to have a successful basketball team. The football coach, Frank Serrao, and Jerry lived about two blocks apart and they drove to school together. What Jerry wanted to know from Frank Serrao was why the football team won so consistently.

Tarkanian: "You'd go to booster club meetings and look at the audience and see nothing but doctors, lawyers, professional people, and clean-cut kids. It also was the smallest school in its league, and it was playing city schools with kids who usually make the best athletes because they are the hungriest. But these teams would run into Redlands on the football field and get annihilated. Redlands had such tremendous pride in its football program. The kids were totally committed to the school, and it was a big deal for a kid to wear a Redlands uniform. Frank Serrao was a great coach. He knew how to motivate the kids and they were dedicated to him.''

The basketball team was a much different story. It would be very kind to say that the team was average, but Frank Serrao wanted a winner on the court and he supported Jerry by going to the games. That was a pleasant change from Antelope Valley, where the football program acted as if the basketball team didn't exist.

In Jerry's first year, the team finished in second place, which was very good for Redlands. Lois, who always got excited at the games, gave birth to the Tarkanians' second daughter, Josephine (Jodie), following the game Redlands lost to give Pacific High first place. The next year, Redlands won the league championship.

Tarkanian: "In those Redlands years we came as close as possible to having a one-man team. Danny Wolters scored over half our points and got over half our rebounds. He was a magnificent player who went on to California-Berkeley. He's a successful businessman now in Stockton, California, and each year comes to the game and visits with us when UNLV plays the University of Pacific.

"I started to think this was it," says Tarkanian. "This would be the perfect place for us to raise a family. We bought our first home. Lois had an administrative job with the San Bernadino County Schools Office. The teachers at Redlands were behind the athletic program. I felt comfortable sitting around the faculty lounge."

The year was 1960, and Tarkanian was content. He even found a unique new image as the only man in basketball who sat on the bench with a towel in his mouth.

Tarkanian: "We were playing in the league championship game against Ramona. It was an afternoon game, really hot. I mean, they had to keep the doors of the gym open to get some air in the place, but nothing helped. My throat was so dry, it was as if I had sand in my mouth. I kept going back and forth between the bench and the drinking fountain, but that was getting ridiculous. To make matters worse, the game went into overtime. I could hardly talk.

"Finally, I just got sick and tired of running to and from the drinking fountain in the middle of the game, so I grabbed a towel, soaked it in water, and carried it back to the bench. Then I'd suck on the towel during the game to get a drink. We won the game and the championship, and since I'm not one to change when something works, I've stuck with the towel ever since. I guess I believe in lucky charms.

Besides, I like having the towel on the bench. I get very nervous during a game and it gives me something to do.''

Redlands was where Lois convinced Jerry to return to school for a master's degree, just in case he ever wanted to coach in college. Also, he would be on a higher pay scale as a high school teacher if he had a master's.

Lois: ''Getting the master's was something Jerry really wanted. He set his mind to do it, and he just went out and did it. One summer he finished teaching at Redlands High on a Friday, and the next Monday he was at Redlands University working on his master's. The first summer session ended on a Friday, and the next Monday he was starting the second session. That second summer session ended on a Friday, and Redlands High began the next Monday. Jerry had no break at all.''

Tarkanian continued in school each term, attending night classes while still coaching. He finished with all A's and one B, his thesis was approved, and he earned a master's in educational administration.

Tarkanian: ''It felt so good to have a master's, and that was something I never dreamed would happen to me when I was hanging around with the guys at our house at Fresno State. Probably none of the guys who knew me as a kid would ever have believed that Jerry Tarkanian could have a master's degree. That's why I know kids can shape up and become decent students. If I did it, I know others can too, and that's part of what I try to tell the kids I coach. It's just a matter of getting your priorities straight.''

3

JUCO Jobs

It's hard to guess how many times in his career Jerry Tarkanian has said, "This is it. This is the job I want. I'll never even think about another one." Then, a few years later, something happens and Jerry starts thinking, "I've got a great job now, but this other job...well ...maybe that would be good too."

Jerry and Lois Tarkanian loved everything about Redlands High School, the city in which it was located, its quality students, and its highly professional teaching staff. But while living in Redlands, almost every Sunday Lois and Jerry would meet Fred and Rita Bistrick. They'd go to church together and then have breakfast. Fred was one of Jerry's old Fresno State roommates and was the football coach at Corona High, which was seven miles from Riverside. The Tarkanians would spend some of those Sundays driving around Riverside, and Jerry would say, "You know, this is a great town. If I could ever get the Riverside City College job, we could retire here. This is a super place."

Then the Riverside job opened.

Tarkanian had won in high school, he had a master's degree, and he thought he was ready to coach on the college level. It wasn't a conscious decision. Jerry never said, "I'll coach in high school for five years, then get a junior college job." It was something that just evolved.

Then there was Riverside's basketball program. It had real problems. It was 10–18 overall and 1–13 in its conference during the 1960–61 season. Riverside had won only one league game in each of the two years before Tarkanian arrived. No one cared about the team—not the students, not the community, not even the former players.

The Riverside City College president, Bill Noble, asked Jerry to interview for the position. Since Redlands was only seven miles away, he knew what Jerry had done in high school and wanted a young coach to pull the Riverside program out of its coma. Jerry's interview was at 1 p.m. on a Wednesday, and by 5 p.m. the interview was over and Bill Noble had offered him the job.

Tarkanian recalls, "I couldn't believe it. I figured that he would have to talk it over with someone, or interview some other people. The last thing I expected was to walk into Riverside and get a job offer. I was so fired up, I didn't think about how bad the program was or that I already had a good setup at Redlands. I just accepted, and that was that."

On Wednesday night, Jerry drove to Pasadena to see his mother and the rest of his family. He was excited about the interview and told his brother, Myron, about Riverside. Myron and Jerry were extremely close; Jerry consulted with him often and respected his opinion.

Myron said, "You're crazy. That place kills basketball coaches. It's suicide. Go to Riverside and it will end your career."

For the first time, Jerry started to have serious second thoughts. He also ran into a coaching friend who told him, "You're nuts. You'll never win there."

Not exactly comforting words.

Tarkanian: "I told myself that Riverside was a great town, that I had some good contacts in the local high schools and I should be able to get enough players so that I wouldn't embarrass myself. Then I got back to Redlands, and I saw that Redlands was a beautiful town and I had great kids to work with. On Thursday, graduation day, the kids were terrific, the town looked more beautiful than ever, and I got very sentimental. I looked at Lois and said, 'I'm not going to take the Riverside job. I just can't leave here. Tomorrow morning, I'm going to call and say I changed my mind.' Really, that's what I wanted to do."

But it wasn't what happened.

On Friday morning, Jerry called Bill Noble, and before he had a chance to say hello, Noble said, "Jerry, it's great to hear from you. Boy, are we excited that you're coming..."

"But I..."

"Listen, Jerry, it's all official. I've got the approval from the board of regents..."

"Maybe we should..."

"We're going to call the papers and announce it right away."

That was it. There was nothing Jerry could say. Bill Noble wouldn't let Jerry get a word in, and Noble's enthusiasm rubbed off on Jerry.

"Bill Noble was an inspiring guy and I just didn't have the heart to tell him that I wanted to stay at Redlands," says Tarkanian. "So I didn't say anything, and that's how I ended up as a college coach. Strange as it seems, if he had let me talk first, I would probably still be at Redlands, teaching driver's ed. on Saturdays."

Lois: "Jerry has never been able to make a clean break from one job to the next. He just drags things out and keeps changing his mind. Riverside was only one of several times that this happened."

Probably the best thing Jerry had going for him at Riverside was that he didn't have a clue about what was ahead. He was well aware that the situation would be bad, but he had worked before in programs that had no basketball tradition. Riverside was worse than he imagined, however, because there was so little talent.

Tarkanian: "We were really starting from scratch. The previous coach, John Matulich, had recruited two kids from Detroit—Joe Barnes and Roosevelt Lee—but they both had to sit out a semester. That was the rule for out-of-state students attending California junior colleges; they had to establish a residence in California before they could play. Counting Barnes and Lee, I had a total of only ten players. If someone got hurt, we had a helluva time trying to scrimmage. We really had no depth. We had only eight eligible players at the start of the season.

"One of them, Louie Davidson, was a pretty good athlete, but he also was an older guy who missed some games because he worked. We opened the season with a game against Antelope Valley College, which was right near Antelope Valley High. And Antelope Valley High was where I had had my only losing season as a coach, so this game was sort of a homecoming for me. We went to Lancaster for the game, and Davidson was at his job and couldn't make it. Two of my players got sick. Suddenly I looked around, and all I saw were five players in uniform. I did have four guys on the bench—the two red-shirts and the two sick kids—but they were in street clothes."

So this was college ball. Five kids, no bench, and not much hope. There were no miracles for Jerry that day at Antelope Valley.

"We got drilled," says Tarkanian. "I don't remember the score and I don't want to. All I remember is that the game took forever and I suffered a lot. That night I thought that my brother and everyone else had been right—I must have been out of my mind to take this job."

The home games were a joke. Wheelock Gym wasn't very big—it

37

sat maybe 2,000 fans. But, Tarkanian says, "you could have fired a cannon into the stands and not hit anyone." Lois showed up with the children, and that was it. "Pam and Jodie climbed all over the bleachers, played hide-and-seek under the stands, and napped on the benches," Lois remembers. "It was as if they had their own private playground-gymnasium."

To add to the problems, Lois, who was in her third pregnancy, developed a blood clot in her left leg and was rushed to the hospital.

Lois: "I don't know exactly how it happened. I just felt a hot, sharp pain, like a bee sting, behind my ankle early in the morning. As the day progressed, the pain gradually began to move further up my leg. I should have called the doctor then, but I was young, had never had any serious physical problems, and thought it was just some pregnancy aggravation that would soon go away. By mid-afternoon, I could hardly move. I called Jerry's office. I remember I was trying to be a good wife and not worry him. I knew he was worrying plenty already about his job. I just asked him to come home right after practice and not stay to talk with anyone. By the time Jerry got home, the pain was excruciating. Our little Pamela tried to console me, but just her touch caused me to scream. Poor Jodie was so small, she just sat there with a frightened look on her face.

"Jerry rushed me to the hospital, where they immediately gave me some painkillers. I felt happy just to have the pain relieved. I remember I was feeling great and Jerry came into the room with an ashen look on his face. He walked over to me and tears came to his eyes. I couldn't understand what was wrong. Then the doctor came in and told me about the clot, and that they would attempt to dissolve it with anticoagulants and heat treatments. But if it had already gone past the leg, it would be difficult to find and could end up in the brain or heart. The doctors were wonderful, and though they prepared me for surgery the next morning, they were able to dissolve the clot that night. Everything turned out fine, except that I had to stay in the hospital for several days."

Tarkanian: "Lois has been with me every step of the way since I started coaching, and that day in the hospital I felt crushed. The one good thing that happened that first season at Riverside was that our son Danny was born eight games into the schedule. Lois had the baby just before our road trip to Utah. I was on top of the world. Our team was beaten badly by Dixie and Snow College, but for once in my life the losses didn't even faze me."

Lois: "Danny was our first son, and the only one of our children Jerry watched being born. Our physician, Dr. Reynolds, had encouraged him to do so. I remember Dr. Reynolds had told Jerry that after two girls, he guaranteed a boy. During the final stages of labor, the nurses and doctors kept talking as if it were a boy for sure. I heard them say, 'He's coming now. He's almost here,' and then I heard one nurse say, 'I think he fainted.' Obviously, I knew that it couldn't have been the baby they were talking about. Evidently, Jerry was keeling over. Just then a nurse shouted, 'It's a boy!' Then I heard heavy footsteps running the length of the hall with a clanging sound. I knew it was Jerry with those heavy gym keys clanging in his pocket. I heard him yell, 'It's a boy! It's a boy!' as he ran to tell our girls.''

One bright spot in coaching was when RCC beat Fullerton City College for the first time in twelve years and 26 games. John Barnicott was the team's best player that year. Things did get better with basketball: Riverside finished 14–13, and at least Jerry had a few substitutes on the bench by the end of the season. Jerry knew this much: he never wanted to be caught so short of talent again.

The 1963 Riverside College yearbook writers were impressed by the 14–13 record. They wrote, "A new coach and new uniforms brought the Tigers a flashing and exciting brand of basketball. Tarkanian moved the team from a cellar-dweller to a contender in one season."

Jerry, however, was fully aware of the lack of community interest. The local newspaper didn't even have a reporter cover the games; one of the RCC coaches had to call in the final scores.

The Riverside job was the first time Jerry realized the power of recruiting. In high school you don't pick your players; the kids are assigned to a school, and they go. About the only thing a coach can do is talk some kid who already is enrolled into going out for the team. But in college, even at a place like Riverside, Jerry had some choice when it came to players. He had a chance to look at all the athletes coming out of the Riverside area high schools and could try to talk the best ones into playing at Riverside City College. That's exactly what he did.

"Jerry had a knack of attracting good, young athletes," said Matulich. "They gave him 100 percent and Jerry would give them 100 percent of his life."

Tarkanian not only persuaded the players who would have been naturals to attend junior college (because they weren't the classic basketball size, or because they were in need of more academic work before attending a four-year school), but he also was out-recruiting four-year schools for the top players in the area.

Tarkanian: "In those days, freshmen were not eligible to play at four-year institutions. So I'd urge players to come to the junior college and play 30 games in a quality schedule rather than play a junior varsity schedule. I told them they could play for a year and then as a sophomore, go on to a four-year school if they wanted. None of them ever did want to leave that second year. In fact, most of those kids will tell you today that those years in junior college were the most satisfying years they had."

By his sheer persistence and enthusiasm, Tarkanian turned Riverside into the place where the area high school players wanted to go, even if they had the grades and the scholarship offers to attend NCAA Division I schools. In five years at Riverside, Tarkanian only missed on one local player he wanted: Jim Barnett, who went to Oregon. Players like Steve Barber, an outstanding Ramona High School athlete who later became a major league pitcher, had the grades and talent to play big-time basketball. He went with Tarkanian instead. Jim Gardner, highly recruited by the University of Southern California, stayed at RCC. Others who also did were Larry Bunce, Larry Bonsoumet, Tom Quast, Ted Page, John Reed, and Bob Glasgow. Probably no other junior college coach had ever controlled his own area as Tarkanian did at Riverside.

There is only one way to do that: work. That's what recruiting always comes down to, and all Jerry did was work.

Lois: "Jerry was gone day and night. He knew every gym and every playground as well as he knew his own living room. If a kid was bouncing a basketball in the summer, Jerry was there to watch. I couldn't imagine how one person could watch so many basketball games—from pickup games to organized summer leagues. He would head out each morning at eight and not be home until 9:00 at night. To keep our family life together, I'd pack up our kids and head to one of the local gyms. Every one of our children enjoyed the games or playing on the athletic fields nearby. Our lives orbited around Jerry and his players.

"I had four children in the first six years of marriage. Riverside was Jerry's sixth year of full-time coaching and his fourth job, so that meant a lot of moving for us. I continued working part-time as a speech and hearing consultant for the San Bernardino County Schools Office. I would go throughout the county helping set up programs for speech-impaired children, interviewing and selecting speech therapist candidates, and giving numerous workshops. Jerry and I were both very busy, but our work and our family were our enjoyments, so we had a good, full family life during those years."

No one had ever recruited in Riverside quite like Jerry. He was highly visible. He knew every player, and the kids saw him every day. There was nothing formal about it, and it was totally different than recruiting is now. Back then, it was a coach hanging around the gym, talking to the kids for a few minutes between games. Few JUCO coaches were doing this. Jerry had especially strong relationships with the black athletes.

In his second year at Riverside, the summer on the courts paid off with winter talent in the Riverside gym. The local kids found a coach from Riverside who wanted them, and they liked the idea of being wanted. Former coach Matulich's Detroit players, Roosevelt Lee and Joe Barnes, were eligible for the full season.

Jerry also used his old Cleveland contacts to bring three more players to Riverside: Tom Crowder, Sam Knight, and Lem Lemmons.

Crowder said recently, "I wish some of those people who sometimes criticize Jerry's recruiting practices would take the time to find out what it's really all about. I know; I was one of his recruits. If it hadn't been for what he did for us, none of us would have accomplished what we have today. I went on to get my B.A. from San Francisco State and a master's from the University of Southern California. I'm now the assistant program supervisor for the Juvenile Division of San Mateo County. Lem Lemmons has his master's, too. Sam Knight is a top administrator for the Chico Rehabilitation Center. Joe Barnes holds a master's degree from Whittier and has been a chemistry professor for years at Pasadena City College. Each of us was the same kind of kid Jerry is criticized for taking. Sure, we played basketball, and that was our main concern at one point of our lives; but he gave us a chance at college and we did something with it. Without that chance, none of us would have the careers we have today."

For the most part, Jerry's teams were composed of Riverside area players. The player who really made the rest of California notice RCC was Riverside's Bobby Rule.

Tarkanian: "When I first saw Bobby, he was 6-foot-7 and about 200 pounds. He and his high school coach didn't get along, and the coach told all the college recruiters that Bobby was tough to handle. It turned out that none of the colleges wanted him. The coach told me, 'Stay away from Rule. He won't work hard, he won't play for you. He's trouble.' But I don't know... I just sort of liked Bobby from day one. He had real long arms. The basketball talent was obvious. He could score, rebound, block shots—the whole package. Lois and I got to know him well, and I was convinced that he got a bad rap. He was a Riverside kid, and I was sure we would have a good relationship."

41

Bobby Rule: "I was a late bloomer. By that, I mean that I grew late physically and developed late as a player. As a junior in high school, I barely played, and averaged something like 2 points a game. The nicest thing anyone could say about me was that I was a big kid with potential. In fact, when I graduated from the ninth grade, I was only 5-foot-9 and I had been cut from my junior high team. I started growing in high school, but my body got out of control. I mean, I was a klutz—two left feet and people making fun of me. Even as a senior I had troubles. I was second in the league in scoring, but I had no rebounding or ball-handling skills. About all I had was a turnaround jumper.

"What might have hurt me the most was that I had no tenacity. Little guys were always taking the ball out of my hands, or I'd just stand there and not even try for rebounds. I knew some of Jerry's players from Riverside, and I used to play in pickup games with them. Jerry would be at those summer games, and I'd be embarrassed, because these good players were making me look sick out there. In fact, I don't think Jerry was all that sold on me at first; he used to tell me that I had to get a lot tougher and play harder. Jerry egged me on a lot by talking about the little guys stealing the ball from me.

"Also, there were some problems between my high school coach and me. We had a personality conflict, and I remember things like a day where I was running laps and he yelled at me. I stopped and yelled 'What?' back at him. The coach told me to run five more laps, and I just walked off. I quit the team right there. My brother had played for the coach ten years before, and he and the coach didn't get along, and I think the coach figured that I was the same. It was like the coach was taking it out on me for what my brother did to him. It was a bad situation, and it didn't help me when it came time to go to college."

Lois: "Bobby had a wonderful mother and a lot of brothers and sisters. His family had little money and they lived in one of the poorer sections of Riverside. They were all good people—very warm and very loyal. Bobby was a big kid, tall and husky. The fact that he was so physically imposing scared some people. Bobby became a close part of our own family. He would baby-sit our kids, and even helped with yard work."

Tarkanian calls Bobby Rule "the greatest player in California junior college history."

Riverside's first season with Rule was in 1962–63, Jerry's second year at Riverside. The record was 32–3. This was when Jerry learned a very hard coaching lesson.

Tarkanian: "Sometimes I get so stubborn that it's just plain stupid. I've never liked a zone defense, for a number of seasons, so we always played man-to-man. I hated the zone so much that we only practiced it for about one week during the regular season, and that wasn't enough. It was dumb coaching on my part. In the California state junior college tournament, we had an 8-point lead against Fresno City College in the second half, and Bobby Rule got in foul trouble. He had four fouls and I wanted to keep him on the floor for his offense. I was afraid that if I kept playing man-to-man, they would isolate Bobby's man and he would pick up that fifth foul, which would have been it for Bobby. So I went to a zone defense, which under normal circumstances was a good idea. Of course we didn't have a zone, so the kids had no idea what I wanted. It should come as no surprise that the worst happened: Bobby fouled out. Our zone was awful and we lost in overtime.''

But it was a year at Riverside unlike anything the college had ever seen before.

Tarkanian: ''What we were able to do eventually was to remove the stigma of going to a junior college. The whole town was into Riverside basketball. It got so that people were lining up for tickets at 6 p.m. for an 8 p.m. game. The gym was built on a hillside, and you had to walk down a long flight of stairs to the gym floor. I remember standing on the floor and looking up at the four transom windows near the roof, which were at ground level outside. Kids would be packed there, hanging from the windows, trying to see the game. We had hundreds of local businessmen who only saw us play on the road—they wanted to go to the home games, but by the time they got out of work at five it was too late for them to get a seat in our gym. We went from just the game scores in the local paper to a few paragraphs, and then a full-time reporter who covered only our team. The writer's name was Ron Shaffer, and he eventually went to work for the Washington *Star*. He was a great writer and he gave us tremendous coverage, always with a lot of pictures and often on the front page. All of our games were on the radio, with a special announcer, Ralph Lawler, just for RCC. I don't think any junior college in the country had as much local coverage and as strong fan support as we did.''

The next year Rule was an even better player. Tarkanian surrounded him with more talent, and Riverside won all 35 of its games, including the California state championship. You couldn't buy a ticket at Wheelock Gym; and when Riverside played on the road, it seemed like a home game, because most of Riverside's fans traveled to support the team.

Bobby Rule: ''We had the right basketball environment at River-

43

side. Our team was very confident, and probably a bit cocky, but the coaches knew to give us room. Jerry didn't scream at us all the time, and he didn't try to coach through fear. Helping Jerry was Rolland Todd, his old friend from Fresno, and Rolland worked a lot with me on my offense. Between Jerry's work on defense and Rolland on offense, we learned a lot about the game. The players also knew each other well, because we played in pickup games year-round. We played tougher ball in practice than in a lot of games, because our second string may have been the second-best team in the league. We practiced for three hours a day, a million drills and as much conditioning as I've ever had—and that includes my seven years in the NBA. All we ever did was run. The big thing was that the coaches had confidence in us. They put us out there and we knew they believed in us. They weren't going to turn their backs on us the moment something went wrong.''

At this point, Jerry also was often starting four blacks.

Tarkanian: ''I never thought much about it, because I was looking for the kids who could win. But once in a while, I'd overhear someone say, 'Why can't Riverside play a couple of white kids?' The old joke would go around that you played three blacks at home, four on the road, and five when you were in trouble. All I looked for was the kids who were committed to basketball. Often, those were the black kids. I certainly wasn't paying attention to who was black or who was white. Now that I look back at team pictures in old RCC yearbooks, it seems our teams were pretty well balanced. We started four blacks when Rule led the team to our first state championship in 1964, and we started four whites when we won the state championship in 1966. After the first few years, about all the good kids from the Riverside area wanted to play for us. They heard our games on the radio, saw the big stories in the paper, and talked to kids such as Bobby Rule, who played at Riverside and loved it. We were a junior college with a major college atmosphere.''

Bobby Rule: ''After playing at Riverside, I had several scholarship offers from four-year schools, but I sat out a year waiting for Jerry to get a four-year college job. I ended up at Colorado State. The coach was older, and he said he would stay only one year and then they were going to hire Jerry. I never knew if that was true or not, but the coach never retired and Jerry never came. I guess the old coach liked winning and wanted to stay.''

Rule was a second-round draft pick by the Seattle Supersonics, and in his first three years (1967–70) he averaged 24 points and 10 rebounds as a 6-foot-9, 235-pound center. Lenny Wilkins was his coach at Seattle.

Lenny Wilkens: "Bobby was on the verge of becoming a great center when he ripped up his Achilles tendon. He had three good years for us, and that fourth season he played four games and I thought this was it, Bob Rule was ready to become one of the premier big men in the league. He had a nice 15-foot jumper, he could really get up and down the floor, and he knew how to get rebounds. When he played a great center such as Bill Russell or Wilt Chamberlain, you could put down 25 to 30 points next to Rule's name, because he really turned on the jets for those guys. He was very popular on the team. He liked to party, but he was a warm guy and easy to coach. It's just too bad he got hurt."

Rule played three more years, but he wasn't the same because the foot injury had severely reduced his mobility. He has had several jobs since leaving basketball, including being a stockbroker and running basketball clinics for the Riverside Parks Department. Now he is a grounds supervisor at Arlington High in Riverside, and he is finishing his degree so he can become a science teacher.

Bobby Rule: "I like working with kids, and I think that goes back to our days at Riverside and the closeness we had on the team. Going over to the coach's house for cookouts, or just sitting around and talking. Lois became very close to players because we could tell her things that we knew would get Tark mad. Lois was a second mom to a lot of the guys."

Riverside was also special to Lois.

Lois: "I tell everyone that those were our golden years, the happiest time of our life. Mention Riverside, and only good things fill my mind. Jerry bought us a home that was a little way out of town. It was on two-thirds of an acre, and we cut a window through the kitchen wall so we could have a nice view of a small valley below. Crossing the valley was an old English-styled train bridge with curved arches. Our kids loved to watch the trains go by every morning during breakfast.

"Our family was growing. George, our fourth child, was born in the summer of 1963. We were delighted to have what we thought was a perfect family: two girls and two boys. It was a time when Jerry actually enjoyed working around the house. He built a pretty good sandbox and drove about thirty-six miles to Palm Springs to get 'the

45

best sand' for his kids. He built them a playhouse, although it was a bit wobbly and it did lose some of its roofing each time we had a heavy wind. The kids had fun with Jerry and called him 'the Fix-It Man.'

"Of course Jerry didn't fix everything just right. One time he tried to fix the kitchen sink. He took the faucet off with a wrench and ended up with water spurting all over the place. Another time, he went to work on the bathroom sink. When he was done with it, we could only use the hot water or the cold water, but not both. So we settled for the hot water in the winter, the cold in the summer. Jerry was so pleased with himself whenever he did anything around the house, he'd go around saying, 'No job is too big for the Fix-It Man.' I told his mother once that I thought it would be easier on all of us if Jerry didn't try to fix anything, but she told me to keep encouraging him and he'd get better. I can't say he really did, though.

"The thing that meant the most to us in Riverside was the closeness we had, in our family and with our team. I remember going for spaghetti dinners at the home of Tom Ferraro, one of our players, and getting to know Joyce Ricci, who had to be the most loyal cheerleader ever. Best of all was our relationship with the players. There was a coach at Fullerton City College, Claude Retherford, who was a really snappy dresser. The man wore $100 suits, which back then was very expensive, and he seemed to have a new suit every week. He knew that a lot of our players had little money, so he'd pass on some of his old clothes to us to give to them. We'd have the kids over to our house and start opening those big cardboard boxes stuffed with clothes, and it was like Christmas morning. They'd laugh in awe and delight at Retherford's wardrobe, trying on this shirt or that jacket to see what fit whom best.

"When the players came by just to see us or to talk about a problem, I always tried to have their favorite foods. I particularly remember stocking our refrigerator with strawberry ice cream for Joe Davis. He loved the stuff and ate it by the gallon. The players would babysit, help with some of the chores, play with our children, and just generally, be near us.

"I'm sure the closeness we all felt for each other helped our teams win so big. I remember that after one of the Ferraro spaghetti dinners, Bobby Rule and Tom Crowder were involved in a severe automobile accident. They were passengers in a car that went forty feet over a ravine. Crowder did not get hurt badly, but Rule ended up in the hospital. Nobody thought the team could stay undefeated without Rule in the lineup, but they all came together to pick up the slack until Bobby returned. Ferraro, who had been averaging 6 points per game scored 20 points in our next game. Rule told us Sam Knight would fill in for him, and he did, getting 18 rebounds. It was incredible. I believe they were able to do it partly because of how much they cared for each other. They ended that year with a 35–0 record.

"We didn't have to worry then about breaking some rule when we fed players or gave them some hand-me-down clothes to wear."

Tarkanian: "Sometimes I wonder if those individuals who make NCAA rules really understand what's happening in some parts of society. I had a great kid on my team by the name of Randy Hoxie. At that point in my career, he was the greatest guard I had ever coached. He was good-looking and intelligent. One day in practice I yelled at him for not running hard, and the next day I really ripped him for doing the same thing. He came into my office that second day and apologized for not going as hard as I wanted. He said he had had nothing to eat in over two days and couldn't sleep well at night. He'd been drinking hot water to fill his stomach so he wouldn't feel the hunger pains and could get some sleep. I felt terrible. I loved that kid and had no idea things were so bad for him. It taught me to look at each player as an individual, and if a kid is not playing hard, to look beyond what seems to be the obvious and find out if something else is wrong. Some of these kids have problems we can't relate to. We need to take the time to get a better understanding of what's happening and relate to those problems better."

Lois: "Jerry was so stunned when that incident with Randy happened. He did everything he could to help him afterwards. Then one day Randy, who also was an excellent baseball player, came to Jerry and said that he had been offered a professional baseball contract. He had another year of eligibility, and told Jerry that if Jerry told him to stay, he would, but that his father really wanted him to sign because the family needed the money. His dad owed back money on his union dues and couldn't work at his job until it was paid off. Jerry did not feel he could hold Randy back, so he told him to do what was best for his family. I was out of town at the time. When I returned and found out what happened, I was furious, primarily because Randy was such a good kid, and I knew he wasn't ready for some kind of pro sports life. As it was, the team sent him to play for a minor league club in the South, where he was thoroughly miserable, and Randy ended up having nothing. When I yelled at Jerry, though, all he could say was, 'Lois, what could I do? You remember when he had to drink hot water. How could I hold him back?' Jerry and Randy remained close friends, and Randy named his first child after Jerry."

*   *   *

After Tarkanian's first year at Riverside (14–13), he had a 131–9 record in the next four seasons, totally dominating California junior college basketball in an unprecedented fashion. In 1965–66, Tarkanian's last season at Riverside, he had what is still considered the strongest team in California junior college history. The starters were all from the Riverside area—Larry Bonsoumet, Jim Gardner, Larry Bunce, Steve Barber, and Lucky Smith. So were his first two substitutes, Joe Stephens and Curtis Cooper, Rule's cousin.

Lucky Smith was a very interesting player. In the Air Force and stationed at March Air Force Base, Smith was married and had a son. Tarkanian spotted him playing in a Riverside city league. Jerry served as a timekeeper for those games and sometimes went out for a few beers with the players after games. In this way he got to know Lucky Smith, and he persuaded Smith to attend Riverside.

Tarkanian: "Lucky was a good player for us. But what really impressed me was that he stuck it out and got his degree. That's not easy when you're 24 and a father. He now earns a high income as a computer entrepreneur in the Silicon Valley. We've stayed close with Lucky and his former wife, Alice, and in 1987, their son, John, became a part of our UNLV team."

In the 1966 California JUCO state tournament, Tarkanian, assistant Ken Krivanek, and trainer Al Boyd had a team with an average victory margin of 43 points. Riverside won the championship game by 30. Tarkanian still liked the pressure man-to-man defense, but he was also winning with a zone defense. It was a 1-2-2 zone he had developed in 1964 when his team started slowly—by Tarkanian's standards—at 5–4.

Tarkanian: "We were a poor defensive team [in 1964] and I was really disappointed with the 5–4 start. Like most coaches in California, I was using the pressure man-to-man defense, which came from Pete Newell. Pete was a great coach at the University of California at Berkeley, and I idolized him. Our Riverside team was going to the Sam Barry Tournament in Glendale, which was a very big tournament because it had the top ten junior college teams in the state. I knew that I had to do something and that I couldn't stay with the man-to-man defense or we'd get creamed, so I put in the 1-2-2 zone.

"Our first game was against Jim Killingsworth's Cerritos Community College team. Jim was one of my closest friends. We would spend a lot of time together talking basketball in the off season. In the Sam Barry game we started in the man-to-man against Jim's team and fell behind. We went to the 1-2-2 zone and won. I really felt embarrassed for having to use a zone, and I remember I apologized to Jim about it after the game. I told him that our team was just so bad in the man-to-man defense that I had to go to the zone to have any chance of winning. In the second game of the tournament, we played Denny Crum's Pierce team. We won, and again I felt bad for the zone and apologized. I just felt that having to go to the zone was a weakness in my coaching, and I had a complex about it. Then we won the third game, and I didn't apologize. I figured that we were on to something. We played the 1-2-2 zone for the rest of the year and won 24 of our last 25 games, and I stuck with the 1-2-2 zone for the next eleven years.

"We became incredibly successful with that zone. Other coaches didn't know how to attack it. They thought there was some secret to it, but there wasn't any. I've always wanted my teams to do only one or two things, but I wanted them to do them well and take pride in them. We liked the fact that although the other coaches knew exactly what we were going to do, knowing gave them no advantage because our execution was so good. I've been told that I almost ruined high school ball in California, because after a while about 75 percent of the high school teams had given up the man-to-man defense and were using the 1-2-2 zone.

"I know that no other junior college team in California used the 1-2-2 zone in the play-offs until we did; and then, about three years later, six of the eight teams in the play-offs used it. Lots of coaches would ask us about our zone, and we gave them all the information that we had. They thought we were hiding something, but we didn't hold anything back. They kept asking about a gimmick, but there was no gimmick. We just played with great intensity.

"After one of our games, Jerry Norman, the assistant coach at the University of California at Los Angeles (UCLA) at the time, asked me to come over to UCLA and talk about the 1-2-2 zone with Coach John Wooden. It was the first time I had ever met Wooden, and I thought being asked to discuss our zone with him was the ultimate compliment."

There were other four-year coaches who were impressed with Tarkanian's zone. In March of 1966 both Tex Winter, then a highly respected coach at Kansas State, and Ladell Anderson, then coach at Utah State and now coach at Brigham Young University, were quoted as saying Riverside had the "best zone defense seen anywhere."

"I think our ultimate use of that zone came in the 1966 state tournament finals in Bakersfield," says Tarkanian. "I know I was quoted as saying that was our best Riverside team ever. I'd never had a junior college team play better. Many thought our junior college team could have beaten most four-year colleges."

49

Coaches, veteran observers, and university scouts in attendance agreed. Riverside defeated three conference champions by a total margin of 118 points in a field that was considered the strongest ever. They beat their first opponent by 41 points, their second by 47, and their third, a highly regarded San Francisco team, by 30.

Tarkanian calls the tournament finals "one of the greatest weeks of my life." The finals were held in Bakersfield; Riverside fans swarmed the city and packed the arena. Orange and black, Riverside's school colors, were everywhere. It was the first and remains the only time that any California junior college had won three state titles in a row.

Shortly after winning the title, Tarkanian was devastated when his mother suffered a severe stroke, never to regain full consciousness. Within a few weeks, she died.

Once again, Tarkanian was about to make a career move and wasn't sure why. Jerry had loved Redlands, remember, yet he left for Riverside. Since it had been from a high school to a junior college, that move could at least be viewed as a promotion.

Jerry says, "Walking away from Riverside for Pasadena City College may be the craziest thing I've ever done. Twenty years later, I still can't figure it out."

Tarkanian thought Riverside had become the best junior college program in the country. He bragged that his assistant Ken Krivanek, an RCC alum who also taught English and German classes, was the most intelligent assistant in the country. Athletic director T. Mark Johnson strongly supported the program. The football and basketball staffs were good friends as well as coworkers. Tarkanian would later recall fondly the beers shared after work with football staff members Bob Dohr, Al Fages, Nate De Francisco, and Don Birren.

Winning a lot of games was part of it. The city itself also played a crucial role. The people loved the players and the team, and they helped to make Riverside the place kids wanted to go to play basketball. In 1964, the community even voted Jerry as Riverside's father of the year, in recognition of his role as father with his own children and also with the players on his teams.

Tarkanian's last team at Riverside (1965–66) had a 33–1 record and won another state championship. Its tournament victories were by margins of 44, 57, and 30 points. Radio announcer Ralph Lawler released a record about RCC basketball titled "Three in a Row." Some people in Riverside even filmed those three tournament games and sold the films. Today, when almost everyone has a VCR, that would be no surprise. But in 1966 that was special, especially for a junior college team.

Then factors fell in place that led to another move.

As usual, little was normal in the way Tarkanian went from Riverside to Pasadena. He wasn't thinking of making a change. He didn't wake up one morning and say, "I'm going to take that Pasadena job." Until he accepted the position, he didn't even know he wanted it.

The president of Pasadena City College was Armen Sarafian, an Armenian. Jerry isn't sure that Sarafian's ancestry had anything to do with why he went to Pasadena, but since Jerry doesn't know why he did go, maybe Sarafian's being an Armenian was a factor. Whatever Jerry thought, Sarafian showed the persistence of his forefathers as he worked upon Jerry's loyalty to his former school and to Armenian relatives living in the Pasadena area.

Sarafian sent his athletic director, Tony Linehan, to the California state junior college tournament in Bakersfield. Riverside's fans were out in full force. The 5,000-seat gym was sold out each evening, and 3,000 of those attending were from Riverside. The RCC team was slicing through the opposition. Tarkanian was sucking on a towel, the crowd was ready to tear down the building, and Linehan knew this was just what Sarafian wanted at Pasadena. In the six previous years, Pasadena City College had won only 41 games, an average of less than 7 wins per season. The current team was 6–22, and PCC hadn't drawn 3,000 fans in its last three seasons combined. Sarafian had plans to build a strong athletic department, and he saw Tarkanian as the man who could be a major factor in doing it. He immediately offered Jerry the job; Jerry immediately declined.

Tarkanian: "I really wasn't interested in Pasadena. I swear I wasn't. But I kept thinking about Pasadena. It was my hometown, and when I was coaching in high school, I'd have crawled on my hands and knees from Fresno to take it. I kept thinking that my mother would have wanted me in Pasadena, where many of my close relatives still lived. But it was in the smog. And it also played games in the afternoon, and no one bothered to show up to watch. The old coach had pulled the team out of a tournament because it was twenty-five minutes away from Pasadena and he thought that was too far to drive."

So why did Tarkanian leave?

Tarkanian: "It started with phone calls. It seemed about every time I picked up the receiver some old friend from Pasadena was on the line telling me that I should come home to coach. The college president was a friend of my family's and my family thought it would be

51

nice if I came back to Pasadena. The president and his wife visited Lois and me, and they gave us a hard sell. The new part of the offer was that I could be assistant to the dean of students, so that when I wanted to quit coaching I could go into college administration."

That part appealed to Lois.

Lois: "Armen Sarafian was a master recruiter and he pulled out all the stops. He told Jerry how much it would have meant to his mother if Jerry had worked in Pasadena, an area she loved so much. He said Jerry's return would be important to all the Armenians living in Pasadena. He talked about how Pasadena would be the perfect place for Jerry to get exposure so he could get a job at a four-year school. If it weren't for Armen Sarafian, we never would have left Riverside. But every time we said no to something, Armen came back with another offer or another reason why Jerry should reconsider. I liked the dean of students position for Jerry because I still looked at him more as a full-time teacher than a full-time coach. Armen also said Jerry would be given time to complete work on his administrative credentials, and that was important to us—we had four children to support. Sarafian even worked out loans for us and extra paying jobs for Jerry so we could afford a nice home."

Despite all that, Jerry insisted he was staying at Riverside.

Tarkanian: "One night I was up until 2 a.m. I had some Riverside reporters at our house, including Ron Shaffer, and I told them that I wasn't going to Pasadena, that Riverside just meant too much to me. But I said I wanted to personally tell the Pasadena president of my decision because I wanted to thank him for the great offer. The next day I went to the Pasadena president's house to say I was staying at Riverside, and by the time I walked out of there I was going to Pasadena. To this day, I'm not sure what happened. But it was done."

Whether Jerry liked it or not, the Riverside era (1960–66) was the past and Pasadena was the present. Before leaving, Tarkanian made efforts to ensure that Bill Mulligan, current coach at University of California-Irvine, was able to get the RCC job.

Jerry had been in difficult situations before. Riverside had problems when the Tarkanians arrived, but Jerry had never seen anything like Pasadena. The team had gone 5–23 the year before. It was in the Western States Conference, and it was a league where no one but current Louisville coach Denny Crum cared about basketball. Crum coached at Pierce College and he had won 44 straight regular-season games. But when Crum's team got into the state tournament, they'd usually lose their first two games and be eliminated because their league was so weak that they weren't prepared for statewide competition.

Tarkanian: "At least Denny Crum was trying to win. The rest of the coaches were retired or something. They liked day games because it gave them the nights free to have dinner and watch television. These coaches didn't recruit, they played golf every day. This should have been the best conference in California because it had the junior colleges with the largest enrollments, but it was the worst because the coaches just didn't care about basketball. They were just plain lazy. My first few months there were awful. I couldn't figure out why I had left Riverside where basketball was so important to the community. I kept asking myself just what had I done. In Riverside, they sold films of our team. In Pasadena, they didn't even charge admission to the games, which said a lot about the lack of fan interest. In Riverside, the sky was clear and driving was no trouble. In Pasadena, there was all this traffic and smog. I thought about it so much that after a while, I felt like I was walking around in a trance."

Eventually, Jerry realized that he could have the same type program at Pasadena as he had at Riverside. Working in his favor was the fact that Denny Crum was the only coach in the league who tried to recruit, so Jerry was able to get the best local kids to attend Pasadena. He knew a lot of high school coaches and they steered players in his direction. Winning leads to great recruiting. Tarkanian won at Riverside and since the move to Pasadena, the kids wanted to go to Pasadena because they thought playing in a strong program would get them a scholarship to a four-year school.

Tarkanian: "As the season drew closer, I settled into Pasadena and I liked it. Sarafian had been right; it was good to be back with old friends and family. I was given an office at the rear of the student union—I also was assistant dean of students. My job was to help the student body function properly. I was adviser to the student government and also worked extensively in keeping the lid on possible riots, since my years at PCC were during the heavy student protest times. I'd chaperon dances and our players would show up too, and we'd have some good times together. I'd brought Joe Barnes, one of my former RCC players, to be my assistant coach. Joe had finished college and gone on to obtain a master's degree at Whittier College."

Tarkanian also was able quickly to assemble a talented team. One member of that team was John Trapp, who was from Detroit.

Tarkanian: "I admit that John did have a chip on his shoulder when I first met him. He'd been dropped out of a couple of schools. He was just an immature kid who had done some stupid things. But John hit it off well with my family. The reason we got to know John and his parents was sort of interesting. George Gaddy, who worked in the

Detroit public schools, sent a lot of players to different colleges in California, and he had sent John to San Jacinto Junior College, which was near Riverside. The coach at San Jacinto was Danny Ayala, a good friend of mine. John had a problem at San Jacinto, and Danny asked me if I would take him. So I took John to Riverside. He sat out a year so he could get his grades in order. That was during my last year at Riverside. When I took the Pasadena job, the Riverside people made it clear that they didn't want to work with John anymore, so I took him with me to Pasadena. His parents liked the way I had handled John, and they decided they wanted both John and his brother, George, to play for me. George at that time was a great high school player in Highland Park, Michigan. Mr. Trapp was able to get a job transfer to an automobile company in Montebello, so he moved his family to nearby Monrovia because they had relatives there. George played at Monrovia High School and John was eligible at Pasadena City College."

Lois: "I heard stories about John. Danny Ayala's wife, Linda, a good friend of mine, was concerned. Part of it was John's very tough looks. I don't blame people for how they felt. After hearing all the stories and meeting John, it was as if there were two different people. John's reputation was bad, but he was a great person for us. He baby-sat our kids. He took our daughters to ballet lessons. He helped around our home. Some of the other coaches' wives would ask me, 'How can you let him take care of your children?' I think the fact that we assumed John wasn't going to be a problem and would act responsibly is part of the reason he did. He was glad that someone gave him credit for knowing how to do what was right.

"Ironically, John became a folk hero for the 'establishment' in Pasadena. When the Students for a Democratic Society (S.D.S.) showed up on campus and planted their flag in the middle of the student square, John Trapp strode over to the flag, pulled it out of the ground, and broke it over his knee. That made a real impression on a lot of people.

"John had been to a couple of different schools, but he only felt good playing for Jerry. I remember reading a *Sports Illustrated* story in which Mr. Trapp was asked why he would move his family from Michigan to California just so his sons could play basketball. Mr. Trapp said that Jerry was the only one who could handle John, and that he would 'move his family to the ends of the earth' so that his sons could play for Jerry Tarkanian. John's case is an excellent example of why we don't always believe what people tell us about kids. We like to get to know them ourselves and make up our own minds. It's too easy to label a kid unfairly."

Pasadena's team began with John Trapp. Jerry then recruited Sam Carter, a star from nearby Monrovia High. Donald Guyton and Phil Vartanian also were team members. What really made the team, however, was Sam Robinson, a great player at Jefferson High in Los Angeles. Sam's older brother, Charles, had at one time wanted to play for Tarkanian at Riverside. That's when the Tarkanians first met the Robinson family. He went on to play at Los Angeles Valley Junior College, but by then Jerry had already developed a special relationship with the Robinsons. So when Sam graduated from high school, it wasn't surprising that he enrolled at Pasadena. The team's point guard was Darrell Evans, who went on to play professional baseball. Thus, Jerry had two junior college players—Steve Barber at Riverside and Evans at Pasadena—who eventually had careers in the major leagues.

At Pasadena, Jerry went 35–1 in his first year and won another state championship, his fourth in a row. "We had mostly local and a few recruited kids on the team, and we won immediately," he explains. "As I said, the league wasn't very good, and that was the only time in my coaching career that I wasn't nervous before games. I just knew we would win."

Lois also liked Pasadena.

Lois: "We did the same things with the kids at Pasadena as we did at Riverside. We had a guest room behind our home in Arcadia. John Trapp and a lot of the other players would come to the house to visit or study and would stay overnight there from time to time. We thought it was great, because we knew where the players were and what they were doing and could influence them more. When you have a player near you and your family, you really get to know him. An inner-city kid sees that there is another way to live and that he can fit in that other way. It is a tremendous education for him, a great learning experience. It was a little awkward because Arcadia was an all-white, relatively affluent city, and I know some of our neighbors weren't wild about our having black kids visiting all the time, but the neighbors really didn't do anything about it other than ask me a couple of times, a little bit tensely, who those kids were and whether I really thought I should let them baby-sit our children.

"I was still doing consultant work with various schools in San Bernardino County. It was a great help that the players and their mothers took turns baby-sitting. You see, that was the thing—it wasn't just us helping the players, but it was the players and their families also helping us. We really were all in it together. We were going day and night, but it never seemed like a job, in the sense of punching a time card and waiting for the hours to pass so you could get away from it. We never were away from the kids and the basketball, but that was how we wanted it.

"Jerry was earning a good salary then, so money wasn't a factor in my working. I mainly continued because of commitments I had made in programs I started for deaf and autistic children. At that time, California was just beginning classes for autistic children, and I was state chairman of a research committee. The San Bernardino County superintendent, Roy Hill, and my immediate boss, Lucy Siegrist, were marvelous in letting me work flexible hours. Of course, we did have four young children, so we didn't have really a whole lot of money, but neither of us ever had rich tastes or wealthy friends, so money wasn't an issue. Our grocery bills were large because players were eating at our house a lot, but I loved those days, and anyway, to me that is what teaching is really all about, mixing what someone learns in school with experiences out of school."

During the 1960s the California junior colleges weren't just feeders for players; a few coaches also moved up. Those who would go on to make names for themselves in four-year schools included Bob Boyd (Santa Ana Junior College), Jim Killingsworth (Cerritos Community College), Bobby Dye (Santa Monica Junior College), Lute Olsen (Long Beach City College), and Denny Crum (Pierce Junior College).

Tarkanian: "I always felt there were some other junior college coaches at the time who were as good as any of us who went on. Two of them were Sid Phelan at San Francisco City College and Bud Presley at Menlo Park Community College. Both of them were great coaches, and it's something of an injustice that they never got the opportunity to move on to the four-year level. It just goes to show you the importance of being at the right place at the right time."

When Jerry coached at Riverside, he did consider leaving the California junior college system for a four-year job. He was contacted by the University of Idaho, Idaho State, and the University of Nevada at Las Vegas. But Jerry thought that if he quit the junior colleges, it would be to coach at a four-year school in California. The Tarkanians at that time didn't want to leave the southern California area, which is why he never pursued those job opportunities.

At Pasadena, Jerry had received a $3,200 raise after his first year, making his salary $18,200. That was more than the coach at Southern

California was earning. In fact, Jerry was probably on a higher salary scale than most of the four-year coaches in the state. The California junior college system in the 1960s was so strong and paid so well that some professors turned down chances to go to four-year schools.

Tarkanian: "I liked being the assistant to the dean of students, and Armen Sarafian was right: it was very rewarding to coach at home before all your family and old friends. Besides, Sarafian became like a second father to me. Being near Los Angeles meant that we started to get a lot more coverage in the newspapers, and that was a boost to the program. I got to know a lot of four-year college coaches, because they would visit me to recruit my kids at both Riverside and Pasadena. Some of those coaches would invite me out for a few beers, and we'd talk basketball until about 2 a.m. Making matters better was the fact that my job was so good at Pasadena that I could set my own hours. After talking to the four-year coaches, or seeing them at a clinic or convention, I'd get all fired up and start thinking about taking a four-year job. Then I'd get back to my junior college coaching, and I'd put it out of my mind.

"In my heart, I never thought I'd coach at a major college program. I lacked the big-time background that most coaches have—I wasn't an All-American, I didn't even play at a big school, and I had no mentor who was a major coach pushing me. I coached at a junior college, which wasn't the primary area from which four-year coaches were hired. Most four-year coaches usually were assistants at four-year schools. I never was an assistant, and I never wanted to be one; I liked running my own program too much to work for someone else. Eddie Sutton has told me he felt the same way. He says the two of us may be the only coaches in the country who never were assistants and who coached at all three levels—high school, junior college, and four-year college.

"I understood that my background had drawbacks, and that's why I never hesitated to take jobs at newer schools. I never expected an established program to hire me, and if I wanted to work I had to go to a place that was starting out. When Lois said my wildest dreams were coaching at San Diego State or Long Beach, she was right. I was sure that an established program would never want me.

"One day I was sitting in the athletic director's office at Pasadena when Fred Miller called. Fred was the athletic director at Long Beach, and he wanted to set up an interview. That night we were playing Denny Crum's Pierce College team. Fred wanted to talk with me immediately about the job, and I wanted to see him right away, too."

To most men, Long Beach would not have been the end of the

coaching rainbow. It had no athletic tradition, a small athletic budget, and 28,000 students, almost all of whom commuted. The campus was called "the mausoleum on the hill."

Long Beach appealed to Jerry for the following reasons:

1. It was near the beach. Jerry liked the fact that there was less smog, and he could go to the beach easily if he wanted to. He thought it would be great for his four children. It also was in California, which was where Lois and Jerry wanted to stay.

2. Most of the Long Beach students started at junior colleges. Jerry had had plenty of experience with junior college kids, and he also knew that he could take his team from Pasadena with him to Long Beach and have instant respectability.

3. As a coach, it was a no-lose situation. Long Beach never had had good basketball teams before, so Jerry knew that anything he did would be a plus.

4. After seven years as a junior college coach, Jerry thought he was as ready as he'd ever be for a four-year job. He was and still is the winningest junior college coach in California history. A four-year job was the logical next step.

Tarkanian: "Fred Miller met with me in a restaurant in the city of Commerce, which is halfway between Pasadena and Long Beach. I thought it was just going to be a normal interview, and then Fred would talk to some other guys and I wouldn't know for weeks, or maybe even months, whether I had the job. But by the end of dinner Fred had offered me the job, and I took it right on the spot. The fact was that this was my first concrete offer to coach at a four-year school in the area where I wanted to live. There had been schools checking on my interest, but no one until Fred Miller had ever said, 'The job is yours if you want it.'

"We kept it quiet through most of the season, but word got out right before the junior college state finals. I had a meeting with the team prior to the game and I told them that I was gone. It seemed to shake up the kids. The timing could not have been worse, but I had no choice. There were radio reports that I was the next coach at Long Beach, and I couldn't go into the dressing room and lie to the kids. We lost in overtime to Cerritos."

Tarkanian had won four consecutive state championships; no one has won more than two in a row before or since. He lost two state titles in overtime by 1 point each at the beginning and end of that string, or it would have been six straight state titles. No coach dominated California JUCO basketball as Tarkanian did. After his first 14–13 season at Riverside, he had 145–12 in the next six seasons. He also coached the junior college team for the 1968 Olympic trials, a team that featured future NBA players John Johnson and Spencer Haywood, along with Pasadena's Trapp and Robinson. Tarkanian guided that team to a victory over the four-year college Olympic trial team, which was considered a major upset.

Of course, what he did in junior college wasn't going to win any games at Long Beach State, and Jerry didn't thoroughly check out the Long Beach program. But that was usual for Tarkanian. When his heart said go, he went, and he worried about it later.

Lois also was in favor of the move.

Lois: "We were very impressed by Fred Miller, because he seemed dedicated to building a strong athletic department. Coaching at Long Beach had been one of Jerry's dreams, so I saw no reason to try and talk him out of it. But I also thought Long Beach would be a good spot for us. The Pasadena president wanted us to stay because he said he had friends at California-Berkeley and that job was about to open, but we went because Jerry wanted Long Beach and felt the chance might never be there again."

Once they arrived at Long Beach, Lois and Jerry were in for some real surprises.

4

First Person: Why I Like Transfers and Junior College Kids

For seven years I was a junior college basketball coach. For three years, I was a junior college student. Just because I finally got a coaching job at a four-year school didn't mean I'd turn my back on J.C. players. I didn't care what other coaches may have said about junior college kids; I liked them.

Hey, I was one of them.

My son Danny went to Dixie Junior College in St. George, Utah. He wasn't sure where he wanted to go for a four-year school, so he went to Dixie for a year and he had one of the best times of his life. He wouldn't trade that year for anything—and Danny was a high school honors student, an honors student at Dixie, and a two-time Academic All-American when he played for us at UNLV. He was even awarded a postgraduate NCAA scholarship.

My experience and my son's have convinced me that a J.C. kid deserves the same chance as any other student. But some people think junior college kids don't deserve the same opportunity, and that's ridiculous. I never had the prejudices that a number of coaches hold about J.C. kids. I knew them too well. When I left Pasadena City College for Long Beach State, there was never any doubt that I'd build the basketball program with junior college players, even though that was in 1968, when very few four-year schools recruited from the junior colleges. I don't think any of the major college programs had a majority of JUCO kids. It just wasn't done.

But we did it at Long Beach. When most basketball people saw that our program was primarily J.C. kids, they said we'd never win. That's part of the reason I was so happy about our success at Long Beach: it showed that J.C. kids could be both productive students and basketball players at a four-year university. We proved a lot of people wrong.

So I was the first seriously to recruit J.C. kids. I was told that you couldn't win with junior college kids because they are hard to coach, because they like to play too much one-on-one, run-and-gun basketball, and they wouldn't learn your system. I found that to be wrong. We couldn't have won at such a high level at Long Beach unless the kids sacrificed and played team basketball.

When other coaches did take J.C. players, it was one or two at the most. That's so the J.C. kids could blend in with the rest of the team, which was mostly four-year students. But in my five years at Long Beach, we had only three players who started with us as freshmen. My first team to make the NCAA tournament, the Long Beach team of 1970, had three kids from Pasadena City College on the front line, a guard from Pierce Junior College, and a guard from Long Beach City Junior College. That may have been the first time a team with a starting lineup of all junior college players made the NCAA tournament. Four of those kids were from the same California Junior College Conference, so don't tell me that you can't win with J.C. kids.

At Long Beach State, a large portion of our student body had previously attended junior college. In California, the master plan for education was that most kids would attend junior college first, many would transfer to four-year state colleges, and then some would attend the university level for graduate work. As I recall, the formula was something like 12½ percent to be admitted to the university level, 37½ percent to the state college level, and the rest to junior colleges. The junior college students would complete an associate of arts degree and move to state colleges for the final two years to finish their bachelor of arts degree. Several of the junior colleges in California offered a higher level of curriculum and a broader selection of courses than many small colleges throughout the country.

When I was at Long Beach, there was another reason for having junior college players, which no longer exists. At that time freshmen were not eligible to play varsity basketball. That meant those kids had to play a very restricted schedule against freshmen teams from other universities. But at a junior college, a kid could play 30 to 35 games a year. He also could practice just about all year, because there were no rules saying when junior college teams could work out. A lot of junior colleges started basketball practice on the first day of school, so a kid had a much better chance of developing his talent because he was playing so much more than a freshman at a four-year school. Now that freshmen are eligible to play at four-year schools, that advantage is gone, but it was very important to me during my days at Long Beach.

I'm not going to use that as a reason for taking JUCO players. It comes down to the fact that I like J.C. kids because I was one of them. In fact, it took me three years to get out of Pasadena City College, so I never considered myself a brilliant student. I was like a lot of J.C. kids in that my main concerns were playing basketball and finding the next party. And I continued to struggle in school at Fresno State until I met Lois and got my priorities in order. Then I went from a barely average student to an excellent one, a guy who even earned his master's degree with honors.

I often mention what I did in school, not to brag, but to show what can be done. A lot of kids I have coached are like me. All they need is to be motivated properly and placed in a good environment in order to do well in school. So when I hear that a kid is having a hard time with the books, I don't just write him off. I want to meet the kid, talk to him for a long time, and see if I can find a way to reach him.

Kids go to a junior college for a variety of reasons:

Maybe they have to work and need to go to a school close to home that won't cost them much.

Maybe they messed around in high school and need to work on their grades.

Maybe they were athletes who developed late physically, or perhaps they didn't start playing basketball until their last couple of years of high school.

Maybe they're just kids who want a little more time before they decide which four-year school they will commit to for the rest of their college career.

The purpose of junior college is to help kids, not stigmatize them. A couple of years ago, I encouraged Indiana's Bobby Knight to take 6-foot-10 Dean Garrett, who was at San Francisco City Community College. Bobby also signed another J.C. kid named Keith Smart, and Smart hit the jump shot that gave Indiana the national title in 1987.

Working with JUCOs is something I have been doing throughout my career. People wrote things about me such as, "Tarkanian has all these junior college transfers," as if it were a disease or something awful.

In the ideal world of college basketball, it would be nice to have all your players come to your school as freshmen who had high grades in high school. But that just doesn't happen. It is true that you get a big turnover every two years, because the JUCO kids use up their eligibility twice as fast as four-year students.

So what are the advantages of J.C. kids?

First, the kid is usually socially and emotionally more mature. He already has been away from home for a couple of years and is over his homesickness. He has adjusted from high school to college life.

Second, watching a kid play in junior college, I usually know him better and can see how he will fit in with my program. This was especially true during my early days at Long Beach, because I had just come out of the J.C. ranks as a coach and I knew all the California J.C. players.

Third—and this is the biggest advantage—they are easier to recruit. When I've recruited J.C. players, I didn't have to beat Kentucky, Louisville, and UCLA. Those schools were concentrating on high school kids. Most of the time, the other schools recruiting junior college players are Oklahoma, Kansas State, New Mexico, Wichita State, Bradley, and some of the schools in the California state system. These places have good programs, but not on the level of Kentucky, North Carolina, and the elite schools.

We always try to get the blue-chip high school player, but it's very hard when one of the other big powers is in the picture. So the junior colleges are a very realistic option for both parties. We can recruit against almost anyone who deals with junior colleges, and we get the kids we want. The J.C. kids and their coaches know that we have taken J.C. players over the years and done very well with them and for them. I have a special relationship with J.C. coaches because I worked the same places they did. We understand each other's problems. When we've recruited high school kids, we've had to deal with a lot of negative recruiting from other colleges, and even sometimes from the kids' high school coaches, because they have such a distorted image of Las Vegas. But when we've recruited a J.C. kid, the coaches have almost always been in our corner.

A lot of times, we don't even have to recruit J.C. kids. They and their coaches call us. This was true for Ed Catchings, Mark Wade, and Sam Smith, who all had good careers at UNLV. Remember that a J.C. kid has been away from home for two years. He has built up confidence in his ability to make decisions, and has more of an idea of what he wants out of college because he already has been exposed to some college life. The high school kid really doesn't know what to expect from college. He is influenced by his high school coach, his high school guidance counselor, his parents, his friends, and so many other people. It's hard to figure out just who will make the decision for the high school kid.

But in the case of the J.C. player, you know that he will make up his own mind. You just have to recruit and get to know him. That makes it so much easier.

Transfers from other four-year schools often are like J.C. players. They usually want to play for us, and they are the ones who make the decision about college. They have been exposed to college, so they are more realistic about it. Both a J.C. kid and a transfer from another school realize that we are giving them a last chance, and they play their hearts out for us. They can reflect back on their first couple of years in college; they can think about what they might have done wrong or what decision they made that didn't turn out as they'd hoped.

In many cases, we get kids wanting to transfer to UNLV whom we first recruited in high school. They went to another four-year college and found out that they had been fed a lot of lies. Then they started to think, "I should have gone to UNLV in the first place." Transfers are not bad kids. Al McGuire always used to take a few when he coached at Marquette. Making the correct choice for college is very hard, especially when a kid is highly recruited and so many coaches are filling the kid's head with all kinds of things.

Once in a while, we get a kid like Anthony Jones, who was a first-round draft pick by the Washington Bullets. Anthony was the high school player of the year in Washington, D.C. We never seriously recruited him because we knew we didn't have a chance to sign him. Anthony went to play for John Thompson at Georgetown, and the pressure of playing in his hometown was just too much for Anthony. One day, John Thompson called me and asked if I would be interested in taking Anthony Jones, because he needed a change of scene. Thompson felt that Anthony would be better off playing in another area of the country; everyone expected too much, too soon from him. John Thompson thought that Anthony was a fine player, but all the pressure had hurt his game. At that time, Anthony was shooting only 50 percent from the foul line, and he certainly is a much better shooter than that. John Thompson thought that UNLV would be a great place for Anthony and directed Anthony here a week before school started in 1983. I was thrilled to get him. He's a good kid and a great player. It was the fact that other transfers had done well playing for me that caused John Thompson to call about Anthony Jones.

The toughest part of being a transfer is that the kid has to sit out a year as a red-shirt player. That means he can practice with the team, but can't play in the games. Sometimes a kid doesn't practice, as was the case with Armon Gilliam, who concentrated on his studies and had an off-campus job. This can be a very difficult year. The coach doesn't get to spend as much time with the red-shirts as he'd like because he is very busy with the guys who are playing that season. This is when I worry about a kid. He probably isn't getting as much attention and supervision as would be ideal. The kid is new to the school and the area. He has few friends. Basketball has always been a big part of his life, but now it's gone because he has to sit out.

If the kid is smart, this can be a very profitable year. He can get straightened out academically because he doesn't have to travel with the team and miss classes. He can make new friends and adjust to his new college without having to deal with the pressures of big-time college ball. In many instances, it's a crossroads year for a kid—he'll get either better or worse. While Gary Graham was not a transfer, he did red-shirt a year, and he practiced with UNLV all season and really developed his guard skills. He also hit the books. But when John Flowers transferred from Indiana, he gained so much weight during his red-shirt year that he had a hard time losing it and was never the same player.

Most red-shirts come through because they know that this is the last resort. If they are ever going to cut it, this is the time. They can't keep going from school to school; they have to make it work at UNLV.

Transfers often show you a lot of loyalty, because they are grateful that you took them. I don't care about a kid's personal problems; if he's loyal you can work with him.

How do you measure loyalty in a transfer?

If a kid knocks his J.C. coach or his first college coach, I won't take him. I remember one kid from the University of Southern California who kept knocking his coach in the newspapers. He decided to quit USC and transfer. One of the schools he said he was interested in was UNLV. Some people close to him contacted us about a possible transfer, but I said no, and I was quoted in the newspapers as saying we didn't want him to transfer to UNLV. If he ripped his USC coach and that program, why would he suddenly be loyal to us?

But if a transfer says that things just didn't work out at his first school, or that he just needs a change of scene, we'll talk with him.

A controversy during the 1986–87 season centered around Lloyd Daniels, a 6-foot-8 guard from Brooklyn who spent part of that school year at UNLV. Although Daniels was never officially a part of the UNLV basketball program, he attended classes at the university hoping to gain athletic eligibility. Daniels had never really had a home. His mother died when he was three and he barely knows his father. His two grandmothers tried to help him, but primarily he grew up on the streets of Brooklyn. He had academic problems almost from the moment he started school, and he attended four different high schools. After arriving in Las Vegas, he was diagnosed as having dyslexia. The reading specialists who diagnosed this problem indicated that if Lloyd followed fully their prescribed remediation, he could be reading on a college level within 18 months.

Lloyd Daniels was dismissed from UNLV in February 1987 after he was arrested by Las Vegas police for attempting to purchase cocaine.

I want to say that Lloyd Daniels is a very nice person. He's not a malicious kid, a violent kid, or a loudmouth. He is a very sensitive but irresponsible kid. Considering the fact that he was on his own since he was eight years old, we could all ask ourselves how we would be if we had grown up the same way. He also is the best basketball player I've ever recruited, one of the best I've ever seen. I think he is in the same class as Magic Johnson. I used to sit up at night thinking about having Lloyd Daniels as my point guard. I wasn't even going to have any plays. I was just going to give Lloyd the ball and tell the other four guys to move.

In the summers after his freshman and sophomore years in high school, Daniels came to Las Vegas to play. He was with the Gauchos, a summer team from New York City coached by Lou d'Almeida. It was the same summer team that Sidney Green and Richie Adams had played for. Lou d'Almeida was impressed by how well Sidney Green and Richie Adams did at UNLV, and Lou d'Almeida and the other people thought that UNLV would also be a great place for Lloyd.

As a junior in high school, Lloyd averaged 31 points, 12 rebounds, and 10 assists a year [at Andrew Jackson High in New York]. He was too good for high school basketball; he just destroyed it. And remember: scoring was the weakest part of his game. Passing was the best part.

We got a call from some people around Lloyd who said that he wanted to go to a junior college instead of his senior year of high school. Lloyd did not have a high school degree, but he was 18 years old. You, your child, or anyone else who applies is automatically admitted to public California colleges after age 18, and Lloyd was 18. So that's how he was able to go to junior college even though he didn't have a high school degree. The feeling was that Lloyd was going to have some grade problems, that he was going to be a Proposition 48 victim and he'd have to go to junior college anyway, so the people around Lloyd thought he'd be better off just starting at a junior college instead of spending his senior year in high school. We were asked to help Lloyd find a junior college, and we responded as almost any college basketball coach in the country would—we said we'd help him.

The summer before he started junior college, Lloyd came to Las Vegas and took two reading courses. In the fall, he enrolled at Mt. San Antonio Junior College. He stayed there for one semester and passed twelve credit hours. While he was at Mt. San Antonio, UNLV assistant coach Mark Warkentien became his legal guardian. Mark didn't try to hide it. Mark made it very clear that he was doing this primarily because he and his wife Maureen had established a good relationship with Lloyd. They wanted to became his guardians so they could more personally monitor Lloyd's academic progress in junior college. Before Mark did this, he checked with our athletic director, Brad Rothermel, who checked with the Pacific Coast Athletic Conference, which checked with the NCAA. He was told that there was no rule against an assistant coach's being a legal guardian. However, about six weeks after Mark became Lloyd's guardian, we received a letter from the NCAA stating that Mark couldn't be Daniel's legal guardian because the relationship might be used for recruiting purposes.

After one semester at Mt. San Antonio, Lloyd decided that he wanted to attend UNLV. Anyone with fourteen college credits and a C average can be admitted to Nevada-Reno or UNLV. No special admission is needed; no committee has to rule on the case. The person isn't eligible for varsity athletics, but anyone with fourteen credit hours can attend UNLV. That's the law. Lloyd had in excess of fourteen credits after his summer work at UNLV and his fall semester at Mt. San Antonio. If Lloyd had wanted to apply to school here and we had wanted to keep him out, we couldn't do it. We'd be in violation of the law.

We knew when we recruited Lloyd that we were taking a real academic risk. Lloyd had trouble reading and had been diagnosed as dyslexic by a clinically certified psychologist in Las Vegas. Once we knew the problem, we were told by a reading specialist that if Lloyd worked hard he could be reading at a twelfth-grade level by the fall of 1988. We believe that our academic support system is one of the best in the country, and we thought that Lloyd had a chance. We have two full-time academic advisers dealing with fifteen basketball players. We have tutors for every single class and for remedial work. We thought that in this environment, Lloyd had a chance. If Lloyd had not been involved in that sting operation and the drugs, I think he would have had a decent chance of making it.

I think we did what most basketball coaches in the country would have done: we recruited Lloyd Daniels when we had the chance. When Lloyd was at Mt. San Antonio, we kept getting reports that other schools were trying to recruit him. Lloyd told us that while he was at Mt. San Antonio, among many contacts, he received a call from Andre McCarter of UCLA, who encouraged him to attend Santa Monica City College, as had Sidney Wicks and other former UCLA players. The day after we dropped Lloyd from UNLV, we received a call from a Kansas assistant coach asking about Lloyd.

Lloyd's case is somewhat similar to Walter Berry [of St. John's and now with the San Antonio Spurs]. Walter was from New York and was not a high school graduate. Walter went to St. John's for his first year, but the NCAA said that since Walter hadn't graduated from high school, he couldn't play. So Walter Berry went to San Jacinto Junior College for a year. Then he went back to St. John's.

No other university or coaching staff would have taken a stronger stance than we did on Lloyd's drug thing. On a Monday night, he was involved in the sting operation, and on the following afternoon he was told he would not be able to become a part of the UNLV basketball program.

People say that Lloyd Daniels didn't belong in college because he didn't graduate from high school. Well, our first All-American at UNLV, Ricky Sobers, also was from New York and didn't graduate from high school before going to junior college and then coming here. Ricky Sobers eventually played twelve years in the NBA, came back to UNLV, finished his degree in secondary education, and now is an analyst on our televised basketball games. Anyone who has met Ricky knows what a fine person he is and what a credit to the program he is. Today he is a solid citizen, a bright guy, and everyone likes him. But he was the same as Lloyd Daniels in that he was a non-high school graduate from New York. Finally, the decision to admit Lloyd was not made by the athletic department, but by the admissions office.

So when people say that Lloyd didn't deserve to be in college, I don't buy that. Like every kid, Lloyd deserved a chance at college and we gave it to him. Unfortunately, he didn't use it wisely. We all still care about Lloyd as a person, and Mark Warkentien remains in close contact with him, helping Lloyd any way he can. The Warkentiens have spent a lot of their own money on Lloyd's drug rehabilitation. Their relationship did not end after Lloyd left Las Vegas.

We still think Lloyd is a good kid with great talent, and we hope things work out for him.

The two biggest parts of coaching are communication and loyalty. If you can talk to your kids and if they believe in you, you can work with kids who may have had troubles growing up or who may have messed up in school. You can help those kids become solid persons in life.

When a kid is loyal, a coach can ask more of him because he knows the kid will respond. And when a kid is loyal, a coach is more patient with him. We realize that kids are just that—kids. They're going to make mistakes and do dumb things, just like I did when I was growing up. We are more patient with kids than some programs. We'll give a kid a second or even a third chance. We know that it takes time to build communication and to make a kid feel good about himself and his school. Pride doesn't happen overnight just because a kid has changed uniforms.

It's the easiest thing for a coach to say, "That's a bad kid; I'm gonna run him off." But why does this have to happen? Why is the coach always right and the kid always wrong? I think a lot of times the coaches cause problems for the kids. So I don't take another coach's word about a player being a problem. If I'm interested in the kid and he wants to talk to us, I'll meet with him. I don't care if he is at a junior college or a transfer from another four-year school. Too many people put the bad rap on a player who may have made just one mistake, and that's not right. If a kid is loyal, I'm willing to give him another chance. That's a lot of what coaching is about.

5

Long Beach

Jerry Tarkanian has never claimed to be a megacoach, that breed who can explain the nuances of the stock market as easily as the intricacies of a zone defense.

"George Raveling, who is coach at Southern California, always tells me that if he were my business manager, he'd make me a million dollars a year," says Tarkanian. "But I don't pay that much attention to the business part of the job. The coaching part consumes me, and when I do get into the other, it's because it falls right in my lap."

But even by Jerry Tarkanian's marketing standards—which admittedly aren't high—he made a terrible financial move by going from Pasadena City College to Long Beach State.

Tarkanian: "When I left Pasadena, I was making $18,200, which was very good money at that time for any college coach, not just a junior college coach. But I got so excited by the Long Beach job that I never negotiated, I just took it. All I wanted was the chance, and I figured I'd worry about the money later. When I was interviewing for the job, I did ask Fred Miller what it paid, and he said about $15,000. I said fine. I had lived on a lot less than $15,000 before. So when I got to Long Beach, I thought I was going to make $15,000. But it turned out to be only $13,300, because an expected faculty raise did not go through. Also, the California state college system made deductions for both social security and the teachers' retirement fund. They didn't do that in the junior college system. When I got my first monthly check, it was so small that Lois thought we were getting paid every two weeks."

So Tarkanian went a few weeks without telling his wife exactly what he earned. After all, it was pretty hard to explain a promotion that led to a $4,900 paycut—from $18,200 to $13,300.

But the surprises were only beginning.

"Guess what our recruiting budget was," says Tarkanian.

Actually, "budget" was hardly the proper term.

Tarkanian: "I had $200 a year to recruit with. What's $200? Maybe one plane ticket? I did have a budget for forty-two pairs of shoes for the team, so I saw that I could get a few dollars from that. I bought only twenty-eight pairs of shoes, and used the money from the other fourteen pairs (about $150) for recruiting. The state college system was not geared for big-time athletics. We were in the California Collegiate Athletic Association. There was no thought of national rankings or things like that. I went to Long Beach with the idea that I could have the best team in the California state college system, because my contacts in junior college would give me an advantage in recruiting. My family would live near the beach and I'd have a place to take some junior college kids who I thought deserved a chance to play at a four-year school. I also liked the athletic staff Fred Miller was molding at Long Beach. The previous basketball coach, Randy Sandefur, took over as volleyball coach, and he was great to me. Miller hired swim coach Don Gambril and track coach Ted Banks from Pasadena City College. Gambril is now coaching at the University of Alabama and has served as the United States Olympic swim coach. Banks moved on to the University of Texas at El Paso, where he won several national track championships before retiring.

"At Long Beach I never had my own personal office; just a little space about half the size of a small motel room, which I shared with two other coaches. We didn't even have a secretary for basketball. Despite all that, everything mushroomed. We started winning, getting ranked nationally, and getting national attention. We didn't make it at Long Beach because the administration or the community was behind us. We made it because we were able to get the best junior college kids in California and they played their hearts out for us."

Tarkanian had tremendous connections with high school and junior college coaches, and the junior colleges were virgin fields of basketball talent. Most coaches wouldn't even recruit a junior college player, preferring to bring in a freshman and work with him for four years. Some coaches thought that junior college players were "problem kids...head cases...not worth the trouble." The few four-year schools that did recruit junior college players usually signed only one or two.

"Most of our Long Beach teams were junior college kids," says Tarkanian. "I knew that we could win with them, and I knew that they were good kids. I mean, I was a junior college coach, so I understood the kids."

By knowing them, Tarkanian could get the best out of junior college players. And there may have been no other coach in southern California who worked as hard as Tarkanian.

"My assistant and I went to every summer league game, and we knew where all the recreation centers were that had good players," says Tarkanian. "UCLA dominated basketball back then. They had John Wooden as the coach and all those national championships. You couldn't beat them on the court or for a kid in recruiting."

But Tarkanian found players whom UCLA either ignored or missed. UCLA saw no need to recruit at the junior colleges, and that left Tarkanian as the man you wanted for your coach if you were a JUCO player. Often Tarkanian and his assistant, Ivan Duncan, were the only coaches at these summer league, junior college, and recreation games. You could find them at Trade Tech, L.A. State, or about any southern California high school gym. They knew every inner-city gym, and at some of them Tarkanian would be introduced and receive a standing ovation from the fans.

The word was out: Jerry Tarkanian took black players, and he wasn't afraid to play four or five at once. He also had a reputation for having a deep interest in his players, and the stories of Tarkanian and his wife having the players over to their house for meals and tutoring were well known. This bolstered his image as a coach who created a family atmosphere on his team.

No other major college coach comprehended the vast talent available in the junior colleges, and no other major college coach went to so many high school, junior college, and recreation league games. Additionally, through his relationship with his current and former players, Tarkanian established a network and credibility within the black community of southern California.

Tarkanian took a dormant Division II program which had had only one winning season in the previous seven and virtually no recruiting budget, and by his second season he had that team in the second round of the NCAA play-offs and ranked among the nation's Top Twenty. In his next three years at Long Beach, Tarkanian's teams were in the Top Ten. This happened for three reasons:

1. Because of his reputation as a junior college coach, many of the best junior college players wanted to play for him.

2. He was willing to go anywhere, anytime to watch a prospective player.

3. He had a reputation in the black community as a coach who cared about his players and who could communicate with inner-city athletes.

Lois: "That first year, most of Jerry's players from Pasadena City College came to Long Beach with us, so that gave us a good team right from the start. Jerry knew the kids, and they knew and trusted him. It wasn't as if he recruited junior college kids from all over the place and had to mold them into a team. He had a nucleus from the junior college teams he knew in southern California. The top seven on that first Long Beach team consisted of only one returning player from the previous coach—Don Nelson. All the others were from junior colleges: Sam Robinson and Tap Nixon from Pasadena, Ray Gritton and Bob Lynn from Pierce, Shawn Johnson from Long Beach, and Arthur Montgomery from Compton. Of thirteen players on the roster, ten were from junior colleges. One of those ten was John Sneed, who went on to become a coach himself.

"Our phone rang constantly. Junior college players called wanting to play for Jerry, and junior college coaches called asking us to take one or two of their players. One day, someone with a draggy, muffled voice called to say that he had heard Tark was going to Long Beach, and he wondered why Tark hadn't called him about coming along. He said he was very hurt about it. I asked who was speaking and it turned out that the voice on the phone belonged to Arthur 'Sleepy' Montgomery, a player at Compton Junior College. Eventually, he became one of Jerry's players, and from the way he sounded on the phone, I knew why he was called 'Sleepy.' Newspapers, of course, eventually had great fun with that nickname, running headlines like: 'Sleepy Wakes Up 49ers.'

"The telephone was one of Jerry's key recruiting tools. He didn't have the budget to hop on planes and go watch kids play, but he called them and wrote them a lot of letters. Our children still remember when Jerry would take them to the Long Beach State gym on Saturdays while he made calls. Pam has said it was just like having your own private gymnasium, because no one else would be there. I am very serious when I say that a day never went by when we didn't do something that had to do with Jerry's job. If we went out of town for a personal reason, Jerry would find a kid in that area that he wanted to visit. I'd bring the typewriter along so we could write letters to recruits. About 90 percent of our players were junior college kids from southern California. Once in a while we'd get a kid from out of state, but most of our players were local. We couldn't recruit like UCLA, Kentucky, and those other schools—where you can fly anywhere in the country to visit a player. We had to recruit in our backyard, and that's what we did. Jerry was seldom home for dinner, because he was out in the evenings at some game or another. His chief assistant coach that first year was John Chambers, a former player from Antelope Valley High School.

"I'll never forget the time I got a call about one in the morning from Jerry. He had been on the go for almost three weeks straight, and that night was seeing a kid in the Ventura area. 'I can't come home,' he said. 'Why not?' I asked. Then he started mumbling something about being stopped by a state trooper who thought he must be drunk because he kept weaving in and out of traffic. The trooper had made him take a sobriety test, including walking a straight line. Evidently, convinced he wasn't drunk but just exhausted, the trooper had escorted Jerry to a nearby motel and told him to get some sleep and not drive anymore that evening.

"We were so young back then, we just did what needed to be done. We never took the time to think, 'Boy, all we ever do is work.' But you know what? About all we really ever did was work. People don't believe it when I tell them about our days at Long Beach. Even before that, we were incredibly busy. I did a lot of typing for Jerry— letters to recruits, scouting reports, and things like that. He had no secretary. We also did a lot of work with the players; I guess you'd call it counseling. We had kids come over to the house when they broke up with their girlfriends, or when their parents had a fight, or when they were lonely. At the same time that this was going on with Jerry, I was working with handicapped children. Jerry and I looked at our jobs the same way—working with kids and helping them. We weren't trying to be martyrs or anything like that. We loved our work and we loved the kids. We spent the time doing something we wanted to do and thought was worthwhile. We did it because we enjoyed doing it.

"It wasn't all work and worry. We had a lot of fun, too. We had the prettiest and peppiest cheerleaders of anyone, the best band—and our head yell leaders had to be the most loyal you could find. The cheerleaders were always trying to think of things that would help everyone support the team better. Our first year it was wooden blocks that we banged together. The league banned them. The second year, it was soda cans filled with rice that we would shake. The league banned them. Next, we tried little dime-store metal clackers. Fiinally, the league did not ban them.

"We had a player who always started the season slow—George Trapp. Jerry said Trapp never played well until after Christmas, so he went on a campaign to have our fans send George Christmas cards in November, and George was floored by all the cards he received.

"Then there was our trip to Mexico. It was the first time a U.S. team had traveled to Mexico for games through a people-to-people program. They were very nice to us, but didn't realize how much U.S. basketball players ate. Our players were hungry all the time, especially for some meat. The game organizers kept promising us that at the next meal we would have some chicken, until it began to be a joke about when the chicken was coming. Finally, one day they served us chicken, but the servings were so small that Ed Ratleff said, 'Are you sure this is chicken? It's smaller than the pigeon that flew by my window this morning.'

"On that trip the only transportation the team had to one game was an open pickup truck. It wasn't so bad until it started to rain. You could see all twelve Long Beach State players standing straight, bunched tightly together in the back of the pickup, trying to pull their brown and gold warm-up jackets over their heads to keep out of the rain as the truck bounced over bumps in the road.

"The referees were interesting on the trip. In one game, we had only four players left in the last few minutes of regulation time. That was the same game where excited fans kept shaking the backboards during our players' free-throw attempts. But all in all, it was a great experience."

Tarkanian's first Long Beach team had a 23-to-3 record, and he put that together under a strange scholarship system.

Since Long Beach was part of the California state college system, the accent was on educating people from the state of California. Tarkanian was allowed eight and two-thirds scholarships for his basketball team.

Every player from California counted as one full scholarship. But if an out-of-state player was recruited, he counted as one and two-thirds scholarships. The idea behind the system was to encourage recruiting in California. It was also designed to discourage recruiting out-of-state players because they counted nearly double (one and two-thirds scholarships). The reason for this was that it cost an out-of-state student more to attend Long Beach than it did a student from California.

In the words of athletic director Fred Miller, "You could play a banjo across the tightness of our budget."

Sam Robinson was the leading scorer on Tarkanian's first Long Beach team.

Sam Robinson: "I always thought we should have gone to the NCAA tournament that year. We were 23–3 and good enough, but no one had ever heard of Long Beach. It was Long Beach's first year as a Division I team, and we didn't have a reputation as a strong basketball school. Maybe some people thought that we should wait a year before making the NCAA play-offs.

I played for Tark at Pasadena and at Long Beach, and there was a difference between the two places. Junior college ball was more fun. We were under very little pressure because we knew that no one in our league could beat us. It was only in the state tournament that we might have had some trouble, and we blew through it—except for the one game when we heard Tark was leaving Pasadena for Long Beach.

But at Long Beach it was more intense. All he did was work, and he pushed us harder than ever. We were starting from scratch. We had nothing. I remember one time, the school wouldn't reimburse me $1.25 I had to pay for a flat tire I got driving myself and other players back from an away game. We had no money, no tradition, and a little gym. In Los Angeles, the only college team they ever talked about was UCLA, and we were in their shadow. Tark's goal was to put Long Beach on the map, and he worked day and night to do it."

In its second season (1969–70) under Tarkanian, Long Beach played in the newly formed Pacific Coast Athletic Association, the same league he would later compete in at UNLV. Assistant coach Chambers moved to a head coaching position at Barstow Junior College and was replaced by Ed Delacey, a Long Beach alumnus. Sam Robinson and the core of Tarkanian's first team were back, and magazines such as *Sports Illustrated* were beginning to notice Long Beach.

"What astounded the people who followed Tarkanian's career was that he so radically altered his style of play at different times," says Pete Newell, the former U.S. Olympic coach who won a national title at California and who is now a scout for the Cleveland Cavaliers. Newell is considered one of the game's best basketball minds, and was labeled as such by Pulitzer Prize winner David Halberstam in his book *Breaks of the Game*.

Pete Newell: "Early at Riverside, Tark's teams played pressure man-to-man. Then he went to a 1-2-2 zone and continued playing a very disciplined offense at Pasadena and Long Beach. In fact, some people give Tark credit for inventing the 1-2-2 zone. Certainly, no one played it as well as his teams did."

Other coaches have raved about Tarkanian's 1-2-2 zone, among them Cleveland State's coach, Kevin Mackey.

Kevin Mackey: "When I was a young coach, I remember looking for an article about Tark's zone. I was coaching high school ball in Boston, and Tark was just starting out with Long Beach on the West Coast, and I heard about that zone. I finally found an article about it and I used it with my teams. The guy was ahead of his time by using pressure, and he was at the forefront of coaching with that 1-2-2 zone."

As Tarkanian entered his second year at Long Beach, he knew that he would have to recruit harder than ever. There are two things to remember when the core of your team is junior college players:

1. They are more mature and tend to be ready to play at the Division I level much faster than freshmen.

2. They come into school as juniors and have only two years of eligibility. That means that every other season is a crucial recruiting season.

Enter Ivan Duncan.

Tarkanian: "Ivan was a guy who was crazier than I was. He had played for me at Riverside City College, and then went on to get his bachelor's degree cum laude in English at La Verne College. He wrote to ask me for a job as an assistant because he wanted to get into coaching. We brought him out even though we could hardly pay him. I think he got $480 for teaching two volleyball classes. He was a graduate assistant, but he would outwork all of us. He was a very intelligent individual, and I always felt he would have earned a lot of money working in another profession. I remember he was a great letter writer. But he just loved working with kids and wanted to coach. He had a philosophy which I carry to this day: Never hire an assistant coach who owns a camper, a set of golf clubs, or a fishing pole.

"My favorite Ivan Duncan story was after our third year at Long Beach. We had had a great season, and a booster named Ralph Snyder took me and my family to Palm Springs. I remember that we were having a good time. I was sitting in a sauna when suddenly, Danny, who was about nine years old, ran into the room yelling that I had an important phone call. I rushed out of the sauna, figuring there was an emergency. I picked up the phone and I heard Ivan say, 'You can't win any games in a sauna.' Then he hung up. Click. That was it. He'd always try to embarrass anyone on the staff who took even a couple of days' vacation. The guy was incredible. I know that I work hard at my job, but Ivan was even worse.

"One time Ivan's wife wanted him to take her on a vacation. 'We don't have time,' he told her, but she kept nagging. Finally, he bought her a fishing pole and took her to the Long Beach pier. He said, 'Here, this is your vacation,' and just left her and then went out to watch some kids play. Having Ivan as an assistant was the reason we were able to get into the national rankings. He was so driven, and all he wanted to do was make Long Beach a national power. Not only was he a relentless recruiter, but once we had kids, he took good care of them. If a kid had a problem getting up for class, Ivan would go to his room and wake him up. Ivan pushed the kids, counseled the kids, did everything he could to help them. Most coaches wouldn't go out to recruit during rush hour in Los Angeles, because all you ended up doing was sitting in traffic. But Ivan would go and sit. He didn't care. Nothing would stop him."

Long Beach easily won the PCAA championship, led by the core of Tarkanian's first team, including the high-scoring Sam Robinson. The major newcomer was George Trapp, younger brother of John Trapp, who had played for Tarkanian at Pasadena. Ironically, John played his four-year college ball at UNLV, where the coach was Rolland Todd, a former Tarkanian assistant at Riverside. Other important recruits were Billy Jankans from Pasadena City College and Dwight Taylor from Compton, California. All but three members of the team had played their high school ball in California.

The team finished with a 24–5 record, and got its first crack at UCLA.

"We always wanted to play UCLA in the regular season, but they didn't want to schedule us," says Tarkanian. "I suppose that was smart. They had nothing to gain if they beat us and everything to lose if they lost."

Officially, UCLA stated that if it scheduled an independent game with Long Beach, then it would have to do the same for the other Los Angeles–area schools, such as Pepperdine and Los Angeles State. But then Tarkanian's team blew through the regular season and earned an invitation to the NCAA tournament. Long Beach defeated Weber State in the first round of the Western Regionals in Provo, Utah, then drew UCLA in Seattle.

"All we ever heard about was UCLA, UCLA," remembers Sam Robinson. "We wanted to beat them so bad, but I think we were just too tight and we didn't play very well."

UCLA took care of Long Beach 88–65.

Nonetheless, Long Beach had never received so much publicity. Two years before it had been playing Division II basketball; now it was playing UCLA in the play-offs. The attention was great for Tarkanian, his players, and the school, but it also was starting to make some other coaches and universities a little nervous. Who was this new kid on the block who showed up and started grabbing headlines and the NCAA tournament berths away from the old guard? And because Junior college players were a sparingly used or unknown quantity, to them, they questioned how Long Beach could win so fast.

In his second year at Long Beach, Tarkanian distinguished himself in another way. It was the spring of 1970, and many of California's campuses were torn by demonstrations and riots. It was the peak of the anti-Vietnam War and civil rights movements in college. Long Beach was one of the few California schools that had a minimum of problems, even though it had one of the highest student enrollments. Part of the credit went to basketball coach and assistant dean of students Jerry Tarkanian, and his athletes, who spoke to a rally of students.

Tarkanian: "Things were starting to get hot. We had some radicals who showed up on campus who wanted to start riots like those that had happened on almost every other state college campus that year. For those guys, the key was getting the black students on their side. So football coach Chuck Boyle, some of my players, and I spoke to the students. We asked them to do whatever they wanted, but just keep it peaceful."

Perhaps Tarkanian has never been more eloquent. The crux of his remarks, as quoted from the *Forty-Niner* student newspaper of May 21, 1970, was as follows:

We've heard cries of peace, but we've had only violence. We've had shouts of 'Power to the People,' and instead we've had intimidation. We've heard pleas for academic freedom and instead we've had tyranny. We've heard only one side of the story, and it's time for the teachers and students to take a positive approach. Nothing is perfect, no school or no country. If you look at faults you can find them in anything, but there are a lot of good things on this campus and in this country. Instead of working to make this a better campus and country, people are working at tearing it down. For 20 years I have worked with young people. You can be the greatest generation we've ever produced, but those of you who like pot and alcohol are playing hide-and-seek with life. You will never solve the problems that now face the world. It's time for faculty and students to pull together. If you look for faults you will find them, but the positive far outweighs the bad.

The 1969–70 season ended with Tarkanian being voted as Long Beach State's professor of the year. When the award was presented at a dinner in Anaheim, it was said that his coaching success had played only a minor role in Jerry's selection. His "general positive influences" on campus were the determining factor in his selection.

The player who really made Long Beach State something special was Ed Ratleff. Unlike Tarkanian's other stars, he wasn't a junior college transfer and he wasn't from the West Coast. Ratleff was a sleek, smooth 6-foot-6 guard from Columbus East High School in Ohio.

Tarkanian: "We ended up with Eddie Ratleff, but his recruiting really started with Bruce Clark. Bruce was the Los Angeles player of the year from Jefferson High, which also was Sam Robinson's high school. Everybody who had a strong program on the West Coast wanted Bruce, who was a 6-foot-8 center. Even though we were still relatively unknown, we had been recruiting Bruce since he was a sophomore, and he loved us. By his senior year, Bruce had narrowed his choices to Arizona State, San Francisco, UCLA, USC, and Long Beach. In the early 1970s, the first four programs made a lot of sense for a kid like Bruce, but no one could figure out how Long Beach got on his list. We didn't have the reputation, the schedule, or the budget of the other schools. We had no tradition or national exposure. We had nothing going for us but the fact that we had given Bruce more attention than all the other schools—and our reputation for having close relationships with the players. Since we had a number of Jefferson High kids playing for us, Bruce had become a Long Beach fan. He'd go to our games and we'd introduce him to the fans. He even went to our basketball banquet during his junior year.

"Ivan and I thought we had a great shot at Bruce Clark. He invited us to his high school graduation, and we were the only two white guys there. We went to the ceremony, to the party at Bruce's house, and everything. When June came and Bruce announced that he was going to Long Beach, that shocked everyone. He even moved to Long

Beach and found a summer job. We spent all day, and I mean every day, with Bruce for three weeks. We had the kid wrapped up. There was a high school all-star game in July in Palos Verdes. Every day my assistant or I went out to watch Bruce practice. During the game, Lois was sitting next to Bruce's mother. The kid had announced he was coming to Long Beach, eliminating San Francisco. He also said he didn't like USC. UCLA had not worked him very hard. In the all-star game, Bruce got 31 points and 19 rebounds. He dominated everyone. After the game, John Wooden went over and introduced himself to Bruce's mother. Right away, I knew we were in trouble. When you are coaching at Long Beach, all it takes is one visit from John Wooden to make you sweat.

"Sure enough, Bruce talked to Coach Wooden and then he told us, 'Right now, you're even with UCLA.'

"I said, 'Bruce, we've been working with you for three years. Then John Wooden comes along and says hello just once and all of a sudden we're even? How can that be? Is that fair?'

"Bruce thought about that and he seemed to feel pretty bad. He said that I was right, that he still wanted to go to Long Beach, so I figured we had him.

"Also after that all-star game, Southern Cal started working on Bruce and they went at him hard. USC was talking to Bruce's father, and we got word that USC was bringing out all its ammunition and it was all over—USC had the kid. Jim Heffner was the USC assistant coach at that time, and Ivan tried calling him for ten straight days. He was never in and would never return the calls. Finally, Ivan called again, and when the secretary said Heffner wasn't in and asked if he wanted to leave a message, Ivan just said, 'Yes, please just tell him Bruce Clark called.' The secretary right away hurriedly said, 'Oh, Bruce Clark, just one moment, I think I hear him coming down the hallway.' Heffner said they were recruiting Clark hard.

"I was ready to give up. Bruce was the biggest recruit we'd ever had, and I thought we had him. It would have been really something for Long Beach to get a kid of his caliber. I kept thinking about all the time and hard work we had spent on the kid, and it was very depressing to know that we had lost him. Well, Ivan Duncan didn't want to quit just yet. Ivan told me, 'Coach, I still think we're going to get Bruce.'

"Ivan went out and spent the night with Bruce's father. They got drunk together on a few beers and a fifth of vodka and talked for a long, long time. By the morning, Bruce was back in our corner."

What Tarkanian and Duncan didn't know at the time was that USC had lined up celebrities such as Sugar Ray Robinson, John Wayne, and Doris Day to call Clark and persuade him to attend Southern Cal.

Tarkanian: "All I know is that USC came back with more ammunition than ever before. They got to Bruce's father again. In early August, Bruce had a noon press conference at Dodger Stadium to announce he was signing with USC. Four hours later, he was in our office at Long Beach, crying and hugging Ivan and me. I reminded him that he had never shown an interest in USC. He used to bring the letters they sent him over to our office, show them to Ivan and me, and tell us how much he didn't like USC. Bruce said that he really wanted to go to Long Beach, but he just couldn't because of the package USC had for his family. He just couldn't turn it down. He kept saying he had to do it for his family. By the end of that meeting, all three of us were crying. I had never been so dejected over losing a recruit. We worked our butts off on Bruce and did everything right, and it just hurt so much to have the heavy hitters come in and blow us right out of the water."

Tarkanian's younger brother, Myron, was a football coach at Pasadena City College, where a Tarkanian named Jerry had once been the basketball coach. Jerry visited Myron in the Pasadena football office and told his brother the Bruce Clark saga. Myron was very sympathetic. There was someone else in the athletic office that day, a basketball player named Vance Carr. Jerry had helped Carr enroll at Pasadena even though Jerry was on his way to Long Beach.

Carr overheard the story of Bruce Clark, and Carr wanted to help Tarkanian, even though he had nothing to do with Long Beach or Bruce Clark. Then Carr did something for which Tarkanian is eternally grateful. He mentioned that he had attended Columbus East High School. Tarkanian may have been in Long Beach, California, but he knew all about East High of Columbus, Ohio, which had one of the strongest prep teams in the country.

"Coach, you should just forget about losing Clark," Carr told Tarkanian. "The kid you really want is Eddie Ratleff. Clark's not half the player Ratleff is."

"We've written to Eddie, we've called Eddie, and we can't get through to him," Tarkanian replied. "We never get an answer."

"Well, I know Eddie pretty well," said Carr. "Why don't you let me call him?"

Tarkanian showed Carr to the football office phone.

Tarkanian: "It went great. The two kids talked for a while, and then Vance put me on the line with Eddie. I couldn't believe how lucky I was, because there was no way I would ever have gotten to even talk to Eddie if this hadn't happened. Eddie and I talked, and I told him that we were very interested in him and that we had written and called him.''

Finally, Jerry convinced Ratleff to visit Long Beach, although Jerry knew that the main reason Ratleff would make the trip was to see Carr, not to check out Long Beach.

Tarkanian: ''But once you get a kid on your campus, then you have a real shot at getting him interested. That's what happened with Eddie. We really hit it off with him and found out that he had some special interests that we could meet.

''First, Eddie wanted to be a professional baseball player. In the back of his mind, he thought he was better in baseball than in basketball. All of the big schools wanted Eddie, but they wanted him to concentrate solely on basketball. He thought he was a very good pitcher. We had a good baseball program at Long Beach, and the baseball team played on a magnificent field. It was the second-best baseball field in the L.A. area, after Dodger Stadium. The athletic complex is so nice that the Rams football team now uses it for its training headquarters. That impressed Eddie.

''This was during the time when freshmen could not play varsity basketball in college. Since so many of our players were junior college transfers, we didn't have much of a freshman team at Long Beach. I told Eddie that he could play freshman basketball and then quit in February when baseball season started. None of the other coaches recruiting him were willing to make him that promise. We convinced Eddie that he could play both sports—baseball and basketball.

''Eddie went home and I got a call from his high school principal, Jack Gibbs. Gibbs was a little concerned because he knew nothing about Long Beach State. He said, 'Eddie loved your school and he wants to go out there, but Eddie isn't going anywhere without our approval, without the vice principal's approval, and without his parents' approval.' He wanted me to send a college catalog, a picture of the arena where we played, our schedule, and some recommendations. We sent everything Jack Gibbs asked for, and I also asked George Trapp's mother and father to call and tell Jack Gibbs and Eddie's parents about Long Beach. I had the president of Pasadena City College, Armen Sarafian, call them. I got a call from Jack Gibbs, and he said that everything looked pretty good, but he wanted me to come to Columbus to meet with him and Eddie's parents.

''I went to Columbus and spent six days there. I spent about three days living with Jack Gibbs. I went everywhere with him. Jack Gibbs was a great guy. His goal was to place all of his kids in colleges, and he spent a lot of his own time working on finding the right school for each kid through a program he had started called Educational Resources. Eddie had agreed to go to Florida State, but he hadn't signed a binding letter of intent with them. Also, Southwest Louisiana was in the picture, and they were pushing real hard. But everything seemed to be going well. The principal liked me and wanted Eddie to go to Long Beach. Eddie's dad wanted his son to go out West. He was worried about his son going to college in the South because this was during the time of all the civil rights demonstrations.

"What changed the picture on Eddie was that Southwest Louisiana wanted to sign almost the whole Columbus East team, not just Eddie. In fact, the only guy they were going to pass on was Nick Connors, who had committed to Illinois. The principal liked the idea that Eddie and two other kids from the Columbus East team would go to the same college. But I talked with Jack Gibbs for a long time, and I told him that I'd find junior colleges for Eddie's two friends. I said that he had to be careful, because once Eddie enrolled at Southwest, there was a chance that the school might dump the other two kids and just keep Eddie. The principal seemed to understand my point, and I went back to Long Beach thinking that we were in great shape with Eddie. In fact, Eddie had made a verbal commitment to us, but I knew, of course, that a verbal commitment wasn't binding.

"After I got home, I made four calls every day—to Eddie, to Eddie's girlfriend, to Eddie's parents, and to Jack Gibbs. This went on for about ten days. While I was gone, Southwest Louisiana was in there, still trying to recruit the whole team. Jack Gibbs called me and asked me to take a guard from Columbus East, a kid named Dwight Lamar. I knew that Jack Gibbs liked me, but he had weakened some on Long Beach because he also wanted us to take Dwight Lamar. The only players I knew on the team were Eddie and Nick Connors. I told Jack that I'd take Connors, but Jack said that Connors was all set at Illinois. He mentioned Lamar again. I thought he was just trying to find a school for Eddie's friend. Under the rules I was working with at Long Beach, each out-of-state student required a one and two-thirds scholarship. I knew that Eddie was worth that, but I didn't know Dwight Lamar, so I passed on him because it would have wiped out our scholarships.

"One day I was in Pasadena with my friends. I got a call from Lois and she said that I should call Eddie's father right away, that it was an emergency. I called the father, and he said, 'Coach, you better get back here to Columbus. Southwest Louisiana is here and they have changed Jack Gibbs's mind. Southwest is willing to take the whole team and they're putting the guilt trip on Eddie, telling him that if he doesn't go to Southwest, some of the other guys won't get scholarships.'

"I was miserable. First I thought we had Bruce Clark, then we lost him at the last minute. Now I was worried that the same thing would happen with Eddie Ratleff. I went to see our athletic director and explained the situation. He said that he understood why I had to go back to Columbus but that there were no funds left in the recruiting budget; I would have to pay for it myself. We had four kids and didn't have any extra money. Then Ivan Duncan called his father, who loaned us the money. If he hadn't written us a check, we never could have gone back to Columbus.

"I called Eddie and told him, 'Don't sign anything until we get there. We're on a midnight flight and we'll be in Columbus by 7:30 in the morning. Promise me that you won't sign anything.' Eddie gave us his word. I was home packing for the trip about 8:30 that night when Eddie's father called and said, 'Don't worry, Coach, you don't need to come out here. I threw Southwest out of the house. I told them that no way was Eddie going to play down there. He was going to play for you at Long Beach.' That was it. Ivan and I were so happy that we took some of the money his dad had given us and went out to Hoefly's bar in Long Beach and celebrated. We closed Hoefly's that night. Of course, we scrimped to pay back his dad later, but it was worth it.

"The funny thing about this story is that I should have taken Dwight Lamar, too. He went down to Southwest Louisiana and averaged about 25 points a game. When Eddie was a sophomore, we went to a tournament in Lafayette, Louisiana. We played Southwest in the finals, and Lamar had a great night—he threw in 46 points and they beat us (90–83). In the airport the next day, we ran into Dwight Lamar and Jack Gibbs. After everyone said good-bye, Dwight told me, 'Coach, I always wanted to come to Long Beach and play for you. Too bad you couldn't use me.' I laughed, but it *was* too bad, because Dwight Lamar turned out to be a great college player. He led the nation in scoring in the 1971–72 season with a 36.3 average. Both he and Eddie went on to be All-Americans."

Tarkanian's recruiting at Long Beach is worth examining in depth, because doing so provides answers to the key questions that have always surrounded his career:

Where does Tark get these players?

How does he get his players?

Who are these guys Tark puts on the floor, and why are they there?

In his five years at Long Beach, Tarkanian had a remarkable 122–20 record and never lost a home game. Three of those teams were ranked in the nation's Top Ten.

If Tarkanian had been coaching at North Carolina or Kentucky, that wouldn't be surprising. In fact, it would be expected, because those colleges had been winning big on the court from about the time man first nailed a peach basket to the side of a barn and started throwing a ball at it.

But Long Beach was a Division II school the year before Tarkanian arrived. Basketball was just something for a few students to do during the winter months. Long Beach was a school with a 2,700-seat gym, a $200 recruiting budget, no money for scouting and recruiting, and a campus that was aimed at commuter students. Moreover, the nation's premier basketball program, UCLA, cast its huge shadow over Tarkanian and his program.

As Tarkanian put it, "Common sense would tell you that there was no way we should have won."

But reality tells you that all Long Beach did was win. And reality is that when a school wins so much, especially when the school never won before, people become suspicious. Other coaches started to whisper about Tarkanian and Long Beach. He had to be doing something to get those players in there. With his strong work ethic, Tarkanian was beating them at their own game—on the court and in the living rooms of the recruits.

The fact was that Tarkanian won at Long Beach without recruiting on a big-time scale because he signed California junior college players.

Tarkanian: "Junior college kids really recruited us. In my five years at Long Beach, we had only four freshman players: Ed Ratleff, Glenn McDonald, Dwight Taylor, and Ernie Douse. Except for Ratleff and McDonald, we never beat a major school for a freshman player. A lot of our junior college kids called us because they wanted to play for Long Beach."

When Tarkanian found a kid he liked, he started asking around. Did he know anyone who knew the kid? What did the kid want out of college, basketball, and life in general? What about the kid's parents? What dreams did they have for their son?

A failure with Bruce Clark ended up as a success with Ed Ratleff. Taking care of a troubled John Trapp at Pasadena Junior College led to younger brother George's playing and becoming a star at Long Beach. The harder you work, the more people you meet. The more people you meet, the more people you know who might be able to introduce you to a player.

There also was Tarkanian's reputation. Other coaches said that Tarkanian did well with kids from the city, kids who might have had some trouble in their past. They also said he was very straight with his black players, that he never prejudged a kid. After a while, coaches and players started coming to Tarkanian, and that is what makes recruiting easier.

Finally, there was Tarkanian's constant communication with high school and junior college coaches, and his presence in the gym with the players. Just watching a kid play day after day in a summer league shows an interest in him without your saying a word. A coach's presence gives a player a strong, positive message. At Long Beach, Tarkanian and Ivan Duncan tried to be everywhere the basketball was bouncing, and this led to their signing some superb players. Here is how Tarkanian recruited a couple of other well-known Long Beach players:

- Nate Stephens: "Nate had played for Eddie Sutton at the College of Southern Idaho," says Tarkanian. "That was a junior college. When Eddie took the coaching job at Creighton, he took Nate with him. One day I got a call from Eddie, who said he had this kid Nate Stephens who wanted to transfer. I told Eddie that I didn't have room for another transfer. Eddie told me that Nate was a 7-footer. I told Eddie that I always had room for a 7-footer. Eddie started to tell me about Nate, saying that he wasn't a bad kid, but that he just couldn't hack it at Creighton, and that a change of scene would do Nate some good. That made me stop a little. I said I needed a few days to think about it. The next morning, I got a call from Sutton telling me that Nate was on a plane to Long Beach. It suddenly dawned on me that when another coach calls you about a 7-footer and then puts him right on a plane the next morning, you've got to figure that something is wrong. Within twelve hours of our conversation, Eddie had the kid out of town. I had wanted a few days to make some calls and do some checking on Nate, but here he was in Long Beach. This was one of the craziest things I've ever seen."

- Glenn McDonald: "Ivan Duncan did a lot of work on Glenn," says Tarkanian. McDonald adds, "Ivan started recruiting me when I was a junior at Jefferson High School and he never let up. At every game I played, Ivan was there. He called me on the phone constantly. He and Coach Tark billed Long Beach as 'The New Powerhouse on the West Coast,' and I liked the idea of going to a program that was on the way up. I knew a lot of the guys who played for Coach Tark, and guys like Sam Robinson and Tap Nixon liked him and said he was a winner. I was being recruited by all the PAC-10 schools but UCLA. Places such as Syracuse also wanted me. But it was Ivan who got me to Long Beach. I just got so much mail and so much attention from them. Ivan would call me every day and say, 'Glen, I just want you to know that I'm thinking about you. We really want you at Long Beach State.' I think that was what did it. Long Beach made it seem like they wanted me more than the other schools, because they worked harder to get me."

Tarkanian resented the fact that his program was sometimes portrayed as college basketball's foreign legion. *Newsweek* magazine was probably the worst offender, dubbing Nate Stephens "the Marco Polo of College Basketball," claiming he had been to seven different colleges when actually he only attended a junior college (Southern Idaho), Creighton, a summer session at Texas-El Paso, and Long Beach.

Tarkanian: "And you can't say I worked hard at recruiting him, since it was Eddie Sutton who called me. I admit Stephens did have some motivation problems, and I probably spent more time talking to him than I did to any other player, but Nate made a sincere effort to be a steady player.

"What disturbed me most about the *Newsweek* article was that Marty Kasindorf, the writer, obviously came to do a sabotage job on our program. He spent a day at practice and saw our game with Cal State-Los Angeles, and then wrote his story. It is strange that a player such as Chuck Terry—our second-leading scorer and rebounder, a unanimous all-conference selection, a starter on the United States Pan-American team, and a leading candidate for the Olympic team—went completely unnoticed by Kasindorf. He also overlooked Eric Mc-

Williams, who had a career high of 17 rebounds in that L.A. game; and Tom Motley, who did an excellent job of handling the ball.

"But Kasindorf wanted to dwell on his own prejudices, I guess. The fact that Terry, McWilliams, Motley, and Lynn were all from nearby junior colleges didn't fit what he wanted to say. We pointed out to him that in the three years I had been at Long Beach before he wrote the article, Nate Stephens was the first four-year college transfer I had. In fact, in my full five years at Long Beach, I only had four transfers from four-year schools. But Kasindorf didn't care. He filled his article with half-statements and innuendos, and that was it. And then later, what he wrote got picked up by other writers who reprinted it without even checking to see if it was true or not."

It is true that Tarkanian only had four transfers from four-year schools during his five seasons at Long Beach. Leonard Gray from Kansas and Lamont King from Michigan were among the four. Most of his players were from southern California, coming into Long Beach either as freshmen, as was the case with Glenn McDonald, or as junior college transfers, such as Sam Robinson and Chuck Terry.

But the reason for the scrutiny—and the sometimes shoddy reporting—was that Tarkanian was moving up fast, perhaps too fast. It may not have been coincidence that the *Newsweek* article appeared the season after Long Beach almost upset UCLA in the NCAA play-offs, or that Kasindorf had been a UCLA student. The first and easiest response when a college team comes out of nowhere is to say somebody is up to something.

Somebody was, and that somebody was Tarkanian, who demonstrated that you could win with junior college players. He was showing that hard work could overcome a lack of basketball tradition. He pushed Long Beach to the point where it became the second-best basketball program in the state, right behind UCLA—and then dared to play the Bruins very close in the NCAA play-offs. As it turned out, certain people at UCLA did not like hearing Long Beach's footsteps.

A man in Tarkanian's position would naturally have very strong feelings about UCLA. His Long Beach team was David; UCLA was Goliath. He was not only the new kid, but the poorest kid on the block. UCLA ran the neighborhood and lived in the biggest house. Year after year, UCLA won and won all the time—in the regular season, in the PAC-10, and in the NCAA tournament. No wonder that Tarkanian is in awe of those achievements and of former UCLA coach John Wooden.

Tarkanian: "There are two basic reasons why UCLA won all the time. First, they probably did have the best talent in the country. But, second, and more importantly, John Wooden did a great coaching job. You can't minimize Wooden's role, because his teams played so un-selfishly. That says a lot for the coach, because he had so many great players that it could have been hard getting them to play together. But John Wooden did that. He convinced them to sacrifice parts of their individual games for the good of the whole team. And he created tre-mendous morale on his teams. There are many coaches who could have had all that talent yet not won as much because they couldn't handle all the egos. And he got his players to play consistently well under tremendous pressure, year after year. And his teams were mul-tifaceted. They didn't rely on just one aspect of the game. It really was remarkable. It was beautiful to beat some of the other strong teams of that era, but it was history to beat UCLA.

"To show you what kind of man he was, I remember that I men-tioned once in one of my newspaper columns that after the Houston loss, instead of pointing out that Lew Alcindor [Kareem Abdul-Jabbar] had an eye injury, Wooden expounded on the play of Elvin Hayes. What Wooden did at UCLA was one of the great sports accomplish-ments of all time. I think we also should remember that he won two national championships before Alcindor.

"Every time I had a chance, I'd watch UCLA on television. They just amazed me, both in terms of individual talent and in terms of how they played as a team. I would watch the games and try and figure out how to beat them.

"John Wooden and I have always gotten along very well. He was great to me, and a man in his position didn't have to be. He didn't have to take time with a young coach at Long Beach State when he had a great program going at UCLA. When I first took the Long Beach job, I was attending a sportswriters' luncheon in Los Angeles and John Wooden was there. I didn't know him well, but he went out of his way to take a few minutes to tell everyone that Long Beach had made a good choice in hiring me. I couldn't begin to say what a thrill it was for me to hear that coming from a man such as John Wooden. It meant so much to a guy who was still in junior college and getting ready to take his first four-year job. During the basketball season, we had those basketball writers' luncheons, and I always made a point to sit near Wooden. The man was always super to me. I admired him greatly, and still do. He is one of the greatest men, in so many different ways, ever to coach."

While the Tarkanians have a sincere admiration for John Wooden, they feel much differently about a few other aspects of UCLA.

Tarkanian: "There is always some bitterness, not towards John Wooden, but about UCLA. In fact, I've always gotten along well with the coaches—Larry Farmer, Larry Brown, Walt Hazzard, and the other guys. In fact, I'm not even bitter at UCLA, but rather at how the NCAA allowed UCLA to get away with so much and then came and tried to bury us at Long Beach. I mean, right down the road at UCLA you had all these things going on—their players drove big cars, they had nice apartments...look, I never would have cared that their kids had it so good if the NCAA and the press hadn't jumped on us at Long Beach. As a coach at Long Beach, I thought I could recruit with any other college and coach in southern California, because we had developed good connections with the coaches, the players, and the black community. But we could never recruit against UCLA's biggest booster, Sam Gilbert.

"I remember once at UNLV when we were very close to signing both Dave Greenwood and Roy Hamilton, who were great high school players in Los Angeles. They had played in high school for George McQuarn, who later became my assistant at UNLV. George's wife was very close to those kids and their families. We were way out in front of everyone else. Then Sam Gilbert got involved, and it was over. Gilbert knocked us out of the box in a matter of hours. The thing is, I even liked Sam Gilbert. He was a contractor in Los Angeles, and he had a lot of connections when it came to getting kids summer jobs. He even helped some of my kids find summer jobs in L.A. Sam just liked kids, and he was good to them. But he was a UCLA guy, and he always took care of them. There was a joke among the coaches: when Sam Gilbert got involved with a recruit, it was time to go home. You could write it down—the kid was going to UCLA.

"You know what? I wouldn't even care about Sam Gilbert if the NCAA hadn't bothered us. But picking on Long Beach and ignoring UCLA, that just hurt me so much. And what they did to the reputation of those great Long Beach kids who had so little just kills me inside. The hypocrisy of it all must be one of the greatest crimes of all time."

Lois: "Jerry is right when he praises John Wooden. He is a class man, a gentleman, and a fine teacher. I feel that he and his wife, Nell, had one of those rare, great loves, because she was with him all the way in all things, and it was obvious how deeply they cared for each other.

"But a few other aspects of UCLA bother me. They had won so

much that some of their fans had become very obnoxious. They thought they were the elite and we at Long Beach were dirt beneath them. They ridiculed the fact that we were a state college and they were a university. They made extremely personal comments about our players. They continually demeaned us. Obviously, I cared deeply about our players and was very proud of the state college system from which I had graduated. To this day, if anyone ever makes personal remarks about a player or shouts raucously, 'We're number one,' or in any other ways demeans the other team, I will personally go to our fans and ask them to stop. I've done this with everyone from individuals to fraternity rooting sections. I will never forget how UCLA made us feel, and I don't want that to happen when we play other teams.''

Award-winning sportswriter Jim Murray of the *Los Angeles Times* echoed Lois Tarkanian's description of old Bruin fans in a February 21, 1988, column:

> The crowd there was like hardly any other in the field of sports. Contemptuous, derisive, abusive...insulting, impatient, intolerant of mistakes. Smug in the knowledge it was the citadel of all basketball. If you didn't play there, it didn't count. Insufferable in victory...mocking of opponents....They came to watch a slaughter, not a game. If the other guys got a basket, they were insulted. They wanted the head of the enemy on a platter. They usually got it....They had the best coach and the greatest players in the business....

Lois continues, ''I remember before a big game with UCLA that their band came to our hotel in Utah and started playing by our players' rooms at five in the morning to wake them up. They claimed that they were practicing—but at five in the morning? And why pick the part of the parking lot to practice where we just happened to have our rooms? That just wasn't right.''

Long Beach player Sam Robinson: ''Our players used to hang out with the UCLA guys. I'm telling you, those guys were well taken care of. They had big new fancy cars, fancy clothes, and they always had money. In fact, when we went out, they came by to pick us up, and they always paid because we were broke. I remember going in to see Jerry Tarkanian and asking him for a few bucks. I figured, why not? They're getting things at UCLA. Tark wouldn't give players any money, and we got mad about it. We resented the guys at UCLA because they seemed to be getting everything.''

Lois: ''Our kids were probably more realistic about UCLA than I was. They were upset that the UCLA kids were being taken care of while our kids had to scrape by as best they could. Only two of our kids had cars, and none of our players lived in nice apartments. Almost all lived in dorms. Our players came from the same neighborhoods as some of their kids—the lifestyles only changed for the players after they enrolled at UCLA."

As mentioned before, UCLA and Long Beach did not play each other during the regular season, but the two teams squared off in the NCAA tournament. During the early 1970s, the field for the tournament was only thirty-two teams; it has since doubled. Also, the pairings were done by regions. That's why Long Beach always ended up in the West with UCLA. Now the pairings are done by computer and other factors, and teams such as North Carolina State can end up in the West, while western teams can go to the South or the East.

In its first meeting with UCLA, in 1970, an inexperienced and nervous Long Beach team was beaten 88–65.

The next game was in 1971, in the West Regional Finals in Salt Lake City, with the winner going to the Final Four. It also gave Long Beach another graphic look at how different life was at UCLA.

Lois: "We were scheduled to be on the same flight with UCLA to the regionals in Utah. When Jerry found out that we were on the same plane with UCLA, he changed flights, because he'd been told the UCLA players would be traveling first class while our kids would be jammed in the back of the plane. We went on a different plane, but because of a layover, we arrived in Utah about the same time as UCLA. While we were waiting for our luggage, the UCLA group showed up. We had one local sportswriter, a radio representative, a few boosters, and some wives and children in our group. UCLA had seven or eight sportswriters, all kinds of television people, and a mass of boosters and others. It was something to see, but understandable because UCLA was the best team in the country. What bothered me was seeing UCLA stars Curtis Rowe and Sidney Wicks wearing cashmere coats, alligator shoes, and felt hats. Meanwhile, our best player, All-American Eddie Ratleff, had on his brown Long Beach windbreaker, jeans, and Converse shoes. I looked at the UCLA guys and I thought, 'Just who is kidding whom around here?' I heard Jerry telling Long Beach sportswriter Loel Schrader, 'Look at our guys and look at theirs, and tell me who has the money. We look like the Salvation Army next to them.'

"Later, a *Sports Illustrated* reporter spoke to me, and I told him about that scene at the airport. He printed it in the magazine. The following year at a play-off game in Oregon, Sam Gilbert came up to a group of us and was talking very jovially. At one point he turned to me and said, 'You shouldn't talk so much,' and then he went on about my quote from *Sports Illustrated*. He proudly admitted that he had gotten the players coats and told me why. He said UCLA had had an earlier game on the East Coast and that the kids had no warm coats to wear. He thought the players deserved the coats, so he got them for them. He also said that he had gone to J. D. Morgan, the UCLA athletic director, and told him about the coats, challenging J. D. Morgan to do something about it. I don't know if Sam Gilbert spoke with J. D. Morgan or not, but I do believe, from all that Sam said, that he bought the coats.

"I knew that Sam and his wife did a lot to help kids. When it was within the area of filling a legitimate need, I couldn't find fault with it. And I don't believe Wooden knew all that Gilbert was doing. Great coaches get so involved with the game that a lot can go on that they just don't pay attention to. It just doesn't register. Wooden and Gilbert were entirely different types of personalities. We even had heard that Wooden would not let Gilbert into his office. Our anger wasn't at Wooden or UCLA, but at the system in general."

Even right before that UCLA–Long Beach game in Utah, Tarkanian and Wooden were very close.

Tarkanian: "The day after we both had won our first-round games, there was a 10:00 officials' meeting and a 12:00 press luncheon. I was going to go back to my hotel between the two meetings, but John Wooden asked me to stay, and we talked for an hour. He told me that he had been offered the job at Indiana, and that Indiana had offered to put into a retirement fund an amount that would match all his years at UCLA. It would almost be like a double retirement fund. He said that he couldn't take the job because of his grandchildren being in California. He also thought the warm weather was good for his health.

"Wooden was originally from Indiana, and he loved the place. He told me how beautiful it was in Bloomington, and then he told me something that really surprised me and made me feel good: he said he had recommended that Indiana hire me. That was a great compliment. He even gave me the name of a person to call, but I never followed up on it. I probably wouldn't have gotten the job anyway, but neither Lois nor I realized then all that Indiana could have provided."

Long Beach sportswriter Loel Schrader: "One day I was in John Wooden's office when he got a call from someone who was pushing Bobby Knight for the Indiana job. Wooden said, 'I've got nothing against Knight, but I can't do that....No, I've recommended Jerry Tarkanian for that position.' You know, Wooden liked Jerry and respected him as a coach. But I also believed that UCLA would have liked to get Jerry out of town. He had become a threat to them. That's also when the talk about Long Beach being a bandit school started. It didn't come from Wooden, but from others at UCLA. Hell's bells, what may or may not have been going on at Long Beach was peanuts compared to UCLA. I saw what UCLA's kids wore and the kind of cars they drove. It was obvious that they were getting greased."

In its second meeting with UCLA (March, 1971), Long Beach was not about to be blown out. Tarkanian's team surprised UCLA by executing its usual 1-2-2 zone to near perfection, forcing UCLA to shoot from the outside. Long Beach kept good pressure on the perimeter shots and took away UCLA's inside game. In the first half, a confused UCLA team could manage only six field goals against Tarkanian's defense.

With 14 minutes left in the game, Long Beach had an 11-point lead, and UCLA All-American Sidney Wicks was on the bench with four fouls. Long Beach alumnus Don Dyer remembers that at this point, J. D. Morgan, UCLA's athletic director, who had been sitting at the scorer's desk yelling at officials, began escalating his remarks at Big Ten official Art White. "He kept yelling, 'Watch number 43,' which was Eddie Ratleff." Did White stick it to Ratleff and Long Beach? Well, only he knows the answer, but Ratleff fouled out, and that was one of the rare times in his college career that Ratleff would foul out. "We always called that game the Art White victory," said Dyer.

Schrader puts it more bluntly "That game was a real screw job. They just took it from Long Beach. I saw J. D. Morgan sitting in the front row, screaming at the officials. J. D. was on the NCAA tournament officials selection committee, and I'm convinced he helped get Art White a job working the Final Four that year because White fouled out Ratleff."

Tarkanian says, "My philosophy is never to complain about officiating after you lose a game, but I have to admit it was very difficult for me not to say anything that year and to keep my mouth shut. I must admit that in following years I did tell White face-to-face about how unfair I thought his officiating was in that game."

Tarkanian took some solace from the fact that UCLA guard Henry Bibby later told him that Long Beach's zone was the toughest he had ever faced. Bibby was amazed that the Long Beach players could cover so much ground, taking away shots both inside and outside.

Many thought this was the beginning of the end for Long Beach, which had come too far, too fast, at least according to traditional basketball powers. Tarkanian had no way of knowing that after that game,

UCLA athletic director J. D. Morgan would begin taking steps against Long Beach, as documents subpoenaed during Tarkanian's case with the NCAA later indicated.

By 1971–72, Tarkanian's recruiting budget had soared all the way from $200 to $2,700. He had eleven full scholarships. He was voted salesman of the year in Long Beach for spreading positive publicity about the community, but the community wasn't responding strongly to the team. Long Beach had moved out of its tiny school gym into the 13,000-seat Long Beach Civic Center, but the average attendance was only 4,700, despite a team that was nationally ranked and almost knocked off UCLA.

Long Beach started the 1971–72 season by winning 16 of its first 17 games, but think about this: Tarkanian almost had George Gervin on the team. Gervin would become one of the highest-scoring guards in NBA history, a svelte 6-foot-7 shooter who is the greatest player in the history of the San Antonio Spurs.

Tarkanian: "I had a great group that season with Eddie Ratleff, Leonard Gray, George Trapp, and Bernard Williams. We had recruited Ernie Douse out of New York City, and we even ended up with George Gervin. Gervin was from Detroit, and it was one of my players [Bernard Williams] who saw George play in a high school game. Bernard told me that Gervin was even better than George Trapp, who was a very fine player for us. I checked around, and Gervin was not written up in any of the major high school scouting reports. He didn't make any high school All-American teams either. I found out that George played in the public school league. Those games were played in the afternoon, because that was during the riots in Detroit. Afternoon games meant virtually no media coverage, so the word hadn't gotten out on Gervin.

"George came out to Long Beach for a visit in the summer. He liked the campus, and we liked George as a kid. His brother also was able to get into nearby Compton Junior College. So George signed with us, and he was in Long Beach for the first couple of weeks of school. It was obvious that he was very homesick. He attached himself to Ivan Duncan, and everywhere Ivan went, George followed. If Ivan was in his office making phone calls George would be out in the hall, sitting on a basketball and leaning against the wall waiting for Ivan to finish. We made a big mistake, however, because we roomed George with Eric McWilliams, who was a junior college transfer.

"One weekend, I told McWilliams to call me if George got homesick, and we'd go see him. There never was any call, but on Monday when I went back to school, I found out that George was gone. Eric

McWilliams had driven George to the airport and put him on a plane back to Detroit. It was only then that it dawned on me: McWilliams and Gervin played the same position. Eric knew how talented George was and was more than happy to give George a lift to the airport. Boy, was I dumb about that.

"Later, George told me that he had made a big mistake in leaving Long Beach. He said his girlfriend was calling him every day, but when he got home they broke up after a few weeks. Isn't that ridiculous? George ended up playing for Eastern Michigan. We could have had Gervin and Eddie Ratleff on the same team. I always kid George about how he cost us a couple of national championships. In fact, my relationship with George Gervin is so close that he was a big help in our recruiting Sidney Green for UNLV. Sidney grew up idolizing Gervin, and George did a great job selling us to Sidney. Every now and then, I see George, and he asks me what he can do to help me and our program."

Even without Gervin, Long Beach went 25–4 in 1971–72 (Tarkanian's fourth season) and had a number-seven national ranking. Once again, a meeting loomed with UCLA in the NCAA tournament. This was when the UCLA band decided to have its 5 a.m. practice by the Long Beach players' rooms.

During the Alcindor years, UCLA had a policy of taking its team off the court during the national anthem because some of its players would not stand while the anthem was played. It was a sign of protest often used in the early 1970s. Long Beach boosters found it ironic that the Long Beach players who remained politely at attention on the floor were often called the bad guys, while the UCLA team was cast as the good guys. Long Beach fans would yell, "Where are you going, Bruins?" as the UCLA team left the court.

This third game between the UCLA and Long Beach teams was a whistle-marred affair won 73–57 by UCLA.

"Going into the game, I thought we had a shot at UCLA even though they had Bill Walton at center," says Tarkanian. "But we never had a chance to find out. We got in foul trouble early and lost the game."

The 1972–73 season was Tarkanian's fifth and last at Long Beach. The core of his team was Eddie Ratleff, Leonard Gray, Glenn McDonald, Rick Aberegg, Nate Stephens, and Ernie Douse. The team ended up with a 26–3 record, and was ranked as high as third in some polls. There was more talk about UCLA, and Tarkanian even offered to play the Bruins in a regular-season game at Pauley Pavilion, but UCLA wasn't interested. Nor did Long Beach get a fourth crack at

UCLA in the NCAA tournament, as Tarkanian's team was upset 77–66 by San Francisco after Ratleff fractured a finger on his shooting hand. "Eddie played tough," says Tarkanian. "He taped the fractured finger to a good finger and did the best he could, but we just didn't have enough to win that day."

Tarkanian's five-year record at Long Beach was an astounding 122–20, and 65–0 at home. Counting his junior college years, that gave him eleven straight undefeated seasons on his home courts.

Tarkanian: "I had better players at Long Beach than I have had at UNLV. Five of my kids became first-round NBA draft choices. That was four in five years at Long Beach, compared to four in fifteen years at UNLV. Also, the NBA had fewer teams back then, meaning it was harder to be picked in the first round."

Ratleff was a major reason why Long Beach became a legitimate power. The 6-foot-6 guard averaged 21.4 points as Long Beach went 74–12 under Tarkanian in those three seasons. He was selected to be a member of the U.S. Olympic team, and went on to play five seasons in the NBA with the Houston Rockets, where he averaged 8.3 points and was known more for his defense than his offense. A back injury caused Ratleff to retire. He obtained his degree at Long Beach, later served as an assistant coach there, and is now managing an insurance firm in Long Beach.

"Eddie's being a great player meant a lot to us, but he was a super person as well," says Tarkanian. "He was the kind of kid you want representing your school. It took guts for him to sign with Long Beach, because we were so young back then. Eddie carried us to another level."

Glenn McDonald, who also obtained his degree at Long Beach State, is now an assistant women's basketball coach at his alma mater. He was a number-one draft choice by the Boston Celtics, and played two years in the NBA. "You couldn't find a better kid in the world," says Tarkanian about him.

Glenn McDonald: "The basketball program at Long Beach has never been the same since Tark left. He just had so much energy. I think that the problem was that we won too much and we weren't supposed to be doing things like playing UCLA close. Tark got the jump on recruiting junior college kids, and he and Lois really worked with us while we were in school. During my freshman year, I got into the habit of going home to L.A. I used to hang around my old high school instead of going to class at Long Beach. Tark found out, and he jumped all over me. He said, 'I don't care so much about you skipping freshman team basketball practice, but I want you in class. If you miss another class, you can find yourself another school. You don't go to school, you don't have a scholarship.' That's why it's just bull when people say that all Tark cared about was winning, or that he didn't pay attention to the academic side of things. He lectured us all the time about school, and Lois was tutoring some of the players. Tark pushed us on the court and in school.''

Tarkanian's coaching style at Long Beach was far more conservative than it is now.

Tarkanian: ''I liked us to walk the ball up the court and work for a good shot under the basket. It seemed that almost every shot we took came from the low post, and you know what? I think I inhibited some of my players. I didn't get the most out of them, because I wouldn't let them run and shoot from the outside as much as they should have. I kept too tight a leash on them. Glenn McDonald was one kid that I might have held back, because he was a much better shooter after I left.''

While Tarkanian is notorious for second-guessing himself, it is obvious that at Long Beach he accomplished one of the most impressive coaching jobs in the history of college basketball—especially when you consider how he made so little stretch so far.

Here are the facts:

Before coming to Long Beach, Tarkanian had won four consecutive junior college championships, something which had never been done before.

He had Top Ten teams for four consecutive seasons on a recruiting budget that started at $200 and never got above $3,000. He never had monies allocated for scouting or filming games.

In eleven consecutive seasons he never lost a home game.

Most of his players came from junior colleges and they weren't heavily recruited. Tarkanian was the first major college coach to recognize the value of junior college players and to use them extensively.

Tarkanian's players were talented, but they didn't compare to the All-Americans at places such as UCLA and Kentucky. Just check how the Long Beach players performed in the NBA. Of Tarkanian's five first-round picks, Ratleff was the only one who had more than a brief career in the NBA. None of Tarkanian's players were of All-Pro caliber. So while he says that perhaps he didn't get the most out of their talent, the facts would indicate otherwise.

Before Tarkanian arrived, Long Beach was a Division II program. Within a short time after his departure, Long Beach ceased to be a national power.

Despite Long Beach's success, however, there was little community support for the team. In his final year as coach, the average attendance was only about 5,000, and the team was even giving away free tickets through a promotion with a local supermarket chain. Long Beach was a state college where the average student age was 24. Over 40 percent of the student body had full-time jobs. Most were not that interested in athletics; they had to concentrate on making a living to support themselves.

No money was available for scouting or filming, and there was only a small amount for recruiting, so all the funds made from a small basketball summer camp were used for scouting and recruiting. Players were given only $5.70 per day in meal money on road trips, which they usually spent on fast food. Tarkanian often has stated that they won at Long Beach "under every conceivable handicap."

Long Beach player Arthur "Sleepy" Montgomery spoke with Lois Tarkanian about getting an academic adviser for the athletes on campus. He had earned his degree at Long Beach and had been appointed chairman of the black studies department. Montgomery went to Long Beach State president Stephen Horn and suggested that since the basketball program was now earning money, perhaps some of it could be used for the students' academics. Sleepy told Lois that Horn denied the request.

"Unbelievable," says Lois. "Here was a man who served on the Civil Rights Commission, and he wasn't sympathetic to the needs of his own minority students; the least Horn could have done was to let us have an academic adviser."

Tarkanian finally was given the use of a small car, but he still had no secretary or personal office. He never earned more than $27,000, the amount he received his last year at Long Beach.

Tarkanian said the Long Beach basketball booster club was "mostly a bunch of nice young guys who liked the game, but like me, they had no money. None of us had much more than a couple of quarters to rub together. They were good guys, fun guys, but they just didn't have much."

There were about eleven USC Trojan clubs throughout California.

The Long Beach Trojan Club would have its weekly meeting at Hoefly's on a Tuesday. They would get John McKay, then the USC football coach, to come and speak, and boosters would donate two or three thousand dollars on the spot. Long Beach State would have its 49ers Club meetings at the same place the next night, and would be lucky to get two or three hundred dollars donated. The wealthy boosters would donate strongly to USC one night and then make a token donation to Long Beach State the next. Their heart and soul were really with USC. They were USC graduates, and many of them had children attending USC. It was only because they operated businesses in Long Beach that they gave even token support to the 49ers. Even the Long Beach football team had more support than the basketball team.

"Don Dyer used to tell me, 'Just wait, Jerry, we're young and we don't have much money now, but we love basketball and some day it will be us who will be running the city,'" says Tarkanian. "He was right, because now those guys do hold prominent positions throughout the city, but then they had very little. That doesn't mean they weren't the best, though. They were. There weren't many of them, but those few bled for our team."

Having no money was a familiar theme with the Tarkanians during their Long Beach days.

"We did have a house in a nice area," says Tarkanian, "because Don Gambril, the swim coach, told me about it and we got into it before prices went up. But we had little in the way of nice furnishings. When the NCAA came down to investigate us, it didn't bother me. We were broke. How could we be doing wrong? We didn't even have enough money to give the kids a first-rate training table as they did at most schools. When the NCAA showed interest, Ivan Duncan said, 'When they get here, they'll see how poor we are and probably hold a banquet for us.'"

6

Going to UNLV

Someone did notice Tarkanian at Long Beach, and that someone had been following Tarkanian's career for quite a while. That someone was a university in Las Vegas that was much like Long Beach: young, looking for an identity, and hoping that athletics could put it on the map. In fact, give the folks at Nevada-Las Vegas credit for making the perfect choice for their next basketball coach, because Tarkanian was exactly what they needed. He had the name and the connections to immediately build a winner, and the kind of personality that would not cause him to be blinded by the lights of the Las Vegas strip.

UNLV was indeed sold on Tarkanian, but selling UNLV to him was another matter.

Tarkanian: "I made up my mind during my fifth season at Long Beach (1972–73) that I was going to leave. We had been in the Top Ten for four years in a row, and we still didn't draw very well. It also bothered me that I had trouble getting the players summer jobs. Our kids really needed those jobs, because they didn't have any money—a lot of them came from very poor neighborhoods. I remember how we looked and looked for a job for Leonard Gray, and he ended up working in a place where he was supposed to clean the inside of cars. The problem was that the cars were compact, real small things, and Leonard was a bulky 6-foot-8. The poor kid couldn't even get in and out of the cars without almost bending himself into a pretzel, and the job wasn't paying much more than the minimum wage. I was disappointed that the community didn't help us more, but I guess that was mainly because Long Beach was still a UCLA and a Southern California town. Their recruits were getting better summer jobs than our players. One summer we helped one of our kids get a job, only to find that a Southern Cal alum had gotten the exact same job for a Southern Cal player, and that player was making $3 more an hour than our kid.

"Long Beach State had been primarily a teacher's college. Those few alums we had did not make the kind of money that would enable them to give much to our athletic program. I really loved Long Beach State and the boosters were great guys. We had a lot of fun together, but there wasn't enough support for us to stay.

"I thought I was going to Arizona State. The athletic director [Fred Miller] who had hired me at Long Beach had taken the Arizona State job, and had said he wanted me to coach the basketball team for him. But the Arizona State coach did not retire as expected, so the job didn't materialize. Then various people from Vegas started calling me. This was the third time UNLV had recruited me for the job. The first was when I was coaching at Riverside in 1963, right after UNLV was founded, but there was a problem about getting me a professorship, so it didn't work out. I recommended Rolland Todd for the position and he was hired.

"UNLV called me again in 1970, but I was just getting the Long Beach program going and I didn't wanted to leave the school or the kids. When UNLV called the third time, it was during the 1973 season. Several UNLV boosters called me. I told them that I wasn't interested, that I didn't think Lois want to move, and that I didn't want to think about anything except coaching Long Beach until the season was over. They kept calling two or three times a week. After we lost in the NCAA play-offs, they called several times a day. They never let up. There was no problem I brought up that they said they couldn't solve.

"Lois and I were new to being recruited so heavily. We'd take all calls and listen to everything people had to say. We didn't realize how that could wear you down. UNLV flew Lois, our daughter Pamela, and Jackie McQuarn [wife of Tarkanian's future assistant George McQuarn] to Vegas for a visit. When Lois and Pam returned, they were still not convinced about UNLV. But UNLV said they'd double my salary. We kept talking, and I started to feel Las Vegas cared more about me than Long Beach, even though I had been at Long Beach for five years. If I asked for something from Vegas, they said they'd do it. I wanted my own secretary and my own office, and they said no problem. I wanted my assistants to work just with basketball and not have to teach classes, which was the situation at Long Beach. All of that was fine with Vegas.''

When Long Beach learned that Tarkanian was seriously considering Las Vegas, some Long Beach businessmen offered to set up a college trust for Tarkanian's children. To help with the attendance troubles, the Long Beach Junior Chamber of Commerce promised to sell 5,000 season tickets.

Tarkanian: ''The only times Long Beach would ever give me anything extra or make a special effort to make me happy was when I was considering another job. One year, I was thinking about a job with the Portland Trail Blazers, and Long Beach got me a small rental car to drive. Another year, when UNLV was talking to me, Long Beach gave a Hawaiian vacation to me and my wife. It wasn't that they didn't care; they just didn't have much to give.

''This time, they knew I was more serious than ever, so they tried to come up with a very attractive package. They arranged to have me involved in public relations work on the Queen Mary. I was going to have my own office and secretary. By the time they were done with everything, their package was pretty close to the one Vegas had offered me. I ended up prolonging my decision longer than the Long Beach president liked. But it was tough because I kept weighing everything and going back and forth. One minute I thought I'd stay, the next I'd go. Decisions like that drive me crazy.

''Then UNLV wanted Lois and me to visit the town and school together. Both of us were pretty sure that we wouldn't take the job, but because all the Vegas people had been so kind to us, we felt we owed them the courtesy of making the final trip. Minutes before we left the house for the airport, we received a call from Sam Cameron, owner of the Long Beach *Press Telegram* and one of the most influential men in Long Beach. He asked us not to take the trip. We told him that it was a friendly gesture, not a commitment to UNLV. He asked us again not to go, and he was very firm about it. We had little time to talk, because our flight was leaving soon and it would have been unfair to cancel the trip on such short notice. We tried to explain to Cameron why we had to go, but to this day I think he felt that we had already decided to take the Vegas job, and that's what appeared in the newspapers.

''In any case, word leaked out that we were flying to Vegas. The newspapers made it look as though we were changing jobs, and no one was reading what we really were saying. I was told later that the publicity about the tug-of-war between Long Beach and UNLV bothered Long Beach State president Stephen Horn. He had told me earlier that week that he could understand if I took a job at Arizona State or Southern Cal, but a move to UNLV was 'a lateral move at best, and a slap in the face for Long Beach.' I didn't think about it at the time, but some people I know from Long Beach told me years later that Horn was embarrassed about losing a coach the community wanted and that he felt the publicity was demeaning to Long Beach State.

"When we returned to Long Beach after the Vegas visit, we were met at the airport by [Press-Telegram columnist] Loel Shraeder and Joyce Ricci, a close friend. They drove home with us and we talked for hours. I went for a long walk on the beach with Danny, who was 11, and we talked about what was involved in moving. Lois was sure about staying in Long Beach, but I hadn't made up my mind. When I woke up the next morning, it was a beautiful southern California day and I was sure that I was doing the right thing by staying in Long Beach.

"A close friend of mine, Vic Weiss, was helping me during this time. He told Long Beach that I'd have a decision by Friday, and he wanted to set up a press conference. We thought the decision would be to stay, but I can see how the Long Beach State people could have thought it would be different. The press conference was to be held the day after the Vegas trip, and the media had written up our trip to Vegas in long stories under big headlines. Horn criticized me in the press for taking too long to make a decision. Long Beach State officials told Vic Weiss that if I was going to stay, I could have the press conference on campus; if I was going to Vegas, I would have to have the press conference somewhere else. Until this time, Horn had done all kinds of things trying to keep me from taking the Vegas job, such as giving me an office and a secretary.

"The media kept blowing things up, saying that I wanted to leave Long Beach but Lois didn't. They made a big deal about the different financial offers, as if one school was trying to outbid the other. Some writers even speculated that with the different packages being offered, the Long Beach basketball coach would earn more than the school president. Horn tried to keep me; then he got on me for taking too long. I thought I had done a lot for Long Beach, and I was insulted that suddenly Horn was trying to pressure me."

Tarkanian felt that he had a real stake in Long Beach. He took pride not only in his record on the court, but in his professor of the year awards and his stance during the days of campus riots.

Tarkanian says, "I couldn't make up my mind what to do and kept going back and forth. The turning point was the press conference. If they had just given me permission to make my announcement on campus, I'd have stayed. I thought they owed me that courtesy. So when they didn't, I left.''

Lois: "Jerry just drags and drags things out. He doesn't do it on purpose, because he is in such agony while it is going on, but it is so hard for him to leave a place and the players that he loves. Not letting Jerry have the press conference on campus was a petty thing to do, and it tipped the scales in favor of Las Vegas.

"But there were other reasons why Jerry left. We all were amazed that we could be ranked third in the country and still average only 4,700 fans. One time Jerry and I were walking out of the arena and Jerry said, 'Can you imagine how embarrassing this is to be number three in the country, with All-American Eddie Ratleff, and still only have 4,700 people in the stands?' I know that upset him. The Los Angeles area had so many professional and college teams. In addition to UCLA and Southern Cal, there were the Dodgers, the Rams, and the Lakers.

"Jerry also saw Las Vegas as a college town. I almost fell over when he said that, but he believed it, and he turned out to be right. Unless you live in Las Vegas, it is hard to realize what the university means to the community. It's the focal point. There were no pro teams, no other universities. We always drew well in Vegas when our Long Beach teams played there. He saw a town ready to explode with enthusiasm.

"As for myself, I didn't want to move to Las Vegas. When I had been there before, it was as a tourist. Jerry had some friends in Vegas and he'd go out to dinner with them. I'd stay in the hotel room and read a book or sit around the pool. I grew up on a farm and loved working in the garden, growing flowers. The desert didn't appeal to me. Later, I found out that you could have a nice garden in Las Vegas and that people there were family-oriented, just like our friends we've had everywhere we lived.

"After Jerry took the job, he went to Vegas to look for a house. I stayed in California with the children. Before, I had been able to move with little trouble, but this time I felt broken up inside. I loved southern California. It's such a diverse and sophisticated place that I could have my own set of friends, people who didn't know me as Mrs. Jerry Tarkanian, or people who didn't even know that my husband was a basketball coach. I was the founding administrator for the first private school for deaf children in California, Oralingua School, located in

106

Whittier. We were in what has since become known as the 'Golden Age of Special Education.' Our staff was just beginning to make some extraordinary breakthroughs in curriculum development and communications strategies. We were very close, and the school was like a child to me. I had helped give it birth; and now that it was starting to receive some national recognition, I wanted to remain a part of it. I had a wonderful group of mentors and friends. I felt at home there.

"In Las Vegas, I was very lonely for a long time. A lot of people offered friendship and were very kind to me, but I just felt out of place for a while, because I was without the network of friends with whom I had grown so comfortable."

Of all the moves the Tarkanians made, this was by far the most painful. Jerry went to extremes to try to make his departure graceful. Several of his Long Beach players wanted to follow him to Vegas. Roscoe Poindexter, considered one of the finest young college players in the country, drove Tarkanian to the airport and asked Jerry to take him along. Roscoe was very close to the Tarkanians and had once gone into the fields with Lois to pick pumpkins in an effort to raise money for deaf children. New York phenomenon Ernie Douse, both Poindexters (Roscoe and younger brother Cliff), and some others also wanted to transfer to Vegas. But Tarkanian urged the players to stay and work hard for new coach Lute Olson.

"I still felt loyal to Long Beach," says Tarkanian. "I could have brought a lot of guys with me to UNLV and we could have had a ton of talent, but I didn't think it was the right thing to do. How could I leave Long Beach and then take their best players? The school had been good to me and I didn't want to hurt it. I wanted to repay them for giving me a chance to coach at a four-year school, and I still cared about the program."

Glenn McDonald says, "Rick Aberegg, our point guard, and I had only one year of eligibility left, so we really didn't think it would be smart to go to UNLV with Tark. About all the other guys wanted to go, but Jerry told them to finish out their careers at Long Beach. He tried to leave a good taste in everyone's mouth, but it didn't happen, although that wasn't Tark's fault."

The players Tarkanian recruited for Long Beach went 24–2 for Lute Olson. The only person Tarkanian took with him from Long Beach to UNLV was Gil Castillo, the team manager, the only one who knew how to fold Tark's towel.

In Long Beach, Tarkanian had become a local hero. After he accepted the UNLV offer, Long Beach State was harshly criticized in the media for not taking steps to keep its coach. The story of Long Beach's refusal to let Tarkanian have a press conference on campus was made public by the media, and that created even more heat for Horn.

"The stage was set for what happened next," says Tarkanian. "The next year was one of the worst times of my life."

Lois: "Being naive or just plain dumb, we didn't put the pieces together of what was happening. A prime example was an incident involving Ernie Douse, one of the few freshmen players Jerry had recruited for Long Beach. He called our Huntington Beach home during the summer and asked for Jerry. I told him Jerry was not home but could meet him during the weekend when he flew back from Las Vegas. I set up a breakfast meeting with Ernie and Jerry and myself at the Hyatt Edgewater Hotel on Pacific Coast Highway. Ernie began by asking Jerry about transferring to Las Vegas. He did not feel comfortable with the coaching staff and felt they did not like him. Jerry explained why it would not be good for Ernie to transfer, because he could be a fine player at Long Beach. Then Ernie said something that should have awakened Jerry and me to what was happening.

" 'Coach,' Ernie said, 'They're asking me to sign some papers and stuff at the college. I don't want to, but they keep pressuring me. They tell me I can't play if I don't.' It was obvious to me that Ernie was distraught as he spoke. You couldn't help feeling sorry for him. 'Do whatever they ask you to do,' said Jerry. 'Just make it easier on yourself. Follow what they want. Keep your nose clean and everything will work out all right.'

"Neither Jerry nor I gave a second thought to what the papers were that Ernie was being asked to sign. We were too focused on Ernie's pain. We didn't even ask him who was telling him to sign the papers. We purposely were avoiding contact with Long Beach players and personnel in order to make the coaching change easier for everyone involved, and Jerry was spending most of his time in Las Vegas. We had no idea that an official NCAA inquiry had been initiated against Long Beach shortly after Jerry resigned."

The NCAA first looked at the Long Beach basketball program in the fall of 1972. It would seem that the investigation was spurred by a complaint from UCLA athletic director J. D. Morgan, who contacted the NCAA on February 1, 1972—less than a year after Long Beach State nearly upset UCLA in the NCAA Western Regional Tournament.

The following paragraphs are taken from a letter dated February 10, 1972, from NCAA Assistant Executive Director Warren S. Brown to Morgan:

"Dear J. D.:

"Thank you for the information which you forwarded concerning Leonard Gray. Please rest assured that the source of this information will remain personal and confidential, as you requested in your February 1 letter, and that the NCAA will take the responsibility of determining whether NCAA rules are involved in this matter."

Gray was a forward who had transferred from Kansas to Long Beach, and it would seem that Morgan was questioning the fact that Gray was in the Long Beach travel party at the NCAA play-offs. The timing of this letter was interesting, because 1972 was the year that Long Beach started to put real pressure on UCLA in the national rankings.

Another item is the NCAA record of a telephone conversation between PAC-8 (now PAC-10) commissioner Wiles Hallock and the NCAA's Warren Brown. The subject was Ernie Douse, a freshman who had accompanied the Long Beach team to an NCAA tournament game in Provo, Utah.

Tarkanian: "Ernie wasn't on the team, because freshmen weren't eligible. But he practiced with us. I didn't try to hide the fact that he was there. I didn't know that it was against NCAA regulations until later. It was just a mistake I made because I wasn't aware of the rule that red-shirts couldn't practice with the team during the NCAA tournament. Neither did any of the other Long Beach officials know about that rule, because they had to approve our travel list. For three straight years, I brought my red-shirts with me to the tournament and no one ever said a word, and NCAA officials were right there watching. All the NCAA had to do was say something, and I would have stopped it right away."

The following is a partial transcript of a telephone conversation between Commissioner Hallock and Brown:

HALLOCK: The name of the freshman who was with Long Beach in Provo was Ernie Douse. The thing here is that I didn't actually see him. A couple of people from UCLA did and UCLA doesn't want to be involved in turning Long Beach in.... Apparently Jerry Tarkanian made no bones about the fact that the kid was there and worked out with them. But he was recognized by...I don't know whether J. D. [Morgan, UCLA athletic director] or what, but somebody recognized

109

him and they knew he was there. I think they would admit it if confronted with it.

BROWN: Well, there wouldn't be any objection on your part at least about contacting UCLA on our own...

HALLOCK: On contacting UCLA?

BROWN: Right. To see if anyone would acknowledge seeing him...

HALLOCK: Well, I think J. D. knows that I was going to report it.

The reason why Hallock seemed surprised that Tarkanian "made no bones about" Douse's presence with the team is that Tarkanian made no effort to conceal it. He had no idea this was a violation. The point of relating this letter and conversation with the NCAA is to show that UCLA clearly played a role in bringing the NCAA to the door of the gym at Long Beach.

Another factor may have been some newspaper columns written by Tarkanian for the Long Beach *Independent*. They concerned one of his favorite themes: the NCAA's selective investigating procedures. Tarkanian wondered why upstart programs such as Western Kentucky were examined by the NCAA while established powers were not. This was a common topic of discussion among college coaches, but it seldom was made public. Tarkanian's columns did not sit well with the NCAA.

In a 1972 column, Tarkanian questioned the heavy sanctions placed on Centenary College. In a January 1973 column, Tarkanian stated:

> The NCAA could take another major step in the right direction by revamping its investigative policies. The NCAA investigated and then placed on probation the New Mexico States, Western Kentuckys, Centenarys and Florida States, while the big money makers go free. It's a crime that Western Kentucky is placed on probation but the famous University of Kentucky isn't even investigated, even though Tom Payne's story has come to light.*

Shortly after Tarkanian's column was published, Warren Brown, NCAA assistant executive director, wrote a letter to Jesse Hill, com-

---

*Payne was a 7-foot star at Kentucky, considered the first black basketball player recruited to the school, who supposedly supported himself in college. After his Kentucky enrollment ended, he made statements admitting he had no money of his own to support himself in school.

missioner of Long Beach's PCAA conference. The January 26, 1973, letter read:

> Enclosed for your leisure-time reading is a copy of a newspaper article...written by Jerry Tarkanian....I wonder whether he considers California State University, Long Beach, in the "big money-maker category."

In the fall of 1972, the NCAA questioned a few members of the football and basketball teams. Long Beach athletic director Dr. Lou Comer told Tarkanian that if there were problems, he would know about it within thirty to sixty days. There was no further word for several months, so school officials believed that they were in good shape concerning the NCAA.

The first notice of a formal NCAA investigation of Long Beach came in a letter from Warren Brown to President Horn, indicating the start of an official inquiry into the basketball program. The letter was dated four days after Tarkanian had left Long Beach.

"Believe me, if I'd known that the NCAA was going to investigate the Long Beach basketball program, I'd have stayed," says Tarkanian. "I don't care what UNLV offered me, I'd have remained at Long Beach to deal with the allegations, but I had no idea they were coming."

Two months after he went to UNLV, Long Beach summoned Tarkanian to answer written questions from the NCAA.

Tarkanian: "Looking back, I feel like I was railroaded. I never got a chance to learn who was accusing me. I didn't even get a chance to go to a hearing and present my side. I just filled out some papers with some questions about things at Long Beach. I wasn't told if my answers were acceptable or not, or if additional information was needed. I even asked to go to a hearing before the NCAA and offered to pay my own way, but the Long Beach officials wouldn't let me. Frankly, I had no idea what was to come."

What was to come was an edict on January 6, 1974, in which the NCAA put the Long Beach basketball and football programs on probation for three years. Long Beach was barred from NCAA tournament and national television appearances.

One implication of the NCAA's statements and the newspaper stories that followed was that Tarkanian had left Long Beach because he knew that the NCAA was about to hit the school with probation. By tying the football and basketball programs together—a tactic seldom

111

used by the NCAA—the NCAA made the basketball program appear guilty of every imaginable sin.

"When the probation was announced, my telephone never stopped ringing. But I had no idea what to tell the reporters because I had not seen the breakdown of the charges in specific terms. When I did learn the details, I flew to Long Beach and held a press conference. A lot of my coaching friends told me that this was a mistake; they said I should just keep quiet and take the probation, that talking about it would make things worse. But I had to say something. At Long Beach, we had won with no money, no alumni support, and very little support from the university. We won because our coaching staff worked our butts off, and because we recruited a lot of junior college kids. The junior college kids came to play for me because I had been a junior college coach and most four-year coaches weren't recruiting the junior colleges. We had nothing that would be considered conducive to winning at the major college level, but we had reached the point where we had replaced Southern Cal as the second-best team in the West behind UCLA. How could I shut up about it? The things they were saying weren't true."

Lois: "I believe quite strongly that Stephen Horn was embarrassed when Jerry left for UNLV. For months after the announcement, Horn told the media and others about coaches who jump from one school to another to avoid NCAA punishment. He sought NCAA legislation to address the situation, bringing additional publicity to his stand. Horn carefully avoided mentioning Jerry's name in any public statement, but the implication was clear. Horn was very smart in not letting Jerry attend the NCAA hearings, because Horn could then control a great part of what was said about Jerry. I think a situation existed where some of the people from Long Beach told the NCAA things that weren't true in the hope that with Jerry gone, the penalty would be made lighter for the school. Jerry offered to attend the meeting, paying his own expenses, but Long Beach didn't want him there. Twice, Jerry called the NCAA, asking to set up meetings with Warren Brown and the investigators so he could explain and discuss the charges, but the NCAA told him that any meeting would have to be arranged by the Long Beach State president, and Stephen Horn did not want Jerry at any meetings with the NCAA."

Tarkanian was quoted in the *Los Angeles Times* (January 19, 1974): "If the school officials were going to take all the blame, I can see why they didn't ask us to attend. But if the blame was going to be directed toward...me, they should have invited us."

*   *   *

112

When everything was finally sorted out, Long Beach State was charged with seventy-four violations—fifty-one against the football program and twenty-three against basketball. It is not worth recounting the football program's alleged transgressions, other than to say that they were the most serious violations.

The NCAA has a way of putting together multiple charges for the same incident, often making the situation appear far more grave than it is. A single charge expands like an amoeba into several charges.

For example, the NCAA said that Tarkanian's assistant, Ivan Duncan, had arranged for stand-ins to take entrance exams for four players: Glenn McDonald, Roscoe Poindexter, Ernie Douse, and George Gervin. By the time the NCAA was finished with that item, it covered fourteen charges. McDonald was enraged by the NCAA's claim.

Glenn McDonald: "I took the test. I signed a sworn affidavit saying I did. I took the case to court and a hearing officer [Helen Gallagher] appointed by a U.S. District Court judge ruled that I took the test and stated that 'a reasonable inference cannot be drawn from the evidence presented [by the NCAA]' that I didn't take the test. My academic status was cleared. What the NCAA said was just garbage. They said my high school records said I couldn't do college-level work, but I got my degree and now I'm an assistant coach of the women's basketball team at Long Beach. Once in a while someone asks me if I was the guy who faked his ACT test. That really upsets me, because the NCAA was dead wrong. I went to court to prove my point, but I still hear about it. It's like I got marked for life. To this day, I'm sure the NCAA was trying to blackball Jerry any way they could."

Gervin told *Sports Illustrated,* "I didn't want to, but they [the Long Beach coaches] made me take it [the test]."

The Roscoe Poindexter charge also was dismissed by the court's hearing officer, but it was far more complicated. Tarkanian had recruited Roscoe Poindexter out of high school.

Tarkanian: "Roscoe signed with us, but it turned out that Roscoe wasn't a college predictor [because of his grades and college entrance tests scores]. We talked Roscoe into attending Fresno City Junior College. We thought that two years of JUCO would help him get squared away academically. After his first year, we heard that Roscoe suddenly was a predictor, and California-Santa Barbara and Fresno State were recruiting him. Supposedly, Roscoe took the test during the summer and scored high on it. A student can take the American College Test (ACT) right out of high school and again a year later. We didn't know that Roscoe was going to take the test again. We called Roscoe, and he said, 'Coach, I took the test and got a 21 on it.' That is very, very high. Anyway, I said, 'Roscoe, we'd love to have you, but I just don't believe that you scored a 21, and I don't think anyone else will either. If you want to transfer to Long Beach now, we'll be glad to have you, but you'll have to sit out a year.' He said that was fine; he wouldn't play that first year. Then he'd have three years left and he could play with his younger brother Clifton, who also planned to come to Long Beach.

"So Roscoe enrolled at Long Beach with the idea of sitting out a year. But a week before our first game [in 1972], the NCAA came to our campus. When they spoke to Roscoe, he told the NCAA that he was sitting out and the NCAA investigator told him that they 'saw no reason why he couldn't play.'

"Roscoe said, 'Coach Tark said I can't play.' The NCAA investigator told Roscoe he could play. Roscoe was very close to Ken Delpit, a coach at his high school. He told Ken what the NCAA had said. Ken gets on a plane and comes to Long Beach. He picks up Roscoe, comes to our house, and starts giving me all kinds of hell because the NCAA said Roscoe could play and I wouldn't let him. Roscoe said, 'You can play me if you really want to. The NCAA man told me so. If you don't want to play me, then tell me and I'll go somewhere else.'

"Obviously, Roscoe's pride was very hurt and Delpit said, 'If you don't want Roscoe, we'll pull him out of school.' I told Ken that we did want Roscoe, but that I had a problem with Roscoe's high test score. Ken kept saying that the NCAA said Roscoe could play, so we should let him play.

"Next, I checked with our athletic director, and he said that he had been told the same thing by the NCAA investigator—there was no reason why Roscoe couldn't play. This was when Roscoe first was on a basketball scholarship, and we let Roscoe play, although he never started for us because he had missed all of preseason practice. Later, the NCAA said that Roscoe's test scores weren't valid and that we had violated the rules. But it was the NCAA investigator who said Roscoe could play in the first place. Obviously, we should have checked with others at the NCAA, but we were inexperienced and no one at our school took that extra step."

The epilogue is that Poindexter also took his case to court and won, just as McDonald did.

The rest of the charges—nine according to the NCAA—were of a minor nature. For example, the NCAA claimed that Tarkanian had offered to move the family of Mississippi high school star Eugene Short to Long Beach and find his mother a job.

"That's just not true," says Tarkanian. "The kid denied it, the mother denied it, and the NCAA offered no proof. They just said I did it."

The NCAA said that Tarkanian gave Ernie Douse $30 while he was still in high school and playing at the Dapper Dan all-star game in Pittsburgh. Douse submitted a sworn affidavit stating that he never received the money. Tarkanian says, "That's just ridiculous. It never happened."

The last charge was that Gervin had spent two weeks in Long Beach during the summer of 1970. Supposedly, Long Beach tried to induce Gervin to attend school by helping to enroll Gervin's brother, Claude, at Compton Junior College.

Tarkanian: "There is nothing illegal about our placing Gervin's brother into Compton College. We didn't pay that kid's way or anything, and he was a legitimate junior college player. The other part of the charge was that George spent more than the required forty-eight hours on campus for his visit. Well, he was in California for two weeks. But George had a brother who lived in Palm Springs, and that's where he was for two weeks—at his brother's house in Palm Springs, California, not on campus."

Thinking about the Long Beach case, what Tarkanian still asks is, "How can they have called these charges 'among the most serious the NCAA ever considered?' What were they talking about? There were no cash payments, except the claim of giving $30 to Ernie Douse, and that was just ridiculous. There were no charges of giving away cars or altering transcripts. They talked to every player I had, and they found no one who would say I gave them a car or money. It left the wrong impression of what the Long Beach program and the players were really all about."

7

Jackie Robinson

An example of the NCAA's investigative tactics in the Tarkanian case occurred in April 1973, about one month after Tarkanian announced he would accept the UNLV position.

The incident revolved around Jackie Robinson, a 6-foot-6-inch senior forward from Morningside High School in Los Angeles. By 1973, the Tarkanian and Robinson families had been intertwined for over ten years. There were eight Robinson children. Jackie's oldest brother, Charles, had been recruited by Tarkanian at Riverside in 1963. The second oldest brother, Sam, had played four years for Tarkanian—two at Pasadena City College and two at Long Beach State. Tarkanian's wife, Lois, and Jackie's mother, Ester, were close friends. Jackie's youngest brother, Angelo, and Tarkanian's oldest son, Danny, had played together since they were toddlers. The Robinson family seldom saw their father, and with eight children, Mrs. Robinson depended primarily upon welfare funds to feed her family.

Jackie Robinson still remembers his mother's kitchen table in their small rental home near the Los Angeles airport. By the time he was 17, he not only knew about driving lay-ups and zone defenses; he had been introduced to life in basketball's big time. It happened at that kitchen table.

"One day a college coach came into our kitchen," says Jackie. "He started laying bills on the table and he did that for what seemed a very long time. When he was finished, there was a large stack of money on the table."

Jackie stared at what was about $10,000, and no words came from his mouth. He had never imagined—much less seen—so much cash. But Jackie's mother did the talking.

"My mother threw the coach out of the house," says Jackie. "She screamed at the man that no one was going to buy her son.

"That's just the thing. Tark was one of the few coaches who didn't offer me anything extra. I'm not afraid to talk about it. It was a long time ago. If Tark had offered me money, I'd say it. I have nothing to hide. But that's the thing—he didn't. No cash, no cars, nothing."

Nothing but a promise, that is.

Jackie Robinson: "Tark did guarantee me that I'd never go hungry. That's also what he told my mother. My one extra benefit was the right to Tark's refrigerator. All his players got the same thing. If we were hungry, we could go over to their house and Tark or Lois would find us something to eat. Sometimes when they weren't home, we'd still find something to eat. One time it was a box of oranges left on their front porch by Tark's Uncle Leo. Gondo [Glen Gondrezick] and I stuffed all our pockets and hands with oranges because we were really hungry and we knew they wouldn't mind."

This is why Robinson is amazed that he was a central figure in the NCAA's investigation of Tarkanian and the UNLV basketball program.

Jackie Robinson: "I'm a guy who went to a school that wasn't buying players, and some still said I was bought. That's not fair to me and it's not fair to Tark. My mother used to baby-sit for Tark and Lois when my brother Sam played at Pasadena. I remember being over at their house while my mother took care of me, my younger brother, Angelo, and the Tarkanian kids. I used to go to almost all my brother's games at Pasadena and Long Beach."

Angelo Robinson: "I'm about the same age as Danny. We were together so much when we were preschoolers that we were like part of the same family. We even shared the same toys. I'd go over to their house for Christmas sometimes, and I remember going on vacation with them one summer in the mountains. I guess I was about 8 then. Danny and I are still close friends; I spent part of last Christmas season at their home. Any time I want to go there and stay, I know I can."

Ester and Lois often went to basketball games together, both at Long Beach and at Pasadena. Ester was there to see her son Sam play forward, and Lois was there to be with her husband the coach. They also spent a lot of their time keeping track of Angelo Robinson and Danny Tarkanian, who found running under the bleachers, picking up trash, and popping paper cups far more entertaining than what was happening on the court.

Lois: "I found myself growing very close to Ester. I worked part-time and she'd watch my children, bringing her youngest, Angelo, with her. We'd always sit together at home games and travel together to away games. It gave us a lot of time to talk, discuss concerns, and get to know each other. We shared a lot of emotional times. We'd talk about raising children and the problems we had, especially since we both had boys the same age. We even talked about our names—her first name and my middle name are the same, and there aren't many Esters around. She'd talk about how it came from the Bible and what it meant. She was a very religious woman and was almost like a second mother to me. I know she gave me far more advice than I gave her. I was young and would get tense over things, and she'd just quote something from the Bible or say something softly to calm me down.

"The Robinsons had little in the way of food and clothes. I remember sometimes I'd drive out to her place just to talk, and I'd pick up something at a fast-food place and make sure there was enough for everyone, because the family was really big. We'd set out that food and you'd think I'd brought a banquet. Her eyes would light up and she'd be so happy, and it just made me feel good. There were other fun times, too. I remember Danny and Angelo dancing round and round her while she sang that Simon and Garfunkel song, 'Mrs. Robinson,' that was popular then."

Sam Robinson was one of several Pasadena and later Long Beach players who used to go to the Tarkanians' home in Arcadia. Lois and one or two of the girls from the junior college would make large batches of tacos and enchiladas. The players would eat about six each and drink about two quarts of milk. When dinner was over and the dishes were cleared away, the textbooks came out. Lois would sit with Sam and other players and tutor them in their English courses.

Lois: "I'll never forget one night when Sam just did not want to bear down on one particularly difficult assignment. I said, 'Sam, I'll be here all night with you until it's finished. I don't care how long it takes.' I don't think he felt I would last, but I was determined. He finally finished it about 2 a.m.

"Another time, in Long Beach, I saved up money so we could serve steaks to the players at a cookout after one of our really good seasons. I wanted to make it something special, but the kids really didn't want the steaks. They asked for hamburgers instead. I was crushed. I'm not really a very good cook anyway, and I felt I must have done something wrong. Ester explained to me that it had nothing to do with my cooking, but that our players came from homes where they didn't have steak. They just had not acquired a taste for it; ground meat had been the best they'd eaten. I learned something very valuable from her: No matter how much you think you know what someone has gone through, unless you've experienced it yourself, you really never can understand it fully.

"To make up for the steak fiasco, I decided to have a soul food dinner. Obviously, I needed help with that, so Ester and some of the other mothers assisted, and we had a big dinner at our home. I remember enjoying the greens, but Ester cooked the chitlins on my stove and a rather unique odor permeated the entire house. Also, I knew chitlins were pig intestines, and I just couldn't eat them. But those were good times, and those are the times you hold on to in your thoughts when some of the other pressures of coaching become almost overbearing."

By the spring of 1973, Tarkanian was leaving Long Beach for UNLV, and Jackie Robinson was 6-6 and 210 pounds, a superb athlete.

Tarkanian: "I never recruited Jackie for Long Beach because I already had a great 6-6 forward in Roscoe Poindexter. Roscoe and Jackie played the same position. It wouldn't have been fair to Jackie or the family for me to bring him in and make him sit on the bench."

Poindexter was a star at Long Beach.

Lois: "I always stayed in contact with the Robinsons, even after Sam had left Long Beach for the pros. I remember Ester asking me why Jerry didn't recruit Jackie to play at Long Beach. I told her about Roscoe Poindexter and Jackie playing the same position, but I'm not sure she really understood. I think she was a little hurt, thinking that Jerry didn't want Jackie. It bothered me that she was upset, so I pressed Jerry on it, but he would only say, 'Lois, you can't bring in a brother of someone who has been a big star in your program unless he will have an opportunity to do equally as well. It's not fair to him.' I didn't say much more after that, but I know that in later years Jerry has kept to that belief about brothers, because he never ever recruited any of the Gondrezick brothers after their older brother, Glen, had been such a big star at UNLV."

One weekend, Tarkanian was visiting the Robinsons, and Jackie, a high school senior, asked, "Coach, are you going to recruit me?" Tarkanian said that he had Roscoe Poindexter, and Jackie would have to sit for two years behind Roscoe. Tarkanian told Jackie that he didn't know if Jackie could handle that.

When Tarkanian left Long Beach for UNLV in March of 1973, however, everything changed.

Tarkanian: "I needed players. I had just accepted the job, and I was in Las Vegas staying at the Circus Circus Hotel. It was about an hour after I'd signed the contract, and I called Lois and about the first thing she said was, 'Now are you going to sign Jackie?' I said, 'Yes.' Right after that, she drove out to the Robinsons' home.''

It wasn't long before the phone rang in Tarkanian's room at Circus Circus. It was Ester. "Thank God you took that job," she told Tarkanian. "The minute I heard you might leave Long Beach, I started praying you'd take that new job. I wanted you to move so you'd take care of my Jackie. I want you to come over real soon and sign Jackie."

Ester Robinson was a deeply religious woman who didn't trust men wearing three-piece suits, carrying briefcases, making lots of promises to her and her son, and putting piles of money on the kitchen table. Instead, she remembered the woman whose children she had helped raise, the woman who at times had put food on that kitchen table out of friendship, not to recruit. And she trusted the coach who made no promises except that her son would not go hungry.

"I didn't have a choice about college once Tark went to Vegas," says Jackie. "My mother said he was a good man and he'd make sure nothing happened to me, and that's where I was going."

But there are several subplots to this story.

The first was a fellow named Jim Harrick, who was Jackie's basketball coach at Morningside High and is now the head coach at UCLA.

Tarkanian: "Harrick was applying for several college assistant jobs. He was indicating to the colleges that he would be able to take Jackie with him wherever he would go. And that probably was true, until I went to Vegas. But when I signed Jackie, Harrick called the NCAA and said I had bought Jackie. It was incredible."

Information made public after Tarkanian's court cases showed how the recruiting process worked, how an 18-year-old was pressured by an NCAA staff member and his high school coach. It showed how he was tempted with illegal offers. Finally, it showed how certain NCAA staff members were not only investigating Tarkanian, but openly recruiting against him and for the man who had complained to the NCAA about Tarkanian.

The following is an abridged transcript of a telephone call, taped by the NCAA, that Jim Harrick made to investigator David Berst:

HARRICK: He [Jackie Robinson] was recruited and signed by Las Vegas, and the problem arises to this day that his mother also was given a trip over there. I know that for a fact, although it would be hard to prove, but she was there and she stayed at the Dunes and was treated very, very nicely and was taken to the Bill Cosby Show and they got to go up on stage....I am his high school coach, and I certainly wouldn't want it to get out that I called....But I didn't think this was the right way to recruit a kid and you know the policy was that in all the years I knew the kid, they said he'd never go with Tarkanian, but he was over there [in Las Vegas] one weekend and he came back signed. Now they're a family on welfare....I can't prove it, but you might be able to uncover this if you were interested....I have no ax to grind because I really don't care....

BERST: Well, we certainly are interested and just the fact that the mother has gone over there on a visit with him is incorrect....Were they flown over there in a private aircraft or commercial?

HARRICK: They went commercial and probably had someone pick up his ticket here, but he would be a friend of Vegas, and that would also be a violation....I have no ax to grind. I just feel bitter that the kids are being used in an unnecessary manner....I would never tell anyone I called, but I'm certainly not ashamed of it and I'm certainly not bitter that he's going there [UNLV], but I'm certainly sure he will not get an education, he won't graduate....That's the thing that upset me....She [Ester Robinson] was mad at him [Tarkanian] for three years, and they would never send another kid to Tarkanian. Never! Never!...I told the kid, don't you go signing anything over there [on his visit to UNLV]....He and I were going to make the decision [about Jackie's college] for three years, all of a sudden, I'm out of it. I hope you don't think I'm bitter, I'm really not.

BERST: No, we are interested in this sort of thing.

HARRICK: If that's not illegal recruiting, I don't know what is. I'm going to get into this [college coaching] and I don't want to be left out in the cold next year.

BERST: Oh, are you moving?

HARRICK: Yes, I am. I'm going to Utah State to be an assistant up there. I didn't recruit Jackie because he was too close to me....I know what a lot of people say, maybe because I didn't get the kid. But it's certainly not like that.

BERST: Is there any indication that he got any cash while he was over there?

HARRICK: No, not that I know of. He would never admit it to me, but he stated to me that they took care of him very well financially, and you know right away, he kind of didn't want to talk about it....I will leave you with that.

The tape ends with Berst, in collusion with Harrick, determining ways in which Harrick could get an NCAA investigator to talk with Robinson without Robinson's knowing the specific reason for the meeting.

This telephone conversation was the start of an intense NCAA investigation into Jackie's recruiting visit to UNLV. It reveals the NCAA's eagerness to pursue Tarkanian over what may have been, at most, a minor violation. The issue was who had paid for Ester Robinson's airplane ticket, since the rules permit the college to pick up airfare only for the player, not his parents. The school could provide accommodations once the parent arrived. A round-trip ticket from LA airport to Las Vegas was in the $50 to $60 range.

The NCAA claimed that Paul Landreaux, an assistant to Harrick at Morningside who had at one time been a volunteer graduate coach for Tarkanian at Long Beach, had paid for Mrs. Robinson's ticket with money from UNLV. Landreaux stated that he paid for the trip himself and produced a credit card receipt to prove it. He also stated that not only was he close to Jackie from coaching at Morningside, but he had been friends with Jackie's family for a long time; relatives of his had played basketball with relatives of Jackie's for years. Knowing that Ester Robinson was suffering from cancer and that she wished to see Las Vegas with her son, he paid for the trip.

"It was a little over $50," says Landreaux. "I went too, because she really wasn't feeling well. It was nothing for me, because I had an old service buddy stationed near there and spent a lot of time with him, but it really meant a lot to her. I'm glad I did it. I think she died within a year."

When the NCAA sent investigator Lester Burks to interview Ester Robinson, his report read as follows:

Mrs. Robinson stated that she was a very close friend of the Tarkanian family....Mrs. Robinson quoted Tarkanian as saying he could not pay for her expenses for the trip to Las Vegas because it would be a violation of NCAA legislation....Mrs. Robinson stated that she did not know whether Landreaux was reimbursed for all of this or not....Mrs. Robinson appeared to the writer to get angry ...asking, 'Are you trying to nail Tarkanian, or nail my son or the University of Nevada?'...Mrs. Robinson stated that Jackie signed tickets for his food and her food and everything else was paid for by Landreaux....Mrs. Robinson stated that Tarkanian is a fair and honest man and he wouldn't do anything against NCAA legislation. Mrs. Robinson is on welfare...is a very religious lady and it appears to the writer that Tarkanian is taking advantage of her. She stated that she can call Tarkanian any time…and she stated Tarkanian even calls her 'Mom,' most of the time…and there was nothing the Tarkanian family wouldn't do for her, all she had to do was call them….Mrs. Robinson appeared to the writer to have held back information because she thought it would hurt Tarkanian or her son.

There was no tape recording of Burks's interview, and no sworn statements. These were just notes made by Burks, based obviously not on what Ester Robinson said, but on what Burks thought she meant and assumed she refused to say.

Another indication of the NCAA's methods in this case can be seen in a sworn affidavit by Jackie Robinson on March 3, 1974, which read as follows:

He [NCAA investigator Burks] talked to me before a track meet and he told me that he wanted to know all the schools I visited. I told him Cal, and he asked what did they offer me, and I said they told me that they would guarantee that I would graduate, no matter what. Then I told him Kansas State and he asked me the same thing…I told him they didn't offer me anything extra….When I mentioned Fresno State, he said I hear they offered you the same thing they offered Cliff Poindexter, and I said yes.

All this time, Mr. Burks didn't say much….Then I mentioned Las Vegas….Then he said, 'I'm not supposed to say this, but I know a guy who attended Las Vegas a couple of years ago and he quit….To tell you the truth, if I were a kid coming out of high school, I wouldn't go there.'…I told him that my high school coach [Jim Harrick] was going to Utah State. He said that was a good school…I said I didn't think the black life was too good there. He said it was good and I should talk to [former Utah State player] Nate Williams.

He asked if any coaches said anything about Tarkanian….I didn't want to say who, but I said the coaches from USC [Southern California] and Fresno had. He asked what they said. I said they said he was cheating…I said as far as I know, they didn't cheat to get me at Las Vegas….He [Burks] said that Tarkanian, he's just one step ahead of us. But we're out to get him and we will. He said he wasn't sure, but he felt there was a good chance Las Vegas would go on probation for two or three years….He asked if Tarkanian had given me any money [on the recruiting trip] for gambling. I said no, but I wish he had.

123

After the track meet, my basketball coach [Jim Harrick] took me out to eat at the House of Pancakes and drove me home. He talked about going to Utah State and said what a good school it would be for me....He said I could still go to Utah State, just tell that man from the NCAA that Tarkanian gave me $5 or something like that. He showed me a letter of intent filled out for Utah State and he said sign this and we can have that man [Burks] take care of the rest."

Ester Robinson also swore out an affidavit, in which she made the following statement:

Lester Burks came to my home on April 27, 1973....He said he didn't think Las Vegas was a good place for a person to go....He said there was too much to distract, too much gambling. He said he knew of players who had played there and had quit and had not gotten an education but instead got jobs in gambling. I said I thought a person could get a good education at almost any school if they really wanted to. He asked me a lot of questions about my trip to Las Vegas and Mr. Tarkanian. He told me they were out to get Tarkanian and would no matter where he went.

I asked him why he was after Mr. Tarkanian and why he talked the way he had to Jackie at school before he came to see me. I told him that he had Jackie all upset and he didn't go to school.

All of these documents reveal the following:

1. Harrick wanted to take Jackie Robinson to Utah State with him. When Robinson signed with UNLV, Harrick called the NCAA.

2. An NCAA investigator was trying to push Robinson towards Harrick.

3. The NCAA talked about putting UNLV on probation three years *before* it happened and two years before an official NCAA inquiry was initiated.

4. The NCAA wasn't interested in Robinson's stories about illegal offers from other schools.

5. Without evidence, David Berst labeled a trip to Las Vegas a violation when it was not.

6. Robinson and his mother both believed the NCAA was determined to find some violations by Tarkanian.

Jackie Robinson on the NCAA's investigation: "It was ludicrous. What were they trying to do? I was a high school kid ready to go to a track meet, and they put me in this room and this guy from the NCAA questioned me hard for almost two hours. It scared me. He even made me miss the team bus and one of the instructors had to give me a ride.

"They kept trying to make such a big deal about my mother going to see a show on that recruiting visit and the fact that we met Bill Cosby. My mother was dying of cancer. She had always wanted to meet people like Bill Cosby. The people at the club were nice enough to let her go backstage after the show. What's wrong with that? Lots of other people were backstage, too."

Lois: "That was not an easy trip for Ester because she was already very ill. She spent most of those two days with me. One day, we started to take a walk around the college, but had to stop because she got too tired. Mostly, we drank coffee and soft drinks and just talked. But I do remember her saying that she wanted to see Bill Cosby, although I'm sure she did not go on stage as Harrick claimed. That was really the only time she went out in those two days. The full impact of her having cancer didn't hit me until that visit—I realized she was going to die. At one point I remember looking at her and seeing how sick she was. I just started crying."

Lois was particularly angered by the Robinson case.

Lois: "We were still living in Huntington Beach when Ester called and told me about Lester Burks visiting with Jackie before the track meet. She was so upset. She told me Jackie had been crying off and on since then, and just moping around his room. I was incensed when I heard what had happened. How could any educator not believe strongly in the rights of students? What gave this organization the authority to go on campus unannounced and disturb a young kid just before he participated in a track meet? Jackie was excellent in track and those meets were important to him. I told Ester it wasn't right, and suggested she report the incident to the school principal. She wanted me to go with her, so I did.

"We spoke with the principal, Mr. Johnson. He agreed that no one should have interfered with Jackie before the track meet, but I could see that his sympathies were with Jim Harrick. Who knows what Harrick told him to prejudice him against anything Ester and I would say? A copy of a memorandum from David Berst of the NCAA dated April 29, 1974, indicated he also spoke with Mr. Johnson. What Berst indicates in that memo certainly did not sound like what Mr. Johnson told us. I don't know if Johnson or Berst told the truth, but I do know that Berst's memo stated that a Ron Jacobs was present. Jacobs was the coach who had taken Harrick's place when Harrick went to Utah State. I did not know Jacobs, but years later he sent us a tape in which he discussed his conversation with David Berst. On the tape he clearly indicated Berst's animosity towards Jerry.''

Ester Robinson told Lois not to get upset; she was sure that Lois was a strong woman and that Lois would take care of things. Ester also said that she was content knowing Jackie would be with the Tarkanians in Las Vegas.

Jackie enrolled at UNLV, and when his mother died, Jerry Tarkanian delivered one of the eulogies. Halfway through, recalls Jackie, Tarkanian burst into tears and could not continue. The Tarkanians offered to adopt Angelo Robinson, who was 12. And yes, there had been times when Tarkanian called Ester Robinson, ''Mom.''

''Jerry and Lois were like a part of our family,'' says Jackie Robinson. ''They did want to take in Angelo, although he went to live with one of our aunts.''

Today, Jackie Robinson directs RKM Financial Services, headquartered in the Valley Bank building in downtown Las Vegas. In the evenings, he supplements his income as a showroom captain at the Aladdin Hotel. Robinson does not have a degree, lacking only his student teaching for a degree in elementary education.

Jackie Robinson: ''After college, I played three years in the NBA, and then I played pro ball in Israel. When I finally retired from basketball, I had these two jobs—at the Aladdin and with the investment company—and I'm doing pretty well. I don't see any reason to go back and student teach, since I'm really interested in business, not education.

''The thing is that when you play at UNLV and if you're a good person, the community is there to give you a chance in business. This city loves the Rebels and it wants to help the former players.

''Tark has done a lot for me since school. He wrote a letter of recommendation to the Aladdin that was very influential in my securing that position. And when we started the investment company, I went to see him. I talked about the company for a minute, and he stopped me and picked up the phone. Then he said, 'Jackie, I trust you. I know that your business is okay. Who do you want me to call? What appointments can I make for you?' Tark is like that for all his former players. He wants to help, and he's willing to work for you. That's why I get mad thinking about the NCAA investigators. They never flinched when I told them about the other schools making offers. All they wanted was Tark, and all Tark was doing was playing it straight. The whole investigation didn't turn up anything.''

8

Early Years at UNLV

The University of Nevada at Las Vegas wanted a big-time basketball program, and Jerry Tarkanian wanted a college town. To Jerry, that meant the elements were there for what he considered to be a perfect marriage.

When most people think of college towns, places such as Chapel Hill, North Carolina; Bloomington, Indiana; and Athens, Georgia come to mind. But Las Vegas as a college town?

"I never would have believed it," says Lois. "I thought Jerry was insane to say that, but he turned out to be right about Vegas as a college town."

Tarkanian says, "The city was hungry for big-time basketball. When I went there with Long Beach State, we always had excellent crowds. The town cared about the team."

Tarkanian wasn't blinded by the neon of Fremont Street and Las Vegas Boulevard ("the Strip"). He knew that two blocks away from the signs and the slot machines were suburban streets that could have been anywhere—Phoenix, Tucson, or Anaheim. He knew that there were 400,000 people who were like people anywhere: they loved sports. He knew that the nearest high-level athletics was a half-day's drive away in Los Angeles, so he had a captive audience. Tarkanian also knew that in a city that billed itself as the entertainment capital of the world, there was room for more—and the UNLV basketball team could be the biggest show of all.

The basketball team would be the focal point of the Las Vegas sports sections, rather than the Dodgers, the Rams, the Lakers, UCLA, and Southern Cal, which ruled the Los Angeles media. Publicity in the papers helps recruiting, builds attendance, and is good for the players' egos. In Los Angeles, Tarkanian and Long Beach had been treated like an interesting off-Broadway play, and were usually relegated to the back pages. In Las Vegas, he and his players were given headliner treatment by the media.

At UNLV, Tarkanian would have a major college budget. He wouldn't have to worry about not being able to send one of his assistants on a scouting trip because that coach had to teach a volleyball class—he would have three full-time assistants. And he wouldn't have to worry about answering his own telephone, because he would have a secretary. In other words, he'd have the same backing as other major coaches, both from the school and from the community.

UNLV had been in existence only since 1957, and it was a university of about 6,000 students when Tarkanian arrived in 1973. The UNLV basketball program had more going for it than Tarkanian found at Long Beach. UNLV had been a Division I school playing in the Western Athletic Conference for four seasons. Tarkanian replaced John Bayer, who had a 44–36 record in three seasons.

Jerry Tarkanian was 43. He was at a program where there was room and resources for him to build. He was in a city that wanted and loved him. All should have been well. Instead, it was miserable.

Tarkanian: "The NCAA stuff about Long Beach just crushed me. I'm a tougher person now than I was back then, and the criticism really stung me. Over and over, I kept wondering how they could hammer Long Beach and not look up the road and see what UCLA was doing. I also know what we did at Long Beach, and I still ask, what did we do there that was so wrong?

"Lois was so hurt by it. Lois was an honor student. She is a devout Catholic. She doesn't go to Mass just on Sunday, but every day. She has always been a person of the highest integrity, and the whole thing hit her so hard that she almost had a breakdown. On top of all that, Lois didn't want to be in Vegas, because she missed her old job and friends. My daughter, Pamela, was 16, and she didn't want to make the move, either. So I had both of them upset with me."

Lois: "We contacted a lawyer, who told us that we should subscribe to a press clipping service in order to keep track of what was written on the Long Beach case. The idea was to get to the bottom of the charges and try to find out who was saying what about us. But what happened was that every day all these newspaper stories would arrive. I'd look at them, and see all the lies and distortions that were getting into newspapers all over the country, and just get sick.''

Tarkanian was in for another surprise—the UNLV program was not nearly as strong as it first appeared.

''I thought the basketball program was in pretty bad shape,'' says Lynn Archibald, Tarkanian's assistant. ''They had a very good player in [6-foot-9 center] Jimmy Baker, and I didn't think most of the other guys were very talented. A real problem was that the players were spoiled.''

Tarkanian: ''When I was talking about taking the UNLV job, I asked several people from the school if the NCAA was investigating it. I was told that wasn't the case. But after I was here for a while, I kept hearing that UNLV was in trouble with the NCAA, and then I was even more worried. I had just left Long Beach, and I knew what the NCAA could do to you. The last thing I wanted was to end up in the middle of more problems.''

In his first year at UNLV, Tarkanian was doing the following:

1. Recruiting a new team for a new school.

2. Trying to see if anything could be done about the NCAA's investigation at Long Beach.

3. Preparing in case the NCAA investigated UNLV.

4. Trying to win immediately. Twenty victories were expected, even though UNLV had never won twenty games in Division I competition.

Even though he didn't take the UNLV job until the middle of March, Tarkanian had one of the best recruiting years in the country. The first player he signed was Jackie Robinson. During that year, he also recruited Eddie Owens, Lewis Brown, Glen Gondrezick, Lawrence Williams, Ricky Sobers, and Jeep Kelly. Four of the recruits were ranked among the top fifty high school players in the nation: Robinson, Owens, Brown, and Kelly.

Lynn Archibald: ''We could have had an even better class, if you can believe it. We had a commitment from Las Vegas native Lionel Hollins, who went on to play in the NBA with Portland. Lionel said he wanted to come to UNLV. He told everyone that was where he was going. Then he saw that we signed Ricky Sobers from junior college. Lionel thought since both he and Sobers were guards, there wouldn't be enough playing time for both of them. Ricky didn't care who we signed. Anyway, at the last minute Lionel backed off and signed with Arizona State.''

When Tarkanian first came to UNLV, the team was still called the Rebels, not the Running Rebels, as it is today. That's because the Rebels didn't run much during Tarkanian's first season.

Tarkanian: "We used the same 1-2-2 zone that worked for us at Long Beach. I still liked the team to bring the ball up the court and work it to the low post so we could get a shot close to the basket. My philosophy was to get a team to do one or two things very well. At Long Beach, we played that 1-2-2 zone and got the ball down into the low post. I can remember going on the road and praying that we'd get the opening tip, because I wanted us to use that first possession to get the ball to the low post for a basket. My fear was always that a team would hold the ball against our zone. This was before there was a shot clock. When teams got ahead of us, they usually stalled, spreading the court and passing it around because they feared our zone.''

Why did Tarkanian stick with his 1-2-2 zone and his low-post offense?

"Because we were winning with it," he says. "Why change when you are winning?''

But that first season did not begin with a victory.

UNLV was upset 82–76 by Texas Tech in Las Vegas. Remember, Tarkanian never lost a home game in five years at Long Beach or in six years as a junior college coach. That meant he was unbeaten at home for eleven straight seasons—so naturally he was devastated by a defeat in his first game at a new school.

Lois: "Here was all this hullaballo about getting this big-name coach, and we lost our first game. Jerry was just sick. That night, he came home and vomited. And Jerry wasn't the only one. Sig Rogich, a major advertising executive and a supporter of the program, told me that he did the same thing. The publicity surrounding Jerry's hiring and his high profile in Las Vegas had created pressure that was horrendous for all of us.''

Even in the worst of circumstances, Tarkanian had always won far more than he lost, and that was what happened in his first season at UNLV. Following the opener, the Rebels reeled off nine consecutive victories. Tarkanian was back on top. The newspapers were calling him a savior.

Tarkanian: "We were going great. Then the Long Beach probation was announced in January. That killed me. I just wasn't the same person after that. It almost destroyed me mentally."

UNLV finished with a 20–6 record, the best in the school's Division I history, but Tarkanian wasn't happy with the team. "We didn't have a good group of kids," he explains. "The players we recruited were great, but a number of the guys who were holdovers just didn't fit in. It was not a close-knit group."

Often, when a new coach arrives and recruits new players, a split can develop between some of the remaining players and the new ones. That is what happened at UNLV. Also, some of the veterans weren't prepared for Tarkanian's demanding practices and strong work ethic. No coach had ever pushed them so hard before. The younger players reveled in it, because Tarkanian was their first college coach.

One of the guys who didn't fit into the system was Jimmy Baker, the 6-foot-9 center who already had the school rebounding and scoring record. "I liked Jimmy personally, but he wasn't happy here," says Tarkanian. "So after my first year, we arranged for Jimmy to transfer to Hawaii, where he would be eligible to play immediately."

Another problem player was Ricky Sobers.

"Ricky was a junior college transfer and he was very disgruntled during his first year," says Tarkanian. "In fact, Ricky's old junior college coach got the job at Oral Roberts, and we did everything we could to try and talk Ricky into transferring to play for his old coach. We thought that might make him happy."

Assistant Lynn Archibald: "We were 20–6 that year, but it felt like we lost twenty games because guys were yelling at each other. The old players didn't want to accept the new players. In addition, all of our assistant coaches were telling Jerry to get rid of Ricky Sobers. We thought he was selfish and a bad kid. But Jerry wouldn't give up on Sobers. He just saw something in the kid that we missed."

It came down to loyalty.

"We had several meetings with Ricky about transferring, but he didn't want to leave," says Tarkanian. "We told him that he would have to cut out a lot of the crap he pulled the first year and have a whole new attitude. We really laid down the law to Ricky, and he said he'd do what we asked."

But Tarkanian's assistants weren't convinced. They still urged him to drop Sobers, arguing that talking a good game was one thing, but playing it was another. Yet Tarkanian was drawn to Sobers for one reason: the kid wanted to stay.

"Jerry said that if Ricky was willing to work with us, we should give him another chance and work with him," says Archibald. "Jerry said there was something about Ricky that he liked. None of us saw it, but Jerry turned out to be right, because the next season, Ricky was our team leader. No one played harder or sacrificed more for the team. It was one of the most remarkable turnarounds I have ever seen in a kid. The assistant coaches were astounded."

In his second year at UNLV, 1974–75, the core of Tarkanian's team were the players he had recruited right after taking the job: sophomores Jackie Robinson, Eddie Owens, Lewis Brown, and Glen Gondrezick. The only senior, Sobers, also was back. Tarkanian added two other key players, Robert Smith and Boyd Batts. This team was the embyro for the Running Rebels, but it took a variety of strange circumstances for that team to be born.

It started with the loss of a 7-footer named David Vaughn, who had red-shirted during Tarkanian's first year at UNLV. Tarkanian thought Vaughn would be eligible during that second season and that he would have a big man to play under the basket—both in his 1-2-2 zone and in his low-post offense. But Vaughn decided to skip UNLV and signed instead with the Virginia Squires of the old American Basketball Association.

"When Vaughn did that, my first thought was that I wished I had Jimmy Baker back," says Tarkanian. "We suddenly were hurting for size."

In fact, he was without a center until the arrival of Boyd Batts, who had been a 6-foot-7 center at the University of Hawaii. There were problems with Batts's transcript at Hawaii, the upshot being that Hawaii had permitted Batts to play when he should have sat out a year. The NCAA stepped in and ruled that Batts could never play for Hawaii. Hawaii was not placed on probation, but it could not have Batts. Batts was permitted to play at any other school. Tarkanian received a call from a friend in Chicago named Shelly Stark, who knew Batts. Stark said that Batts was interested in attending UNLV. Since Tarkanian was losing starting center Jimmy Baker to Hawaii as a transfer, he was more than willing to take Batts.

As for Robert Smith, Tarkanian had recruited the 5-foot-10 point guard out of Crenshaw High in Los Angeles.

Tarkanian: "Actually, we were talking to Robert mostly because he was a close friend of Marques Johnson [who later became an NBA all-star]. This was when I was still coaching at Long Beach. But after I took the UNLV job, Marques Johnson went to UCLA. The new Long Beach coaches weren't interested in a 5-foot-10 guard like Robert

Smith, so he went to Arizona Western Junior College. He was a very nice kid and I didn't want to see him caught without a place to go to college and play ball. At Arizona Western, Robert had a good year, but he wasn't an all-conference player and he wasn't being recruited much. I went to see his team play, and when I walked into the arena Robert saw me and he suddenly broke into a huge grin. Now, a lot of other coaches were telling me not to take Robert, that he was too small and not really that good a player. But this was during the time when we were having troubles with some of the kids that first year at UNLV. Also, the NCAA stuff about Long Beach had hit. I looked at Robert and thought, 'I don't remember the last time anyone seemed so happy to see me. No one has smiled around me in months.' So I decided to take him. I just wanted a kid with that kind of smile on the team.''

When Jerry Tarkanian opened practice for his second season at UNLV, he looked around and started worrying. Where were the big men?

"We had one," says Tarkanian, "Lewis Brown, who was extremely talented but inconsistent in his play."

Tarkanian knew that he couldn't count on the 6-foot-10 sophomore night after night.

"I was thinking that UNLV had brought me here and the people had been so good to me," says Tarkanian. "They were paying me a lot of money. There was a lot of publicity. There was no way we could have a bad season."

Most coaches believe the name of the game in basketball is rebounding. If you control the defensive boards, the other team is limited to one shot. If you control the offensive boards, you can miss your first shot and still score off the rebound. Most second shots come from less than a foot from the basket—which means that when a player gets an offensive rebound, the odds are overwhelmingly in favor of his putting the ball in the basket. After all, most second shots are lay-ups or dunks.

But if you have no size, the opposition gets a lot of second shots, which translates into easy baskets. And if you have no size, your second shots (and easy baskets) are limited, and Tarkanian was in that situation.

Tarkanian: "I looked at our team and saw that we had two things: good athletes and good speed. Our guards were Sobers, who was 6-foot-3, and Robert Smith. The rest of the guys—Eddie Owens, Jackie Robinson, and Glen Gondrezick—were in the 6-foot-6 range. So we asked ourselves what we could do with a bunch of guys who were

133

6-foot-6 and could run. Since we also had great quickness and good perimeter shooters, we reconstructed our game. We felt we had to play at an up-tempo pace, utilizing our quickness and minimizing our lack of size. To play an up-tempo game you have to play man-to-man pressure defense. If you play a zone, your opponent can determine the tempo of the game. It wasn't easy for me to drop the zone, because we had played it for so long, but I knew it wouldn't work. I felt we could win some games just because our kids were going to be in better condition than the other teams, and that would give us an edge if we ran on offense. That meant they had to work hard, run more, and practice longer. If you have a good group of kids, you can get them to make that sacrifice.

"I figured that if we got the bigger teams running, it would take away their size advantage. Rather than work the ball around the perimeter, I wanted us to get the ball up the court as fast as possible, and then take a quick jumper before the defense could set up. Speed would be the determining factor in the game. The team that got the rebounds would be the one that hustled for the ball more and reached it first. So rebounding became more of a matter of hustle and quickness than size in our style of game."

So the Rebels became the Running Rebels not so much because Tarkanian wanted to have a team that racked up 100 points as because it was their only chance of winning.

"Boyd Batts was our center," says Tarkanian. "Boyd Batts was 6-foot-7. Walking the ball up the court with a 6-foot-7 center is not how you win many games, and Batts wasn't even going to be eligible until January."

Over the long haul, the new Running Rebels would be a stroke of genius. But in UNLV's early games, it looked more like an act of desperation, and not a smart one at that. The Rebels lost two of their first three games.

"At that point, we were scared that the whole thing would blow up in our faces," says Tarkanian. "But we had no other choice. Our kids weren't going to get any taller. Three games into the season is no time to start putting in a whole new coaching system. So we stuck with our plan."

And it worked.

UNLV finished the season at 24–5, meaning it went 23–2 after those first three games. The Rebels were picked for fifth in the Western Athletic Conference, and they won it with a 13–1 record.

Tarkanian: "We hit our stride in January. In the second half of the season, we averaged over 90 points and only 9 turnovers per game. That shows we did more than just run up and down the floor. All the conditioning paid off. In practice, the kids ran sprints. We had blocks on the floor and they had to jump over them. No matter what team we played, we ran for the whole game. When the other teams started to feel tired, our guys were still going strong.''

More impressive is the fact that UNLV used only seven players, meaning Tarkanian's first five were on the floor for most of the game. You can get by with a thin bench when you walk the ball up the floor and slow down the pace, but to have an effective running game and still use only two substitutes is mind-boggling.

"Ricky Sobers made it click for us," says Tarkanian. "He was the point guard, and the only senior on the team. He averaged 18 points and could have scored a lot more. But he made sure that the other guys got the ball. Sobers also worked very hard on defense. He was great on the press. Ricky became our first All-American and he was a first-round draft pick by Phoenix. To this day, I think Ricky Sobers in 1974–75 had one of the best seasons of any player I've ever coached."

Once the Rebels started to run, there was no turning back. In Tarkanian's first season, the team averaged 78 points. The average jumped to 91 points the second season, and the fans were in love.

"I liked it too," said Tarkanian. "We had good athletes and we let them show what they could do. Sometimes I wish I had run more with our teams at Long Beach, because now I think that I held some of the guys back."

Veteran basketball coach and scout Pete Newell was amazed at Tarkanian's new style.

Pete Newell: "For years, Tark was the best zone coach in the country. He had a very controlled offense. In one year, he ripped up his whole book of coaching and tried something entirely new. There aren't too many coaches who would have had the courage to try that, because if you flop, it looks like you lost your mind. Most coaches make the players adjust to their system—and that is especially true of successful coaches. Often they believe in their system as much as they believe in their players. But Tark saw that his system didn't fit the players, and he threw it out. He coached in a way he had never tried before. Very few coaches have ever made such a radical change as Tark did between his first and second years at UNLV."

And with the exception of the grim days of probation in the late 1970s, the Rebels would always be running for Tarkanian.

9

First Person: Coaching Means Pushing the Hot Button

I don't care what you try or what happens to be your job—the key to success is motivation. If a person wants something, and wants it more than anything else he has ever wanted in his life, then he has a very good chance of getting it. Everyone connected with sports talks about athletes giving 100 percent, even 110 percent or more. Well, 100 percent is all a person can give because it is all a person has.

But it just doesn't happen. People don't give all they have every day, because it is hard and it hurts. In some ways, pushing yourself to the limit is against human nature; most people just don't do it. Ask yourself: If you work or go to school, did you give everything you had every day last week? Did you try your hardest and not take any shortcuts? Did you give 100 percent? Very few of us can give 100 percent every day for a week. There usually is some point where we let something slide or cut a corner.

Well, it's the same thing with basketball players. Basketball is their job. It's what they do and what they think about every day. They don't just wake up in the morning and go out and give 100 percent. They may be self-motivated and extremely dedicated, but they still probably won't give 100 percent that day unless someone helps them.

That's where the hot button comes in.

Every person has one, and it is a coach's job to find it and push it. In fact, it's probably the coach's number-one job. Every coach says, "We have to play hard." But playing hard doesn't start on the court. It begins the first time the coach meets a kid. It is a product of the rapport between the coach and the player, and of how they feel about each other.

In 1986–87, our team went to the Final Four and came very close to giving 100 percent. It didn't happen all the time, but that team understood that you don't win games unless you play hard every minute. And you won't play hard in the games unless you play hard in practice. You can con your boss in the office by saying all the right things and wearing nice clothes. Maybe you can con your history teacher by sitting in the front row and asking a lot of questions. But you can't con the game of basketball. Athletics is the ultimate test of a person's work ethic and desire. Every day is a test. It doesn't matter what you wear, what you say, or what your name is; you have to produce on the court. Appearance doesn't mean anything; dedication and effort are what decides who wins and who loses.

I can't stress motivation in coaching enough. That's because players don't motivate themselves. They tend to play in a comfort zone. They push themselves until it starts to hurt, until their legs get a little heavy or they begin to feel like they're getting a little short of breath. Then they back off. It's the same thing for the average guy when he decides to go outside and jog. He'll run until it hurts, then he'll stop. Then he'll go in the house and tell everyone how hard he worked.

Players don't know that they are loafing. They think, "I'm playing hard. I'm giving all I can give." People in business often feel the same way when they are at their jobs. But in both instances, a person has a lot more effort they can put out.

You can really see it in basketball. In a playground game, they don't play hard; they just run back and forth and score baskets. At most schools, they don't play hard all the time. In fact, I think that there are only four or five college teams in any given season that consistently play hard.

To be successful, you have to play through that comfort zone and into the next level. Most players don't want to reach that point. That's why if a coach can get his team to push itself, he has a tremendous advantage. His team will give an extra effort while the opposition won't, and at times that can make up for a lack of talent.

When we start a season, I only have one goal for our kids: that they play hard. I don't talk about winning a certain number of games. I don't talk about winning a league title or getting to the NCAA tournament. I just want the kids thinking about one thing: playing hard.

Some of my best friends are football coaches. I like football coaches. But football coaches amaze me with all the goals they have. They set goals for when they want their kids to wake up, when and what the players are going to eat each day, and about everything else under the sun.

I ask only this from my kids: be totally prepared physically, mentally, and emotionally. Now, you might say that every team does that. Well, I'll say that every team probably does that in the big games—the game on national television or the games against great teams. That has nothing to do with what I'm talking about. I want my kids up for the first day of practice and for every practice after that.

Basketball is a game of habit and reflexes. It is unnatural for kids to work hard every day in practice. Odds are that they didn't do it in high school in sports or anything else, so why would they just automatically start doing it in college? The body gets used to reacting a certain way and putting forth a certain level of intensity. The more a coach demands, the more he will receive. But if a team is used to taking shortcuts in practice, it will do the same thing in games. There are some days when you can walk into practice and just see the kids' faces and know that the kids are feeling lackadaisical. We try to guard against that, and when it happens, we raise hell with the kids. And there are a few days when no matter how much you talk, what you say, or how many hot buttons you push, the team is just flat. But if you stand by and do nothing, you are condoning it. If you let it go by once, the odds are it will happen again. And soon, your team will form all kinds of bad habits.

Our approach is very basic: play hard in practice.

So many things happen in a game that a coach can't control. There are bad calls from the officials, crazy bounces of the basketball, or freak injuries. But a coach can strive to have his team prepared to do their best mentally, physically, and emotionally.

Sometimes, your kids just can't win a game. The difference in talent is too great; or perhaps one of those other things, such as officials' calls, enters into the game. That's why you can't tell your kids, "You have to win this game." They just may not be able to do it. They may play their hearts out and still get beat. You should not jump on your team if they played hard but still lost. It's not fair to the kids.

The worst thing a coach can do is to blame his players for a loss. When your team wins, give the credit to the kids. When they get beat, you should take the heat. Remember that the people you are coaching are still kids, while you as the coach are the adult. Of course, nothing much helps when you lose. I know how terrible it feels to lose, and that's why I always say something nice about the other coach and players after we win a game. I know how depressed and how much pressure the other coach is under.

I also know how bad a coach can feel when his team doesn't work hard. At UNLV, I've had three teams where I felt that most of the kids didn't put out maximum effort. Two of them won 20 games, and my son Danny played point guard on one of them. But in those three instances, I didn't have a banquet at the end of the season for those teams, because I couldn't say much that was positive about a team that doesn't work hard.

There are many forms of motivation, and I don't think it is right to say one way is the best.

Perhaps the greatest football coach of all time was Bear Bryant, and he motivated through fear. Bobby Knight is one of the greatest basketball coaches ever, and does the same thing. When a kid plays for a coach who motivates through fear, he is afraid of making a mistake. He is scared to death of seeing the coach after he has messed up. It is the fear that makes him concentrate more and work harder than he usually would.

But each coach must motivate according to his own personality. My personality won't let me motivate through fear. Too many coaches try to copy other coaches, and you can't do that, because the kids can see through you and they know you are a phony. My way is to get very close to my kids. I like my kids, and I want them to play well, because it helps them and the university. We try to build a team with kids who want to be the best they can. It starts with pride. We often talk to the kids about their responsibilities—to themselves, to their parents, to the community, and to the university. They represent all these people when they step out on the floor. The kids have to feel that they are part of something that is important. That's why they have to push themselves.

If I have the right kind of kids, I like to appoint team captains, to have seniors who are team leaders. In 1986–87, our captains were Gary Graham and Mark Wade, and they were captains because they were the two hardest-working kids we had. They were very vocal, too. So they were a great example not only on the floor, but in what they said to the other kids. You hear a lot of coaches talking about "what it takes to win." That's because most players don't know what it takes to win. They figure if they go out and they play, they'll be successful. But at the higher levels of basketball, it doesn't work like that. A real captain knows how to prepare himself emotionally, mentally, and physically for each practice and game. He understands the importance of practice; he knows that how you practice will dictate how you play in the games. When I find a kid who does know these things, I like to put him in a leadership role.

Another factor is morale.

A team can't play hard consistently unless the kids get along and pull for each other. Practice habits will become game habits. Basketball is a game of habits. That's why you can't have a bunch of guys who bicker, or who are malcontents. The kids at the end of the bench are very important to the team, because they have to give maximum effort in practice even though they seldom play in the games. They can make or break a team. One clubhouse lawyer can wreck a season. That's why we tell the kids, "Listen, this is your team. Don't fight among yourselves. You guys have to guard against that. Sometimes, we don't know all that is going on. If you are aware of what can happen, you can end it before it becomes a problem."

Basketball is such an emotional game. On the road, there sometimes are 15,000 people screaming at the kids, calling them names, maybe even throwing things at them. That's why good teams are very close. The players believe in the coaches, the coaches believe in the players. And the players also respect each other. That's how a team overcomes adversity. If these relationships exist, then your team will take that extra step to give 100 percent.

Defense

One of the biggest myths in college basketball is that a team automatically is playing good defense and showing a lot of discipline in a game if the score is something like 45–43. What a joke. A disciplined team is one that plays the way it practices. If your plan is to pressure the ball on defense and run on offense, and when the game starts you press and run, then you are a well-disciplined team and it doesn't matter if it becomes a 100-point game. If I wanted to, I could make our games be in the 50-points range. All a coach has to do is to tell his players to walk the ball up the court and pass it around until the shot clock is about to run down. But that has nothing remotely to do with defense. That's just keeping the score down by holding the ball on offense.

Most of our practice time, probably 60 percent, is spent on defense. That's because defense is unnatural, sort of like playing through that wall you hit at the end of the comfort zone. Kids have spent their lives on playgrounds and in gyms dribbling the ball, passing the ball, and shooting the ball. But they don't think about guarding anybody. Many coaches like to rely on gimmick and combination defenses. By "gimmick," I mean a zone defense or a man-to-man defense where the players do a lot of switching from one guy they are guarding to another. In a combination defense you play part man-to-man defense and part zone. The idea is to fool your opponent so he won't immediately know if you are in a zone or man-to-man, and thus to confuse the offense.

We go in the opposite direction: practically all individual man-to-man defense. Our theory of defense starts with the idea of guarding the guy who is dribbling. We don't want that guy to beat us on the dribble and drive to the basket. When you are beaten on the dribble, there are problems. Either the guy can go all the way to the basket and score, or else someone must leave his man to switch to the guy with the ball. That means there is always an open man.

So we want to pressure the ball, take away the guy's dribble. It sounds simple, but it takes a lot of effort and concentration. We don't go into a game trying to trick anyone. Some coaches want their players in a box-and-one or a triangle-and-two. There is nothing wrong with that—those defenses have been used by many great coaches—but it's not my coaching style. We believe in intensity and pressure. We take great pride in the fact that the opposition will know exactly how we're going to play, but we'll outwork them. Each player works hard on defense so he won't get beat individually. That's how a man-to-man starts—all five players playing great individual defense. "Pride" is the key word. We take pride in being able to play defense, in having good footwork and other defensive techniques. We concentrate on being able to grind the opponent down. When the coaches talk about "Rebel Pride," that's what they mean. We go into the game with the idea that we will play harder than our opponent will and we will pressure the ball all over the court. I think that when you try to outsmart the other team, it takes away from your intensity. And there is only one way to play good defense: play it hard every second on the court.

There are a lot of different styles of defense. Ours is playing hard, but one of the basic ideas I have about coaching is that no one strategy is right for everyone. The key to defense is technique, developing proper work habits and being intense. We put great emphasis on technique—stance, footwork, balance. The better the technique, the better the chances are of a player's stopping an opponent one-on-one. It also is how hard the kids work and how much they concentrate. It comes down to intensity. If your kids are intense, you'll play good defense regardless of the style.

I really don't worry about how a kid played defense in junior college or high school. Some guys will tell me that a kid is a great player;

he does everything but he won't play defense. Well, if a kid has good basketball skills and natural athletic ability, he can learn to be a good defensive player.

The reason why most college teams don't play man-to-man defense is that they don't work on footwork and technique. That means their players are always getting beat on the dribble, and if you can't stop the man with the ball, then you can't play a pressure man-to-man defense. After a while, a coach just gives up and goes to a zone. But if you stick with it, you can get kids to play that intense man-to-man. You have to do it every day in practice, and do it a lot. But I'm convinced defense can be taught.

Offense is more complicated than teaching defense. You have to try to mold each player's skills into a team concept, and at the same time develop a great sense of unselfishness. Every player must sacrifice his personal goals for team goals before the offense can function at a maximum level.

Remember this: the more you give a player to think about on defense, the slower his feet become. That's because he is hesitating. He is trying to remember, and he becomes tentative. Using too many defenses just confuses the kids so they don't play with their natural quickness and reflexes. So we keep it simple. Play hard, guard your man, and don't let your man beat you on the dribble.

Basketball Is Instinctive

I am convinced that the more you make your basketball players think on the court, the more you hurt them. You take away the one ingredient every great player has: instinct, the ability of a player to make a move or throw a pass because it is natural. The more you ask a player to think, the more he will be tentative. If a shooter hesitates, he misses. If a passer hesitates, he throws the ball away. If a defender hesitates, his man dribbles past him.

For most players, their natural style is to get up and down the court fast and take the first open shot. That's how they grew up on the playgrounds, and the ability to run and score in an open-court game is what made them good players to begin with. So that's how we play. We get up and down the court and we try to take a shot before the defense sets up, so long as it is a good shot. I'm not into passing the ball around forever and watching the shot clock run down. I'm not into patience just for the sake of patience. We do ask our players to sacrifice for the team, because we demand that they play tough, aggressive man-to-man defense. That is something they usually aren't accustomed to when they come to UNLV. So there is a bit of give-and-take. We let them run and shoot, but to do that they also have to play defense.

When I coached at Long Beach, I put too many restrictions on our players. I had better players at Long Beach than I have had at UNLV, but I didn't let the Long Beach kids run, and I didn't let them shoot as much from the outside as I should have. Some guys would say that we did a much better coaching job at Long Beach, because the team had more discipline. That's not true. We felt that our 1–2–2 zone defense at Long Beach was the best in the country, but it put too many restrictions on our offense.

When a team faces UNLV, we try to take them out of their game and make them play up-tempo with us. We want to force the other team to run with us. We do that by taking quick shots, and by playing the pressure defense. We'll get the ball up the court in a flash and shoot it. That's our style. A lot of teams aren't used to playing like that, and they are lost when they are forced out of their usual deliberate pace.

Some coaches are afraid of the running game. They think that they will lose control of what the players are doing on the court. So they slow up the game. As a result, many great players have ended up in situations where they have not been allowed to utilize their tremendous natural gifts. A team playing at a slow pace may look good, because it seems the coach knows his X's and O's. The team may seem well drilled. But the kids aren't allowed to play and utilize their skills to the maximum.

You can be organized and well drilled and still have a running game. One of the biggest fallacies is that if you run, your team is out of control. Remember: you play like you practice. Well, we practice the running game. The kids learn how to fill the lanes, what we think is a good shot and what isn't, and things such as the numbered fast break. We do those same few things over and over, and then the kids don't have to think about what to do—they just do it.

Another thing is that I don't believe in chalk talks. Kids don't learn much from staring at a blackboard and watching a coach write down a bunch of X's and O's. Most of the time, a chalk talk will break the kids' concentration. We use it at pregame for review, but that's all.

Kids need to visualize what will happen on the court. That's why we don't put it on the blackboard. We take the kids on the court and walk through everything. That way, they are doing the plays, seeing where they are on the court, instead of just trying to imagine it from what was written on a blackboard. Again, I want to keep the kids' heads clear so they can go out and play on their instincts.

I can tell you several excellent benefits of our style of play.

One is that the community loves to watch us play. Ask most basketball fans if they'd rather watch a 45–43 game or a 100–98 game. They'll pick the high-scoring game, because it's fun to watch the kids run and shoot. Nobody likes to watch a game where a kid stands at the top of the key about 35 feet from the basket dribbling the ball until the shot clock ticks down. So the Running Rebels' style of play has been a big hit with the community.

Another factor is recruiting. Since most kids grow up playing the running game, that's what they want to do in college. Well, when a kid comes to UNLV, he knows he will get to run. That is a real advantage. All coaches say they like to run, but when you look at some of their programs, you see that they don't. At UNLV, running is at the center of our program. Just watching one of our games will show you that we are committed to getting the ball up and down the court and giving the kids freedom to play.

The Roster

In major college basketball, I think the ideal situation for a coach is to have eight players he can use and count on. But that means eight players available for every game. Sometimes, you hit a weekend where one of the kids gets sick, another sprains an ankle, and all of a sudden you're ready to play a Top Twenty team on national television and you have only six experienced players ready—five starters and one on the bench. So you're caught short and you get beat.

This has forced most college coaches to overrecruit. College basketball has turned into a big business, and there is a lot at stake with all the money a school can earn by going to the NCAA tournament. One bad week can knock you right out of the NCAA tournament picture, and that can cost your school over $1 million. So that often leads to overrecruiting.

I believe that you can only use eight players and give them enough minutes to make them happy. That's what I try to do: set up eight guys who are going to see most of the minutes. Even though we use only eight players in most games, we try to have ten quality players available. Our fast-break style allows us to substitute more than most teams, and this gives more kids a chance to play. The fatigue factor in a fast-paced game such as ours means the bench is very important.

Another thing I like to do with my roster is take a couple of walk-ons. These kids don't have basketball scholarships, but they are very solid people and they just want to be a part of the program. They are good people on the end of the bench because they keep up the team morale. They may not have as much ability as the scholarship players, but that doesn't bother me. They work hard in practice and they are happy. They are having the time of their lives, an experience they'll always remember. A coach can't play everyone, so there is a need to have kids who will be content just to be on the team and help out in practice. In several cases, kids who started as walk-ons have worked out so well that we've put them on scholarships. That always makes me especially proud.

Role Players

At UNLV, we realized that we couldn't recruit like North Carolina, Louisville, and Kentucky. We were not going to get the great high school player, the kid who is the complete package and can do everything. But we can find the player who has great talent in one or two areas, and if you find that type of player, you can still have a strong program. That is what has happened at UNLV. We've been at the school since 1973, and we've had only four McDonald's high school All-Americans on our roster. It's not uncommon for the top schools to have as many as ten high school All-Americans on their team at one time. But we've been able to compete with those teams because our kids have played hard and utilized their skills.

It works like this: If you have a bunch of very good role players and they do exactly what you ask of them, you can beat one of the elite teams on any given night—but only if your players do what they are capable of doing and don't try to do the things that are beyond their capabilities. In a seven-game series, it wouldn't happen. The other side's overwhelming talent would make the difference. But on one night and in one 40-minute game, you've got a shot to upset them if your kids are playing hard and playing smart.

The hitch is taking a player with talent in one facet of the game and selling him on the idea that he should not try things that are out of his range. For example, when Mark Wade was our point guard, he was a tremendous passer. He knew how to move the ball around and

145

where and when his teammates wanted a pass. But Mark was not a very good outside shooter. So he concentrated on passing and defense and shot about three times a game. He was a perfect example of a player understanding his role and playing it.

But that isn't easy for a lot of kids. When some kids are told not to shoot, they get upset and say, "The coach is taking my game away from me." You hear it all the time. So the coach has to communicate with the kid, he has to motivate the kid to play to his strengths. Mark Wade took great pride in his passing, and he didn't worry about scoring. That's what a player must learn: to feel good about doing the things he does best. As for the player's weaknesses, we don't dwell on them. We just tell the kid that we don't want him trying those things he can't do, and it's never mentioned again unless the kid forces us to bring it up.

As I said, the players recruited by the elite schools can do everything—pass, dribble, shoot, run, jump, and play defense. Sometimes, players we recruit *think* they can do everything on the court. It is up to us to show them that they have to do what Mark Wade and so many others did for us—they have to learn their roles and play to their strengths.

When our team was ranked number one in 1983, it happened because the kids understood what we expected of them. My son Danny was the point guard. Danny was a great point guard in terms of passing, handling the ball, and defending. His shooting was not as strong. So like Mark Wade, Danny took care of the ball, and the other guys shot it. Our other guard that season was Jeff Collins, who was not a good outside shooter but was extremely quick. He could play defense and run the fast break as well as any guard in the country that year. So when we got a defensive rebound, the kid under the basket threw the ball to Danny, Danny pushed it up the court, and Jeff Collins filled one of the lanes. Jeff would break to the basket and Danny would hit him with a lob pass. We also used Jeff Collins to defend the opponent's best scoring guard.

Our center was Paul Brozovich, who couldn't shoot well, but set great screens, knew how to pass, and took up a lot of space under the basket. We told Paul what we wanted him to do and he did it. He didn't think, "Well, I've got to get my shot." He just thought about passing, setting screens, and rebounds.

Our shooter was Larry Anderson. We got him the ball on the wing, and he knew to take the shot. Don't hesitate, just shoot. That's what he did best, and we didn't get on his back if he missed three or four shots in a row. If you believe in a kid as a shooter, you've got to let him shoot and not clutter his mind.

Sidney Green played under the basket and was a strong, inside player. Danny knew where Sidney wanted the ball, and we worked the ball inside to Sidney. Also, Sidney knew that we wanted him under the basket, not shooting 20-footers. Sidney and Larry knew that they were the shooters, and they shot with great confidence. The whole team wanted them to shoot the ball. Everyone was happy because each kid played to his strength, and we ended up with a very good team.

If you can't recruit the all-around players, then you have to get specialists at each spot. What's the sense of having players who can run and jump if you don't let them play in a running game? What's the sense of having a kid with a good jumper if you put a harness on him and make him always look to pass the ball inside? What's the sense of having a kid who is a great one-on-one player and not letting him sometimes isolate his man and beat him off the dribble to the basket?

Let the kids do what they do best.

Point Guards

The ideal point guard is a guy like Isiah Thomas or Magic Johnson. They can pass, they can score; they are all-around players.

We've rarely had a player like that.

Our best point guards recently have been Mark Wade and Danny. They ran a team as well as any point guard in the country. They handled the ball the majority of the time and made very few mistakes. Their ratio between assists and turnovers was outstanding. First Danny set an NCAA record for assists in a season, then Mark broke it. Mark and Danny would never be considered great shooters, but they didn't often shoot. Since they didn't get out of their roles, we didn't talk about their shooting. Instead, we praised their passing skills.

In the middle 1970s, we had Robert Smith as our point guard. Robert had a nice jump shot and he averaged 15 points for us. We let him shoot because it was something he could do.

We don't make it a rule that our point guard doesn't shoot. That only applies if shooting is not a strength. But my main priority in finding a point guard is to get a kid who understands how to pass, how to play defense, and who is an excellent leader. If he can shoot, it's a bonus. If he can't, we are able to make adjustments.

Shooters

The shooters usually are our shooting guard and small forward. Freddie Banks was a great shooting guard for us. He knew he was out there to take the outside shot. All the guys on the team knew that Freddie was there to shoot. We encouraged Freddie to look for the shot, and when it was there—don't think twice, just take it.

This is the same role that Sam Smith, Anthony Jones, Larry Anderson, and Tony Smith filled for us over the years. They were on the floor to shoot. We didn't ask them to worry about passing inside all the time, or to always take the ball to the basket. Our shooters shoot the ball; it's that simple. We tell our kids that, and it's understood. That is how a coach can eliminate the problem of players complaining that one kid is always looking to take a shot. Well, shooting is this player's job. And if he takes too many shots, that's my responsibility. It also is my responsibility to make sure that we create the right opportunities for the kid to shoot. We have to find ways of getting our shooters the ball.

Sometimes, your wing men—the small forward and the shooting guard—may not be good natural shooters. You need a couple of guys who can hit from the outside, or you're going to lose a lot of games. So you figure out which kids have the best chance of becoming shooters, and you work with them. You tell them that they are great shooters. Over and over you tell them that you believe they will make the outside shot. So much of shooting is confidence, anyway, so you work with them and make them believe they can shoot. If a kid has some ability as a shooter, he can become a very good one if he believes that he can make the shot. If a kid's confidence is high, his shooting level will rise. When he begins to have doubts, the shots stop falling.

When Anthony Jones transferred from Georgetown to UNLV, he was shell-shocked. He had had a tough first year at Georgetown because he was a Washington kid and was under a lot of pressure to play well immediately in his hometown.

But we were convinced that Anthony could be a great shooter. We gave him the green light. We kept telling Anthony to put the ball up. In his first year with us, it didn't always work out well. He was still having problems with his confidence, and that carried over to his shooting. But in his second year, his senior season, Anthony believed he could score and he did. That led to his being a first-round draft choice by the Washington Bullets.

Sometimes, you can even change a player's role. Early in his career, we didn't want Gary Graham shooting the ball. But he worked on his shooting, both in practice and on his own, and really improved. So in his last two years, we let Gary take some outside shots. Just as kids have to adjust to the coach, the coach has to adjust as his kids change.

Inside Players

If a coach had his choice, he would like both his center and his power forward to be able to score. In our program, that seldom happens. In 1987, We had Armon Gilliam at power forward and Jarvis Basnight at center. Armon had a super jumper, so we let him shoot. Jarvis wasn't a scorer, so we told him to concentrate on rebounding and pressure defense. Jarvis also would pop outside from under the basket, catch a pass, and then pass it to a player on the other side of the floor—in other words, he helped us reverse the ball. During his first year, Basnight concentrated on catching the ball, passing it, and reversing the ball to the other side of the floor. The next year, his role switched. He worked very hard on his shooting and became one of the nation's leaders in field-goal percentage.

We've never had that 7-foot, All-American center at UNLV. It's just so hard to recruit those kinds of players, because everyone in the country is after them. I'd love to have a 7-footer like David Robinson, who blocks shots and can score. But we've never been able to recruit one. That means we make adjustments. We get a kid like Richie Adams, who was only 6-foot-8 but could jump out of the gym. He blocked shots and got rebounds, and he usually did it against bigger guys. You make the most of what you have.

10

Recruiting Reggie Theus and Building the Running Rebels

The Running Rebels were born with Ricky Sobers, but they grew up with Reggie Theus. Just listen to Jerry Tarkanian talk about the 6-foot-7 guard now with the Atlanta Hawks.

Tarkanian: "I'll never forget what Reggie meant to the school and the basketball program. He was so much more than a great player—he was a great person. What I admire most about Reggie is that he was so unselfish. That's why I laugh when some people in the NBA say that Reggie worries about his scoring too much, because I know that isn't true.

"When Reggie came to our program as a freshman, he was good enough to start on most teams. But we had a veteran team and he played only 12 minutes a game for us. Yet Reggie never complained. As a sophomore, Reggie was our most talented player. I knew that and he knew it, but he didn't start, because a senior, Sam Smith, was playing in front of Reggie. Then there was a span of about seven games when Sam was hurt and Reggie took over. Well, Reggie was our leading scorer in most of those games. I mean, he was tremendous. But as soon as Sam got well, I put him back in the lineup and Reggie was back to coming off the bench. After that taste of starting, he accepted the role as our sixth man and he always worked hard. That's why I admire Reggie so much: he was willing to come off the bench even though he knew he was better than some of the guys playing in front of him. He helped the morale of the team, because the other guys saw how he was willing to sacrifice.

"Another thing about Reggie is that he was an excellent defensive player. Some NBA people say that Reggie can't play defense. Well, that's not right. He is a great defender when he is guarding the man with the ball. He had some trouble when he was away from the ball, but I still remember an NCAA tournament game where North Carolina's Phil Ford started running the four-corner offense against us. We put Reggie on Ford, and Reggie gave him fits. People said that they had never seen anyone pressure Ford like Reggie did, and Phil Ford was a great college point guard.

"During his junior year, Reggie started for us and was sensational on the court. But it is the off-the-court things I remember the most. He is so outgoing and personable. People meeting Reggie for the first time always like him. Everyone loved him in Las Vegas. I still tell my players about what he did at UNLV."

Reggie Theus grew up in Inglewood, and he grew up poor. His parents were divorced when he was 6. Sometimes he lived with his mother, and sometimes with his father. Theus has a deep respect for his father, who worked as a custodian and often had two jobs.

Lynn Archibald was the UNLV assistant coach recruiting Theus. "Mr. Theus was working day and night," he says. "The way I understand it, Reggie came home one day and found his father dead on the floor."

Theus says that his father "basically just worked himself to death."

UNLV had been watching Theus's progress longer than any other college. When Lynn Archibald was in the neighborhood, he made a point of stopping by Inglewood High to visit Reggie and his high school coach, Leon Henry. This was when Theus was a junior and receiving virtually no attention from college recruiters. Reggie lived primarily with Leon Henry.

"Before his senior year, most people thought Reggie was a good high school player and that he could play at the major college level," says Tarkanian. "But I don't think anyone saw him as a great college player who would have a long career in the NBA."

The year was 1974, and Theus was just starting his senior year of high school. He was considered a good college prospect, but not exceptional.

Tarkanian: "We were way out in front when it came to recruiting Reggie. His high school coach had played for me at Pasadena City College. Leon and his wife had a tremendous influence on Reggie, especially after his father died. We got a big break when UCLA and

John Wooden weren't interested in him. I heard that Wooden didn't like Reggie's style of play. And not many black kids were going to Southern Cal back then, so we felt we had Reggie all the way."

Reggie Theus had a superb senior season, and John Wooden retired as the UCLA coach and was replaced by Gene Bartow.

Lynn Archibald: "During Reggie's senior season, Leon Henry asked us to call him only once a week. He didn't want Reggie bothered while he was playing, so that's what we did—we called Reggie once a week. We did talk to Leon Henry every few days, but we pretty much let Reggie just play basketball and enjoy it without putting any pressure on him. But by the end of Reggie's senior year, the recruiting had gotten very intense. Tark and I started to get worried because UCLA was in there heavy. Gene Bartow loved Reggie."

Tarkanian: "Whenever UCLA comes into the picture with one of the players we're recruiting, I get nervous. But Bartow was on the scene late, and we were way out ahead on the kid."

Then came San Francisco.

Tarkanian recalls, "What a run they made at Reggie. I mean, they were all over the kid. They brought out all their heavy ammunition."

Lynn Archibald: "When San Francisco came into the picture, it got dirty. They really ripped us at UNLV. I mean, they even brought up the fact that I was a Mormon and they asked Reggie if he, as a black man, could actually play for a coach who was a Mormon. Reggie told me that they were offering him everything under the sun—a bank account, you name it. I told Reggie that I would never blame him if he took it."

Theus says, "The key to my recruiting was my relationship with Lynn Archibald. Tark recruited me a little bit, but it was Lynn who did most of the work and I really grew to like Lynn. He was always at my games. One school was offering me so much that I couldn't believe it was true. It was wild. I'd ask for something, and they'd say fine. Then I'd ask for something else, and they'd say they could take care of that, too. I ended up with a list of about twelve things, and they said yes to them all. I couldn't believe what was happening."

The fact was that Theus wasn't very comfortable with the offers. He had developed a trust in Leon Henry, who had nothing but praise for Tarkanian. And he respected Lynn Archibald, because he was the one college coach who had been interested in Reggie longer than anyone else.

Reggie Theus: "My recruiting got almost scary, the way people were talking. In the end, I just went to UNLV because that was where I

Jerry Tarkanian, 1988. *(University of Nevada-Las Vegas Sports Information Office)*

Tark on high after winning the 1966 state championship with his Riverside City College team—their third in a row. *(The Riverside Press-Enterprise)*

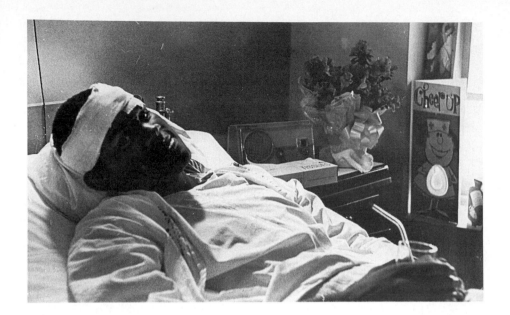

Bobby Rule of
Riverside, *above*,
whom Tark called
"the greatest
junior college
player ever,"
suffered only one
setback in his
college career: an
auto accident in
the year his team
went undefeated.
*(Author's
collection)*

In 1964, Jerry
Tarkanian was
chosen Riverside
County Father of
the Year. *Left to
right:* Dan, Jerry,
George, Pamela,
Lois, and Jodie.
*(Jurupa Hills
Newspaper, Jurupa
Hills, California)*

Jubilant in victory: the 1967 Pasadena City College team, *above*, after winning the California state championship. *Left to right:* Tap Nixon, John Q. Trapp, Tark, Willie Betts, Donald Guiton, and Darrell Evans (wearing glasses). *(Pasadena City College)*

The first victory in the Long Beach Arena, *right*, came against Tulsa, 1970. *(Long Beach State Sports Information Office)*

Jerry and Danny watch time tick away at the NCAA play-offs. *(Deseret Newspaper, Salt Lake City, Utah)*

Rival coaches in a friendly moment: Tark with Al McGuire, head coach of the Marquette University basketball team, 1969. *(Author's collection)*

The 1975–1976 Running Rebels in front of the saucer-shaped Las Vegas Convention Center, their home before moving to the Thomas and Mack Center. *(UNLV Sports Information Office)*

Robert Smith, Lewis Brown, Glen Gondrezick, Eddie Owens, and Sam Smith paced the high-flying 1976–1977 Final Four squad that averaged 110.5 points per game, an NCAA record.

Jerry, in 1977, with Reggie Theus, one of his favorite players, who now plays with the Atlanta Hawks of the NBA. *(UNLV Sports Information Office)*

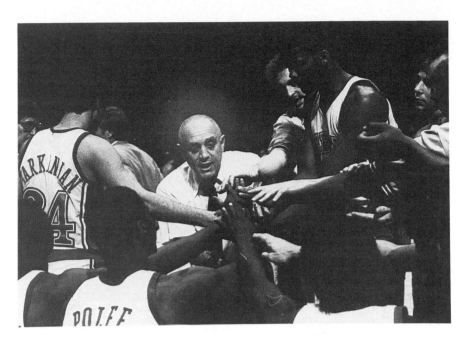

Tark shows his intensity in the huddle. *(UNLV Sports Information Office)*

The Tarkanian mask made its first appearance at the Utah State game in February 1987. *(Greg Wyatt Productions, Inc.)*

A tough day at the gym, 1978. *(Author's collection)*

Tark calls the offense as assistant coach Ralph Readout, *to Tarkanian's right,* charts the play. *(Greg Cava, UNLV Sports Information Office)*

Danny Tarkanian's 1984 graduation with honors from UNLV. *(Author's collection)*

Pamela Tarkanian's wedding. *Left to right:* Dan, Jodie, Lois, Pamela, son-in-law Eric King, Jerry, and George.

Jerry and academic adviser Ann Mayo with five graduating members of the top-ranked 1986–1987 UNLV team. *Left to right:* Freddie Banks, Leon Symanski, Eldridge Hudson, Armon Gilliam, and Gary Graham. *(UNLV Sports Information Office)*

Jerry with Willie Shoemaker, 1988. *(Las Vegas News Bureau)*

One of the Rebels' most illustrious fans, Frank Sinatra, with Jerry in 1976. *(Author's collection)*

felt I should go from the beginning, and there were three reasons for my choice.

"First, I didn't want to go far from home. Vegas was four hours from L.A., much closer than San Francisco. At UNLV, I could go home every weekend if I wanted to.

"Second, I knew some of the guys who played at UNLV, and they liked it.

"Third, I liked Tark's style of basketball. His team ran with the basketball, and I was best in the running game.

"When I was a kid, UCLA was all you ever heard about in college basketball because they won all those national championships. But to me, UCLA was John Wooden, and when he retired, it sort of lost its magic. I did meet with the UCLA athletic director, but I got bad vibes. I also wasn't into prestigious schools, anyway. My high school was small. We were a basketball power, but we weren't an elite school or anything."

Theus's first meeting with Tarkanian wasn't ideal.

"One of the first things Tark said to me was that I reminded him of Eddie Ratleff," says Theus. "I knew that Ratleff was a good player during Tark's days at Long Beach, but I really didn't know much about him. I was never a big sports fan. I liked having my own identity, and I never saw myself in terms of another player. I suppose some guys like being compared to other players, but it always bothered me. So I wasn't thrilled when Tark started talking about me and Ed Ratleff. I suppose the fact that both Eddie and I are about 6-foot-7 and light-skinned might have made Tark think there was a physical resemblance. Our playing styles might have been similar. But truthfully, I didn't care about Ed Ratleff or the fact that Tark thought that Ratleff and I were a lot alike."

So why did he go to play for Tarkanian?

"I did like the man," says Theus. "I also decided that no school was going to buy me. When I was offered all that money, I kept thinking, "What will these people expect from me?" What they were saying was too nice, too good. There are always strings attached to any deal. I wasn't going to let anyone say that I owed them anything. I never took a dime at UNLV, and neither did the other players when I was there. We were a very tight group. If one of us had been getting something, the others would have known. The only time I ever took anything from Tark was when my car ran out of gas. He lent me five bucks to get back to my room, and I paid him back the next day.

"I get tired of people accusing Tark and UNLV of buying players.

153

There are a lot of envious people out there, people envious of Las Vegas and of Tark's success. They say things like nobody would want to go play ball in the desert unless they were getting something. Well, they don't know what they're talking about. I had a car when I was at UNLV, and people kept insisting that the school got it for me. It used to irritate me, and I'd argue about it. Finally, I just said, 'The hell with it,' and stopped arguing. But the truth was that I bought the car and made the payments from the social security check I got each month, and that check came to me because my father died. So if you really want to know who paid for my car, it was my father's death.

"But the bottom line on UNLV was that nowhere else could I have grown as much as a player and a person. My relationship with Tark grew after I got to Vegas. We—by that I mean the team—spent a lot of time at Tark's house, watching tapes of games or movies on TV. Lois became a very important person in my life, because she tutored me. We also would have group discussions about books and plays, and I love to argue. She'd provoke me, just to make me think. I'd say one thing, and she'd play the devil's advocate just to get me going. I could get very hard-nosed. I wouldn't back down and neither would Lois. We had some great debates.

"As for Tark, he is just so sincere. If something was on his mind, he'd just say it. If he thought I'd done something great, he'd say, 'Reggie, I love you. You'll always be a part of my family. I'd like my son to grow up like you.' If I messed up, he'd tell me how bad I stunk and exactly why he thought I was screwing up. He had a way of making me like him and get mad at him at the same time. But I don't think any coach ever got more out of me than Tark.

"My whole experience at UNLV was terrific. Las Vegas is a paradise for a young kid. The school is good, the basketball program is great, and the community loves the team. You are a hero when you play for the Rebels. Also, if you have a few bucks, you can eat in the best restaurants in the whole world because the food is so cheap. I went in as a naive kid of 17 and I knew how to handle myself like a 35-year-old when I got out."

As Tarkanian started his third season at UNLV (1975–76), he had Reggie Theus enrolled. As mentioned, Tarkanian also had signed Robert Smith, because the little point guard had smiled at him when he needed desperately to see a friendly face. Jackie Robinson had come to UNLV because of his family's relationship with the Tarkanians. Boyd Batts had transferred from Hawaii after there was a problem with his transcript. This is how Tarkanian describes assembling the rest of what would become college basketball's highest-scoring team ever.

- Lewis Brown: "Lewis played for George McQuarn in high school. George and I were good friends, and he would later become my assistant. My relationship with George was key to our recruiting Lewis. George had played only baseball in college. But when Verban Dei High in Los Angeles opened, George was made the basketball coach. He knew that he had a lot to learn, and wrote letters to all the coaches in the area asking them to send him anything that would help him start a basketball program. I was at Long Beach at the time, and I was about the only guy who mailed George anything. I sent him books, folders—almost everything I had. He called me and we got to be good friends. He came to my practices; we talked a lot. His team became a national power. He had a 6-foot-10 center named Lewis Brown, and early on I knew all about Lewis through George. We recruited Lewis from the time he was a sophomore. We were very close to him, and we didn't have to beat UCLA for him because he had made a negative comment about UCLA that Wooden didn't like. Also, UCLA was getting Richard Washington out of Portland at the time, so they didn't need Lewis, and that meant we could sign him."

- Sam Smith: "Sam was not a highly recruited player. He was raised in Las Vegas and went to Seminole Junior College in Oklahoma. He came to us. In fact, he was home from Seminole for Christmas break and showed up at one of our practices. He saw me and came running onto the floor. He said, 'Coach, I think I'm coming here.' I said, 'Oh yeah, good.' But I kept looking at him. I didn't know who he was. Sam said, 'You guys have been writing me all year.' I said, 'Is that right...who are you?' He said, 'Sam Smith.' I said, 'Oh, great, Sam. That's great.' I knew that we had been writing a Sam Smith, who was a 6-foot-2 guard with a great outside shot. But I had never met him until he came to see me, and he turned out to be a magnificent kid as well as a great player for us."

- Larry Moffett: "Larry was from Gary, Indiana, and he wasn't a great high school player. He originally went to Murray State, and he had a few personal problems there. The coach from

Murray State called us because he knew that we had been successful with transfers. The call was the first time we had anything to do with Larry Moffett. We directed Larry to Compton
Junior College. He didn't have a very good year. He wasn't an
all-conference player or anything, and we were ready to back
off from him. But Lynn Archibald went to see Larry play in
the California JUCO state tournament, and Lynn said that the
kid was all over the floor, playing hard. Since we needed a
backup center to Lewis Brown, we took Larry. Larry couldn't
shoot, but he was a 6-foot-8 shot blocker who loved defense.
He had a bad reputation at Murray State, and that's why no
other school was really interested in him. When Larry came to
UNLV he was a great kid, one of the most coachable players
I've ever had. When they saw Larry play for us, the coaches
from Murray State couldn't believe he was the same kid. The
coaches from Gary, Indiana, couldn't believe it either.''

- Glen Gondrezick: "Gondo was from Boulder, Colorado. A
friend of Gondo's knew a lawyer in Vegas. Gondo's friend
wrote the lawyer, and the lawyer came to see me with this
letter about a kid named Glen Gondrezick in Colorado. Until that point, I had never even heard of Gondo. So I went to
see him in Boulder. I still wasn't sure what kind of a player
he was, but Gondo struck me as a great kid. I knew we
couldn't go wrong with that kind of person on the team. The
University of Colorado wasn't interested in him. No major
college coach was except Dick Harter at Oregon. Gondo was
ready to go to Oregon, but Harter kept putting him off.
Harter thought he was going to sign Adrian Dantley, and he
was saving the scholarship for Dantley. Gondo was being
held in reserve in case Oregon couldn't get Dantley. Gondo
kept telling Harter that he wanted to sign, and Harter would
tell him to wait another week. Finally, Gondo's dad got tired
of the whole thing. He called me and I went to Boulder and
signed him.''

- Tony Smith: "Tony was from Saginaw, Michigan. Unlike
some of the guys on this team, Tony was a great high school
player. We recruited Tony, but he went to Houston. He
wasn't happy there and was looking to transfer. One day, I
got a call from Bill Frieder, who was then an assistant coach
at Michigan. He told me that Tony wanted to transfer, but
Frieder was scared that Tony was going to transfer to

Michigan State, Michigan's rival. Frieder didn't want that
to happen, and it didn't because Tony called us and said he
wanted to come to Vegas.''

• Eddie Owens: "He was an outstanding player at Wheatley
High in Houston. We never even tried to recruit Eddie, because I just don't go into Texas. There is too much going on
down there in terms of recruiting for us to get a Texas kid.
I just haven't had much success recruiting against Southwest
or Southeast conference schools. And Eddie was from
Houston; all the top kids from that town went to the University of Houston. I was at the Dapper Dan Classic, which
is a high school all-star game in Pittsburgh. I was with George
Raveling, who was then coaching at Washington State.
George said I should recruit Owens because he was a great
shooter. I said that Owens was a Houston kid and I never
could get a kid out of Texas. But George said I should check
on it. During one of the practices, I sat with Eddie's high
school coach. I asked him if the University of Houston had
Eddie locked up, and the coach said, 'Absolutely not.
Houston is the one place Eddie won't go. I can promise you
that he isn't going to Houston.'

"Apparently, Dwight Jones was one of that coach's players who had gone to Houston, and something had happened
to Dwight that really bothered the coach. Anyway, Houston
was out. So I asked the coach if I could talk to Eddie, and
the coach set it up. Eddie and I hit it off well, and he came
to UNLV for a visit. So far, everything was going great.

"Eventually, it came down to us and Oral Roberts for
Eddie. Eddie's mother was a very religious woman, and Oral
Roberts had her in his hip pocket. But Eddie wanted to go to
Vegas. He called me and said he was ready to sign. I went to
see Eddie, and the kid wanted to sign but his mother wouldn't.
I sat in that house for four and one-half hours, but his mother
wouldn't sign. She kept talking about Oral Roberts. I was trying to reason with her. She wanted to wait another day because
Oral Roberts was flying in to visit her the next day. But Eddie
was saying he didn't want to go to Oral Roberts. It got to the
point where Eddie went into his bedroom and wouldn't come
out. That left Eddie's mother and me alone, and I had no choice
but to try and convince her that Eddie would be fine at UNLV.

"Finally, Eddie came back into the room and said, 'No way

157

am I going to sign with Oral Roberts.'

"Still, his mother wouldn't sign. Eddie and his mother started having meetings in the kitchen, then they'd come out and talk to me.

"I thought that if I sat there long enough, the mother would have to sign. Finally, she did. It was about one in the morning. I had a tremendous headache when it was over, but I'd pull out the signed letter of intent and look at it, and that would make me feel better."

In Tarkanian's third year at UNLV, he kicked the offense into high gear: it was man-to-man defense, push the ball up the court, and the first guy who was open should let a shot fly. It was run, run, run. College basketball had never seen anything like the UNLV teams of 1975–76 and 1976–77. Anyone who had watched the Long Beach State teams of the early 1970s and then these UNLV teams found it impossible to believe they were coached by the same man.

Tarkanian says, "We concentrated on rebounding and then getting the ball up the court as quickly as possible. We would time it in practice, and we could get the ball up the court and score in four seconds. Our fans went nuts that year. They just loved how we ran."

College basketball wasn't ready for these Running Rebels. While it was true that they averaged 91 points in Tarkanian's second season, 91 points was just getting warmed up for this group.

How does a per game average of 110.5 points per game sound?

How does scoring at least 100 points in 23 out of 31 games sound?

How does a 164–111 victory at Hawaii-Hilo sound? In that game, UNLV had 85 points at halftime. Sam Smith nailed his first seven shots, all from at least 20 feet. At one point, the score was actually 16–16 as the local officials in Hawaii were playing *Can You Top This?* when it came to calling fouls and turnovers against the Rebels. Tarkanian is normally very patient with officials, but he threatened to pull his team off the floor unless the guys blowing the whistles settled down and called a decent game. The game was played in a tiny gym that sat 2,512 fans. The scoreboard was numbers hung on pegs under one of the baskets. So the site of the highest-scoring game in NCAA history was a humble facility on an island 4,000 miles from the mainland.

Pete Newell: "When I think back on those Vegas teams, I am truly amazed. They scored 110 points without a shot clock. They scored 110 points on a 40-minute clock, not the 48 minutes and the 24-second clock that the pros have. By NBA standards, that would be like scoring 135 points a night. And the thing was, those kids really did play intense defense. Tark had the best press in the country at that time, and he totally caught everyone off balance. No one had any idea how to defense UNLV or how to slow them down, and no one knew how to run with them, either."

The Rebels began that season with 23 consecutive victories, before losing 93–91 to Pepperdine when Dennis Johnson hit a shot with three seconds left to stop UNLV's streak. The Rebels finished the season ranked third in the country. After defeating Boise State (103–78) in the first round of the NCAA tournament, UNLV was dumped 114–109 in overtime by Arizona. Tarkanian still thinks about that game.

This was the season when the Hardway Eight came into existence. Tarkanian has often said that the ideal rotation for a coach to use is eight players, because that is the greatest number of players who can receive meaningful minutes on the floor. With this team, Tarkanian had what he considered eight starters. His only senior was 6-foot-7 center Boyd Batts. He had six juniors: Sam Smith, Lewis Brown, Eddie Owens, Robert Smith, Glen Gondrezick, and Jackie Robinson. The only freshman was Reggie Theus, and he played the least of the Hardway Eight.

The sleek 6-foot-7 Owens averaged 23 points, shooting 54 percent from the field and 81 percent from the foul line—and remember, most of his points came from the outside. Sam Smith's 20- to 25-footers were good for a 16-point average and a 52 percent mark from the field, and he scored the first field goal in 22 of UNLV's 31 games. The Rebels made a point of getting the ball to Smith on their first possession, so he could unleash a jumper from the Utah state line and immediately get the crowd into the game. As for Theus, he averaged 5.9 points and concentrated on passing and defense. That's why Tarkanian so reveres Theus: on a team where the offense was run-and-gun and where Reggie Theus could run-and-gun as well or better than anyone on the roster, Theus made a point to get the ball to the upperclassmen. That was a major concession from a kid who averaged 28 points as a senior in high school. When the 1975–76 season went into the books, UNLV had set seven NCAA season records for scoring average (110.5), points in game (164), points in a half (85) and 100-point games (23). Their record was 29–2, and all but the points-in-a-half record remain.

As the 1976–77 season approached, Jerry Tarkanian should have been happy. But there were constant rumors, and there were too many phone calls delivering the same message.

"Over and over, I kept hearing that the NCAA was out to get me," says Tarkanian. "People would call me and say that they had talked to an NCAA investigator, and that I had better be careful because that investigator was saying right out that they wanted to nail me."

Sound a bit paranoid?

Not if you listen to these accounts:

"Right after I signed with Vegas, a guy from the NCAA came to see me and asked if Vegas gave me any girls or money," Eddie Owens told reporters in 1977. "I hadn't even started school there, and I was being questioned. I told them that UNLV had come clean with me and the guy couldn't believe it."

Glen Gondrezick recalls, "I know people talked about us getting things at UNLV, but that just didn't happen. One month we were so broke, all Jackie Robinson and I could do was go to the Jackpot Casino, because they were selling hot dogs for a quarter, and that included a Coke. We each bought five and got sick as dogs during practice."

But when the players told the NCAA those stories, all the investigators did was stare in disbelief.

Here is another example of what Tarkanian considered harassment:

Sports Illustrated visited the UNLV campus in October of 1976. The *SI* reporter, Barry McDermott, said he was there to do a story about UNLV being selected as the number-one team entering the season. Eddie Owens was supposed to be on the cover. UNLV sports information director Dominic Clark said he was told this by the *SI* reporter. Owens said he was given the same information by the *SI* photographer.

But a few weeks before the story was to run, Clark received a call from *SI* saying that it was canceling the Eddie Owens cover and turning to another team as its number-one preseason pick. Clark said that *SI* claimed it had a reporter in Kansas City who had learned from the NCAA that UNLV was about to go on probation.

This same Kansas City reporter was mentioned again later when there were premature news releases about UNLV's having problems with the NCAA. Royce Feour, a sportswriter for the *Las Vegas Review Journal,* called the reporter in Kansas City. Feour's notes on the conversation indicated that the reporter told Feour that he spent a lot of time at the NCAA's office in Shawnee Mission, Kansas, and this enabled him to sometimes get information before it was released. These conversations and reports about UNLV's problems with the NCAA occurred before the UNLV case was heard by the NCAA infractions committee, and thus before any decision was made about UNLV's guilt or innocence.

Despite the rumors, it made sense that UNLV was highly regarded. Its record the year before was 29–2 and it had lost only one player—center Boyd Batts. The core of the team was six seniors. In addition, highly regarded transfers Tony Smith and Larry Moffett had become eligible.

But there were other grim signs.

The Tarkanians recall that a production company named TVS was filming and doing features on teams that might end up in the 1977 Final Four at the Omni in Atlanta. UNLV was slated as one of the teams to be covered, but Jim Maroney of TVS told Jerry Tarkanian that he had spoken with an NCAA official about the teams he would film, and the NCAA official had told him to skip UNLV because the team was about to go on probation.

No UNLV games were included on NBC's national or regional schedule, because of rumors that the program was headed for probation. UNLV was a natural for television because of its running game. This was during the snoozeball era of college basketball, when coaches had become enamored of the stall and the four corners offense. UNLV's playing was a welcome relief, which was why the networks wanted the Rebels.

There also were several newspaper reports stating that UNLV and Tarkanian were in trouble with the NCAA.

Tarkanian: "The bad thing was that we weren't on probation, no ruling had come down, and people were acting like we were on probation. We were being treated that way by magazines and television networks."

The Tarkanians were convinced that the NCAA was consistently leaking the probation story to places were it would hurt UNLV the most—*Sports Illustrated,* NBC, and other national media outlets.

UNLV assistant coach Lynn Archibald: "I couldn't believe what they were doing to us. It was like we were being convicted before there was a hearing or anything like that. We didn't even know what we would be charged with, yet people were acting like we were guilty. The thing is, I know exactly what we did to get Reggie Theus, Jackie Robinson, Ricky Sobers, and about every other player in Jerry's early years at UNLV. We were careful. Because of the NCAA's interest in Jerry, we knew we had to be careful and not even have the hint of any impropriety. But as it turned out, none of that mattered. No matter what we did or didn't do, the NCAA was after Jerry, and that was all there was to it."

*   *   *

Tarkanian still had the Hardway Eight as the 1976–77 season began, but two of the names were different. Batts was gone, replaced by senior Larry Moffett. Jackie Robinson had a severe ankle injury and was red-shirted. His place was taken by transfer Tony Smith.

This was an interesting group of players.

The starting center was Moffett, a thin, 6-foot-8 pogo stick who relished rebounding and blocking shots. He was perfect for the Rebels, because it was his board work that started the fast break. All teams say that they want to run, but running begins with rebounding. If you don't rebound, the fast break is just a rumor. With Moffett, the Rebels could rebound. Making it even better was that Moffett wasn't especially interested in scoring. He was content to rule the boards, and that was ideal, since Tarkanian already had enough guys who could shoot. Moffett averaged 8.0 points and 9.2 rebounds.

Six-foot-ten Lewis Brown was the other center. Brown had a pro body, and at times he played like an All-Pro. But those times weren't often enough. Tarkanian used him wisely. He put Brown into the game in settings where if he succeeded, he was a wonderful contribution to the game; but if he wasn't in the flow, UNLV's game would not be jeopardized.

Tarkanian calls Sam Smith "not just the best long-range shooter I've coached, but the best I've ever seen. He was only 6-foot-2, but he threw in 25-footers as if they were lay-ups." Sam Smith averaged 14.8 points and shot 52 percent, which was remarkable accuracy considering where the shots were being launched.

Robert Smith was the 5-foot-10 point guard who brought structure to the offense. Left open, he could hit from 18 feet. He also made a point of learning where and when his teammates wanted the ball. Robert averaged 12.8 points and 6.6 assists, shot 49 percent from the field and 93 percent at the foul line, and set a team record for steals. "Most of all, Robert was one of the hardest workers I've ever had and a super kid to coach. His smile lit up the room. I just liked being around the kid," says Tarkanian.

Eddie Owens was a 6-foot-7 forward who was a natural scorer. According to Tarkanian, "he could do it inside or outside." Owens averaged 21.8 points.

Glen Gondrezick was a 6-foot-6 forward who took an average of four charges a game. How do you take a charge? You stand there and let the guy with the ball run over you. It is a good way to get a footprint on your chest. That didn't happen to Gondrezick, but he did develop a cyst on his chest that had to be surgically removed. It was a product of all the pounding his body had taken on the court. Tarkanian loved Gondrezick for his relentless defense and his fearlessness.

Tony Smith was the third of what was known as the "Smith Brothers," along with Robert and Sam. He was a 6-foot-2 guard who averaged 14 points.

Theus still didn't start, but the 6-foot-6 guard averaged 14.5 points and shot 50 percent.

Reggie Theus: "We really didn't have that much size. But we could score on anyone, and man, did we ever work on defense. In my three years at UNLV, I never played a zone. Not once! It was all tough man-to-man defense, and we ran a full-court press for the whole game. The college game had never run into anything like those teams we had. Back then, people tried to write us off as gunners, saying that we didn't pay attention to defense. But the defense triggered the offense. We'd get a steal, throw a pass, and a guy would catch it down at the other end of the court for a dunk. We forced teams into 28 turnovers a night, teams that usually turned the ball over half that amount. All some people saw was that we'd win 120–105, but that was because a running game creates so many more possessions and more shots. It means more opportunities to score."

The Rebels racked up a 29–3 record and averaged 107 points.

Reggie Theus says, "We really had it going that year. When other teams came to our gym, it was a nightmare. The light show really got to the guys on the other teams. I mean, the whole place would be dark, the crowd would be on its feet, clapping, and each player would go out on the floor covered by a spotlight. Every night the building was packed, the crowd was going crazy. Vegas is a big-time town, and the players feel it because of the exposure the players receive. Our team was so close. The guys were together; it was like we had a sixth sense of what it took to win on the court and to be a part of the community. We made a point of taking time to sign autographs and to make appearances at schools. It was the greatest college basketball situation you could imagine."

It turned out that the television people from TVS were right: UNLV was destined for the Final Four. It was Tarkanian's initial trip to college basketball's hallowed ground.

Their first NCAA play-off game was against San Francisco. The Dons had 7-footer Bill Cartwright in the middle and were ranked second in the country. The game was in Tucson, and UNLV stunned tournament officials by taking 7,000 fans along. The Rebels also unloaded on the Dons by a 121–95 count. In a span of 90 seconds the Rebels scored 12 points. They were in front 63–44 at the half, and ended up forcing San Francisco to throw the ball away 32 times. Reggie Theus had 27 points in 23 minutes. Tarkanian had stressed to his players that they could beat the more talented and bigger Dons just by playing harder. He said that San Francisco had periods where it became vulnerable because it lost interest in the game and let down. He talked press and he talked sweat. He made his team run extra sprints in practice, telling them that it would pay off because San Francisco was not making the same extra effort.

Tarkanian: "Getting to the Final Four is sort of a dream for every coach. But a lot of luster had come off it because there were all the rumors about the NCAA and the talk about probation. That's all the reporters wanted to talk about, and that was so sad for the kids because they had worked so hard and done nothing wrong. They deserved to be able to savor that moment at the Final Four. The only NCAA charge against anyone on that Final Four team was that Eddie Owens used someone's car during his 48-hour recruiting visit to drive another recruit from a party back to his room. That's why it hurt when those kids had to take abuse. They didn't do anything."

UNLV met North Carolina at the Omni. This time, Tarkanian told his players that they had to play hard for all 40 minutes, because he knew that Dean Smith's players were ready to do exactly that. Smith and Tarkanian went out of their way to praise each other to the press. UNLV took a 49–43 lead at the half and was in front 56–46. But Larry Moffett went to the bench for several minutes with an injury that first appeared to be a broken nose, and the Tar Heels reeled off 9 unanswered points. The game remained close, but North Carolina prevailed 84–83, thanks primarily to being perfect on all sixteen of its second-half free throws. In fact, the game was decided at the foul line. North Caroline was 18 for 28 from the foul line, while UNLV was 1 for 5.

Former UNLV assistant coach Al Menendez: "I can still picture Tark after we lost to North Carolina. Jackie Robinson was injured that year and he was in his street clothes. Jackie had his arm around Tark, helping him off the floor. Tark looked like the saddest man in the world. It was how you would expect a guy to look if his whole family had been wiped out in an accident. It was the look of a guy who thought there was no justice in the world."

11

The NCAA Strikes Again

While Jerry Tarkanian was coaching UNLV to its first appearance in the NCAA Final Four, he and his family were, as he said, "going through the most excruciating time of our lives."

Tarkanian continually heard that he was being investigated by the NCAA and that some of the investigators had a vendetta against him. "I was sure that once the facts came out, there wouldn't be any more problems between UNLV and the NCAA," he says ruefully. Tarkanian also had confidence in NCAA investigator David Berst, whom he considered a good guy.

Lois was worried; she didn't have the same faith in the NCAA and Berst.

Lois: "Almost every day we'd get a call from someone telling us that Warren Brown, David Berst, or someone else with the NCAA was saying something negative about Jerry. The clippings we were getting from the service were devastating. Between the telephone calls and the newspaper stories, it was really getting to all of us. One story out of Arizona that scared me was written by Rich Rickert in January of 1974. It said, 'An NCAA spokesman, obviously miffed that Tarkanian had moved in time from Long Beach, was overheard saying that Nevada-Las Vegas was being investigated....' I learned from some reporters that the investigator was David Berst. Jerry and I argued over what I considered his blind faith in Berst, and what I thought was his obstinacy in not facing the fact that the NCAA enforcement staff was out to get him. I thought he was living in never-never land.

He is as apolitical as you can get, and he just wouldn't listen. Meanwhile, I felt like our whole world was about to cave in on us."

Then, in the middle of the 1977 season, the Los Angeles Lakers contacted Tarkanian and offered him a solid, five-year deal to coach a team with Kareem Abdul-Jabbar at center.

Tarkanian: "When you have Kareem, you're pretty sure that you'll win a lot of games. The Lakers job had a lot going for it. The salary wasn't that high by pro standards—$70,000 a year with increases of $2,500 a year—but no other coach in the NBA had a guaranteed five-year contract. Jack Kent Cooke was the Lakers owner, and I met with him several times. He was a unique guy and we really hit it off. He was into secrecy. His favorite saying was, 'Less is more.' In other words, the less you say, the better.

"He would call me on the phone and try to disguise his voice. He'd say, 'Jerry, I'm calling from the *Los Angeles Times*. Is it true you are interested in the Lakers job?'

"I was under orders to always say no comment, so I'd tell him, 'No comment.' Jack Kent Cooke would laugh and say 'Atta boy, Jerry,' and hang up. Then he'd call back a little later and say, 'Jerry, remember that less is more.'

"At first, I turned the job down. Then Jack Kent Cooke came to Vegas and stayed at the Tropicana Hotel. He was a great salesman, and I finally agreed to take it. I was staying at the MGM Grand to hide from the press, with my close friend Vic Weiss, who handled the contract talks for me."

Lois: "Jack Kent Cooke was an intriguing man, very courtly and sharp. He took us to a home he had bought in the Scotch 80s section of Las Vegas and told us that the house had been designed by Frank Lloyd Wright. He gave us a complete tour of the home and spent hours talking with us. We explained our situation with the NCAA, and he said that the NCAA was a very small part of the world. He said we'd be better able to get out the true information if we weren't under their jurisdiction. If Jerry were a winning pro coach, he could speak out on anything he wished. I told Jerry that I liked Mr. Cooke and thought he made some excellent points.

"My instincts told me that Jerry would not get a fair chance with the NCAA. The pieces were beginning to fit together.

"As usual, Jerry wavered back and forth about a job change. I think he was driving Cooke crazy. Vic Weiss said that after the fourth time Jerry changed his mind, Cooke told him, 'Jerry is a genius on the basketball court, but flaky off of it.' But Cooke never pressured Jerry and was very patient with him. Vic and I thought we had convinced Jerry to leave UNLV.

"Then Jerry suddenly decided to call David Berst. I couldn't believe it. Jerry kept insisting that Berst was a good guy; I remember him saying, 'I can ask him if they can put you on probation even if they can't find any evidence. There can't be evidence if I didn't do it.' I asked Jerry if he was crazy. Vic Weiss also told Jerry that it wasn't a good idea to call Berst. But Jerry picked up the phone and called him, explaining the Lakers offer and asking Berst several times if he could be found guilty if there was no evidence. Berst said they needed proof. I almost got sick thinking that Jerry would trust that man. Finally, Vic and I convinced Jerry that he should take the Lakers job no matter what, and we went to bed thinking that was the case."

Tarkanian: "The whole time these talks with Jack Kent Cooke were going on, I was thinking, 'I don't want this job. I let these people talk me into it.' Vic Weiss had handled the negotiations for me, and he thought I should take the offer. Lois also thought I should take it.

"People kept telling me, 'Take the job and get out.' They said, 'You'll get buried if you stay at Vegas. The people will say that they'll stand by you, but when the shooting starts you'll be in the trenches looking around, and you'll see that you're all alone.' The feeling was that once the NCAA came in, everyone would desert us and leave us to take the heat. But I kept thinking, 'I don't want this job. I don't want to run from the NCAA, because once the infractions committee sees our evidence, I'll be cleared.' It was a long night; I kept thinking about the job, going back and forth. My oldest daughter, Pamela, was staying in California at that time. She called me at the MGM at one in the morning.

"Pamela said, 'Dad, it's all over the television about you taking the Lakers job. You told me that you didn't want it, so why are you taking it?' I said, 'I don't know. I don't want the job. I don't know why I'm doing it.' Pamela said, 'Then don't do it. Do what you want, Dad.'

"So I decided to stay. If it weren't for that phone call at one in the morning, I would have gone. Pamela and I talked for forty-five minutes. When I hung up, I called Jack Kent Cooke and told him that I wasn't taking the job. He got all upset and he told Lois, 'How can Jerry be a coach? He can't even make a decision.'

"I didn't want to run out on what was happening to UNLV. If I had been guilty, maybe I would have gone, but I knew I had done nothing wrong. Also, it seemed that the whole state of Nevada was trying to get at the truth. The state of Nevada's attorney general's office got involved when they were asked to conduct the investigation for the university, a state institution. All their evidence showed that the charges were false. The university hired an attorney, Mike Leavitt, to examine the case. He couldn't believe what the NCAA was doing, because there was no substance to their charges. So everybody felt that the enforcement staff was out of line and that once the charges went in front of the NCAA's infraction committee, the charges would be dropped. I felt people were behind me, and I was going to stay and fight it out.''

Tarkanian: ''But when I and others from UNLV went in front of the infractions committee, they didn't really consider our evidence or listen to us. They just were a rubber stamp for what the investigators wanted. It was an awful time, because I knew something bad was coming from the NCAA, but I didn't know what the charges would be. All I could be sure of was that the NCAA was going to say we did something. Later, there was a period where my attorney, Lois, and myself were the only ones who knew that the NCAA was planning to get me suspended. Lois and I didn't want our children, or players, or anyone to know. We kept it quiet. My attorney said they couldn't do it, but in the back of my mind I kept thinking, 'What if my attorney is wrong? What if the NCAA can get me fired? What would I do without basketball?' Basketball is my whole life. It was a real hard time, because I thought about that every day. I'd wake up early in the morning and go to school. After practice, I'd go to the Jockey Club and work out. Then I'd sit in the sauna all by myself and I'd ask myself how this could be happening to me, why the NCAA would want to take away my job.''

On August 26, 1977, the NCAA released this statement:

The University of Nevada, Las Vegas, has been placed on probation for two years by the NCAA as a result of violations which occurred over a four and one-half year period [1971–75] in the conduct of the University's intercollegiate basketball program. ...In accordance with the ''show cause'' provision of the NCAA enforcement program, the University must also take appropriate disciplinary and corrective actions against individuals directly involved in the case, including a former head basketball coach, a former assistant basketball coach and the present head basketball coach.

It was also made clear that the action against "the present head basketball coach" was a two-year suspension from college coaching for Tarkanian.

Tarkanian: "As I walked out of the hearing, one of the NCAA investigators told me that the two years would go like 'water under the bridge.' I said, 'If I have to be out two years, I'll never coach again.' The guy repeated the line about water under the bridge. I hated him for saying that. Couldn't he see that if I didn't fight the suspension, I would be finished in college coaching? Couldn't he understand what being a college basketball coach meant to me? The negative publicity from the probation and the suspension would finish me. It made me a marked man. The NCAA was trying to ruin me.

"When the whole NCAA thing started, some coaches had told me, 'Shut up. You can't fight them. You'll never win. They have unlimited funds. They'll bury you and they're vindictive as hell. If you speak up, they'll make an example of you. Just keep quiet and eventually they'll go away.' But I couldn't keep quiet. It hurt too much and it was so unfair. But those coaches were right. When we went to the infractions committee, there wasn't a shred of evidence to back up the charges. We had all the proof, not the NCAA. Then they suspended me anyway. I couldn't back down."

The NCAA made thirty-seven charges against UNLV. Seventeen of them went back to the previous coach's tenure.

There were ten charges made specifically against Tarkanian and ten others against the program in general. Three of the charges against Tarkanian were pro forma charges related to the seven other allegations against him: he was cited for having signed compliance forms in 1974 and 1975, stating he was unaware of NCAA violations, and a general charge of improper conduct was brought because of alleged violations.

Of the seven charges against Tarkanian, one of the most serious was the charge that he had arranged for a player named Robert "Jeep" Kelly to obtain free airline transportation home during his freshman year and had reimbursed him in cash for his return trip.

Kelly had quit the team a week before the first game in his freshman year, and had gone back to Pittsburgh. When he returned to UNLV, he was not allowed to play, or even dress for, the first game. Instead, as official game records showed, he was relegated to the junior varsity to work his way back up again. Tarkanian had allegedly arranged the trip by providing Kelly with the name of an individual who operated gambling junkets to and from Las Vegas, and by reimbursing Kelly with cash when he returned. Although Tarkanian pointed out that it was "ludicrous" to think he would arrange airline transportation for a player to leave his team and equally "ridiculous" to think he would reimburse the player to return and then not let the player rejoin the team, the NCAA insisted the charges were true. Their evidence? NCAA investigator David Berst said that he recalled having a conversation with Kelly in 1975 during which Kelly said he was unhappy at UNLV and wanted to go home, but that Kelly later changed his mind and wanted to return to UNLV. He states that Kelly said Tarkanian had told him to call the junket operator, who would arrange for Kelly to receive a free ride on a junket from Pittsburgh to Las Vegas. The Kelly case was broken down into nine violations against Tarkanian and others.

The university countered the charge with the following:

1. A deposition and a sworn affidavit from Kelly denying the charges and stating that he had purchased a commercial airline ticket to his home in Pittsburgh by selling his season tickets (which at that time were given to players before the start of each season); that Tarkanian had never reimbursed him with money; and that the return ticket was obtained through the help of his high school principal, Dr. James Robinson.

2. A sworn deposition from Dr. James E. Robinson stating that he had authorized the Schenley High School treasurer to write a check for Kelly's return ticket. The money had come from the school's general fund, which could be used at the discretion of the principal for assistance to students and former students.

3. A sworn affidavit from Kelly's high school coach, Spencer Watkins, stating that he and Dr. Robinson had urged Kelly to return to UNLV to complete his first year in college and that they had made arrangements for his return to Las Vegas and the purchase of the plane ticket.

4. A letter from Garin F. Veseley, athletic director of Kelly's high school, in which Veseley stated that, as authorized by Dr. Robinson, he had purchased an airline ticket for Kelly on November 30, 1973.

5. A copy of a Schenley High School payment order requesting the issuance of a check in the sum of $135.00 to be made payable to cash "in payment of traveling expenses RJK," to be charged to the general account and dated November 30, 1973.

6. A letter from the accused junket operator stating that for the time period in question, the companies with which he was associated had conducted no aircraft flights between Las Vegas and Pittsburgh, or anywhere near Pittsburgh, and no flights at all on the dates when Kelly would have left Las Vegas. Flight manifests supported the information he gave.

Almost nothing matched.

Lois: "When Jerry told me what happened, I couldn't believe it. Berst claimed that Kelly had told him that he was afraid, yet at that same time Kelly was calling us frequently on the telephone and coming over to our house to see the children when he was in town. It didn't make sense. If Kelly had wanted to hurt us, why would he have given such inaccurate information? He knew that he had taken a commercial flight to Pittsburgh and that lots of people were involved at his high school in getting him back to college. If he purposely wanted to hurt us, why wouldn't he make up something where there wouldn't be so much evidence to prove it wasn't true?"

After months of frustration, university lawyers found out the reason for the Kelly contradictions. A former assistant UNLV coach who had recruited Kelly to UNLV and had not been rehired contacted the attorney general's office. The former assistant stated under oath that it was he, not Kelly, who had given the information to Berst, and that on the date Berst claimed Kelly had given the information, Kelly had been present but the former assistant had done the talking. Kelly's friendship with the assistant coach had kept him from interfering. The meeting had been arranged and conducted in such a way that Berst could tell the infractions committee that Kelly had given the information, and thus keep the former assistant's name out of it. He stated that he had been bitter about his job situation and had wanted to get back at Tarkanian. He regretted his action and then wanted to clear up the situation. Unfortunately, he stepped forward too late for the university to utilize effectively the information he provided.

Berst's "recollections" of conversations were the only evidence the NCAA had to weigh against the university's several affidavits, letters, canceled checks, and other sworn testimony.

Another allegation against Tarkanian was that he had arranged for a part-time instructor at UNLV to give a student named David Vaughn a B grade in a black studies course, with the understanding that the student would not have to attend class or complete any work. The NCAA based this charge on a conversation investigator Hale Mc-

171

Menamin said he had with the instructor. UNLV produced the following evidence to support Tarkanian's claim that the charge was not true:

1. A sworn affidavit from the part-time instructor stating that he had never made an arrangement with Tarkanian or any-one else from the UNLV athletic department for Vaughn or any other student to receive special treatment or grades.

2. An affidavit from the student athlete stating that Tarkanian had made no special arrangements with his teacher and that he had attended classes and done the required work.

3. Letters from five students (not athletes) who said they saw the student athlete in class and that it was easy to notice him because he was almost 7 feet tall.

4. A statement from a female student in the class that she had typed the player's final paper for him and had been present in class when he had orally presented the paper.

5. A polygraph test in which the instructor stated that he had made no special arrangements with Tarkanian concerning Vaughn or any other student.

6. A voice analyzation that supported the instructor's polygraph test.

The only evidence the NCAA staff presented to back up their charge was investigator Hale McMenamin's "recollection" of conversations. It was never explained why a teacher would provide to a complete stranger self-incriminating information that was damaging to the teacher's professional reputation.

To show how inaccurate McMenamin's "recollections" could be, UNLV produced the following evidence: In a report concerning another allegation, McMenamin had told the infractions committee that a Las Vegas sportscaster had told him that he was reluctant to talk with the NCAA because he "was born and raised" in Las Vegas and "depended on the university to make a living," but that he had filmed an alleged incident and broadcast it on his "5 p.m. and 10 p.m. sports shows that night." The sportscaster denied having made those statements to McMenamin. He pointed out that as a matter of record, he had been born and raised in Los Angeles, California, and had not moved to Las Vegas until he was an adult; that the alleged incident occurred on a Sunday and his program was not broadcast on Sunday; and that the regular newscasts were at 6 p.m. and 11 p.m., not 5 p.m. and 10 p.m. Obviously, McMenamin's "recollections" were not reliable.

Such was the situation with each of the charges against Tarkanian: the NCAA's sole evidence was an NCAA investigator's recollections of conversations; the university's evidence was a substantial amount of sworn testimony and documented information.

UNLV requested that individuals named in or offering hearsay evidence be called to appear before the infractions committee to personally respond to questions. This request was denied by the committee as being "too expensive."

How did investigator Berst explain the contradictions concerning his "recollections" of conversations? He claimed that Tarkanian had contacted Kelly and his aunt to discourage them from giving truthful information. This claim of Berst's resulted in another charge against Tarkanian: obstructing the investigation. Berst had written memos of the alleged content of those conversations. In other situations pertaining to the UNLV case and in other university cases, Berst had at times tape-recorded conversations with individuals, often without their knowledge. No such tape-recorded transcript for any of the supposed Kelly conversations was presented.

Infractions committee records show that UNLV personnel were shocked at the extreme disparity between evidence they had collected and Berst's recollections.

By this time (late in 1977), UNLV was in the midst of its appeal to the NCAA council. An attempt was made to clearly show that Berst had misled the entire investigation in the Kelly situation, but Walter Byers, then executive director of the NCAA, strongly objected to any assertions of wrongdoing on the part of his investigative staff. Byers, who said in a 1987 *Sports Illustrated* article that he had never intervened personally during a university's appeal before the NCAA council, had in fact intervened during UNLV's appeal, a fact established during court proceedings.

In its case against Tarkanian at UNLV, the NCAA showed the following pattern of bias:

1. The only evidence presented by NCAA investigators to support their charges during the Tarkanian tenure at UNLV was

their recollections of conversations held years before. Their memos from the supposed conversations were dictated after the interviews occurred, sometimes months afterward, often without benefit of notes. Where notes had been made, they were destroyed prior to the hearing. The individuals interviewed never had a chance to see the notes or to review the information to check for accuracy. Neither UNLV nor Tarkanian nor their legal counsels were ever allowed to see or obtain copies of the memos, despite their repeated requests to do so.

2. After the regular hearings, UNLV obtained additional information clearly demonstrating that NCAA investigators had provided false and misleading information to the committee. The information included a tape recording secretly made by Rodney Parker in December 1976, while Parker was being questioned by David Berst. Parker was a New York basketball enthusiast and playground coach featured in a book, *Heaven Is a Playground,* written by Rick Telander of *Sports Illustrated.* The tape recording clearly demonstrated that at the infractions committee hearing, Berst had attempted to discredit sworn statements obtained by UNLV, and the objectivity of UNLV's investigation, by misrepresenting statements Parker had made. What Parker said to Berst, as the tape recording showed, was directly opposite to what Berst had told the infractions committee.

3. UNLV requested a special hearing at which it could question the NCAA staff about what appeared to be staff lies concerning facts and information sources. At that hearing on March 13, 1977, the NCAA investigators claimed they had the right to misrepresent the facts concerning their sources of information because of an unwritten and/or unpublished committee policy regarding confidential sources. The infractions committee backed them up on this. When Tarkanian's counsel attempted to question NCAA staff about these, he was told they were confidential. The infractions committee upheld this claim and prevented further questioning.

4. Neither the infractions committee nor the NCAA council made any investigation of their own into the matters concerning the investigative staff.

Neither UNLV nor the Nevada attorney general's office ever received a copy of NCAA infractions committee policies, procedures, and guidelines so that they could investigate the charges in the proper manner, even though requests for these items were made numerous times. Lyle Rivera, chief deputy of the Nevada attorney general's office, initiated the requests shortly after the university received the official inquiry. During subsequent meetings and correspondence with NCAA staff, UNLV personnel were told the following:

1. Such information was available in the NCAA Manual, pages 116–123. (Those pages, however, gave a sequence of actions, not procedural guidelines.)

2. No such information was available.

3. The committee policies and procedures were in written form and were transmitted upon request of an institution.

4. Warren Brown, NCAA assistant executive director, could not remember stating the guidelines were available.

5. The procedural guidelines were being compiled.

6. The guidelines were being submitted to council and could not be distributed.

7. UNLV did not need the guidelines because all questions had been answered and if they had additional questions, they could forward them to NCAA staff.

UNLV's counsel, Mike Leavitt, traveled to Colorado and Kansas City in attempts to meet with NCAA officials and get a copy of the rules and procedures. "Finally," Leavitt said, "we were told by David Berst that the infractions committee had decided to deny our request for policies and procedures, notwithstanding the fact that we had been promised them five months before." In other words, UNLV had to conduct its own investigation not knowing what the rules were of this very high-stakes game.

Lois: "I believe all of this was a purposeful action orchestrated by Warren Brown, who was in charge of enforcement at the time. If a university is given very little concrete guidance, mistakes are more likely to be made, and they can be construed by NCAA investigative staff to indicate a lack of objectivity on the part of the university or an act of obstruction on the part of the individual. For example, early in the investigation, we were receiving numerous calls from individuals concerning actions of NCAA investigators. I would make notes on these calls and give them to university personnel. Then I realized that NCAA investigators were trying to make it appear that we were influencing what these people said. After that, whenever we got a call, I immediately gave the caller the telephone number of the university lawyer and asked the person to call the attorney.''

Tarkanian was both angry and hurt by the NCAA. He wondered why the NCAA investigators were ''making things up.'' He wondered why they were calling him vile names, why they wouldn't accept the answers they received from the various players. He thought that the NCAA would only listen to the answers they wanted to hear and that they ignored anything to the contrary. Ultimately, Tarkanian was convinced that he was being harassed by the NCAA, and he planned to battle them for both his job and his reputation.

Tarkanian believes that the NCAA's investigation of him was more than business; it was personal. One piece of evidence comes from the autobiography of former UCLA star Bill Walton, which was co-written by Jack Scott. Scott wrote, ''UCLA players were so well taken care of—far beyond the ground rules of the NCAA—that even players from poor backgrounds never left UCLA prematurely [for the pros] during John Wooden's championship years. If the UCLA teams of the late 1960s and early 1970s were subjected to the kind of scrutiny that Jerry Tarkanian and his players have been, UCLA would probably have to forfeit about eight national championships and be on probation for the next 100 years.'' Walton himself commented, ''I hate to say anything that may hurt UCLA, but I can't be quiet when I see what the NCAA is doing to Jerry Tarkanian only because he has a reputation of giving a second chance to many black athletes other coaches have branded as troublemakers. The NCAA is working day and night trying to get Jerry, but no one from the NCAA ever questioned me during my four years at UCLA.''

If Walton had been questioned by the NCAA, it would have been something he'd never forget. Here is Reggie Theus's account of being interrogated by the NCAA:

Reggie Theus: ''The NCAA was looking into UNLV. I was called into the president's office and there was a big round table full of people sitting around it, and they all fired one question after another at me. The NCAA was something else—they tried to make it look like the Contras investigation or something. I can't remember most of the specific things they asked me, but I remember their tone. They tried to trap me into saying things. They wanted to sucker me into saying what they wanted to hear. They'd ask me if I was getting money or something and I'd say no. A minute later, they'd ask me the same thing again in a slightly different way. They refused to accept what I said and they tried to make me feel like I'd done something wrong. It was awful. The NCAA had a terrible attitude. They really wanted to scare and intimidate you."

Al McGuire had this to say about the NCAA in the November 28, 1977 issue of *Sports Illustrated:*

The main thing they should change is the way they can blackmail a school on probation into releasing its coach. You shouldn't take a man's livelihood away from him....The NCAA does it like Pontius Pilate; it pretends to be washing its hands when it is really saying, "Crucify that guy." My main problem with the NCAA is that it has no respect for coaches. If a coach went to a leper colony, they wouldn't send him five dollars.

The NCAA has incredible powers to force a school to inflict punishment upon a coach or player. The University of Minnesota case is a notorious obvious example. When the University of Minnesota was found guilty of NCAA violations, the university was directed by the NCAA to take certain actions against three student athletes. University president John McGrath stated that due process hearings would have to be held at the university according to school policy. Before a 1977 congressional subcommittee, McGrath stated that a top-ranking NCAA official told him to go ahead and hold the hearings, "then you reach the right decision."

As it turned out, the due process hearing did not result in suspension of the players. The NCAA then directed that not only the Minnesota men's basketball team but all men's teams at Minnesota would be on "indefinite probation" until the "suggested" punishment of the NCAA was met. Still Minnesota did not buckle under, so the NCAA went further. Citing an obscure "Section 10" ruling that any member of a conference had to be in good standing with the NCAA, it directed that all schools in Minnesota's Big Ten conference would be ineligible for post season competition if they played Minnesota. With that, President McGrath stated that ashamed as he was, he had to give in to the dictates of the NCAA and make those players ineligible.

Tarkanian had announced that he was leaving Long Beach for UNLV on March 23, 1973. NCAA records show that six days later, the UNLV files were reopened ("activate case No. 443") by the enforcement staff. Appearing in those files was a March 24, 1973, newspaper article detailing Tarkanian's move to UNLV.

These are some of the reasons why Tarkanian has long insisted that the NCAA had a vendetta against him. He has a file cabinet jammed with sworn affidavits to prove it.

Here is a sampling:

I was summoned by [NCAA investigator] David Berst to meet with him and [NCAA investigator] Lester Burks about their investigation of violations of NCAA by Long Beach State College.... Berst stated that they wanted me to assist them in the investigation of Tarkanian because they heard I was unhappy with him and they wanted to get Tarkanian. I explained that I knew of no wrong things by Tarkanian and asked who told them that I had bad feelings toward Tarkanian. They said they would not reveal this information. Lester Burks stated that Tarkanian was exploiting black athletes. Berst said that they didn't have enough on Tarkanian yet, but they really wanted to get him.... In another meeting, Berst told me to tell other players that if they gave [the NCAA] information on Tarkanian, the player would get immunity even if the school went on probation. He [Berst] would see that [the players] would get into another college.... As I recall, Berst said something like Tarkanian was obsessed with abusing athletes from junior college all the way up and that the NCAA had a responsibility so stop this. Tarkanian would be an example to show the NCAA doesn't give up and this would deter other coaches.... He said, "It's the Big Guy I want."... He said that Tarkanian didn't belong in coaching because he abused black athletes and that he'd make sure the NCAA followed Tarkanian wherever he went.
—*Arthur Montgomery [Dr. Ahman Rahn], a former Long Beach player under Tarkanian and later chairman of the black studies department at Long Beach State, November 9, 1976*

An NCAA investigator came to see me and told me that a lot of ballplayers in Long Beach were unhappy and that the NCAA was trying to get evidence against Tarkanian. He told me: "Why do you want to stay loyal to Tarkanian? All he ever did was screw you. Look at what he did to you. We're out to get Tarkanian and we're going to hang him."
—*Dwight Taylor, a former Long Beach player, February 8, 1974*

On May 5, 1973 at approximately 11:45 at Long Beach City College while I was attending the Southern California Interscholastic

Basketball Coaches Clinic, the following statement was made by [college coach] Jim Harrick: "An NCAA investigator was on campus talking to Jackie Robinson...when he was down, he said the NCAA was checking up on Tarkanian, and that they were out to get Tarkanian."
—*Robert Espinoza, a former basketball coach at San Dimes High School, April 4, 1974*

Investigator David Berst talked with me when I left UNLV [and transferred to Hawaii] and threatened me that if I did not cooperate with his investigation, I would not be able to go to any other school under the jurisdiction of the NCAA.
—*Jimmie Baker, former UNLV basketball player, June 17, 1976*

David Berst told me that Tarkanian was a man who shouldn't be in basketball. He said, "Tarkanian is bad for the game. Personally, I don't like the man."...He said, "I'm out to get Tarkanian." He later told me, "I've got you now. I got all the stuff against you. You're dead...Roscoe, if you help me get Tarkanian and Long Beach, I won't submit enough evidence to convict you and you'll still be able to play....I'm going to get Tarkanian if it takes the rest of my career."...This made me feel like I should make up something [on Tarkanian] to keep him [Berst] off me.
—*Roscoe Poindexter, a former Long Beach player, August 31, 1976.*

When Jerry Tarkanian and Long Beach were under investigation by the NCAA for alleged rules infractions, Investigator Berst questioned me and examined some of my records. Upon his departure, after finding everything in order, he stated to me that: "This time you had time to doctor the records, but don't worry, some day I am going to get you and your friend." The friend he had in mind was Jerry Tarkanian.
—*Vic Weiss, a friend and adviser of Jerry Tarkanian, May 5, 1976*

Many other affidavits make the same point.

One of the most telling revelations about the NCAA's case against Tarkanian came from veteran college basketball coach Norm Sloan, who testified under oath in front of the United States House of Representatives Oversight Committee during its hearings on the NCAA in 1978. Sloan told the committee that assistant NCAA director Bill Hunt had visited him in his office at North Carolina State. Sloan testified that Hunt said, "We're not only going to get him [Tarkanian], but we're going to run him out of coaching." Sloan said that Hunt's face turned red when he discussed Tarkanian.

Sloan, who was subpoenaed to appear before the subcommittee, said he was shocked that Hunt would make such a statement. He also testified that he had hesitated about coming forward because he did not want to anger the NCAA. "The NCAA is very powerful and has a good deal of influence in my life or that of any other coach. I just don't think it is a healthy situation to have those people upset at you."

Tarkanian was obviously upset by the things he heard, and he kept hearing them day after day, night after night, year after year, almost from the moment he left Long Beach for UNLV. One former player remembers an NCAA investigator saying, "Tarkanian is like a pimp to you players." David Berst had referred to Tarkanian as a "rug merchant."

Furthermore, the NCAA continually asked Tarkanian's former players if they received cash, cars, or clothes while they played for him. The players continually denied the charges. After a while, the NCAA attacked the players for "protecting" Tarkanian. In one instance, NCAA investigators questioned former University of San Francisco center Bill Cartwright, asking Cartwright if Tarkanian had given him $10,000. At that point, Tarkanian had never talked to Cartwright and had not recruited him, which is what Cartwright told the NCAA.

Between 1973 and 1976, rumors and NCAA leaks continually appeared in newspapers, hinting that the NCAA was about to lower the boom on UNLV. When the charges finally came out, they covered five years, two different athletic directors, two different coaches, and two different university presidents.

UNLV president Donald Baepler: "After all the years of rumors of impending disaster, it was almost a relief to find out what we were being charged with. But it was especially frustrating to the university investigators to find out that the NCAA would furnish no specific information to aid the university in its own investigation. We found no evidence to support the NCAA's charges. The NCAA's sources were not revealed, and the NCAA did not cooperate in giving the university a copy of the procedures to follow."

Tarkanian and his lawyer, Sam Lionel, worked quickly. UNLV's probation and the NCAA's order to suspend Tarkanian for two years were announced on August 26, 1977. A week later, Congressman James Santini (Democrat, Nevada) said that the House Oversight Committee would start investigating the enforcement and investigation practices of the NCAA.

Santini and the House were beginning to put some political pressure on the NCAA. The legal pressure came from Sam Lionel, who filed for an injunction in a Clark County district court to protect Tarkanian's job. Both Lois and Jerry describe Lionel as a "savior." "His intelligence, commitment, and caring saved us," said Lois.

On September 30, 1977, Judge James Brennan ruled against the NCAA and ordered that Tarkanian remain as coach at UNLV. This is an abridged version of Brennan's ruling:

> The case against Tarkanian was incredible....The evidence the NCAA presented was 100 percent hearsay without a scrap of documentation in substantiation....The evidence shows that every fundamental principle pertaining to the plaintiff's due process rights were violated. The Committee on Infractions and its staff conducted a star chamber proceeding and a trial by ambush against the plaintiff....The plaintiff was denied the specific charges against him and the facts upon which such charges are based. The plaintiff was denied the right to present evidence and call witnesses in his behalf. And most important, he was denied the right to be confronted by the witnesses against him and cross-examine them....
> The Committee on Infractions allowed a staff investigator, who the evidence clearly shows, swore he would get Tarkanian if it was the last thing he ever did, to act as investigator, judge and jury....
> The so-called Pink File...shows how David Berst threatened, coerced, promised immunity, promised rewards to athletes in his effort to obtain derogatory information against the plaintiff. There is strong evidence which suggests that in their zeal to "Get Tarkanian," the investigative staff tried hard to divert athletes away from UNLV and Tarkanian, to other institutions, who had offered these athletes patently illegal considerations in exchange for their athletic talents....The record is replete with lies, distortions and half-truths....The evidence clearly shows Berst as a man possessed and consumed with animosity toward the plaintiff....There is no legal credible evidence to support the findings and action of the NCAA.

As an interesting sidelight to this case, the NCAA had decided not to be a part of the court action. So the NCAA ordered that UNLV suspend Tarkanian. That's why the Clark County court case was *Tar-*

kanian v. UNLV, although university officials believed that their coach was innocent of the NCAA's charges.

Lois: "Judge Brennan's decision was a relief. I don't recall our being in court for anything before, and to be involved in an actual trial of such importance to our family was a tremendous strain on all of us. The day after the trial result appeared in the media, we received dozens of calls from people supporting us. About mid-morning someone called for Jerry. I explained Jerry was not home at the time and asked who was calling. 'Frank,' the caller said. 'Frank who?' I asked. 'Frank Sinatra' was the reply. I couldn't believe it at first. Sinatra went on to say how pleased he was with the trial result and that we had his full support. He was extremely cordial and sincerely interested in what was happening to us. That call wasn't all he did. During the congressional hearings, he had an attorney, Vince Chiefo, attend the sessions with us as we attempted to determine what would be the best direction to take legally."

The NCAA wanted UNLV to appeal Judge Brennan's ruling in the Nevada state district court, which UNLV did. The ruling was appealed to the Nevada Supreme Court, which took a very narrow legal stance. It ruled that the NCAA should have been a party to the case along with UNLV, since the NCAA's investigation had led to Tarkanian's being suspended by UNLV. Then the Nevada Supreme Court ruled that the case be returned to the district court, with the NCAA as part of the action, meaning that Brennan's ruling stood.

The ruling was made on May 17, 1979, nineteen months after the first district court ruling. So what happened in those nineteen months? From a legal standpoint—nothing. Tarkanian was still the coach at UNLV because of the injunction order by district judge James Brennan. But the other NCAA sanctions against UNLV—no postseason play and no national television appearances—were in force.

In between the two court rulings, the House Oversight Committee began its investigation of the NCAA. The hearings began on February 27, 1978, with a variety of coaches appearing from such schools as Mississippi State, Michigan State, and Minnesota. The message from the coaches and other university officials was the same as Tarkanian's: the NCAA doesn't inform the institution of the charges in advance; often the charges are leaked to the press before being presented to the schools; the school does not have a chance to learn the identity of its accuser or to cross-examine its accuser; the NCAA's evidence is often hearsay and recollections of conversations that investigators had with witnesses. NCAA investigators Berst and Bill Hunt admitted under oath that "no" institution, or "perhaps one" in their memory, had ever been found completely innocent once the investigative staff had initiated an "official inquiry" on campus.

According to Arthur Reynolds, chairman of the NCAA infractions committee when the UNLV case was heard, "It is well understood by the enforcement staff that when a violation is not admitted by the institution, the enforcement staff must carry the burden of proof and they must convince the Committee on Infractions that the available evidence supports the finding of a violation." That just wasn't the procedure in the UNLV case and in some other cases, which appalled the House Oversight Committee.

Tarkanian appeared before the House Oversight Committee on June 9, 1978. His message was a strong one: the NCAA rules don't allow a coach to do as much for a player as a professor can do to help a regular student. Tarkanian talked about his philosophy of coaching—that a coach has to be involved in the lives of his players, that there must be a real closeness. "The NCAA takes the humanism out of coaching," he said. Once again, problems with the NCAA investigative techniques were discussed.

What were the results of the hearings?

The House committee made several recommendations to the NCAA, suggesting basically that the organization adopt a more legalistic approach to its investigations, such as giving the school under investigation certain due process rights. There were several specific suggestions about how the NCAA could achieve this, some of which were adopted and some of which weren't.

Remember that the NCAA is the most powerful athletic entity ever to exist. Consider all the universities that come under its jurisdiction. Also, it has an iron grip over its members. A school can withdraw from the NCAA, but where can it go? If a university wants to play major college athletics, it must play ball with the NCAA. It has no other choice.

Lois: "I think that the congressional hearings did some good. They provided a forum where complaints about the NCAA could be made public, not just by UNLV but by many schools. The NCAA was worried about the hearings. They care about what Congress thinks about them, and the NCAA did change some of their procedures after the hearings. Of course, the NCAA said they were in the process of making the changes anyway, but I believe the hearings had a lot to do with making the NCAA adopt some reforms.

"For years, NCAA enforcement officials, including Walter Byers, had ridiculed any criticism of the enforcement process by stating that only those caught cheating complained. Yet under oath before the congressional subcommittee, highly respected individuals never investigated by the enforcement staff told of their concerns about NCAA enforcement practices. This group included former NCAA president John Fusak. Mickey Holmes, then Missouri Valley Conference commissioner and current College Football Association president, told of requesting a blue-ribbon committee to evaluate the NCAA enforcement program. He told of the resistance he met from executive director Walter Byers and his assistant Bill Hunt.

"A megaton of facts taken under oath and subpoena was collected during the subcommittee hearing, and subcommittee counsel, particularly John Adkinson and James McLain, did an excellent job in the hearings and in preparing a set of recommendations. The sad thing is that so little of that wealth of information was given much exposure in the media. But anyone following the hearings or reading through the transcripts would find a very insightful, well-documented picture of how the NCAA enforcement process works. They also would find a perfect example of a phenomenon described by management specialist Peter Drucker: service 'line' specialists becoming overly powerful in bureaucracies that grow rapidly in size and complexity.

"But much has changed in the NCAA since the hearings. The most promising change is the fact that William Shultz is now the executive director. There always have been many good parts to the NCAA, and now Jerry and I both feel that Shultz will make the good parts even stronger and also not be afraid to objectively assess the weak areas and correct what needs to be corrected. We believe he will take a more humanistic direction while still maintaining integrity. We met him personally and he seems to be someone who really understands what it is like being a student athlete, a coach, or an athletic director. He has the leadership ability, strength, and caring to make a difference. I only hope he doesn't get swallowed up in it all."

The *Tarkanian v. UNLV-NCAA* case didn't come to court again until June of 1984, when Nevada District Court Judge Paul Goldman came out strongly in favor of Tarkanian. He said that the NCAA's tactics "might be considered efficient, but so was Adolph Eichmann and so is the Ayatollah," and that the NCAA "entertained actual bias and prejudice" against Tarkanian.

Judge Goldman was livid about David Berst's reference to Tarkanian as a "rug merchant," considered an ethnic slur toward Armenians. Goldman told Berst, "The name of the Plaintiff is Tarkanian. The name of the Chief Justice of the State of Nevada is Noel Manoukian and the name of the Governor of the State of California is George Deukmejian. All are Armenian and there isn't a rug merchant among the three."

Berst also was scolded during the trial for continually answering questions by saying, "I don't recall." Judge Goldman even threatened him with contempt of court in order to make him more responsive. In addition, the verdict brought an award of $290,000 to Tarkanian to cover his legal fees to be paid by the NCAA.

The frightening thought is that this trial took place eight years after UNLV was placed on probation—and twelve years after the NCAA first started investigating Tarkanian. The NCAA had lost not once but twice in court. But it appealed again, this time to the Nevada Supreme Court. In this case, UNLV refused to be a party, so it was *NCAA v. Tarkanian*. And in 1987, the Nevada Supreme Court ruled in favor of Tarkanian. That didn't discourage the NCAA, which appealed the case for a fourth time—to the United States Supreme Court, which is expected to hear the case in the late fall of 1988.

The United States Supreme Court refused to hear the case on five of the six issues on which the NCAA appealed, but did agree to hear the case on the issue of whether or not the NCAA was "state action." An organization considered to be "state action" is required by the U.S. Constitution to provide certain rights to individuals, including due process. Private organizations are not required to do so. The United States Supreme Court let stand the Nevada Supreme Court ruling that Tarkanian had been denied his due process rights.

So the Tarkanian case has gone far beyond the issue of a coach's suspension, and may even occasion a landmark decision regarding the protection of individual rights.

The Lakers came calling again for Tarkanian in the summer of 1979. Jack Kent Cooke had sold the team to Jerry Buss. Like Cooke, Buss wanted Tarkanian for his coach. The reasons were obvious:

- Tarkanian is colorful and good with the media.
- Tarkanian coaches the running game, which is crucial to life in the NBA. Tarkanian also knows that it is the players who

win, not the coach. He gives the players freedom to use their great gifts and doesn't let his coaching ego get in the way of the athletes.

Buss had several meetings with Vic Weiss, Tarkanian's lifelong friend who also handled some of his business dealings.

Tarkanian: "The first time the Lakers offered me the job, it was a five-year deal for $350,000. This time, it was still five years guaranteed, but the money was $1 million. That was exactly what I told Vic Weiss I needed in order to take the job, and Vic called me to say that the Lakers were willing to pay. The only loose end was season tickets. They were offering me four, and I wanted ten. For every two season tickets you get a car. So four tickets meant two cars, but I wanted one for my daughter, one for my wife, and one for myself. I also wanted tickets for my brother. When Jerry Buss bought the team, I met with him and we got along great. Looking back, I think I should have taken the job right on the spot. I wanted it. The money was what I had asked for. Magic Johnson was coming out of Michigan State, and he was ready to join the team. I knew that Magic had a chance to be the greatest player ever, and I used to stay up at night thinking about how it would be to coach him. I knew the timing was perfect."

Vic Weiss had one last meeting with the Lakers about the season ticket question. The Tarkanians drove from Las Vegas to the Balboa Bay Club in Newport Beach, where they were supposed to meet with Weiss for dinner. Weiss was supposed to bring the final copy of the Lakers contract for Jerry to sign. Amazingly, the news had not leaked.

"Then Vic never showed up," says Tarkanian. "That was unlike Vic, but he had told us he was meeting his wife, Rose, in Pasadena later in the evening, so we just thought that he had been delayed with Buss and had gone directly to meet Rose. We spent the late afternoon and evening at the Balboa Bay Club.

"Then at two in the morning we received a call from Rose. She asked if Vic was still with us. My heart sank. I knew that Vic would never miss meeting me and Rose too."

Tarkanian made several calls, but no one had seen or heard from Vic Weiss. For three days, he was missing. Then his body was found in the trunk of a Rolls Royce in the parking lot of the Sheraton Universal, a hotel near Universal City Studios. Weiss had been killed and the murder is still unsolved. Police said that Weiss had no criminal record and no connections with organized crime. They thought the killing might somehow be related to professional boxing, as Weiss had managed several fighters.

"Vic wasn't an agent, at least not like you think of most agents," says Tarkanian. "He was just a kid I grew up with. He lived two blocks away from me in Pasadena. We used to go to school together and we became very close friends. He was a successful businessman. He owned a couple of automobile dealerships. He became a millionaire and he loved sports, so he'd come to a lot of my games. He negotiated my contract with UNLV. Vic also was involved in the fight game, and many people think that it was his connection with the boxing world that led to his being killed. His death shattered me."

It also caused the world to know that Tarkanian had been talking to the Lakers, since it was reported by the newspapers that Weiss was last seen driving away from the Beverly Comstock Hotel, where he had just met with Jerry Buss and Jack Kent Cooke.

"For a couple of weeks, I didn't want to think of any job," Tarkanian remembers. "I was just shocked by what happened to Vic. But in that time, the people from Vegas had learned about the Lakers' offer and they went to work trying to keep me. A few UNLV boosters, particularly Irwin and Susan Molasky, said things that really opened my eyes. These people had stuck by me during my trial with the NCAA and then during the probation. They said that we were going to court again with the NCAA, and this time we would really beat them. My attorney said that if I left now, after all the work he had done, the NCAA would claim that they had won and I was running away to the pros. Another booster said the timing wasn't right for me to leave, not after the whole town—make that the whole state of Nevada—had backed me. So I went to Jerry Buss and told him that I wanted to take the offer, but I felt an obligation to the people of Vegas to stay because they had stood by me. I said I wanted to get my case with the NCAA resolved, and then maybe I'd like a shot at the Lakers job. But that never happened, because Magic Johnson came in, the Lakers became a great team, and that was that. They didn't need another coach. Had Vic Weiss not been killed, I would have been gone. But after he was murdered, there was time for me to think, and that's when I changed my mind."

Danny Tarkanian: "I remember Dad saying that he was going to stay at UNLV and fight the NCAA until death if necessary. That was how strongly he felt about winning his case. He said he'd rather beat the NCAA than win an NBA championship."

During the 1970s, the Tarkanians had their emotions under siege. Not once, but twice, they had to decide if they should jump to the NBA

187

and the Los Angeles Lakers. Then there was the death of Vic Weiss. But what really took away a piece of their heart was the fight with the NCAA. It hurt Jerry, but it almost destroyed Lois.

Lois: "Jerry felt bad during the investigation, but he really didn't know how to fight it. He wasn't much help when it came to learning how the NCAA worked and what was happening to him. That pretty much fell to me. What we did in fighting the NCAA was what the American ideal tells you to do. They came after us, and we thought we had been wronged. So we took it to court and we took it to Congress. That's how it works in this country. We fought to protect our name and our integrity. We did everything we could to protect ourselves from these attacks. But even though we won in court, I don't think you ever win totally. Some people will always attach a stigma to us. I suppose that's one of the things that bothers me the most.

"During this ordeal I became an expert on the NCAA. I was obsessed by it. It was the only thing I did. I wasn't doing any real work professionally; I wasn't keeping a clean house; I wasn't an especially good mother or wife. For me, it was all the NCAA. I read every book I could on the organization. I kept volumes of information. I had real periods of depression. It was like a cancer for me. I didn't go out, and day and night all I thought about was what the NCAA was doing to us. I'd say it wasn't fair, I'd say it wasn't right. Over and over, I thought that. Then I'd cry. That didn't make me a very effective person. From about 1974 until 1979, all I did was work on our case with the NCAA. At the end of that time, I hit bottom.

"What saved me was that a friend of mine, Dr. Joan Owen, who was a psychologist, talked me into going to work on my Ph.D. I have always loved school and education, and it was great going back to classes, to be with all kinds of new people. These people weren't associated with sports. They didn't care what happened to the basketball team or what was going on with the NCAA. They were in school to probe different facets of life. I attended a small university in San Diego where the programs emphasized psychology and appropriate use of human resources in management and education. A part of me started to rekindle that I had let die. I was challenged again to think, to read deeply, and to produce papers.

"Sure, I still thought about the NCAA. Some of my studies were related to it. One of my classes was on conflict, and I wrote about conflict with the NCAA. I studied the subject of power—its acquisition, uses, and abuses. When it came to the NCAA, I was at first irrational. I thought the NCAA must all be bad guys, to have let our situation happen, not to have cared enough to take the time to examine all the facts carefully. Then I began to realize that in our situation, the real problem lay in the closeness between the NCAA investigators and the infractions committee members. They were friends. They worked together for years at a time. They socialized. How could the committee be objective? They were certainly going to believe people they'd worked with a long time, rather than strangers who were appearing before them for the first time and about whom they'd already been given negative misinformation. David Berst stated at the 1977 congressional subcommittee hearings that he had just spoken earlier to a 'friend,' and then went on to reveal that the 'friend' was an infractions committee member. It's difficult to obtain an objective hearing concerning accusations against you if your accusers are 'friends' of those who determine guilt or innocence.

"And then, when we began to present our information about improper actions of the investigative staff, I think the committee took a defensive posture. One infractions committee member frankly admitted in court that he had made up his mind against UNLV before any hearings took place because of UNLV's attacks upon the NCAA staff.

"I think a defensive posture became the mind-set with the infractions committee and the NCAA council. Rather than question with both sides present, the NCAA council questioned only Byers and his staff, and naturally, got answers supporting the staff's point of view. A few brave souls questioned what happened, particularly James Frank, who eventually served as NCAA president; but Byers vehemently protected against any outside, objective evaluation, and no one challenged him.

"It appears that NCAA staff members do not hold the same standards for themselves as they do for athletes. And this is what still bothers me. I remember what happened to our players who went to the 1977 Final Four. They were among the greatest kids in the country, and they worked so hard to reach that goal. The NCAA hounded them with questions and requests, and they investigated those kids more than any other group had been investigated. Those players and their girlfriends and wives spent days and sometimes weeks finding canceled checks or receipts to prove they had paid rent and utilities two or three years earlier. Because of 'leaks' to the media, these young men were never given the respect they deserved and were usually regarded with suspicion in the media. When we got to Atlanta for the Final Four, it was worse. We lost by one point to North Carolina. I keep thinking that a partial release of that pressure on them could have resulted in a couple more points.

"And what violations did the NCAA find after the most extensive—

and expensive—investigation of these young men? In the end, only one charge was made regarding any member of that team. The charge was that Eddie Owens had been 'provided an automobile for his personal use for an evening at no cost to Owens' during his official visit to UNLV. Eddie denied that charge, and so did another recruit at the time who was with him, but again there were those 'recollections' of supposed conversations, and they carried all the weight.''

The probation also staggered the UNLV basketball program.

"We had Albert King all lined up,'' says Al Menendez. "He was ready to come to Las Vegas until the probation came down. Then he went to Maryland.''

The Rebels' first year (1977–78) under probation was the last season for Reggie Theus at UNLV. As a junior, he averaged 19 points for a team that was 20–8.

Reggie Theus: ''Probation was probably the main reason I went into the NBA hardship draft. I knew it was going to be a bad situation for the program. I had accomplished quite a bit at UNLV. I was already an All-American. There wasn't much more for me or the team to do, because probation meant we couldn't take part in the NCAA tournament. When I told Tark that I was going into the draft, he didn't believe me at first. Then it sunk in that I was leaving, and it shook him up. I know he was hurt because he thought I had been an integral part of the program, and the last thing he needed was to lose me on top of all the trouble he was having with the NCAA. So I guess it should be no surprise that he wasn't happy when I told him that I was leaving. Tark saw me grow up, and he thought, 'Reggie would never do that to our program.' But it reached the point where Reggie had to start thinking about Reggie first, and Reggie Theus knew that the NBA was the next stop for him. Also, I knew that I could leave Tark, because we had a very good, up-front relationship. He was always straight with me and I was straight with him. As I said, I never took any money or anything from him or the program, so I didn't feel obligated to stay. And with what the NCAA did to our program, it was time for me to leave.''

So the NCAA's probation probably cost UNLV one more year of Reggie Theus. And who knows how else the two years without national television appearances or NCAA tournament appearances cut the heart out of Tarkanian's program?

Tarkanian: ''It knocked us for a loop, because we were on the verge of becoming a national power. Our running style of play was attracting a lot of attention and a lot of good high school players. When people saw us run and press on television, they liked it. But the probation killed that exposure. There were rumors that I would leave UNLV for an NBA job, or that the NCAA would get me fired. So when we recruited a kid, it was tough. The kid may have liked our coaches, our school, and our program, but assistant coaches from other schools would come in and tell the kid, 'You don't want to go to Vegas. Tark won't even be there. The NCAA is trying to get him fired. He might go to the pros.' So we ended up taking kids who were pretty good athletes, but were hard kids to coach. They just weren't solid people, and it is the only time when I was at Vegas that I could say we didn't have all good kids on the team. Some of these kids just weren't fun to coach and they weren't fun to be around. I know we won 20 games with them except for one year, but that didn't change the fact that coaching them wasn't fun.

"With me, the most important thing is playing hard. But you can't build pride with kids who aren't solid. If they don't have pride, they won't play hard. I mean, some of our kids were just plain goofy. You can't deal with a goofy kid, because to him, two plus two isn't four. And I don't mean intellectually. It's a way they look at life. You can't reason with a person who doesn't understand that two plus two is four. If you have a couple of these kids, you can surround them with good people and bring them around. But we had five or six at a time, and that was too many. That's why it was such a relief when the probation period was over [in 1979]. Then I knew I could go out and really recruit some good kids and get our program back where it should be."

12

Recruiting

Unlike some coaches, Jerry Tarkanian doesn't mind recruiting.

Tarkanian: "I've heard coaches say that recruiting is the most difficult and the worst part of coaching, but I don't look at it that way. I like
going out and meeting the kids, their parents, and their coaches. It's a
nice break from the other aspect of college coaching. You have three seasons: the coaching portion, when you have practice and games; the part
of the year you spend at clinics and speaking engagements; and the recruiting segment. I like going out and watching kids play. I enjoy sitting
down with a player and his parents, talking about basketball, school, and
life in general. Usually I feel very good about recruiting.

"What I don't like is negative recruiting. How can you go into a
family's home and tell them how great your school is, how much character you have, and how much you value integrity, and then in the
next breath tear down another coach and his program? What do you
really know about the other coaches and programs?

"Finally, what does negative recruiting say about the people who
use it?

"I won't recruit a transfer who knocks his coach. If I were a kid,
I wouldn't consider a college whose representatives knock other
schools. Not everyone uses negative recruiting, and I won't allow it
at UNLV. I strongly believe that a coach should concentrate on selling his own program, explaining the merits of his university and his
basketball team. It's important for a kid to understand how he would
fit in at the school and with the team.

"At UNLV, we have been the victim of some negative recruiting. Some people wonder about going to school in Las Vegas, and they wonder if there really can be a legitimate university in a town like Las Vegas.

"Two kinds of people ask these questions:

• People who have never been to Vegas.

• People who spent a weekend in Vegas and never left the Strip.

"I know what kind of program we run and what kind of university we have. Las Vegas is a great town. It has 600,000 people, 12 high schools, more churches and Boy Scout members per capita than any city its size in the country, and a clear, blue sky almost every day.

"What about the casinos?

"Hotels, casinos, and tourists are some of our main industries. They are what steel was to Pittsburgh and the auto industry was to Detroit, and it's not fair to judge Detroit or Pittsburgh just on the areas where you find the mills and factories. The hotels are our factories. That doesn't mean that people in Vegas are compulsive gamblers—far from it, as most people who live in Vegas only visit the casinos when they have out-of-town visitors. In all my years of coaching at UNLV, we've had only one scholarship player with a gambling problem. Remember, in Las Vegas, the players can't hide. Everyone knows who they are because of the tremendous exposure the program receives on television and in the newspapers. Besides, if you're 6-foot-9, you don't exactly blend in. We have friends in every casino in town, and I'll get a call within ten minutes of the first time one of my kids sat down to gamble. The people in the casinos know that we don't want our kids gambling, and they make sure that the kids don't.

"The kid we had problems with was a good player. He was our sixth man and the next season he was going to start as a senior. I got three reports that he was gambling, and I raised hell with him each time. The kid denied it. He said, 'It wasn't me. I was in bed. They must be talking about another player.' You get the idea.

"Well, I was pretty sure that the kid was gambling, and the guys who called us said they knew who he was. I wanted to be certain, so I had one of my assistants follow him, and we caught the kid at 2 a.m. gambling. That was it. We wouldn't let him play his senior year. From a basketball standpoint, that hurt, because he had talent and would have made a major contribution.

"There are certain things I won't tolerate. Gambling is one, and buying players is another. We don't buy players for several reasons. First, I don't believe in it. Second, it's against the rules. Third, it just isn't right.

"Our program is based on the philosophy that we play harder than anyone we face. If you buy a kid, he won't play hard for you. I'm convinced of that. He may look great on national television or in big games, but game after game and practice after practice, the effort just isn't there. He is not a consistent player throughout the season, because he is playing primarily for himself and not for his teammates or the university. That's because he doesn't have loyalty to his coach or his university. That type of player is at a school not because it was the school he would have picked, but because he was paid to go there. So he frustrates the hell out of a coach. You have no idea if he will be paying attention or if he will be thinking about something else. That is why certain teams with great talent are so inconsistent. They beat a Top Twenty team one night and lose to a very weak school the next.

"I'm committed to loyalty. I won't take a transfer if he bad-mouths his coach or the school. I can understand if his first choice of schools wasn't the right place for him. It's so hard for an 18-year-old kid to make the right decision about college, especially when recruiters are smooth-talking him, making him promises that can never be kept. Sometimes, a kid gets in a bind. There are a lot of problems. The money has to look good to these kids. So they take the money, go to a school they didn't like in the first place, and they hate it. Or you get a kid who was recruited by one coach, and after a year that coach leaves and the kid is left out in the cold because the new coach wants to bring in his own players. Some of these kids have so many problems we can't comprehend. That's why I'll accept a transfer, but not if he rips his old school or coach. I can cope with a kid who had a tough life growing up, a kid who perhaps got into a little trouble, as long as he is loyal and has a sincere interest in UNLV.

"Loyalty also is why I seldom travel to visit recruits during the regular season. My first concern is the players we have. If a coach is constantly on the road during the regular season, how can he also take care of his team? I let my assistants take care of most of the regular-season recruiting. I'll call recruits, but I won't visit them until the spring.

"What often works for us is that other people help us recruit. Most are former players. I'd say nearly all of them are totally loyal to our program. When a recruit visits a campus and meets the current players and the former players, that often is the moment of truth. One kid will not lie to another kid. Not about the college and the coach. The loyalty of our former players and the high school and junior college coaches who have sent us players is the reason our program didn't completely crumble during the probation, and why we came back so strong. I feel particularly good when parents send both of their sons to play for me, as was the case with Sam and Jackie Robinson. Some of my former players are now coaches, and they send me kids. That's why I say loyalty is the crucial factor—from the former players, the parents, and the teachers with whom a coach has worked. That's what makes or breaks a program over the long haul, and you can't buy it.

"People ask why players are being bought in some areas of the country rather than others. Why does it happen so often in the Southeastern Conference, but not much out West? That also has something to do with loyalty. In some areas of the country, especially the South and the Southwest, kids are born dreaming of playing for their state university. Their parents, maybe even their grandparents, went to the state university. The mothers sing the school's fight song to them when they rock the kids to sleep. Children go to games with their parents from the time they're three years old. These kids grow up and attend the state university. By now, they are fanatics. They sit in the student cheering sections and they yell their lungs out. Hey, that's great; that's how it's supposed to be. Then, the kids graduate and they go into business. And then they become boosters. They love their school and they'll do anything for it, and they sometimes get carried away. Giving large sums of money to a player becomes a natural thing for them to do. They don't see anything wrong with it. That's when there's trouble. That's also why we don't usually bother to go into the South to recruit a kid. I figure we just can't beat those schools for a player.

"Most West Coast schools don't have many fanatical boosters, because most of the people are new to the area. You don't have generation after generation of families from Las Vegas or Fullerton or San Diego. The school may become important to them, but it's not in their blood. Their daddies didn't go there, and often they didn't even go there. They sort of adopt the college where they live, and that's what has happened with UNLV. The majority of our fans may never have taken a class at UNLV, but they have come to love the college because we are an important part of the community.

"Local loyalty played a part in our recruiting of Freddie Banks. Just as it is almost impossible for us to go into Kentucky and recruit a kid away from Eddie Sutton, it was tough for other schools to try and get Freddie Banks away from us. Freddie was a Las Vegas kid. His parents wanted him to play close to home and he grew up hearing about UNLV basketball. Freddie played it cool, and for a long time he refused to say where he would go, but I never had any doubts.

195

Unfortunately, there are fewer than 1 million people in Nevada, so we don't have the number of local recruits that can begin to compare with schools in bigger cities and states.

"Byron Scott, now a guard with the Los Angeles Lakers, is an example of what often happens in recruiting. He was a Los Angeles kid from Morningside High, the same school from which we signed Reggie Theus and Jackie Robinson. We had a tradition of getting kids from that high school, kids who liked our program and did well. Byron seemed to be another in that same line. He visited the campus, he talked to the coaches, everything was great. He stood up at a school assembly and announced he was going to UNLV. I was convinced that we had him, because we had been recruiting Byron for two years. We spent more time with him than any other school. Well, after he announced for us, an assistant coach from Arizona State convinced Byron to go to Tempe for a twenty-four-hour campus visit. I got really worried. Here was Arizona State coming out of nowhere, and they talked the kid into a visit. Byron goes there for one day, comes back, and says that we're out and Arizona State is in. I was amazed by what happened. It seemed strange that they got this kid in one day, after we had recruited him for two years and after he had said he was going to UNLV. The same thing happened with Michael Cooper. He had committed to us and then he disappeared to New Mexico at the last second.

"So what's the key to recruiting?

"The answer is short: you work like hell. But that hardly means it's simple. With our current budget, we can go anywhere to recruit. Travel is no longer a problem as it was in my early days at Long Beach, but I still believe that some of your best recruiting is done by telephone and through the mail. Mark Warkentien, our former recruiting coordinator from 1980 to 1987, did a great job on the phone for us. During the 1987 NCAA tournament, he had a list of five kids, and he called them during halftime of each of the games just to give them a progress report about how we were doing and to let the kids know that we were interested in them. As Mark said, it might sound strange for a coach to make a telephone call in the middle of the game, but his job was recruiting and working on the academic side. While our other coaches were handling the strategy, instead of just standing against the dressing room wall and nodding his head, he wanted to make a real contribution to the program, and the phone calls were a way to do that.

"Now that's good, aggressive recruiting. I believe in giving my assistants a lot of room to recruit. They are the guys in the field. They know what's going on, and they don't need me breathing down their necks every minute. I keep close tabs on how we're doing with the recruits, but I'll never make one of my assistants give me a minute-by-minute account of what he's doing.''

Mark Warkentien: "People laugh when I say that the elite schools such as North Carolina and Indiana don't recruit; they draft. But they do, at least when it comes to kids in their own regions. For example, Gene Bartow has done a great job at Alabama-Birmingham. On the court, his teams usually can compete with the University of Alabama. When it comes to recruiting against Alabama for the top kids in the state, Bartow probably gets about one out of fifteen. And it will never change, because Alabama-Birmingham is a relatively new school and Alabama has been there forever. Somewhere along the line, there is an Alabama alumnus or fan who has an influence on the kid. It may be his father's boss, his high school coach, or the guy down the street who buys him cheeseburgers and Cokes. But there is an Alabama guy in there somewhere, just as there is a North Carolina guy or an Iowa guy when you recruit a kid from those states. Those schools control their regions. Consequently, they have a good chance to sign the best kid in the state every year; and that means they may have three or four outstanding players from their own state on the roster in any given season.

"At UNLV, we have to go into someone's backyard every year and find a kid who is overlooked by the local schools. It means we have to out-evaluate the other schools, out-recruit them, and outwork them. We may not get the best player in the state, because he's usually locked up, but sometimes we can get one of the top five, or a kid the local college just missed. We have had a lot of kids from the Baltimore/Washington area lately—Gary Graham, Anthony Jones, and the James brothers [Keith, Karl, and Spoon]. Washington and Baltimore have never been controlled by the University of Maryland for some reason, and that makes it a great spot for us. Georgetown usually can get the best player in the area, but there is so much talent that there are plenty of good players who are interested in looking at UNLV.

"Pittsburgh also has been a good spot for us, because of Larry Anderson. We got Larry to come to UNLV, and he had a good career. Now he can help us in Pittsburgh, and so does his high school principal, Dr. Jim Robinson. When we were recruiting Armon Gilliam, things were looking good until the last minute, when people started to throw rocks at us. Armon's father is a minister, and he was worried about some of the things he heard. It was Dr. Robinson who spoke to

197

Reverend Gilliam on our behalf, and it eased Reverend Gilliam's mind. Once we have gotten a player, we usually have the total support of his family, and that is a major asset when we recruit another player from the same area of the country.

"When I go out to recruit, my first job is to figure out what the kid wants. Some kids immediately agree to a visit, because coming to Las Vegas for a few days sounds like fun. They have no intention of signing; they just want a vacation. The University of Hawaii has the same problem. They can get the top twenty players in the country to visit, but none have any intention of actually going to Hawaii. Some recruiters brag about how many homes they visited, or how many kids they got to visit their campus, as if that means something. All that matters is if the player wants to go to your school and signs.

"Sometimes a player blatantly has his hand out. He's just out to get the most he can, almost as if it were an auction. Fortunately, that doesn't happen very often. The real trouble often is someone around a kid—a parent, an uncle, a friend, a guy he calls 'my man.' I really start to worry when I hear a kid tell me that I had better talk to 'his man.' That usually means that this guy is going to try and hit us up for something, and that means the end of our recruiting.

"There are several groups of people who can be around players. The first group is the fathers, mothers, older brothers, high school coaches, and others who have the best interest of the kid at heart. They've known the kid for a long time and they really don't want anything. They are the obvious people you figure would be involved in recruiting.

"Another group is playground guys and recreation center people. One example is Lou d'Almeida, who is a very wealthy real estate developer in New York. His organization is called the Gauchos. He is a man with a social conscience; he's in it because he loves basketball and kids. He'll help stars, and he'll help those you've never heard of and never will. His main goal is to get a kid into a university or a junior college, to get him out of the slums of New York so that he has a chance to become something. Another person like that in New York is Joe Bostic. His heart is in the right place: helping the kids. Both of these men like kids and enjoy talking to big-name coaches.

"The summer coaches have become very important, because in some ways the early-signing rule has eliminated part of the control the high school coach had over recruiting. In the past, you could only sign a player during and after April of his senior year. Now the NCAA allows a kid to sign a letter of intent in November of his senior year, before he has even played a game as a senior. This has pushed recruiting up a year, and now coaches are paying close attention to kids during their sophomore and junior seasons. The early-signing period has made the summer a crucial recruiting time. You can't talk to a kid face-to-face, but you can watch him play in summer camps, AAU tournaments, and so on. That's where you meet guys like Joe Bostic. They're coaching the summer teams. The high school coach can't practice his kids in the spring and summer, and most high school coaches don't spend a lot of time watching the camps and summer leagues. Meanwhile, the kid is playing in summer league all-star tournaments at places like the University of Kentucky, or even UNLV. The kid gets a look at the campus and the city because he is there for the tournament.

"The college coach needs the summer league coach. You want the summer league coach to think well of you and your school, because he can talk to the player all the time. In most cases, the summer league coach doesn't have enough power to tell a kid where to go, but he has the influence to eliminate a school. A summer coach is with the kid all the time, which means a lot more than a couple of visits to a kid at his home or school. These guys sometimes sense their power, because a big-name college coach can't talk to their players, so they talk to them. That can be a pretty heady experience for guys who in real life have ordinary jobs, never coached at a school, and never were much in the way of players themselves. The summer coaches are, as I said, usually very good guys, and the high school coaches are very reliable people and have the kids' best interest at heart.

"What worries most coaches are the hangers-on. These guys might be from the neighborhood. They have nothing to do with basketball, and they make life miserable for the player's parents, his high school and summer coaches, and the college recruiters. These guys are the ones who cause trouble. They try to hook on to the kid and get what they can out of him. They'll call themselves agents or advisers, and they really are nothing but leeches. You can always tell who they are because they are the ones asking for money. They don't know NCAA rules and do nothing but drag a kid down.

"As a recruiter, my biggest battle is to get parents to believe that 600,000 people actually live in Las Vegas, and that they are normal people with normal jobs and enjoying their lives. What do many people think of when they hear Las Vegas? If they've never been there, they imagine the casinos, the neon signs, and the high rollers at the crap tables. That's what they see on television. If they have been here, the odds are that they rarely stepped out of the casino. Some coaches will use that negative Las Vegas image to try and keep a recruit from signing with us. This is where our current and former players step in and help us. They can give the kids and their parents a true picture of the town and the university, because they've been here. They also are the reason we've been able to overcome the negative recruiting.

"The reason we get hit with this stuff is because they can't challenge us on the major issues:

1. Coaching: Jerry Tarkanian has the winningest record ever of any college coach, and our former players love the coaching staff and our program.

2. Style of play: We like to run, and most high school kids like the running game.

3. The arena: We have one of the best facilities in the nation in the Thomas & Mack Center.

4. Fan support: We have some of the best fans in the nation. They pack our 18,500-seat arena, and they go nuts during our games. You won't find a better atmosphere for college basketball.

5. Academics: We've made such improvements and have spent so much time, effort, and money on it that we have one of the best academic support systems in the country.

"When some people visit Vegas, they act as if they have a fever. All they think about is gambling. It's like they have a monkey on their back. I'll tell recruits from California that every time they drive past a racetrack, they don't stop the car, run inside, and play the daily double. When you live near a racetrack, after a while you don't even notice it's there unless you get caught in a traffic jam. The same holds true for casinos. When I was an assistant at California-Fullerton, I drove past Disneyland every day when I went to work. That didn't mean I had to stop or that I wanted to. The fact is, a lot of people like to throw stones at UNLV. We have so much going for us—a lot more than most other schools. So the only way the other school can look good is to hammer away at us.

"The biggest problem in college basketball is that too many kids are being bought. The coaches know it, the kids know it, and I'm sure the NCAA knows it. I'm not going to name the schools that regularly buy players, because I refuse to get into any sort of finger-pointing and name-calling contests. A few years ago, there was a great high school player whom I thought we had convinced to come to UNLV.

The kid loved our running style of play, our campus—everything. I spent as much time recruiting this kid as I ever did to get a player. I felt we had him. He was talking UNLV all the time. Suddenly, we went from the top of the list to completely off the page. That's because his mother wanted money.

"Late in the recruiting season, she told me that she would give us a bargain. On a slip of paper, she wrote down, '$10,000,' and she named a certain car that she wanted in certain colors. I looked at this and told her that she had the wrong school. She said that she could get a lot more from other colleges, but her son really wanted to go to UNLV so she was making us this offer. I told her that it would never fly. The next day, I went to the house, but she wouldn't let me in. She wanted to talk to me on the front lawn. I had seen another car parked in front, so I assumed another recruiter was inside. I told her that we loved her son, but we weren't going to buy him or anyone else. I thought she might get mad or feel insulted because we were turning down her request. I was shocked when she smiled and said, 'That's all right. Those people inside will give us twice that.' She asked only that we stop talking to her son.

"A few days later we announced that we were no longer recruiting the kid, and it was picked up by the wire services. The kid let me know that he still wanted to come to UNLV, but he couldn't go against his mother, so what was he supposed to do?

"When I was hired in 1980, we were just coming off probation. Things were pretty bleak. [UNLV assistant] Tim Grgurich and I always call those the Dark Days. For years we had to operate by signing junior college transfers, kids who had left other four-year schools, and some overlooked high school players. I remember that the coaches had a meeting in 1981, and we said that if we did this right, worked our butts off, we could have the best program in the West. Ever since John Wooden left UCLA, there has been a void when it came to the best college team on the West Coast, and our goal was to become the team that the players out here thought about when someone mentioned college basketball. We weren't talking about national rankings or the Final Four, just to be the best in the West. We used to ask if a player could help us be a good team out West.

"Since we've had so much success, being ranked number one, going to the Final Four, all that has changed. Now, we look at a kid and ask if he can get us to a national championship. In one respect, the winning has made recruiting easier, because we have more legitimacy and can get into more kids' homes. But it also has made it more difficult, because we are going after a much higher-caliber player. The last couple of years, we've been trying to get the blue-chippers, and we finally have a shot at some of them.

"The kids are interested in us because they like to win and they like the national exposure. We have that, especially since most of our independent games are on national television. Also, 38 of our games in the 1986–87 season were televised either regionally or nationally. The players also like the running game, and we are among the highest-scoring teams in the nation every year. Some teams talk about running, but when you watch their games the score is 28–25 at halftime. In recruiting for UNLV, the basketball end has never been a problem.

"Sometimes it's tough to figure out what the players want. They all want to play for a good team and they don't want to sit on the bench. But after that, a lot of them aren't sure. They let recruiters come in and sell them. It's sort of like going out and buying a car. If you don't know what kind of car you want in the first place, odds are that someone will come along and sell you a car with a bunch of junk in it that you don't need, and a month later you wonder why you ever bought it in the first place. Some kids don't know what they want or need from a school, and that causes them to make bad decisions.

"So what does that mean for the coach?

"Our approach is to show the kid what we have and how that meets his needs. That's why the campus visit is crucial to us. We'll always be fighting the Las Vegas image. We encourage recruits to bring their parents along for the visit, so we can show them how the people in Vegas live. Even if they've been here before, they've never seen the real Las Vegas. A problem is that the NCAA allows you only to pay for the kid's visit, and many parents can't afford to pay for their own travel.

"On the visit, we take the recruit to the campus. It's on Maryland Parkway, and when you drive up and down that street you'd never know that you were in Las Vegas. There are no casinos, just regular stores and houses. It looks like Anaheim, California. We take the kid to all of the coaches' houses, so the recruit can see that there are neighborhoods here like in any other city. If we have a kid who is pretty sharp, I'll show him my house and say that it cost me only $60,000. Put that same home in L.A., and it will run you $100,000. It's cheaper to live out here, and we have the same kind of weather that you'll find in much of California.

"We want the kids to get to know not just the coaches, but the coaches' wives and families. We are the people who will be here if the kid needs us. One of our strongest points is that our program is like a family, and that's the last thing people expect in Las Vegas. We want

202

kids to feel free to drop over to a coach's house when they're lonely or have a problem.

"Las Vegas also appeals to black inner-city kids because there are other blacks living here. This is not a small, rural college town where the only blacks you see are on the basketball team. Also, our streets are safe, meaning kids don't have the problems found in the inner city."

Tarkanian: "Mark is right. The visits are crucial to recruiting, both our visit to the player's home and his visit to our campus. It comes down to developing a rapport with him. It works like this. First, you hear about a kid who is a good player and whom you might want to see. Next, you watch him play. If you think he would be right for your school and fit into the program, you make contact with him and try to get to know him. After talking to the kid a few times, even if it's mostly on the phone, you get a feel for him and can start to measure his interest. If he seems to like your school, you arrange a home visit in the fall of his senior year. Usually, that period is between September 17 and October 7. That's when you can walk through any major airport in the country and see college basketball coaches running from one plane to the next. We all put in a lot of air miles, or a lot of miles behind the wheels of our cars. Usually, my recruiting assistant goes with me on the visit, because I don't like to drive—I tend to get lost.

"On the home visit, we sit down with the recruit, his family, and sometimes his high school coach. That's when you start to tell the player what you think of him as an athlete and as a student, and how he would fit into the basketball program and the university. You also do a lot of listening, because the kid and his parents should have a fair number of questions. The kid usually wants to know about all the players you have coming back, and if he has much of a chance to play. He also wants to know about getting a degree.

"I like to use the visit as a time when we get to know the recruit and his parents, and they get to know us. This is a crucial step in recruiting. If the home visit goes well, then you'll have the player interested in making a visit to your school. If the home visit doesn't go well, it's pretty much over. Some recruits will have as many as fifteen coaches visit their homes, but a recruit can only visit five colleges.

"When a recruit visits UNLV, we like him to meet with our players and our ex-players, because they can sell the program better than anyone. Those kids played for the Rebels; they know what the school is like in terms of basketball and academics. The former players also know about the business opportunities in the community, and that's one of our selling points. Former UNLV players are wanted by local businesses because UNLV is such a high-profile program. Las Vegas is growing rapidly, with many different kinds of companies, and this provides a tremendous job market with a lot of different opportunities for players. It is one thing for me or one of my assistants to tell a recruit about the school, the community, and social life, but it makes more of an impact when a player or a former player talks to the kid. Players are honest with each other and they trust each other.

"At some schools, they have videotape presentations to show to recruits. They are almost like television commercials. But I really don't like those videos. I believe in personal contact—talking to a kid in my office or my home. I like visiting his home, talking to him on the telephone, or writing him letters. I don't mean form letters, because those are like the television commercials. Rather, I like to write a personal letter, even if it is just a note with a couple of lines. Letters were one area where boosters were a big plus in recruiting, but that has all changed because of a new NCAA rule. After August of 1987, only coaches and faculty members can write recruits, and that rule has hurt us. People in the community used to write a kid and his parents, the idea being to show what life is like in Las Vegas. Here is an example of a letter mailed to James Moses, a guard from California:

ERNEST A. BECKER ENTERPRISES
50 South Jones Boulevard, Suite 100
Las Vegas, Nevada 89107-2699

May 19, 1987

Mr. James Moses, Jr.
1662 Cyrene Drive
Carson, CA 90746

Dear James,

I understand you are considering joining our fabulous "Runnin' Rebels" at UNLV this Fall, but are concerned about the quality of education and life in Las Vegas.

As a businessman who has made his home in Las Vegas since 1952, and having raised four fine sons here, I would like to offer a viewpoint of our city and university other than the "bright lights" and "sports" that you undoubtedly have heard from others.

True, those of us who have lived here for many years are proud of our Rebel teams, but we are even more proud of the city we helped shape, including one of the finest universities anywhere. By most standards, both Las Vegas and UNLV are young, especially when compared to the older "traditional" cities and schools. That means, however, that we are able to shape our destiny as we like, not being hindered by "tradition."

Accordingly, we have set out to become the best, and actively and willingly support both the community and the university. Both have been growing at an incredible rate for many years, both in size and in quality. We have a clean, wholesome community that extends far beyond the lights of the casinos that made Las Vegas famous, and I urge you to look beyond the "razzle-dazzle" to find the best place to complete your education.

Welcome to UNLV and welcome to Las Vegas.

Very truly yours,

Ernest A. Becker

"The letters were very effective, especially with parents. They showed that people did more in Las Vegas than work in the casinos. Our basketball team also gets a lot of fan mail, especially from little kids, because our players make a lot of volunteer appearances in local elementary schools. It's good for the young children to see the players, because the players are heroes in this town. And it's great for the players to talk to the kids, because they discover that they have attained a certain stature in Las Vegas. Little kids look up to them, and that means the players have a responsibility not to let the kids down. We used to mail recruits copies of letters like this one:

Dear Rebles

I feel sorry that you lost. I am happy for the people that are going to grauate. You Guys got a reward didn't you? I think you're The Best Basketball players I was hoping you would win. Tark The Shark is the most lovable shark.

from
Michelle M.
Don Deru School
5-14-87

"The spelling and grammar may not be perfect, but the heart is in the right place. The little kids and the letters they write are fun, and they mean a lot to our players.

205

"Now, only university faculty and staff can write players. Here is a letter from Dr. Jerry L. Crawford of the theater department to Don MacLean, a 6-foot-10 player from Simi Valley High with a 3.2 grade point average. He is a true student athlete, the kind of player we welcome at UNLV:

COLLEGE OF ARTS AND LETTERS
DEPARTMENT OF THEATRE ARTS
University of Nevada, Las Vegas
4505 Maryland Parkway
Las Vegas, Nevada 89154

June 16, 1987

Don Mac Lean
c/o Coach Bob Hawking
Simi Valley High School
5400 Cochran St.
Simi Valley, Ca. 93063

Dear Don:

I learned from my friends Jerry Tarkanian, Mark Warkentien, and Ann Mayo that you are considering UNLV for your undergraduate education, but have questions relative to the quality of education one might anticipate at our university. Please permit me to offer a comment or two on the subject.

I have taught at UNLV for twenty five years, coming here after taking my BFA at Drake University, my M.A. at Stanford University, and my PhD at the University of Iowa. In the early years of our young school, we struggled with budget and facility limitations to develop programs in solid academic foundations. It took nearly two decades to realize, but excellent state governmental support has permitted us to now stand as an urban school rivaling the university system in your home state. Our professors hail from the likes of Harvard, Yale, Stanford, and other leading training centers; all of our programs are solid and, indeed, such areas as Hotel Management, Desert Biology, Business, and the Fine Arts rank among the best in our nation. We are fully accredited with the Northwest Accrediting Association; our facilities are second to none; our community is essentially conservative and extremely supportive; and, as you know, we harbor one of the finest basketball programs anywhere. Jerry Tarkanian and his wife, Lois, take pride in the academic progress of that program. Five of our recent seniors recently graduated; our tutorial system is solid; our athletes not only go to the Final Four, they get a quality education. Despite nonsense images of Las Vegas and our school from a hype-oriented press, I can assure you that we do not "buy" athletes or use them up and discard them. We care for athletes as students and human beings, and the factual record will prove that assertion.

Select your area of academic interest, Don, and look into UNLV with care and deliberation. I believe you could not select a better basketball program or academic institution.

With warm personal regards.

Cordially,

Jerry L. Crawford, Ph.D.

"So that's how we recruit. I stress persistence. In the summer our top recruits receive four to five letters a week. We call the kids, and our assistants watch them play. We want them to know us and to know Las Vegas. I want players to realize that we won't run them off if they get hurt or have some troubles. If we recruit a kid and he has a problem, then it's our problem, too. The only things I won't tolerate are using drugs or gambling.

"There is nothing tricky about our recruiting. That's why I laugh when I'm portrayed as some hotshot recruiter who can talk anyone into anything. I wish it were that easy. I wish all I had to do was open my mouth and kids would come to UNLV. But recruiting is a long, sometimes agonizing process. The kids are overwhelmed by promises from the coaches; the coaches worry that someone will buy a kid right out from under their nose. The kids will change their minds 100 times during their recruiting, and the coaches will wonder what they can tell the kid so he will sign a letter of intent. After a while, it is enough to drive everyone crazy."

13

Courting Sidney Green

It was January of 1979, and in three months, Jerry Tarkanian and the University of Nevada-Las Vegas would finally be off probation.

What did NCAA probation mean to UNLV?

Two years of no games on national television.

And what else did it mean?

Two years of being banned from the NCAA tournament.

And what does that add up to?

Tarkanian: "Death when it came to recruiting. I'd go into a home to talk to a kid and I'd spend the whole time explaining myself. The probation gave assistant coaches at other schools a chance to tell kids that I was going to take an NBA job, or that the NCAA was going to get me fired. Then we weren't allowed in any postseason tournaments ...it was a terrible combination. For two years, we just couldn't get anyone."

But Tarkanian realized that at the end of the 1978–79 season, the shackles of probation would be lifted.

"It was time to recruit," says Tarkanian. "I knew that we had to get out there and work harder than we ever had before to get the right kind of kids if we were going to get the program turned around."

The 1978–79 season may have been the best-ever for high school centers, and there is no better way to immediately revive a team than to sign a big man. In Harrisonburg, Virginia, there was 7-foot-4 Ralph

Sampson, who was supposed to be the next Kareem Abdul-Jabbar. In Lebanon, Pennsylvania, there was 7-foot-1 Sam Bowie, who some scouts thought would rival Sampson. And in Brooklyn, New York, there was 6-foot-9 Sidney Green.

"We never had a shot at Sampson," says Tarkanian. "We had been writing Sidney and keeping track of him, but we didn't know where he would go. Suddenly, Bowie popped into the picture."

The courtship of Sidney Green didn't get really serious until after the romance of Sam Bowie, and that romance started with a computer. Bowie had gone into his high school guidance office and filled out a form stating that he'd like to major in hotel management and was interested in a big-time basketball program where he could play immediately.

"UNLV popped out of the computer," says Tarkanian. "We weren't even recruiting him. Suddenly, Sam comes out in the newspapers and says that UNLV is one of the schools he is considering."

Naturally, Tarkanian was very happy to consider Bowie, who had not only a center's size, but the ball-handling and shooting skills of a guard.

Tarkanian: "We got Sam to come out to Vegas for a recruiting visit, and he loved it. I thought we had a real shot at him, and we set out to let him know that we really wanted him. Four times that year, I caught a midnight flight after one of our games and I'd fly all night just so I could get to Lebanon the next day at about ten in the morning. I'd sleep for about three hours, then head over to his high school to watch him practice, and to talk with him and his folks. Then I'd take another plane and fly all night to be back in Vegas in time for practice the next day."

What did Tarkanian learn from this?

"There is no quick way from Las Vegas to Lebanon, Pennsylvania," he answers.

What else?

"The best place to stay in Lebanon is the Roadway Inn."

And what else?

"Oh, do I hate to recruit against the University of Kentucky."

That lesson was driven home dramatically.

"One afternoon, we got word that Sam's father was sick," Tarkanian recalls. "I called Sam and he told me that his father was in the hospital. I told my assistant, George McQuarn, to get on a plane and go see Sam's dad."

About seven hours later, Tarkanian's phone rang.

"It was George McQuarn," says Tarkanian. "He said, 'I just got to the hospital and you won't believe this.'

"I said, 'Won't believe what?'

209

"George said, 'Kentucky is here already.'

"That's when I knew we never would beat out Kentucky for Sam. They just had too much ammunition. I mentioned that I used to stay at the Roadway Inn when I went to see Sam. Well, so did Kentucky. Leonard Hamilton was then an assistant coach at Kentucky in charge of recruiting Bowie. So I'd call him when I was in Lebanon. He always was registered, but a lot of times he was never in the room. Later I asked Leonard about that, where he was all the time. Leonard said, 'Oh, there were times when I wasn't in town. We just decided to rent out that room at the Roadway for the entire recruiting season so we could get in and out to see Sam with no problems.'

"Think about that. *Kentucky rented a motel room for the entire basketball season just so they could recruit one kid.* Boy, did that show me something about life in the big time."

The setting switched from Lebanon, Pa., to Brooklyn, N.Y., from the Roadway Inn to the apartment of Winston Karim.

Tarkanian: "After losing Bowie, we knew we had to go hard at Sidney Green. We also knew that the only way we could get a kid the caliber of Sidney was to have an in with him. We needed to know someone in his family, or someone close to him."

That someone was Winston Karim, a native of Trinidad. In the spring of 1979, he was working for a shipping company in Brooklyn. Today, he is a limousine driver.

Winston is well known to college recruiters and Brooklyn playground phenomenons. He likes kids, they like him, and sometimes he can help a kid find a college or help a coach find a player.

Winston Karim: "Some guys hanging around the playgrounds sell players to colleges. I never took anything more than some T-shirts from a coach. I do it because I like basketball. I want to help kids get into school."

It was Albert King who made Winston Karim someone college coaches needed to know. The younger brother of Bernard King of the Washington Bullets, Albert was a star from the time he was 13; he now plays for the Philadelphia 76ers.

"Albert was recruited by about a dozen different high schools," says Winston. "They were offering him money, everything. I'm talking about high schools now, not colleges."

Albert King attended Fort Hamilton High in Brooklyn, and during his last two years in school, he lived with Winston.

The home situation in that family wasn't very stable," explains Winston. "Albert said he could trust me, and asked if I would take him in. So I did. That's also when I got to know college coaches, including Jerry Tarkanian."

It was the summer of 1977, and Albert King was the subject of one of the most intense recruiting battles in the history of New York City.

"Colleges were offering me and Albert everything," says Winston. "I never would have believed it if I weren't in the middle of it. Albert didn't like dealing with recruiters that much, so he asked me to talk to a lot of the coaches. One school offered to set me up in a house and get me a $25,000 job if I could deliver Albert to them. Another school offered me a racehorse. I told the school, 'I'm from Trinidad, I live in Brooklyn, what am I going to do with a racehorse?' It was crazy. Albert was 6-foot-7 and he had pro talent at 16. Coaches were killing each other trying to get him, it was like *Can You Top This?*

"One day, Jerry and UNLV representatives came in to recruit Albert. Until I met Jerry, I had always pictured him to be like some guy from the Mafia. I had read what people wrote about this guy, what the NCAA had said, and I figured he was real shady.

"So Jerry is in there talking with me and Albert, and I keep waiting for the other shoe to drop. I mean, Jerry wasn't saying anything bad about the other schools. He wasn't criticizing the other coaches. He just talked about himself, his family, and UNLV. I kept waiting for the question. By that, I mean when coaches ask, 'Winston, what's it going to take to get Albert? Money? Cars? What?'

"To this day, people don't believe me when I tell them that Tarkanian was one of the very few coaches—and I mean very few—who was totally clean with Albert King. Almost everyone else was cheating their asses off, trying to get Albert King, but Jerry was totally clean. Frankly, I was shocked. He wasn't anything like his reputation, and it really made me wonder. Other coaches were ripping him, the NCAA was on his back, and he was playing it straight.

"You know what? Jerry would have signed Albert King, too. But it was 1977, and that's when the NCAA put UNLV on probation. The probation was the only reason Albert passed on UNLV and went to Maryland.

"Of all the major coaches I've met, the guy I feel most comfortable with, the guy I trust the most is Jerry Tarkanian. After Albert King went to Maryland, Jerry would still call me, just to see how I was doing. He didn't even ask me to get him players. Other coaches would call only if they thought I had an in with this guy or that guy. If I wasn't involved with a player, I never heard from most of them, but Jerry was different."

*   *   *

It was two years later, the spring of 1979. UNLV's probation was coming to an end, Albert King was finishing his sophomore year at Maryland, Sam Bowie was headed to Kentucky, and Sidney Green was averaging 35 points and 25 rebounds at Thomas Jefferson High in Brooklyn.

Winston Karim: "Sidney had heard from Albert King that I was a help during the college recruiting. I'd go by the playground and Sidney would yell to me, 'Hey, Winston, make me famous like you did Albert.' We used to get together and talk about college.

"Sidney was a special kid, a good kid who craved attention. There was no father in the home. His mother was a great woman, but she was from South Carolina and not used to how things worked in Brooklyn. Sidney lived with his mother and several brothers and sisters on the border of Queens and Brooklyn, known as East New York, in a little house they rented. It wasn't the worst part of Brooklyn, but it was a ghetto."

Sidney Green: "I came up tougher than most guys. If you grew up in my part of Brooklyn, you were one of two things: on drugs and stealing or a fast talker and a bit of a con man. I was a guy who could talk his way out of a lot of jams. You have a hard time trusting people. They always seemed to be jiving, to be trying to get something out of you. I learned from the guys on the street and I promised myself that I'd never make the same mistakes they did."

Sidney Green learned about the streets the hard way.

Winston Karim: "During the spring of his junior year [on May 1, 1978], Sidney and his older brother Len were walking out of a store. These guys came up from behind Len. Len turned around, put out his hand, and they shot him. Killed him right there on the sidewalk. It turned out that they knew Len, but they were junkies and they needed money to feed their habits. They were just going to rob Len, but when he put out his hand, they panicked and killed him. They were too high to even know who they were shooting. But when they saw that they had killed Len, a guy they knew, and then they saw Sidney, they just took off. Addicts are like that. They just shoot anybody. They could have killed Sidney, too.

"Sidney really admired Len, who was about seven years older. He obviously was upset having seen his brother murdered, and he even talked about quitting basketball, quitting school, going to work and supporting his mother."

Green says, "Brooklyn was too tough. I just wanted to get my mother out of there."

Winston and others convinced Green to stay in school and to keep playing ball.

"That was his only way to realize his dream," says Winston.

Sidney's mother, Lucretia Green: "I used to call Sidney 'Goofy,' because he was so tall. I love him so much. He would walk through the house, making me promises. Telling me that things would get better. He'd stop by a window, look out, and say, 'Mama, I'm gonna get outta Brooklyn. I'm gonna get us a new house and make things nice for you.' I loved it when he said those things, and I'd say, 'Well, honey, hurry up and do it.' I'd laugh, but I knew he was serious, and that made me love him even more."

Tarkanian: "We really went after Sidney in January of 1979. But we had no idea if we had a shot at the kid. Sidney and Tony Bruin, another good player, were close friends, and they played together on the Riverside Church teams in the summer. The word was that they both were going to South Carolina."

Winston Karim: "There definitely was some sort of package deal in the works for both Sidney and Bruin at South Carolina, but I never knew the details. All of a sudden, it fell apart. Everyone was talking about how South Carolina played a real slow-down game, and Sidney wanted to run."

Tarkanian received a call from Winston, updating Green's situation. South Carolina was out. But North Carolina State and Louisville were going at Green hammer and tong, and UCLA also was creeping into the picture.

"The first time I heard about UNLV was late in my junior year," Green remembers.

Winston says, "That's right. He got a letter from George McQuarn. Sidney said, 'Forget these guys.' He started talking about the probation. I told him not to judge UNLV and Tarkanian so quickly."

Tarkanian and his staff continued to write Green, and eventually his attitude toward UNLV softened, especially as the probation came to an end.

Sidney Green: "I loved the way Coach Tark recruited me. He'd come to my house and he'd talk and talk and talk. He never ran down another school or coach, and I respected him for that, because it seemed like all the other coaches were degrading each other. Listening to that stuff makes you sick after a while. I remember telling one school that I planned to visit UNLV. The coach ripped into Coach Tark, into Las Vegas, into everything that had anything to do with Jerry Tarkanian. One coach said that if I went to visit UNLV, I'd be awed by all the bright lights and the casinos and I'd sign with them right on the spot.

"All that negative stuff is part of the reason I decided to visit Vegas, and I loved it. The whole program seemed like a big family, and I especially liked Lois. The town was crazy about the team. I remember Coach Tark telling me, 'Sidney, you'll be the guy here. Why go to a school where you'll be a small fish in a big pond? This can be your pond. You come here, and you'll be the big fish.' That idea appealed to me.

"Another time, we were walking around Vegas and Coach Tark said, 'Sidney, I don't buy players. I won't give you anything extra, because we don't operate that way. But if you play hard here for four years and if you keep your nose clean and do what's right, after you graduate, this town can be yours.' Just walking around, I could see all the business opportunities."

Tarkanian: "Sidney loved his visit and he kept telling me that he was coming, but I couldn't get him to sign. He just went home to Brooklyn, and I didn't know what would happen."

Winston Karim: "I told Jerry that if he wanted to get Sidney, he had to come to Brooklyn and just stay here. You have to show Sidney that you want him. He has to see you day after day. You can't just send some assistant coach out here a few times and expect Sidney to sign a letter of intent."

Tarkanian spent a week in Brooklyn.

Tarkanian: "As usual, Sidney was telling me that he was coming to UNLV. I'd ask him to sign, but he'd say he needed more time. Finally, I had to go home for a few days because my son Danny was getting an award."

Frightened that Green would sign with another school while he was gone, Tarkanian told him, "Sidney, you gotta sign with me."

Sidney said, "I don't want to sign until May 1."

Tarkanian continued to talk with Sidney about a commitment.

Finally, Green said, "I'll sign a note."

Green scrawled a note that read: "*Coach, I'm coming. Sid.*"

To make matters worse for Tarkanian, Green handed him the note and said he wanted to visit UCLA.

"I kept thinking about all the kids I'd lost to UCLA over the years," says Tarkanian. "Never once had I beaten UCLA for a kid. I knew he would meet Sam Gilbert, and it would be over."

After another week in Las Vegas, during which Tarkanian would stare at Green's note, knowing it was worthless and also knowing that Sidney was visiting UCLA, Tarkanian made a decision: he was going to Brooklyn, and he would stay there as long as it took to get Sidney Green signed.

The month was April, and Tarkanian moved into Winston's apartment.

Winston Karim: "I was working for the shipping company then. I decided to really help Jerry. A lot of schools were trying to buy Sidney, and I didn't want that to happen to him. I trusted Jerry and I believed Jerry would be like family to Sidney. So I took two weeks of vacation to help Jerry with Sidney."

Winston and Tarkanian settled into a routine.

"Every morning, we'd get up early and go to a diner on Utica Avenue that Jerry loved," says Winston. "Jerry would say, 'Now we have to plan our day.' But it was always the same. We'd sit in my Grand Prix and follow Sidney around. We watched Sidney go to school. We hung around the school in case Sidney felt like stopping by between classes to say hello. We'd follow Sidney to the playground after school. When Sidney went home, we'd call him on the telephone. It was like this day after day, yet Jerry always talked about planning it. We could have taken our plans out of a Xerox machine."

Tarkanian: "It was amazing. A lot of times, we'd sit around the guidance counselor's office, and there were always some other coaches around, guys from Oregon, Louisville, North Carolina State, and we'd have to set up appointments to see Sidney. It could be Louisville at two, us at three, Kansas State at four, and so on. Big-name coaches were coming in from all over the place just to get a couple of minutes with Sidney."

For Tarkanian, the idea was to be seen.

"All I wanted Sidney to know was that I was there," he says. "Sometimes, he'd see me and stop by to say hi. Other times, he'd come over and we'd have a long conversation. From day one, I had a good rapport with Sidney. He liked talking to me and I liked talking to him. During the season, I'd call him all the time. Sometimes we'd talk for a few minutes and sometimes for an hour. That's why I felt good about our chances of getting him. It came down to this: I knew Sidney liked me."

Tarkanian was far from the only one on the Sidney Green trail. Louisville had been "real strong in the picture," according to Tarkanian. Or as Winston put it, "Man, Louisville was in there heavy, very heavy, pulling out all their big guns to get Sidney."

Shadowing Green for Louisville was Otis Wilson, who had attended Green's high school. Now a linebacker with the Chicago Bears, Wilson was playing football for Louisville at the time.

Tarkanian: "Otis and I used to talk all the time as we sat around waiting for Sidney to get out of class or to finish playing his game on the playground. After a while, Otis and I would meet and go to the park together to watch Sidney. We got to be good friends."

Tarkanian was subtly recruiting Wilson.

"One day, Otis said to me, 'Coach, if we don't get Sidney, I hope you do,'" Tarkanian remembers.

Lucretia Green: "From the moment I saw Tark, there was something special about him. All those other coaches, they had fancy suits and shoes and it was hard to get to know them. But Tark, he was just so lovable, with those sad eyes. You see a man like that and you just want to walk over and hug him, to make him feel better. A lot of those other coaches, I just didn't trust them, you know? Too much fancy clothes, like I said, and too much fancy talk. And they were saying such terrible things about Tark and Vegas. It was always Vegas this and Vegas that, Tark this and Tark that. They kept pressuring Sidney, 'Sign now, sign now.' Over and over. But that Tark, he just sat there and waited. He always talked to me. You know how you can just look at some people and know you can trust them? That was how it was with Tark."

When Winston and Tarkanian weren't with Sidney or Lucretia Green, they drove around the streets of Brooklyn.

"I took Jerry to the worst neighborhoods," says Winston. "I wanted him to know what kind of place Sidney came from."

One day, Tarkanian saw apartment buildings with no windows.

"Winston, do people live in there?" he asked.

"Of course they do," said Winston.

"But Winston, there's no windows."

"That's right."

"What do they do in the winter?"

"What do you think, Jerry? They freeze."

There was a long silence.

Finally, Tarkanian said, "Now I know why Sidney wants to get his mother out of here."

Winston Karim: "That really upset Jerry. He couldn't believe that people lived in such poverty. The ghettos in New York are much worse than those on the West Coast. Jerry just kept looking at those blown-out buildings and shaking his head."

Winston and Tarkanian spent a lot of time visiting various playgrounds, including Brooklyn's Foster Park, which was featured in Rick Telander's book, *Heaven Is a Playground.*

Winston says, "The first time we went to Foster Park, everyone thought we were undercover cops. I mean, what else would a white guy in my Grand Prix be doing in that part of Brooklyn? Then Jerry got out of the car, and this 10-year-old kid spotted him and ran over screaming, 'Tark The Shark! Tark The Shark!' All of a sudden, Jerry was surrounded by all these little kids wanting autographs. Jerry kept saying, 'Winston, I can't believe all these little kids know who I am.'"

Sidney Green remembers, "All the older playground legends knew Coach Tark, and they all went over and shook his hand."

And Tarkanian seemed honored to talk with guys named Helicopter and Cleanhead.

Sidney Green: "The playground guys knew that Coach Tark let his players run-and-gun, that he didn't take the game away from them. They had seen Coach Tark and his teams on television. Besides, the playground guys liked the way he looked. One guy told me that he thought Coach Tark had the look of a tough little thug, someone you wouldn't want to mess with. Sort of like Carmine Gallante or somebody. Of all the coaches who recruited me, the playground legends liked Coach Tark the best. They said he understood what life was like on the playground."

Tarkanian and Lucretia Green used to have philosophical discussions.

Lucretia Green: "He always told me not to let anyone buy my child. He said men would try to do that. But Tark, he always talked about the pot of gold at the end of the rainbow. That's something I'll never forget, all that talk about the pot of gold. Because you know what? Tark was right. We had to wait, but there was a pot of gold for Sidney."

Winston Karim: "Everyone knew that Sidney was getting all kinds of offers—money, cars, you name it. After a while, Sidney was almost getting immune to it, and I think Jerry caught his attention by not offering anything extra."

Lucretia Green: "All Tark ever said was that Sidney would have another family in Vegas, that he and his wife would make sure Sidney had someone to talk to, someone who cared about him. I liked that, Sidney having a family where he went to school."

Lois Tarkanian remembers receiving nightly calls from Brooklyn. It was Jerry with the progress report on Sidney.

Tarkanian usually said things like this:

"I think Sidney really likes me."

"I really like his mother. You'll like Mrs. Green—she is a very good woman, a sweet woman."

"Lois, you ought to see this neighborhood. It's terrible. I feel so sorry for these people. I've never seen anything this bad."

"I'm really worried about UCLA. They're coming at Sidney real hard."

"Sidney gave me his word. He says he'll sign, he just needs a little more time."

"I don't think he would say he'd sign if he wasn't going to do it."

"I'm so nervous, I can barely sleep."

"Lois, you should see these playground guys. They all know about us in Vegas. They love our team. These guys are something else."

"Do you think Sidney would say he was going to sign and then not do it?"

"His mother is very important. He loves her so much, and I've gotten to know her well. I know she wants Sidney to sign with us, but she won't tell him what to do."

"Lois, some of these schools could really turn his head. They're putting a lot of pressure on the kid."

"I know he'll sign, I just know it. I've just got to wait it out."

Then came the day Tarkanian feared.

Winston Karim: "Sidney and I were sitting on the front steps of his house and a car pulled up. Two coaches from a school got out, and one had a briefcase. They said hello to Sidney and asked if they could see Sidney alone inside the house.

"Sidney said, 'Yeah, come on in.'

"The assistant coach said, 'Well, what about Winston?'

"Sidney said, 'If you can't talk in front of Winston, you can't talk in front of me.'

"I said, 'Sidney, go inside. I'll stay out here.'

"I waited a few minutes, then Sidney came out of the house. He was all excited. 'Winston, they opened up a briefcase and it was stuffed with money. They say there's $15,000 in there and I can give it to my mother right now. They said there will be more for me later.' This wasn't just a promise of money, it was right there for Sidney to take.

"I told Sidney, 'If you take their money, you're letting these people buy you.'

"Sidney kept saying, 'Man, it's money. Money, you know? They say everybody does it.'

"Now, you can't blame Sidney for being excited. His family was on a fixed income. His brother had been shot right in front of his own eyes. All he ever wanted to do was to give his mother something. And his mother—she is such a nice lady from South Carolina, she didn't know what was going on.

"Anyway, I told Sidney, 'If you let those guys buy you, I'm going home.' I started walking down the street toward the subway station. Sidney follows me, and those two idiot coaches are alone in the house with a briefcase full of money. I mean, how dumb can you be, walking through Brooklyn with that much cash in a briefcase? Talk about being desperate—and those guys were from a well-known school, a basketball power.

"I know those coaches overheard me and Sidney talking outside the house. But I didn't care. Later that night, I went to see Sidney and his mother, and I told her that if she let these guys buy her son now, she'd never get him back. I talked to her for hours.

"Frankly, I didn't think they could turn down the money. Put yourself in their position. You take the $15,000, and who will ever know? Suddenly, you finally have money after never having anything.

"Naturally, Jerry heard what was going on, and he got real scared. He wanted to do something, but there was nothing he could do. Jerry wasn't going to start bidding on the kid. There wasn't anything more he could say to Sidney or his mother. All he could do was wait for their decision."

Sidney Green verifies the story: "I remember wanting that money so bad. The bills were itching in my fingers. My mother and I talked about it, and then we made a decision."

Lucretia Green approached the coaches and asked them to leave.

So it was established that $15,000 in a briefcase wasn't going to get Sidney Green signed. But what was?

After eleven consecutive days in Brooklyn, and seventeen overall,

Jerry Tarkanian was beginning to wonder. Finally, it came down to one last night.

Sidney Green: "Coach Tark was like a piece of furniture that night. I mean, he was in the house and he wasn't moving until he got me signed."

Tarkanian and Winston began their vigil at Sidney's home at 5 p.m.

Winston Karim: "Man, it was so hot that day, probably about 85 outside and 95 in that little house. It was dark inside, bad lighting. And there were no fans or air conditioning. I mean, the humidity just hung in the air. Everybody's shirt was soaked from sweat. Jerry was getting really tired by now, and I could see it.

"Jerry said to me, 'Winston, he's gotta sign tonight.'

"I said, 'Jerry, don't worry, he'll sign.'

"Sidney's mother was in the rocking chair, very serene, saying things like, 'Well, whatever my child does is what he does. I know my son will make the right decision, but don't worry, he'll sign with UNLV.'

"Then Jerry said to me, 'Winston, he's not gonna sign. All the blue-chippers tell me they're going to come, but they never come.'

"Sidney showed up in the room and took the letter of intent from Jerry. He stared at it, and I swear he was about to sign when the phone rang. It was the Louisville people, giving Sidney their last shot. Jerry was sitting there, looking at Sidney, and he knew it was Louisville on the phone. He almost had Sidney signed; now Sidney was talking to Louisville.

"While Sidney was on the phone, all these guys from the neighborhood started to drop by the house. They wanted to say hello and wish Sidney well, wherever he was going. You had cousins, people with crying babies. One guy started telling Jerry, 'How much are you going to give Sid? I've been doing my homework and he should get...' On and on it went, crazy things like that. We're all sweating; his mother was still in the rocking chair, going back and forth, back and forth. Guys were asking Jerry for money; Sidney was on the phone with another college...

"Finally, Sidney hung up and Jerry was about to talk to him again. Sidney said, 'Hey, Coach, I know I'm gonna sign with you, but I need a little more time.'

"Jerry said, 'What do you need more time for? If you're gonna sign, go ahead and sign.'

"Then the phone rang again. This time, it was UCLA. In fact, it was Arthur Ashe, the tennis pro, calling for UCLA. About the first thing Sidney said on the phone was, 'Well, I didn't make up my mind. I still haven't signed with anyone.'

"I looked at Jerry sitting on their sofa and I thought he was going to have a heart attack."

Sidney Green remembers the UCLA call, too.

Sidney Green: "Poor Coach Tark, he was trying to look real relaxed on the sofa, but he was so nervous inside. I could see little beads of sweat popping up on his forehead. And he kept getting up and going to the bathroom. My mother counted that he went to the bathroom eleven times in the two hours I was on the phone with UCLA."

When Sidney hung up with UCLA, he told Tarkanian, "Right now, you're even with UCLA."

Tarkanian: "I told Sidney, 'Even...Even? How can we be even, Sid?' Sidney started telling me about his visit to UCLA, how he had gone to a party at [former football star] Jim Brown's house in L.A.

"Sid told me, 'I've never seen so many pretty ladies in my whole life.'

"I told Sid, 'All you need is one. More than one causes you too much trouble, anyway. I'm sure there is one pretty lady in the whole city of Las Vegas who can make you happy.'"

Then Winston came up to Sidney and the two went into another room.

Winston Karim: "Sidney told me, 'Winston, I think I want to sign with UCLA.'

"I said, 'Fine, go tell Jerry and let him leave. You've been putting him through this all night. He's sweating like crazy; he's going to the bathroom every five minutes. Crazy people are coming by and saying crazy things to him. Jerry is a friend of mine; just let him go home if you won't sign.'

"Sidney said, 'Man, I just don't know.'

"I asked Sidney, 'Why do you want to go to UCLA?'

"Sidney said, 'Well, they got nice weather out there. The ladies are pretty.'

"I said, 'What about the coach, the team? How come you're not talking about that?'

"Sidney said, 'I need more time.'

"I said, 'How much?'

"Sidney said, 'Another week.'

"I said, 'Sidney, you can't have another week. You can't keep putting people through all this.'"

Once again, there was a telephone call. It was UCLA again. Former UCLA assistant Larry Farmer told Sidney that they would come to New York and sign him, but first they wanted to go to Bridgeport, Connecticut, to sign another high school phenomenon, Rod Foster.

Tarkanian: "When I heard that, I knew I had a chance. I told Sidney, 'Why would they go sign a guard first?'

"Sidney said, 'I don't get it.'

"I said, 'Sidney, these guys are going to sign a guard before they sign you.'

"He said, 'Oh.'

"I told Sidney, 'I've been here two weeks. How can we be even? I went to the park with you. I went to school with you. I'm here right now, telling you I want you. They're in Los Angeles and they're talking about going to Bridgeport to sign someone else before they even get to you. You can't let them come in at the last minute like this...'

"Sidney looked at me and said, 'You're right, Coach.'

"Then, believe it or not, he took the letter of intent and signed."

Sidney Green: "I kept looking at Coach Tark's sad face, those droopy eyes, and I could see that the man was suffering. When I signed the paper, my mother jumped up, hugged Coach Tark, and said, 'Thank God.' I knew that was where she wanted me to go, and I knew I trusted Coach Tark more than the other guys."

When Tarkanian had the signed letter of intent, he turned to Winston and said, "Winston, take me home. It's over. It's finally over."

Winston Karim: "When Sidney signed, it must have been about 1 o'clock in the morning. It was one of the most memorable times of my life. I call it the night of all nights. Sidney went through three T-shirts before he signed, because he was sweating so much."

Sidney Green: "I wish I had a videotape of Coach Tark recruiting me. I loved those days."

Sidney Green was the starting center for UNLV for four years. He was there for some of the best and some of the worst times of Tarkanian's coaching career. During Green's sophomore season, the Rebels were 16–12; it was the only season in Tarkanian's career when he did not win 20 games. Green also was there in 1982–83, when UNLV was 28–3 and reached number one in the college rankings. He left the school as its second all-time leading scorer and top rebounder, and was named to several All-American teams.

Sidney Green: "When I first committed to UNLV, some people thought I had been bought, especially other college coaches. I've always resented that. Believe me, if I had wanted to get bought, I could have done it easily.

"That first year, I really was lonely. I spent a lot of time at Jerry and Lois's home, and I got to know Danny real well. I felt like part of their family, and Lois really worked with me on my school stuff."

Winston Karim: "UNLV was the first place where Sidney had to hit the books. In Brooklyn, he was just a basketball star, and basketball stars wear gold chains, green tennis shoes, and don't go to class. They figure they're headed straight to the NBA."

Sidney Green and Lois became very close during his freshman year. They had long talks about life in Brooklyn, about his brother who was murdered, and about getting his mother a new house.

Sidney Green: "My one regret at UNLV was that I didn't take more advantage of Lois. She helped me so much with my studies, but she was willing to do even more. If I had listened to her, I'd have gotten my degree on time. Instead, I had to go to summer school to pick up the last few courses. Lois and Jerry gave me something all those schools with their money couldn't: loyalty and friendship. When a school tries to buy a player, it tells you how they view people. When a coach spends seventeen days in a Brooklyn ghetto—and they were seventeen days of hell for Jerry—it tells you something about loyalty and being wanted."

The Chicago Bulls made Sidney Green their first-round draft pick in 1983; he was the fifth player selected overall. At last, the money came—not in a briefcase, but in a sizable check.

Winston Karim: "Sidney went to work on getting his mother that house. He found one in Pittsburgh, because that was where Sidney's sister lived, and his mother wanted to be near her.

"I remember one night when he brought several of us over to a suite at the Hyatt Grand Central Station. Sidney was playing for the Chicago Bulls, and the team was staying there. He had the deed and all the papers for the house, and he was pointing to places for his mother to sign, and everyone was so happy and crying. It was amazing."

Sidney Green: "I don't think I've ever felt prouder than when I was able to buy her that house. It was a great feeling, to set out to do something and then do it. My mother kept talking about it being the pot of gold at the end of the rainbow."

Sidney Green's pro career has taken him from Chicago to the Detroit Pistons to the New York Knicks. He has drifted in and out of the starting lineup, but remains a gifted rebounder who probably will have a lengthy NBA career. He also returned to UNLV and earned his degree in 1988.

"I like the NBA, but I loved playing at UNLV," says Green. "I was so close to Coach Tark and Lois. I made a lot of great friends in the community, and the feeling that you get playing for the Rebels ...You know what I miss? Walking around campus the day after you win a big game, and having everyone come up and pat you on the back and want to talk about the win. That's what I loved most about college."

14
Danny

At some point in almost every speaking engagement featuring Jerry Tarkanian, you can count upon hearing this exchange:

QUESTION: Coach, who's your favorite player of all-time?

ANSWER: Danny Tarkanian.

Listen to him talk about his son.

Tarkanian: "I love all my players, but I've never loved a player as much as I love my son, and I never hide that fact from anyone. That's why Danny's playing for me could have been a real problem. A father and a son can have a great relationship. A player and a coach can have a great relationship. But when the father is the coach and the son is the player, that's a different story. When Al McGuire coached at Marquette, his son Allie played guard for the Warriors. Al told me that he'd never do it again; that it was tougher on the kid than it was on the coach. And Allie was a very fine player at Marquette, good enough to start at about any college program. Al said his son was under a lot of pressure, and that made it hard for both of them.

"Danny's playing for me was a success. I don't say that it was easy, and Danny certainly put tremendous pressure on himself. But when it works, when the son is the player and the father is the coach and the team wins, it is one of the greatest feelings in the world for both people. The victories become something the father and son can share and always treasure. That's what happened with Danny and me. If your son is going to play for you, these two things are a must:

"First, the team had better win. If you lose, both you and your son are going to catch hell. The critics will be after you both and your lives will be miserable.

"Second, the kid has to play an unselfish role on the team. Danny was our point guard for three years, from 1981 to 1984, and all he thought about was getting the ball to the other guys on the team. He took only a few shots each game. His mind was always on making the team better. He passed, he played defense, and he hit the floor for loose balls. He was willing to sacrifice. When the son does that, the other players gladly accept him. He's doing the dirty work so that they can take the shots. But if the son is a scorer, and if the father is drawing up plays so that the son gets a lot of shots, there is going to be trouble. There will always be some kid on the team who thinks that he should be getting the shots, instead of the son. And he'll think that even if the son is an All-American. No matter how much the son scores, there will be a kid who thinks he could score more if only he had the same opportunity.

"At UNLV, we won big with Danny, and part of the reason was that Danny was a great passer and knew how to make the guys he played with happy. But it was Danny who kept it all together and he did it through hard work. In practice, he pushed himself to the limit. When we ran sprints, he won 90 percent of them, and he wasn't even close to being the fastest kid on the team. He just worked and worked, and he did everything full-speed. When other guys were tired, he was reaching back and finding something inside him that enabled him to go harder. All the other players saw how Danny pushed himself in practice, and no one could question his work ethic.

"I think the greatest tribute to Danny came during his junior year. We were playing West Virginia in Morgantown on a nationally televised game. Danny had a severe virus and during the week had been in the hospital because his body was so run-down. The day of the game, Danny was still in bed at 6 p.m. He didn't even feel strong enough to go to the pregame meal. Lois was there in his room, trying to get some food down him. Before the game, I mentioned that we probably couldn't start Danny. He was just too sick. One of our forwards, a great shooter named Larry Anderson, grabbed me and took me into the men's room. Larry said, 'We need Danny. This game is on national TV. This is a big chance for me to get some exposure. I want Danny in there because he gets me the ball.' That was a wonderful compliment to Danny. It showed how he had adjusted to his role and how his teammates respected him.

"But I'd still agree with Al McGuire. In most cases, it is not a good idea for a son to play for his father. It's one thing for the coach

226

to be on the front line and to have the critics taking shots at him. That comes with the job. But the son also ends up in that same situation, and that's not fair to the kid. Thank God Danny is Danny, a kid who knew what he had to do and had the discipline to do it. You have to know Danny to realize why it worked so well.

"Danny was both a fine student and a fine athlete at Bishop Gorman High in Las Vegas. I was never more nervous before a game than when Danny played quarterback. When we were going through the NCAA probation and receiving a lot of bad publicity, the one thing that kept me going was watching Danny play football. I had become sort of a recluse. I stopped going to a lot of coaching clinics and conventions because I was feeling so depressed about what had happened with the NCAA. No matter how bad I felt, though, I didn't miss a single one of Danny's games. If I had to go somewhere, I took a midnight flight after one of his football games and traveled all night. His senior football season was the most fun I've ever had in athletics, and all I did was watch. I loved his whole team. The summer before, he and teammates Frank Fertitta, Mike Brascia, Steve Gradyian, Ken Sullivan, Keenan Raftery, and Brad Ezor were at our home talking about how they were 'going to win state' their senior year. Lois and I looked at how small some of them were and we felt bad, because we knew how excited and happy they were then and how sad they would be when the season started and reality hit. But those kids were really something. The courage and determination they showed against teams from larger schools was unbelievable. Bishop Gorman's team went undefeated and won the state championship. They shocked all of us.

"I love high school sports, and I'd rather watch a high school game than a pro game any day, just because the high school kids put their hearts and souls into every play. It's a great feeling sitting in the stands on a fall Friday night watching high school football.

"At Bishop Gorman, Danny was a right-handed quarterback and was picked the MVP in the state. The amazing thing was that he never practiced football. All he played on his own was basketball. The reason he went out for football was that some of his friends were on the team. I watched him play both football and basketball, and I thought he was 100 times the athlete that I was. He also was 100 times the student that I was. He had something like a 3.7 grade point average at Bishop Gorman. But I'm his father, and I know that fathers aren't always the most objective people when it comes to evaluating their sons. For what it's worth, I think Danny was a better football player than anything else."

*   *   *

227

Danny had his own ideas.

Danny: "My heart always was in basketball. Until I left UNLV for law school at the University of San Diego, I never went more than two days in a row without playing basketball, and I started out playing when I was about four years old. We had this little basket, and I'd shoot a volleyball into it underhanded. When we were in Long Beach, I'd shoot around with Dad, and I played on a recreation team coached by Gary Redmond. I did go to Dad's summer basketball camps, but he never pushed basketball on me. Basketball was something I always wanted to do. I just grew up with it and I've always loved it. I'm a driven person, and once I start something, I keep at it.

"My father loves football, and he had a lot of friends in college who were football players and ended up coaching football. I remember when we'd take vacations during the summer, Dad and I would play catch with a football. For our vacations, we'd get into a borrowed camper and travel to spots where Dad was involved with clinics or coaching, places such as Estes Park, Colorado, or Flathead Lake, Montana. Whenever we stopped the camper, we always had the football with us, and no matter how short our stop we always got in a few throws. Those were great times.

"Dad and my brother George would try to catch a fish every year. I know my father didn't like fishing that much, but George loved it, so Dad joined him. They tried all kinds of different poles and what seemed like hundreds of different baits and hooks. Every place we'd stop, they'd ask the people how the fish were biting. They spent hour after hour on the banks and in boats. One year, George finally caught a fish, but Dad never did.

"My father would be speaking in Washington or Utah, and we'd drive there. It was a chance for the whole family to be together. Dad's always had two loves: his family and basketball. He spends a tremendous amount of time on basketball, but it was never anything that we children resented. Rather, we shared it. Our family is as close as it can be, especially since the problems with the NCAA. That's what really brought us together. We've taken a lot of shots, and a lot of lies and unfair things have been said about us. Dad would always try to shrug it off. If there was a bad newspaper story or something, he'd say, 'Don't pay attention to that. It doesn't matter. Don't worry.' But we knew that it hurt him. Some people talk about Dad being Tark the Shark. The guy who named Dad Tark the Shark was a friend of ours [writer John Hall, who was with the *Los Angeles Times*], and he did it because of the rhyming of 'shark' and 'Tark,' and because we lived by the ocean and Long Beach State played right at the edge of the ocean. It was a compliment, and we still don't think there is anything negative about it.

"You can't underestimate all the pressure we've been through because of the NCAA. I remember Dad not being able to sleep at night. He and Mom used to get into arguments about little things, or they'd argue about the NCAA. The pressure really got to Mom, and it took a toll on her. It is amazing that their marriage survived. Very few marriages could have withstood all that, but they stayed together because they loved each other and they are very loyal to each other.

"The other thing was, we knew what was going on at other colleges. I knew that we had no money at Long Beach State. We couldn't have bought a kid even if we had wanted to, because we had nothing to pay him. After a while, you become bitter and you begin to dislike the people taking shots at you. As a family, you either split apart or you grow closer when something like this happens.

"The comments may have been about Dad and the basketball program, but that's really 'us,' our family, because we've always been in it together. We've jumped into his profession and given him our full support. That's because he is always there for us, so we want to be there for him and his basketball.

"At our Christmas dinners, all we talk about is the season—how it is going, who is playing well and who isn't. At Easter dinner, we talk about what players we'll have next year, who we will play, and what some of the older players are doing. It's a unique situation—all basketball. I've been out of school for a couple of years, but I go to every UNLV game I can. The whole family is there for the games. No matter how tense he is before a game, Dad always knows if we're all there. Each of us knows how much we mean to him.

"One morning, we were all at the breakfast table looking at the newspaper. That was during the Gary Hart scandal. My sister asked Dad what he thought about Gary Hart. Dad looked up and said, 'Who's Gary Hart?' We all laughed so hard, because we knew that he had no idea who Gary Hart was or what had happened. Politics is not part of his tunnel vision, even if it is on the front page of the paper.

"That's how it was in our house when I grew up. Dad's life was our life, and Dad's life was basketball. But Dad never said that he wanted me to play for him, and I never mentioned it, either. In fact, we always talked about me going to other colleges, not UNLV. At the time [1980], UNLV would not have been a good spot for me. Dad had Michael Lloyd as his point guard, and he was a starter the year before. He also had Greg Goorjian, who was a transfer from Arizona State. In high school, Goorjian had been the leading scorer in California

229

history. So those two guys were the point guards, meaning I'd have to sit behind them for two years. Maybe I could have beaten those guys out, and maybe not; but I didn't want to put myself and Dad through all that. I saw that there was no obvious need for me at UNLV, so I was thinking about other schools."

Tarkanian: "Danny was right. When he was in high school, we didn't talk about him going to UNLV. I wanted Danny to go to Redlands University, where I got my master's degree. I thought that would be a great school for him. He'd get a good education. He could play football and basketball and not be under a lot of pressure. He could join a fraternity and chase girls."

Lois: "Danny was such a good student that I wanted him to go to Stanford, because that was the strongest school academically on the West Coast. I wanted Danny to go to the best school possible. I didn't care what sport he played in college, or even if he played anything at all. I had seen a lot of what big-time college athletics does to kids, and I didn't want Danny to go through all that pressure."

Tarkanian: "At one point during his senior year at Bishop Gorman, Danny thought about playing college football. He even visited a few schools, but the interest was never strong. A few schools wanted to sign him, and he went to Nevada-Reno on a recruiting trip. But Danny didn't want to make the decision right away. One day, he told me, 'Dad, just tell them I want to play basketball in college.'

"I thought Reno would have been a good spot for Danny. He could possibly have played both basketball and football, or at least picked the one he liked best. It was a Division I program, yet Danny would not have been under the gun there as he would at some other schools. As far as basketball went, I liked Reno's coach, Sonny Allen. They ran the numbered fast break offense that we even picked up and used at UNLV. I thought Reno's style would be good for Danny as a player. Also, he wouldn't be so far from home, and we'd be able to go see him play a lot."

Danny liked the University of Southern California.

Danny: "My mother wanted me to go to Stanford or Harvard. She talked a lot about getting the best education. I wanted that; but I also loved basketball, and I wanted to play in the NCAA tournament, maybe even get to the Final Four. I knew that Harvard and Stanford were never going to the Final Four, so I ruled them out. My mother wasn't thrilled, but that's how I felt.

"I was born and spent part of my life growing up in southern California, where most people follow Southern Cal or UCLA. I liked

Southern Cal, probably because we always had a strong rivalry with UCLA when we were at Long Beach.

"I had a lot of respect for Stan Morrison, the University of Southern California basketball coach. He seemed liked a great guy, and he showed a lot of interest in me. They had me in for a recruiting visit and offered me a scholarship. I was ready to sign with them right away, but Dad wasn't that enthusiastic about USC. He said that they had a transfer from Kentucky coming in, Dwight Anderson, who was a guard. Another great high school guard, Dwayne Polee, also had committed to USC. The ironic thing is that Polee changed his mind and came to UNLV for a year, then he transferred to Pepperdine. As far as USC went, Dad was worried that they were loaded at guard.

"Looking back, I can see that Dad did little things to change my mind. Suddenly people I respected, such as Jackie Robinson, who was from L.A. and had played for Dad, would ask me about college. I'd say I was thinking about USC, and Jackie would say that USC has a problem in this area or that area. He never said, 'Don't go to USC,' but he'd say I should look at the situation again. Meanwhile, my dad had a lot of nice things to say about Reno. It came down to those two schools—USC and Reno. On signing day, I called up Stan Morrison and told him that I had decided on Reno.

"Dad was right. Reno's style of game—the fast break—would have been good for me. Sonny Allen's son, Billy, was a point guard who had committed to play at Missouri, and Billy called me to tell me that I should play for his father at Reno. So I committed. Reno sounded good. About three days before I was supposed to leave for school, there was a story in the paper that Billy Allen had transferred to Reno to play point guard for his father. That really made me mad—not that Billy transferred, but that I had to read about it in the newspaper. No one took the time to call me. At this point, I was tired of all the recruiting and everything. I figured that I had committed to Reno, so that's where I was going. Sonny Allen called me to say that I could play together with his son. I wasn't so sure, because I'm 6-foot-1 and Billy is 5-foot-11, and that would make for a very small backcourt."

Tarkanian: "When I read about Billy Allen transferring to Reno, I was in Hawaii at a Nike coaching clinic. I immediately called Danny and told him not to do anything until I got home."

Danny: "There was no way I wanted to wait anymore. I just wanted to get to Reno and start college. I had a feeling that Dad would talk me out of it and I'd have to go through the recruiting thing again. I decided that I was going to take off early. My best friend, Keenen

Raftery, also was going, and we planned to drive up before Dad got home from Hawaii. We had the car packed and everything, but I got sick the night before and was too ill to drive.

Tarkanian: "When I got home from Hawaii, Danny told me that Sonny Allen had called to say that Danny and Billy Allen could play together. I told Danny that what Sonny Allen said might sound okay to most people, but I'm a coach and I know that you can't play two point guards at once. I told him, 'What will happen is that he'll move you out of position, to the shooting guard, and leave Billy at the point. That will hurt your game because you're not a shooting guard.' I also talked to Sonny, and he told me how he planned to use Billy and Danny together. To me, it just didn't sound right."

Danny: "Every day for a straight week I made plane reservations to Reno, and every day I canceled them. Dad kept telling me to take my time, to think about where I wanted to go to school. Stan Morrison called again and said he still wanted me for Southern Cal, and he even flew in to see me, but he did say that I might have to sit on the bench for a while. I also got a call from Texas Christian, which previously had recruited me heavily. School had been in session about two weeks, and I still hadn't gone anywhere. Finally, I ended up at Dixie College. I had several good friends who were going there: Ed Rugerrolli, Mike Gomez, Chi Chi Bengochea, and Russ Malloy."

Tarkanian: "Dixie College is a junior college in St. George, Utah. A lot of guys from Danny's football team were going there. It's about 100 miles from Las Vegas. I knew the Dixie coach very well from various basketball camps. When the papers said that Danny wasn't going to Reno and that he had committed to Dixie, Stan Morrison came to see him about Southern California. That really impressed Danny; I think he might even have gone to USC except he didn't want to change his mind again. He was afraid that would make him look bad."

Lois: "In the long run, Danny made a great decision. Jerry and I have never looked down at junior colleges, because we know how good they often are. We don't take an elitist attitude. We realize that a junior college can serve as a place where a kid can relax and adjust to college life. Dixie was right for Danny because he wasn't under the microscope, and there was no pressure of big-time sports. St. George is a quiet place, almost out of the 1950s. Danny always said that the most beautiful girls he had ever seen were at Dixie. It is a strong Mormon town, but they embraced Danny even though he is a Catholic. Everything worked out for him. He did well in the classroom [3.85 grade point average] and well on the basketball court [15 points, 7 assists]. He was voted the freshman of the year. Jerry and I were very proud of Danny because he was happy and flourishing in that environment.''

Tarkanian: "While Danny was having a great year at Dixie, the 1980–81 season was our worst at UNLV; we went 16–12. We had problems at point guard because the team didn't play well together. I have a policy that when I don't like a team, I don't have a banquet for it at the end of the season. This was one of only three teams in my career that didn't have a banquet.

"So what we did was plan for the next year. We needed a point guard desperately. I was going to recruit one. I also knew that Danny could do it for us. But I wasn't going to force Danny into coming to UNLV. I saw him play a couple of times at Dixie, and he looked very good. Then again, I was his father, so I knew that my opinion was biased. To make sure I was right about Danny, I sent my assistants up to see him, and both Mark Warkentien and Tim Grgurich were very impressed by Danny. The coaches kept telling me that we should bring Danny to UNLV.

"I was just happy that Danny was having fun at Dixie. He talked about going back there for a second year, playing both football and basketball, and hanging around with his buddies. It sounded pretty nice.

"Arizona was interested in Danny, and they offered him a recruiting visit to Tucson the weekend of the Arizona–Notre Dame football game. Danny turned them down. When he did that, I thought he might be thinking about coming to UNLV, because it isn't easy for a strong Catholic kid to pass up a chance to see Notre Dame play football. Meanwhile, we were recruiting a point guard from El Camino Junior College, who we thought was the best junior college point guard in the country. I didn't want to sign this kid if Danny was coming to UNLV; on the other hand, I didn't want Danny to feel pressured into making a decision before he was ready."

Lois: "That season was so hard on Jerry. Our team had some talent, but it was like a body without a head. None of Jerry's point guards had a feel for running an offense. The ball never went where it was supposed to go, and that drove the coaches crazy. Jerry kept experimenting with different players at point guard, and it kept getting worse. The fans were on us all the time. Jerry's sister, Alice, was at a conference that year in Los Angeles. During a break in her meetings, she overheard someone from Las Vegas saying that Jerry was "over the hill." Naturally, the man didn't know who Alice was. But remember, this was the only season at UNLV that Jerry didn't win 20 games. In the life of a coach, the fans only remember what you did in your last game.

"I really didn't want Danny to play at UNLV, because I knew the pressure would be tremendous. Jerry took the losses so hard, and I didn't want Danny to go through the same thing. Danny was suffering with UNLV even though he was 100 miles away and playing for Dixie. Every time Jerry lost, Danny felt it. I remember driving up for a holiday tournament at Dixie to watch Danny play. That same night, I listened to the UNLV game on the radio. UNLV lost to Air Force, 51–50. That was an awful defeat, because we really had better talent than Air Force. That night, Danny was named to the all-tournament team. After the final award ceremonies, I went up to congratulate him, and I saw that his eyes were cloudy, almost teary.

"Danny said, 'Mom, is it true? We lost to Air Force?'

"I said, 'It was on the road in Colorado; the high altitude might have had something to do with it.'

"Danny said, 'But Mom...Air Force? How could we lose to Air Force?'

"I think it was then that I knew Danny was going to attend UNLV."

Sidney Green: "I helped recruit Danny. I had gotten to know him from hanging around Coach Tark's house, and Danny and I hit it off. The year Danny was at Dixie, our team stunk. We had no point guard. Guys wouldn't pass the ball or run the plays. We just had some selfish people on the team. I told Danny, 'If you come here, we can turn this thing around. Man, we need you. We're not going anywhere without a point guard, and I'll tell you this—I have two years left, and if we don't get a guy to pass the ball, I don't want to spend those last two years at UNLV. You and I can help change our whole image.'"

Danny: "I grew up with UNLV, and I honestly believed that as long as Dad was the coach, they'd be a Top Twenty team and win 20 games a year. I couldn't believe what had happened. The point guard situation was bad, and the team had just stopped running. It was unlike any UNLV teams I ever knew. I love my father, and I'm convinced he is a great coach. There is no doubt that he is as good a coach as Dean Smith, Bobby Knight, and the other great coaches. His record is as good as anyone's, and he has had to make do with far less talent.

"The whole thing really came to a head when UNLV was playing Utah in Salt Lake. [Utah coach] Jerry Pimm was recruiting me; I was at that game to look at their program. UNLV was up about eight points at the half, and then we just quit. I mean, we got beat bad [95–83]. I couldn't believe how those guys let Dad down. I was crushed.

"When we did talk about it, Dad said, 'I'm not going to tell you that we want you here, and I'm not going to tell you that we don't want you. It's your decision. If you come, we'll be more than happy to have you. If not, we have this other junior college player who everyone tells me is a great player.'

"I thought it over and thought it over.

"Dad said, 'If you do come, you have to understand that you'll hear me yell a lot. You'll see me in situations like you've never seen me before.'

"But I had been around Dad's teams all my life. I knew that he yelled and I knew how he acted. That didn't bother me. It came down to the fact that I wanted to help him. He needed a point guard and I could fill that role. He liked to run on offense, and that was my game. I wanted to play in the NCAA tournament, and I knew that with players such as Sidney Green and Larry Anderson, we could get there. This was the perfect situation for me. I knew I'd come in and play, and I knew that my dad needed me, even if he never said so. That's why I went to UNLV. I grew up with my father and with Rebel basketball."

Tarkanian: "Danny's first season at UNLV [1981–82] was difficult for him because we thought we'd have one of our greatest teams. The talent was there, with players such as Sidney Green, [Michael] Spider Man Burns, and Dwayne Polee, who was the southern California high school player of the year. Our final record was 20–10, which was better than the 16–12 the season before, but I was still very disappointed.

"I don't judge kids on winning and losing; rather, I ask, 'Are they playing hard?' This team just didn't play hard. We were capable of putting forth extra effort one night, and then we'd act like we were asleep the next night. When a team won't give 100 percent, I find it hard to like them. So for the second year in a row, I didn't have a team banquet.

"As for Danny, I thought he played very well. He ran our offense, he set a school record for assists and steals, and he handled the pressure of being the coach's son very well. I believe that the point guard is the most important position on the floor. If you look back at some of our best teams, each one had a tremendous point guard. The team that went to the Final Four in 1977 had Robert Smith, who later played in the NBA. The 1983 team that was ranked number one had Danny; and the 1987 Final Four team had Mark Wade, who broke Danny's NCAA assist record. So when I say I didn't like this team, it wasn't a reflection on Danny's play or effort. He gave me all he had.''

Danny: ''I knew that playing at UNLV would be hard. I was the coach's son, and that meant that the newspapers and some people in town might give me problems. I suppose it's only natural. But I also believed that I could help bring the team together.

''Michael Lloyd was one of the point guards from the year before, and he was in a serious auto accident. When Michael did come back to play, he had lost some of his quickness. The other point guard was Greg Goorjian, who was really a shooting guard. He had been a shooting guard all his life and he averaged over 40 points a game in high school. He never played point guard until he came to UNLV, but in our offense the point guard is not supposed to shoot much. When a point guard is shooting, the other guys get frustrated and start standing around; before you know it, your offense just stops. Greg later transferred to Loyola Marymount where his dad, Ed, was the coach.

''As for my dad, that 20–10 year really wore him down. He had a team with some players other coaches wouldn't touch. It got so bad that Dad even said things like, 'I don't know how long I can keep coaching. The fun has just gone out of it.'

''I had never heard him talk like that before. When we lost, he watched tapes of the games over and over, trying to figure out what went wrong. He refused to blame the players for getting beat. In his head he kept asking, 'What did I do wrong? What could I have done better?' Dad wanted to win so bad, and I saw some games when his players just quit on him. I couldn't believe it.

''It seemed that even when we won there were problems. I remember when we beat Texas A&M at home. Texas A&M was loaded that year, and they were favored to win. After the game I was going nuts because I was so happy.

''Dwayne Polee was our top freshman recruit and the biggest name we had signed since Sidney Green. He wasn't playing well early in the season, and this led to his playing time being cut. Twice during the year he got homesick and left the team. But after that Texas A&M game, when everyone was so happy, Polee just sat there and didn't say a word. He left after the game, and no one saw him again for a couple of days.

''Our center, Richie Adams, also got homesick that year and went home to New York for about ten days. We lost Michael Burns at midseason because of grade problems. What I'm trying to say is that team morale was a mess. It's very hard to imagine all the turmoil.

"Before I went to UNLV, I didn't think I'd have a problem listening to my father yell at me; I figured he would only yell at me if I were loafing or forgetting how to run the plays—you know, things like that, mental mistakes. I busted my butt every day. You could ask anyone. We'd go to the track for conditioning drills and I'd win almost all the races. We'd start with a mile run. Then we'd run six 40-yard dashes, six 60-yard dashes, a 220-yard dash, and cap it off by running up this big hill seven times. By the time we got to the hill everyone was dead. I mean, guys could hardly stand up. But I won the races on the track and I won them on the hill. I wasn't going to let anyone beat me, because I didn't want anyone to say I was getting off easy because I was the coach's son.

"Well, I got yelled at anyway. I don't think he got on my back more than most guys. He was in a bad mood all year because we were losing, and the team wasn't hustling, and some of the guys were having problems off the court. So we all caught it from him. But during that time it seemed as if Dad was riding me a lot harder than he did the other guys.

"When he would yell at me, I'd say something under my breath. I wanted to yell out, but I never did. I never walked away from him, either. I just stood there and took it the best I could. Coach Grgurich said I used to make certain faces at my father when he got on my case. Coach Grgurich would make the same faces at me, and I'd laugh, but I know it wasn't funny when it was happening.

"It was all right when one of the assistants yelled at me, but when it came from my father, well, it bothered me a lot more. I suppose I let him get to me. I felt I was playing as hard as I could, but he was still unhappy.

"A lot of it had to do with the team. Dad was upset at the overall attitude, which was pretty rotten. He never blew up at us in the dressing room during the games, but he got on us pretty good during practice. It's not like he cussed at us; he doesn't swear that much. The worst thing Dad can call you is a jackass. If you're a jackass, you're in deep, deep trouble—the worst thing on the face of the earth. When he said that word, you knew Dad was reaching the boiling point.

"He hardly ever cussed at me, but he would say things like, 'Danny, what kind of pass is that?' I wouldn't say anything because I didn't want to get in trouble. Dad would say, 'Tell me, what kind of pass was that?' I'd say, 'I thought...' Dad would yell, 'Don't talk back to me.' I'd shut up because you're not supposed to talk back to your coach. A second later, Dad would say, 'Danny, what kind of pass was that?' And the whole thing would start up again."

Larry Anderson: "At first we were very suspicious about Danny. We didn't know how it would be to have the coach's son on the team. I remember at one of Danny's first practices, Coach Tark got on him about a pass and Danny didn't say anything. Coach Tark said something else to Danny, and Danny said, 'But Dad...' Then he shut up, because he knew he had said something wrong. Everybody in practice kind of stopped and looked at Danny and Coach. That might have happened once or twice more, but after that, Danny always called him 'Coach,' and Danny wasn't a problem for the rest of the guys. If he heard someone complain about Coach Tark, he didn't run to his father and tell him. I ended up as Danny's roommate on the road, and the guys liked Danny because he passed them the ball. They respected him as a person."

Sidney Green: "At first, a few of the guys didn't accept Danny. They were jealous because he was Coach Tark's kid; but these were the same guys who only cared if they got their 15 or 20 points. I had no use for them, because they couldn't see what Danny did for the team. These guys really didn't care whether we won or lost; all they wanted was their shots and their points. It's a good thing that these kids washed out of the program, or quit, or whatever. And all I know is that I never wanted to be in Danny's shoes that first year. No matter what Coach Tark says, he was tougher on Danny than on anyone else. Sometimes they would get so upset with each other during practice that they wouldn't say a word. They would just stare at each other. They were both so intense and they both wanted to win so badly that they got on each other's nerves."

Tim Grgurich: "I don't know how Danny and Coach made it through that first year. Most fathers and sons probably would have ended up killing each other. We won 20 games that year, but it seemed like we lost 20. In Vegas, winning 20 games sometimes isn't enough. The fans expect more, and they were all over Coach and Danny. If the Tarkanians weren't such a strong, close-knit family, they never could have handled it. Instead, Danny and Coach showed me that they were very tough people and that they loved each other very much. That's why they survived."

Danny: "The fans were all right as long as we won. But when we started to lose, I could have been tarred and feathered. The newspapers were OK to me, and most of the guys on the team were very good. But the fans—I couldn't understand some of them. I was out there diving for loose balls, taking charges, and I led the team in steals and assists. I worked as hard as I could.

"I guess I was a little naive. I figured that if I hustled, everyone would see and appreciate my style. I remember how the fans loved Glen Gondrezick, and I grew up watching Glen and he played as hard as anyone I've ever seen. Gondo was on the 1977 team that went to the Final Four. They won, and perhaps that was the difference.

"In my first year, the fans used to get on me because I didn't shoot that much, only taking about three shots a game. I'd catch a pass and be looking to hit the open man, and all of a sudden some of the fans would just start yelling, 'Shoot it, shoot it, will you?' It's tough to make a shot when people in the gym yell for you to shoot. That was the worst year of my life."

Sidney Green: "That 20–10 season was my junior year, and I just couldn't wait for it to be over. We had some jerks on the team; I guess they were the last holdovers from the probation era. Well, they were leaving, and Danny had survived his first year, so I figured things were looking up. Some of the veterans, such as myself and Larry Anderson, knew what Danny could do for a team. He really was the missing ingredient. Then Coach Tark had some transfers who became eligible— Jeff Collins, Eric Booker, and Paul Brozovich. These were good guys. The funny thing is, they weren't as talented as the last bunch of players we'd had, but they knew what it meant to play like a team. It wasn't that Coach Tark just couldn't get through to the last group, or that Danny was a problem. Nobody could have reached those guys. In my opinion, Danny kept that season from being a complete disaster."

Tarkanian: "That first season, Danny and I learned that there are some people who just root for you to fail. I guess they like to see people miserable. Danny heard some of the fans booing him, although I don't think it was nearly as bad as he believed. But he worked so hard on the court that it was impossible not to like him. At least that's the way I saw it."

Danny: "At the start of my second year [1982–83] the fans still weren't thrilled about me. They knew we were coming off a disappointing season and didn't think we were going to have a great team this time. The turning point for me was the Rebel Roundup Tournament in Las Vegas. In the opening game, we beat Long Island University [101–78], and I shot 1 for 3 from the field and had 18 assists. The next night, we beat Baylor [77–65] to win the tournament. I was 1 for 6 shooting, but had 20 assists. The 18 assists was a single-game record for UNLV, and the 20 assists was an NCAA record. I was named to the all-tournament team over Eric Booker, who shot well in both games. When I went out to get my award, I was booed. I couldn't believe it. We'd played at home and we'd won, and some fans still weren't happy. Maybe I was too sensitive. My folks told me the booing wasn't nearly as bad as I thought it was, but it still bothered me.

"My sisters were great. I remember Pam and Jodie telling me they would go up to the concession stand at halftime to get a Coke and they'd hear some guy ripping me. Well, they would just yell at the guy and tell him to shut up. I liked how they defended me, but the situation just seemed to be getting stranger and stranger.

"I never thought about quitting the team, but I sort of wondered what was going on. Finally, two things made it better. First, I did a better job of putting the fans out of my head. I really made a point of trying to keep things from bothering me.

"Second, we started to win, and that was a big help. The other players had an important role, too, because they started telling reporters that they appreciated my contributions and my style of play, and that led to some very nice stories. I was leading the nation in assists for much of the season. The best part is that the team just came together. We kept winning and winning, and soon everyone was behind us. No one was saying anything about me being the coach's son. They weren't knocking Dad, they weren't knocking the players, they weren't knocking anyone. We won 24 games in a row to start the season, and were on cloud nine. I was so proud when we were voted number one in the country for a couple of weeks."

Sidney Green: "Danny was the heart of the team that year. The credit for our playing so well went to Larry Anderson and me, because we scored the points. Larry and I had good seasons, but Danny made the difference in the team. I didn't care if he never took a shot or scored a point; when Danny was on the floor, I knew we had a great chance to win. If he wasn't out there, I worried. Our other guards just turned it over, or they passed it to the wrong guy, or the play just was not run correctly. The team didn't run smoothly. I knew that Danny could deliver me the ball—and when you're a big man playing near the basket like I did, that's all that matters. I was so happy for Danny, because I'd told him that we could turn this program around, and we did.

"That first year, there were about four guys on the team who didn't want to accept Danny. They just froze him out. They did everything they could to make his life miserable. Well, when those guys left, we found out who was the problem, and it wasn't Danny. If you look at the record from Danny's first year to his second year, that tells you the story.''

One of the people who saw Danny play quite often at UNLV was Pete Newell, former basketball coach at California, now a scout for the Cleveland Cavaliers.

Pete Newell: ''When I first heard that Danny was going to play for his father, I had my doubts. It had nothing to do with Jerry or Danny. Rather, I've always thought that fathers coaching their sons was an impossible situation, especially for the kid. This relationship between Danny and Tark may be the best example of a son playing for his father that I've seen.

''For a player to have to go into a dressing room after a practice or a game and see a couple of guys who are upset with the coach, and when the coach is the kid's father—that's tough. What does the kid do if another player says something against his father? Or what happens if the other players are afraid to speak freely because they don't want the son telling the coach what happened in the locker room? That tension can be unbearable, and in almost every instance I can think of, it just didn't work because it was unnatural. I've always thought that the dressing room was the players' sanctuary and they should be able to say what they want in there. That's why none of my sons played for me when I coached. I didn't want to put them in a setting where they could be ostracized by their teammates because of their father.

''The fact that it worked at UNLV says a lot for Danny and Tark. If Danny weren't Tark's son, he would have gotten a lot more credit and recognition. He was the perfect point guard for those Vegas teams. But instead of talking about Danny's guts and what he meant to UNLV, the tendency was to dwell on the fact that he was the coach's son. That's an interesting story, but it overshadows the fact that Danny was exactly what a coach wants in a point guard. He was one of the best I've seen at taking the coach's game plan off the blackboard and having it run on the floor. Sure, Danny wasn't much of a scorer, but that was about the last thing Tark needed.

''I've asked myself why Danny and Tark were successful when so many others weren't. I think it was because the players had so much respect for Jerry. They knew that he wanted to win more than anything else, and that he wasn't going to play favorites. But they also saw Danny working harder than anyone. Danny is very intelligent, and he was sensitive to what the other players were thinking, so he never did anything to cause second thoughts. No one could say that Danny was getting away with something because he was the coach's son. My goodness, Danny was working twice as hard as anyone on the team.''

Lois: "One day, Jerry came home late from practice with this big smile on his face. He told me that [Boston Celtics president] Red Auerbach had been at practice and was amazed at how hard Danny was working. He asked Jerry, 'Who's that white kid? He's a real hustler.'

"I asked Jerry if he told Red Auerbach that Danny was his son.

"Jerry said, 'No, I just smiled,' but Auerbach then figured out who Danny was.

"Jerry didn't tell Danny, and I thought he should have, because it was a wonderful compliment and Red Auerbach is a basketball legend. I'm sure that if Danny hadn't been Jerry's son, Jerry would have talked about it to everyone in town. But since he was Danny, Jerry kept quiet about it.''

Assistant Tim Grgurich: "The more I saw Danny and Coach together, the more I grew to admire them. You can't believe what Danny meant to the program. Everyone knew that Danny was an exceptional kid and a great student. When he came into the program, we were taking a lot of shots because it was the end of the probation period. But the fact that Danny went to UNLV helped our recruiting. Other assistants could have said, 'If UNLV is supposed to be a good academic school, why doesn't Tark's kid go there? Why is he somewhere else?' But Danny took care of that kind of negative recruiting. Then, by playing so hard and being unselfish, he won even more fans for us.''

Lois: "I was against Danny playing for his father, but I guess it was inevitable. Ever since Jerry moved us to Las Vegas, all Danny ever heard about was UNLV basketball. Really, it was inevitable. But it also made us even more vulnerable. I don't care what anyone says; a son playing for his father at any level is asking for trouble. At a place such as UNLV, where the fans almost treat basketball like a religion, it could have been a disaster. I've gotten somewhat used to people saying things against Jerry. It still hurts when it happens, but I deal with it the best I can. I'm probably like the typical mother when it comes to handling criticism of her children. It's like the old saying, 'Say anything you want about me, but be careful what you say about my husband and don't you dare say a word against my children.' With Danny being the point guard at UNLV, I knew that he was going to be criticized.

"I don't think it was as bad as Danny thought. The newspapers really didn't knock Danny or Jerry. There were some fans who booed, but I don't think it was a majority opinion or anything like that. But I admit I hated it when anyone said a word against Danny. And once we started to win, that took care of the issue as far as the fans were concerned.

"Now, I think it was good that Danny played for his father. It was something Danny and Jerry both wanted. Jerry honestly thought that the best kid in the country he could get at that time to be his point guard was Danny, and Danny had always wanted to play for his father, even though he never said so. Academically, Danny was an excellent student—he had a 3.86 grade point average and was a two-time Academic All-American, a Rhodes Scholar candidate, and a recipient of an NCAA postgraduate scholarship. He showed that the kind of education you get is up to the student. Just because you go to Stanford or Harvard doesn't mean you learn a lot. And just because you go to a state school doesn't mean you're cheating yourself in the classroom.

"The reason why Danny did so well in basketball and in school is that he's a lot like Jerry. When he sets his mind on something, Danny gets tunnel vision and he works like crazy. You have to understand that Jerry and Danny are very intense. They hate to lose. They equate losing with death, and they suffer so much. But when we won, the family treasured those times even more. Danny wasn't living at home; he stayed near school and roomed with some of the players. But he came home a lot, and the victories tasted even better when Danny was playing.

"Maybe that's why Jerry and Danny were both almost fanatical about finding ways to make Danny a better player. At times, I just felt sorry for Danny. He was wearing special shoes with high heels that were supposed to strengthen his arch or his ankles and help his jumping ability. Danny also wore this strange mouth guard to straighten his teeth, because one of the theories on jumping was that if you had even the smallest offset in your dental bite, it hurt your shot. Don't ask me what that thing was about, but Danny tried it.

"Most people don't realize that Danny never should have played his senior year. He had terrible bone spurs in his ankle, and he was in a lot of pain. The summer before Danny's senior year, he had played for a U.S. pre-Olympics team that toured the Orient. The condition of his ankle grew progressively worse, and by the time he came home it had reached the point where we decided to take him to a specialist. The doctor took x-rays, and he told me that he couldn't believe Danny was able to walk into the doctor's office on his own because the ankle was in such terrible condition. The pain wasn't the problem with Danny—he always played hurt, and he played through the aches and everything else and never complained. But the bone spurs severely hindered his ability to make sharp turns and quick cuts on the court. But it didn't matter. Danny had that fire in his eyes, and he was going to play no matter what. That was his personality.

"One of the craziest things was his shooting. That was the weakest part of Danny's game. Danny kept switching back and forth—I mean, one year he was shooting right-handed, the next year he was shooting with his left hand. I don't claim to be a basketball expert, but I had never seen anything like it. I kept telling Jerry to just let Danny alone, he was making Danny's shot even worse. But they just kept messing around with it."

Danny: "I started playing basketball when I was so small that I used to shoot the ball underhanded, which was a two-handed shot. Then I went to a two-handed set shot, and it seemed like my left hand kept slipping behind the ball while my right hand stayed on the side, meaning I was drifting towards becoming a left-handed shooter. So left-handed was how I shot through high school. But when I went to Dixie College, Dad thought I should try shooting right-handed. I was surprised at how fast I was able to switch from left-handed to right-handed, and my shot was pretty good—or at least, I thought it was. I was hitting pretty well from 18 to 20 feet, and I averaged 17 points at Dixie. I have to admit that it was a strange-looking shot, and it took me a long time to get it off. When you're shooting, the hand you have on the side of the ball—the guiding hand—has to come off the ball first. Well, since I was used to shooting left-handed in high school, the left hand was the hand that came off the ball last, which was as it should be. But when I switched to right-handed at Dixie, my left hand was supposed to come off the ball first, but sometimes it wouldn't. That makes for a shot that is kind of weird-looking. Dad thought that if you were going to be a great shooter, your shot had to look good. I shot right-handed my whole year at Dixie.

"After I transferred to UNLV, I thought I was going to shoot right-handed, because that was what I had been practicing. But about a month before the season, I went back to shooting left-handed. By then I had no confidence whatsoever in my shooting. When the games came, I didn't want to shoot. I thought the other guys were better shooters, and the last thing I wanted to do was screw something up and cost us a game. During my junior year, I went back to shooting right-handed.

"It was Dad who kept switching me back and forth. Another thing was my foul shooting. During my junior year, I had the best foul-shooting percentage on the team. I used to shoot with both feet parallel to the line. Then Dad said he talked to someone from Weber State, where the guys all stood at the foul line with one foot in front and the other in back. So he had me switch my foul shooting, and that was a real mistake. Because of the bone spurs in my ankle, I couldn't bend my foot as you needed to in order to shoot that way. But I kept plugging away and practicing. By January of my senior year, I was shooting 48 percent. I had lost all confidence in my foul shot. It was really embarrassing. Then I went back to my old way of shooting and hit about 75 percent at the line for the rest of the season.

"Once I got through that first season at UNLV, I loved playing basketball for the school and for Dad. Looking back, I don't think a college basketball player can have a better experience than I did at UNLV. Everywhere you go, you're recognized. I used to get letters from little kids, telling me that they thought I was the greatest and that they loved the Running Rebels. I'd look at the letters and feel really good. I mean, what did I do to get some little kids to write to me? But it was nice that they did.

"The home games were the most amazing thing. When you're introduced, you run out to the middle of the floor on a red carpet. There are 20,000 fans screaming. They play the school fight song, and they have this great light show. Then they shoot off fireworks inside the building. Even now, when I think about it I get a special feeling inside.

"After college, I was drafted by San Antonio in the eighth round, and I went to summer rookie camp with them and was cut. Then, I went to veterans camp with Portland. There were seventeen of us, and after two weeks I was one of three guys who were cut. I thought about going to play pro ball in Europe, but that didn't materialize. I also considered the Continental Basketball Association, but minor-league basketball is mostly one-on-one. Nobody cares if the team wins or loses. Most guys are out for themselves, and you can't make any money.

"But sometimes I wish that I had gone to Europe to play. I have a lot of friends playing overseas and they love it. I had an offer to play in Switzerland, but I went to law school instead. I remember the 1987 play-offs, when I was watching the Lakers play Denver on television. There were a couple of guys, such as A. C. Green and Mark Alarie, with whom I had played on summer all-star teams. I kept thinking that I was studying ten to twelve hours a day and those guys were playing ball. I really missed the game.

"I remember seeing the movie *Hoosiers*, where one character says to the other, 'What's so great about basketball? You're a hero for a couple of years and after that, no one knows you.' But most people would do almost anything to have those few years. That's how it was when I played at UNLV."

15

Rebuilding the Rebels

The next great 7-footer Jerry Tarkanian has will be his first.

Think about that for a moment. If you want to win, then you want to be big. A major part of the game of basketball is rebounding, and the easiest way to rebound is to be taller than anyone else. The difference between a 6-foot-9 player and a 7-footer is more than just three inches in height. It is about a half-foot in arm span. The taller the player, the longer his arms. And the longer the arms, the higher a player can reach for a rebound.

So that's why height is treasured by coaches. The saying is that you can't coach height. Either a kid has it or he doesn't.

For the most part, Tarkanian's teams have been small.

Sidney Green is 6-foot-9, and he was the man in the middle for the 1982–83 Rebels when they were ranked number one for a few weeks. Green is now a power forward in the NBA with the New York Knicks. Some NBA scouts have said that Green eventually will have to play small forward, because the league gets taller each season.

The center on UNLV's Final Four team of 1976–77 was Larry Moffett, who stood all of 6-foot-8. Moffett was a second-round pick by the Houston Rockets, and played only 20 games before being cut and then continuing his career in Europe.

The center on the 1986–87 Final Four team was 6-foot-8 Jarvis Basnight. That's right—the Rebels were 37–2 with a 6-foot-8 center.

Where are the Bill Waltons or the Ralph Sampsons? How about the Brad Daughertys, the Danny Mannings, or the Pervis Ellisons?

You found those players at UCLA, Louisville, North Carolina, and the other traditional elite basketball powers.

"We've never been able to recruit the blue-chip big man," says Tarkanian. "Believe me, we've tried. We've just had to learn to live without them and make the best out of what we've had."

Call it ingenuity or making a little go a long way, but that has always been Tarkanian's trademark. He has taken players who weren't tall enough to be centers, and played them at center. They've played well there, because Tarkanian has convinced them that they could do what others said they couldn't: outjump, out-rebound, and out-hustle more talented and physically gifted opponents.

The key to Tarkanian's success has been his ability to work with players like Richie Adams.

Who is Richie Adams?

"A kid who needed someone like Jerry Tarkanian in his life," according to Cleveland State coach Kevin Mackey, who knew Adams as a high school player in New York. Mackey says, "Richie is a street kid, and you can't con a street kid, because by the time they're 12, they've heard every con job in the world. Street kids know if you care about them or not. Tark cares about those kids. He trusts them and he has patience with them. I'm convinced that no coach could have gotten more out of Richie Adams than Tark."

Adams was a 6-foot-8 leaper who played for the Rebels from 1982 to 1985. A strong case can be made that Adams was UNLV's best center. He also is one of Tarkanian's finest coaching jobs.

Kevin Mackey: "I recruited Richie Adams when I was an assistant at Boston College. His neighborhood was the worst. Remember the movie *Fort Apache, The Bronx,* where the police station was in the middle of a gang-infested area with buildings burning down all the time? Well, that was Richie's home, Bedford-Stuyvesant. The kid had no father in the picture. In his neighborhood, you have junkies, thieves, murderers. The cops just pick up the bodies. In many ways, it's an amoral atmosphere. People rob each other. They kill each other for no reason. It is a society unlike any most of us will ever know. He started from so far back, as behind as you can get. Believe me, when you take a kid like Richie and get as much out of him as Tark did, you're talking about a miracle.

"Adams was a great high school player at Benjamin Franklin in New York. Everyone knew about Richie. As a player, the kid could just hover. I mean, he would jump and just stay up there indefinitely.

He was a leaper, a playground legend in New York. But he had limited academic skills. Tom Davis was the head coach at Boston College when I was there, and we both liked Richie. We put him at Massachusetts Bay Community College so he could get his grades together.''

In high school, Adams averaged 18 points and 15 rebounds for a prep team that was ranked second in the country. He was even better in junior college, averaging 25 points, 18 rebounds, and 10 blocks a game. Most centers are happy with 3 blocks, but Adams was swatting away 10, which is considered an unofficial junior college record.

After Adams's first year at Massachusetts Bay Community College, Tom Davis took the Stanford coaching job, and Boston College stopped recruiting Adams. Davis still wanted Adams, but Adams lacked the academic credentials for Stanford, even though he had performed relatively well in junior college. It was at this point that UNLV assistant coach Tim Grgurich laid the recruiting groundwork to bring Adams to UNLV.

A key person in convincing Adams to attend UNLV was Joe Bostic, who teaches math at Junior Academy in Brooklyn. Junior Academy includes grades three through eight, and is the largest black-owned private school in the state of New York. Bostic also was a coach of summer league teams in New York and that's where he met Adams.

Joe Bostic: ''I was happy when Richie told me that he was interested in Vegas. There aren't that many college coaches I trust—Dean Smith, Louie Carnesecca, Tark, and a few others. With those men, their word is their bond. Tark told me that they would get tutors for Richie. He said they would treat him like part of their family. I knew he would, too. So I pushed Richie to play for Tark.''

As for his relationship with Bostic, Adams has said, ''Joe is like a father to me.'' On parent's night, it was Joe Bostic who was standing on the court next to Richie Adams.

But Adams's first season at UNLV was not what Tarkanian, Bostic, or even Adams hoped.

Joe Bostic: ''First of all, I think Richie was suffering from culture shock. All he knew was New York and the East Coast. He was used to the city—and to a kid from the Bronx, Las Vegas is not a city. He also was used to being the main man, the big star. But when he got to Vegas, Sidney Green was the main man. Hey, Sidney should have been; he earned it. But Richie was jealous of Sid, and Richie started acting like the biggest idiot in the world.''

Danny Tarkanian always was Adams's closest friend and strongest supporter. It's an intriguing combination. You have Adams, a black kid with no stable home and from the worst part of New York City.

He was not a serious student, nor interested in much of anything but basketball. Danny Tarkanian was a white, middle-class kid who became a two-time Academic All-American. On the UNLV team in the early 1980s, they were the odd couple.

Danny: "That first year, Richie did act strange a lot. More than once, he told me that he was a manic-depressive. During some practices, he would just go sit in the corner and not talk to anyone. I mean, he wouldn't move. Guys would say things to him; Dad would try to get him on the floor; but Richie just sat there. He wouldn't even act like he heard you. It was as though he were in another world. He hated everyone. Of course, that 1981–82 team had a bad attitude. Richie was always a follower, so he fell right in with the guys who did all the complaining.

"After his first year at UNLV, Richie went home for the summer. He had registered for the fall semester, but while he was in New York, right before he was supposed to come back to start school, his grandmother died. Richie was close to his grandmother because she had raised him. Then, a few days later, the mother of Richie's girlfriend died. He had been going with this girl for years, and that upset him. He wouldn't go back to school; he wouldn't even leave their apartment. Richie's mother called Dad and said, 'Please get Richie to come back to school. All he does is sit in his room. He won't do anything.' The coaches talked to Richie and he finally came back to UNLV in November."

Since Adams never attended the classes he had registered for, he was withdrawn as a student. He tried to re-enroll, but he was suspended because he missed too many classes. He returned to New York and sat out the 1982–83 season.

Tarkanian: "While Richie was gone, we made it to number one in the country. I think that really amazed him. Richie knew he had tremendous talent, and he found it hard to believe we could win that much without him. That just blew his mind, and he started calling me to come back."

But no one wanted him.

Not assistant coaches Mark Warkentien or Tim Grgurich, who had originally recruited him. Not Tarkanian, who places so much emphasis on working hard in practice, and had to endure a pouting Adams disrupting what he was trying to do.

But Danny Tarkanian had other ideas:

Danny: "I told Dad that Richie was a follower. While he sat out, we had completely changed the personality of the team. The last of the guys recruited under probation were gone, and we had a lot of good people. I told Dad to think about how we would have reacted if we had grown up like Richie did and if our grandmother and our girl-friend's mother had died within a few days. I told Dad that if he died, I wouldn't feel like going back to school for a few months. I'd be de-stroyed. Well, Richie was the same way. The coaches were mad at Richie, first because he didn't practice hard; then, because he was late reporting to school when his grandmother died; finally, because when he did get to Vegas, he turned around and went home to New York after he was suspended. The coaches wanted him to stay in town, but he was homesick. If he couldn't play for UNLV, he saw no reason to stay."

Tarkanian: "Danny is the reason I brought Richie back [in 1983–84]. My coaches didn't want him; even most of the people in town didn't want him. But Danny kept saying that Richie would be a good person if he was surrounded by good people. Danny even offered to live with Richie. I said, 'Hell no, you're not living with Richie.' But we did set up one of our graduate assistants to live with Richie, and we told Richie that he would be under close supervision all the time. If he messed up, that was it. There would be no more second chances. He accepted that and came back. And Danny was right; Richie was a totally different kid. He went to class. Because of his background, he was never going to be a great student, but he tried like hell."

As the 1983–84 season started, the Rebels had lost Sidney Green and Larry Anderson, their two leading scorers, who were taken in the NBA draft. In many ways, it was a transition season. But Adams came through for both Tarkanians. He had a Tarkanian named Danny pass-ing him the ball and a Tarkanian named Jerry setting up the plays. Adams responded by becoming the Pacific Coast Athletic Association player of the year as the Rebels were 29–6.

Danny: "I just wish we had had Richie that year when Sidney Green and Larry Anderson were seniors. "I'm convinced that we would have gone undefeated with him. Richie did just what I thought he could: he blended in with the team because he thought the guys liked him. In-stead of people filling his head with garbage, Richie had guys telling him to push himself in practice, to go to class, and to play team bas-ketball."

In Adams's senior season [1984–85], he repeated as the PCAA player of the year, averaging 15 points and 8 rebounds as UNLV went 28–4.

Tarkanian: "What pleased me is that Richie was so happy. The town loved him, and we found something that really interested him: working with kids. He used to go to elementary schools so he could be with children. Richie just loved little kids. After most games, there were twelve to fifteen kids waiting for Richie. He walked from place to place in the gym, and little kids would follow him as if he were the Pied Piper or something. Other players went off with their girlfriends; Richie went to get ice cream with the little children. On Senior Night, the people stood and cheered and cheered for Richie. There were tears running down his face. All these little kids were going crazy. Richie is one of my favorite people, because he made such an unbelievable turn-around.''

Adams was drafted in the fourth round by the Washington Bullets in 1985, and he didn't last long in training camp. Out of the structured and nurturing environment of UNLV, Adams was "a lost soul," according to Joe Bostic.

"When Richie got out of school, I begged him not to go back to New York," says Tarkanian. "Everyone knew that if he went back to New York, he'd end up with the wrong people and there would be trouble. In his neighborhood, there is nothing but trouble. He wanted to go home. I said, 'Richie, Vegas is your home. Stay here. This is where people care about you.'"

But Adams went back to the Bronx.

Joe Bostic: "Tark kept calling me, wanting me to get Richie back to Vegas. I told Tark, 'I don't want Richie in the streets, either. As long as he is in the streets, anything can happen.' But Richie is a hero in New York, even if all he does is play in summer leagues. The neighborhood tournaments are very macho things. A lot of these summer league coaches want to get good players, and they slip the kids money. The good playground players are celebrities. The bad thing is that some of the guys hanging around these athletes are dope dealers and crooks. They want to drag the players down with them. In New York, Richie reverts back to his old ways; he wants to hang around the playgrounds and play ball. That's not all bad. But the people who are hanging around the playgrounds can get you in trouble. And Richie did eventually get into trouble.

"Tark has set up a job for him in Vegas working for the recreation department. It would be perfect for Richie because he would be with kids. Tark has no stake in the kid; he is out of eligibility. He gave Tark some real headaches early in his career. Most coaches would disappear, but Jerry didn't."

Lois: "The problem is that the good period Richie had at UNLV wasn't long enough to overcome all those years in New York. Jerry begged Richie not to go back to New York, but he said he was home-sick and wanted to see his friends and family. It is like he is two different people—a good kid in Vegas and a kid who is vulnerable to outside influence when he is in New York. When he was in Vegas, Richie worked with a child who had learning disabilities. The boy's father thinks that Richie is the greatest, and working with that boy made Richie a better person. Jerry lined up a job for Richie in the recreation department, where he could take advantage of that gift he has for working with children. Richie could develop a solid future for himself in Las Vegas. All Richie had to do was move here and take it, but he couldn't seem to pull himself away from New York.''

Adams has spent several winters playing pro basketball in Argentina. He says he is thinking about returning to Vegas.

Sidney Green: ''I grew up in Brooklyn, so I know how it is for Richie. You have to tell yourself, 'I'm going to leave the street behind.' Then, that's it; you just do it. On those few occasions when I have been back in Brooklyn, I've seen the same guys doing the same things they were doing ten years ago. They were in trouble then, and they're in trouble now, and they'd like nothing better than for me to get down with them. Now, it's up to Richie. Tark has given him a chance at a new life. The Tarkanians have done everything short of adopting him. They are the only real family he has, and he should realize it.''

The Rebels never made it to the Final Four with Danny Tarkanian, Sidney Green, or Richie Adams.

''Dad wasn't disappointed that we didn't get to the Final Four, but we all knew that it was his dream,'' says Danny. ''You can't imagine how important getting there is to him and therefore to our family.''

Here's how Danny Tarkanian characterizes the effect of the Final Four on Tarkanian and UNLV.

Danny: ''First, when you're winning, you get very little bad publicity. If you win game after game in the NCAA tournament, reporters around the country tend to write nice things about you. That's because they get to see Dad and talk to him. They find out that he is a nice guy; that our players are good, articulate kids; and that the team isn't like the image most people have of Vegas. Sure, there are a few exceptions. Some guys will take their shots at you no matter what, but for the most part, the publicity is excellent.

''Second, we—the players and the family—feel that Dad hasn't gotten the recognition he deserves for the job he has done, not just in one year, but throughout his career. The man is the winningest coach in major college basketball. That's a fact, not an opinion. But when Dad goes to the Final Four, people start to see that he is a good coach.

They start to examine his record and say things like, 'This guy must have been doing something right all these years to win so many games.' People start to respect him as a coach.''

Sidney Green, Larry Anderson, Richie Adams, Anthony Jones, "Spoon" James and Danny Tarkanian formed the core of the teams that brought UNLV out of the dark ages of probation. From 1983 to 1986, they helped Tarkanian to records of 28–3, 29–6, 28–4, and 33–5, along with four appearances in the NCAA tournament. While the Rebels never quite made it to the Final Four, those players and others gave the program legitimacy. They set the stage for the 37–2 team in 1986–87, featuring seniors Freddie Banks and Armon Gilliam.

Banks was a 6-foot-2 guard from Valley High School in Las Vegas. Growing up, Banks imitated UNLV guard Sam Smith. The bigger Banks became, the more he practiced his jumper, and he shot from long range—after all, Sam Smith uncorked 22-footers as if they were lay-ups. At Helen C. Cannon Junior High, Freddie Banks averaged 42 points a game, a remarkable achievement since those games consisted of four 6-minute quarters. That meant Banks was racking up those 42 points in 24 minutes. At Valley High, Banks led his team to three consecutive Nevada state titles. When Banks played in high school, his coach tried to harness Freddie's Sam Smith shooting tendencies. As a sophomore, Freddie was told to shoot from no farther than 15 feet. As a junior, it was moved back to 18 feet. As a senior, Freddie was let loose and had several games over 30 points. This led to letters from 162 colleges and a berth on the McDonald's high school All-American team.

Tarkanian: "We watched Freddie grow up. His dad [Tilmon] works at the Hacienda Hotel and his mother [Martha] works at the Union Plaza. They had six children and they were great parents. They made sure those kids went to school every day and that they were polite and did their schoolwork. You won't find a better family. We are talking about great, great people. That's why Freddie is a coach's dream. He would do anything he was asked.

"When he was a senior, there was talk that Freddie would go here or there—a lot of colleges wanted him. Supposedly, Oregon State and Nebraska were strong in the picture, but we went right to Freddie's mother. Freddie's mother loved us from day one, and so did his father. The Banks family is so close; they didn't want their son going to play somewhere across the country. Freddie is a homebody, and I knew his mother would not let him be talked into leaving the area. Freddie was a good kid and a decent high school student. All we had to do was show that our program was solid and that we could do a good job with him academically. We had just built a new arena. Everything was on the upswing. Some people were surprised when Freddie signed with us, because there were rumors that he was going elsewhere. But I never had a doubt about the kid.''

At Vegas, Banks surpassed his hero, Sam Smith. He steadily built his scoring average, from 4.9 as a freshman coming off the bench to 19.4 as a senior in 1986–87.

"I called him 'Fearless Freddie,'" says Tarkanian. "It started when Freddie was a freshman and we were playing at Utah State. It was late in the second half, and I had run out of players because of foul trouble and injuries. I had to use Freddie almost the whole game. The score was close, and the Utah State coaches were screaming, 'Foul the freshman,' meaning foul Freddie, because they thought he'd miss like many freshmen would in that situation. But Freddie just kept hitting the foul shot. He was a great clutch player for us from the start, a player without fear. Some 7-foot, 250-pounder would come down the lane, and Freddie would put that skinny 155-pound body of his right in front of the guy. Freddie would know he was going to get run over, but he'd take the charge and then bounce right up off the floor. In a close game, he wanted to take the last shot. A lot of guys run from the ball in those situations; they don't want to be the guy who gets blamed if they miss the last shot. But Freddie was willing to take that responsibility.''

On six different occasions, Banks hit shots in the last few seconds that either won games or forced an overtime.

"He was amazing in the clutch,'' says Tarkanian. "That's because he is a tremendous kid. His family is right behind him, and he knew that. The parents were at every home game. When we came off the road, his mother picked up Freddie at the airport. That means a lot to a kid. It really helps his self-image when the parents are there.

"Freddie had some tough times. There was a period during his junior year when he was having trouble scoring and was forcing some bad shots. Some of our assistants got on him a little bit, and it psychologically affected him. The key to being a good shooter is having great confidence, but Freddie was starting to have some doubts; he was being torn up inside. He was worrying that his shooting was hurting the team. We needed Freddie's outside shooting to win. I told my assistants to leave Freddie to me. He was better off being left on his own. If he took a couple of bad shots I'd live with that. We wanted him playing naturally, free and easy.''

That's what Banks did during his senior season as he averaged 19.4

points. He was impressive from 3-point range, hitting 41 percent. In practice, Tarkanian used Banks as an example.

"He worked so hard, showed so much desire," said Tarkanian. "That was the thing about Freddie. He already was a great player at UNLV, and probably the greatest high school player ever to come out of Las Vegas, but he worked hard in every practice. The other guys saw it, and they did the same thing. That's being a leader—putting yourself on the line every day in practice. I love Freddie for that."

Tarkanian felt the same way about Armon Gilliam, a 6-foot-9, 240-pound power forward.

This was a kid who didn't start playing basketball until his junior year at Bethel High in Pittsburgh, and he wasn't even on the varsity. In fact, he was the sixth man on the junior varsity squad. He was a football player, a tight end who was recruited by Clemson and other prominent schools. He also received some other college scholarship offers, but they were for wrestling, not basketball.

But Gilliam fell in love with basketball. As a senior, he started on the varsity and averaged 13 points and 10 rebounds. His high school coach, Red Ryan, remembers Gilliam as a big kid who liked to shoot from the outside. That isn't exactly the ticket to major college basketball. At this juncture of his career, Gilliam was, in basketball terms, "a body." That means he had size, and he had strength, but he also had little idea of what to do with it on the court. His next stop was Independence Junior College in Kansas, where he was spotted by Mark Warkentien.

Mark Warkentien: "Armon wasn't a starter. When I first saw him, I was at a game to scout Spoon James. Then I saw this kid come on the floor. He had a body. I told myself, 'This kid's body will play.' I mean, when a kid is 6-foot-9 and 240 pounds of muscle, you have to take a chance on him, no matter how far behind he is in terms of basketball skills."

Tarkanian: "Mark was so excited the first time he saw Armon, and the minute I heard Armon was from Pittsburgh, I knew we had a shot at him. Tim Grgurich is from Pittsburgh, Larry Anderson is from Pittsburgh, and so are a lot of other people who have been involved with our program. Armon told us that he wanted to leave Independence after a year, so we pretty much had him locked up. But right at the end of the summer, [former Maryland coach] Lefty Driesell heard about Armon. Lefty had never even seen the kid play. He just heard that UNLV wanted Armon, so he figured that Armon must be pretty good. Armon's father is a minister, and he had some concerns about his son going to school in Las Vegas. It was the same thing we often run up against in recruiting. But we had so many people who knew us well talk to the father, and since these people were from Pittsburgh, it had an impact and we were able to hold off Maryland. One person who really helped us was Dr. Jim Robinson, Larry Anderson's old high school principal. Dr. Robinson is very respected in the Pittsburgh black community, and he had a big influence on Armon's father.''

Obviously, signing Banks and Gilliam meant a lot to UNLV on the court and in the record book. But they also were a plus to the program's image—just like Sidney Green, Danny Tarkanian, Larry Anderson, and the other players who helped UNLV reach number one in 1983.

If the Rebels had lost Banks, a heavily recruited local kid who was a respectable student and had a wonderful family, it would have been used against them when they recruited other players. Assistant coaches from other schools would have said, "If Vegas is so great, how come they couldn't keep Freddie Banks from leaving town?" Just as those coaches would have said, "If Vegas is so good, how come Tark couldn't even sign his own son?"

But Tarkanian did sign Danny and Freddie Banks. And in Gilliam, he signed a player whose father was a preacher. That struck a real blow to Las Vegas's "Sin City" recruiting image.

Added to the mix of Gilliam and Banks was Jarvis Basnight, a 6-foot-8 leaper from Pittsburgh who averaged 9.1 points and 4.9 rebounds. The other key players were Mark Wade, Gerald Paddio, Gary Graham, and Eldridge Hudson.

Wade had a remarkable season in 1986–87, breaking Danny Tarkanian's NCAA assist record. He had attended Oklahoma for a year, but the Sooners had no plans for a 5-foot-10 point guard who wasn't a strong shooter. His next stop was El Camino Junior College.

"Mark always wanted to be a Rebel," says Tarkanian. "But we were recruiting some other people we thought were better, and we kept putting him off. We wanted to sign Tommy Lewis. When Lewis picked Southern California instead of us, we turned to Wade."

Tarkanian never regretted it.

Eldridge Hudson was a premier high school player from Los Angeles, who ripped up his knee after his freshman season. The knee was surgically reconstructed, and there were fears that Hudson might never play again. While he lost some of his mobility and leaping ability, he remained a trusted veteran whom Tarkanian brought off the bench. Paddio was a transfer from Seminole Junior College in Oklahoma.

Gary Graham had known about Las Vegas for years. His older

brother Ernie Graham was a fine player at Maryland. At one time, Ernie had contacted Tarkanian about transferring to UNLV. Tarkanian had told Ernie to talk to Maryland and try to resolve his problems before transferring, and that was what happened. But when it came time for younger brother Gary to attend college, he already knew about UNLV, and that's where he went.

So the team that went 37–2 and made it to the 1987 Final Four had one high school All-American—Banks. It had another player considered a high school star—Hudson; but Hudson's emotional swings caused many colleges to decide against offering him a scholarship. Also, Hudson was not the same player after his knee injury. Graham was a good complementary player on a great Dunbar High team in Baltimore. The other three players—Gilliam, Paddio, and Wade—were junior college transfers, and not among the top JUCO players in their respective classes.

"I know UNLV was ranked number one for much of the season, but I don't even think Tarkanian had Top Twenty talent," says Pete Newell. "Banks was the only kid with a big reputation in high school."

By major college standards, UNLV's talent is pretty good.

But great?

Hardly.

So why does Tarkanian win?

Pete Newell: "He was ahead of a lot of the other coaches. When the NCAA put in the close 3-point line [19 feet, 9 inches], Tark immediately recognized what that would mean. That rule transformed college basketball from a game where the emphasis was on inside offense to a game where the emphasis was on outside shooting. He saw that the new 3-pointer was a good percentage shot for some guys. He also knew that a 3-point play is like a punch in the stomach to the other team. So he took Banks and Paddio and he put them on the wings, right behind that 3-point line. He told those guys to shoot and shoot and not to worry if they missed. He built up their confidence, convincing those kids that they were great outside shooters. Next, he had Wade delivering the ball. Wade was one of the most selfless kids ever to play college basketball. Under the basket Tark had Gilliam, and Gilliam had developed into an excellent shooter from the 10- to 12-foot range. Also, Gilliam was like a bull; no one could move him. Finally, he had Basnight on the boards for rebounds.

"Think about what Tark set up. In Banks and Paddio, he created a dangerous outside game. If you give them room from 20 feet, they take the shot. If you go outside to cover them, that opens up Gilliam in the middle of the key. What's more, you had Wade, who knew which players should get the ball, and he got them the ball at the proper spots on the court. Only Rick Pitino at Providence took advantage of the 3-point rule as much as Tark.

"I've always been a Tarkanian man because of the adjustments he has made over the years. His record obviously establishes him as one of the top coaches, but what I really admire is how he has evolved as a coach. In junior college, he was a running-style coach. At Long Beach, he played that 1-2-2 zone and walked the ball up the court on offense. At Vegas, he went back to the running game. Then in 1987, he carried the running game one more step. Instead of his kids driving all the way in for lay-ups, they stopped at the 3-point line and took the jump shot. Instead of tailoring his players to his style, he changed his style to fit the players. A lot of coaches won't do that. Their egos say their system is bigger than the players, and the players should learn to play within that system. Tark puts talent first. He coaches to suit his players."

Oklahoma City coach Abe Lemons: "Jerry Tarkanian is the most misunderstood coach in the country. The damage the NCAA did to his reputation was severe, and it was done for no reason. It upsets me just to think about it, because it was true injustice. A number of years ago, Digger Phelps and Marv Harshman wouldn't vote for his team in the polls because UNLV had been under investigation. What kind of garbage is that? Those coaches were totally out of line, and what they did to Jerry was terrible. Those guys barely knew Jerry, and they were making judgments about him. Anyone who knows Jerry has to appreciate him, because he wins gracefully and he loses gracefully, and he wins with almost no blue-chip players.

"Teams such as North Carolina and Indiana have more high school All-Americans on their roster in any given year than Jerry has had in his career at Vegas. With Jerry, there is almost no ego involved—and that's saying a lot, because the coaching profession is filled with guys who have huge egos. As for Jerry as a coach, no one has dominated a league as he has the PCAA. He has been in it for six years and won six titles. What could be better than that?

"The impressive thing is that he has won it every single year. That's because Jerry's kids play so hard. He takes no one for granted, and he has gotten his kids to look at it the same way. That's one of the hardest parts of coaching—keeping your kids from having a letdown. Furthermore, every league game Jerry plays is the biggest one for his opponent, because they all are aiming to knock off UNLV. What really strikes me about Jerry is that he and his kids win the games they should win. They almost never are upset, and they also win a lot of games where UNLV is clearly the underdog.''

Purdue coach Gene Keady: ''One of the most amazing parts of Jerry's coaching has been how he has radically changed his style of play to suit his kids. That's something I don't know if I could do. But no matter what offense or defense his kids play, they play hard. Every coach will tell you that the key to winning is intensity and getting your kids to play hard. That has always been the trademark of Jerry's teams. But why does it happen? I think part of the reason is the kids Jerry takes. Many of them are transfers from junior colleges or other four-year schools. A lot of coaches are afraid of transfers, but Jerry never has been, and neither have I. Jerry and I were both junior college coaches. We know that JUCO kids often have academic or social problems, or else they just weren't that talented when they came out of high school. But we also know that when those kids come to you, they usually are willing and ready to listen. Their backs are against the wall. They can't keep transferring from school to school. At some point, they have to buckle down and do the work, and Jerry is the perfect guy for a kid in that situation. He pushes those kids, he demands a lot, but he also is patient with them. So the kids not only know that Jerry is their last chance; they know that he will give them a real chance to make something of themselves.''

Kentucky coach Eddie Sutton: ''The thing that sticks out the most about Jerry is that he and I are the only coaches I know who have never been assistants, and we have been head coaches at every level—high school, junior college and four-year college. I'm sure that we could have learned something from being an assistant under a major head coach, but the lessons we learned by running our own programs taught us more. We learned the game from the bottom up. We taped ankles, did the laundry, and raised money to buy our kids tennis shoes. We did all our own scouting, recruiting, and academic work. Now when you tell some young men that they should start out as a high school coach and work their way up the ladder, they look at you as if you're asking them to go slumming. They all want to be a graduate assistant, then a full assistant, and then a head coach, and they all want to do it on the major college level.

''The fact that Jerry worked in the high school and junior colleges is a tremendous asset, because it brought him close to the kids. He was there to listen to all their problems, because they had no one else to turn to. There were no academic counselors or assistant coaches. Working in that kind of grass roots of coaching means that Jerry developed a special sensitivity to the needs of kids. It also meant that Jerry was recruiting JUCO kids before anyone else. Now it's fashionable to recruit the JUCOs, but Jerry was there from the start. So why does Jerry win? To me, it's simple. He's paid as many dues as anyone in the business.''

Detroit Pistons assistant Dick Versace: ''Jerry is a very intriguing personality. On one hand, the man *is* UNLV basketball. There was no real basketball program of national consequence before he arrived, and it's hard to say whether UNLV can continue to win as often if Jerry ever leaves. There are two kinds of programs. The first is found in places such as Indiana, North Carolina, and Kentucky, where the basketball tradition is rich, the leagues are prestigious, and no matter who is the coach, the school is guaranteed a certain degree of success. Those schools recruit for themselves. Certain leagues such as the ACC, the Big Ten, and the Big East also recruit for themselves. Then there are schools where the man, the coach, is the program. That's Jerry and UNLV. The reason why UNLV has prospered in the desert and playing in a young league such as the PCAA is Jerry. He made the program.

''Yet Jerry's personality is very low-keyed and self-effacing. All he cares about is winning and making his kids better, and he is so sincere. Because he isn't interested in making himself famous, he has time for his kids and he likes them. He likes being around them, and that's not true of every college coach. Jerry maximizes his kids' skills. For example, Freddie Banks and Gerald Paddio were not great percentage shooters, maybe hitting about 43 percent. Yet Jerry has built up these kids' confidence to the point where they were good 3-point shooters. He is a master of taking a kid who is a good athlete, who has a skill in one area, and hiding the player's weaknesses while using his strength.

''Like Jerry, I coached in junior college, and then when I coached at Bradley, I had to work with JUCO kids, kids who may have had a problem along the way. But when these kids come to Vegas, there is a tradition. First, he has made UNLV into a winner, and these kids desperately want to be associated with a winner because it makes them feel better about themselves. Second, Jerry has a reputation as a coach kids can trust because of all the good work he has done throughout the years. They say, 'If you can't play for Tark, who can you play for?' This means that kids go into his program with the right attitude. The kids see how hard Jerry's players work, how they act, and a lot of that swagger goes away. Jerry's former players also play a big role. They tell the recruits that they like and trust Jerry. They also tell the recruits that this is how it is: if you play for Tark, you better be ready to work harder than you ever have in your life. That's the message you get from his program."

Former UNLV assistant Bud Presley: "I coached in junior colleges for over twenty years, and I always wondered how Jerry got his kids to play so hard. Then I spent a year [1983–84] as Jerry's assistant, and I think I found the answer. He is like a daddy to his players, and a lot of his players haven't had father figures in their lives. He openly shows that he cares about his players, and they don't want to disappoint him, because he has given them one last chance to make something of themselves. They don't just play hard to win; they play hard to please Jerry. The other factor is that Jerry is so single-minded. Twenty-four hours a day, it's nothing but basketball. His assistant, Tim Grgurich, does the same thing. So the players see two of these guys doing nothing but eating, thinking, talking, and even sleeping basketball, and it rubs off. Because the players like him, they start acting and thinking the same way. Soon, he has the whole team on a mission."

North Carolina State coach Jim Valvano: "Some people say that Jerry has tunnel vision; I prefer to say that he is focused. Every person who has been great in a field—whether it's writing, acting, politics—has been focused. Jerry Tarkanian is a BASKETBALL COACH in capital letters. Basketball and his family are all he cares about. Have we ever had a conversation where basketball wasn't mentioned? Sure, we've talked about academics, about business, and a few other things, but you know what? It usually was how academics related to basketball, or how business related to basketball. With Jerry, everything in life comes down to hoops. That's why it doesn't matter where he has coached, what players he coached, or what style of play he used—Jerry has won. The game has changed over the years, and Jerry has done more than change with the times—he has kept ahead of the other coaches.

"A key to his success is his family. They are as dedicated to basketball as he is, and that's saying a lot. How he ever convinced a bright, dynamic woman like Lois to marry him is beyond me. You know that still stands as his greatest recruiting job. Talk about a mismatch! But what happened was that Lois and his children pulled together with Jerry to help him with basketball. They have created that family atmosphere, which now includes all of his former players. That's not the case with other coaches' families. He has the reputation of running a family program, of being the great hope for the junior college player or the kid who maybe got in trouble once in his life. When you play for Jerry Tarkanian, you know that the past is the past. It doesn't matter what you did yesterday; what is important is working hard today and tomorrow.

"Frankly, I don't have Jerry's focus, his stamina for basketball. I don't know how he has done it for all these years. Away from basketball, he moves through the world in a state of bewilderment. You say something to him and Jerry says, 'Is that right?' I mean, you can tell Jerry that the sun rises in the east and he'll say, 'Is that right?' as though he never heard it before.

"Jerry is very funny, and a lot of it is unintentional humor. It's his facial expressions, or the way he seems amazed to hear the most obvious things. At the coaches' clinics, we'll be sitting around the pool and Jerry will be picking all the other coaches' brains. I mean, these guys are .500, and he's listening to them. But that's Jerry—other guys do all the talking, and he does all the winning."

LSU coach Dale Brown: "There aren't many coaches I talk to. Most coaches are petty, jealous people. They talk behind each other's backs. They say that this guy cheats, that guy can't coach, or this guy is a bad person. Then they tell you how great they are. Well, what about the man who is without sin casting the first stone? A lot of people forget that. I like Jerry because he doesn't blow his own horn. You run into a coach and you'll ask how things are going and he'll say, 'Oh great. The kids are wonderful, everybody is going to class and on the honor roll, and all my players are about to be canonized as saints.' Well, that's not the real world. On every team there is a kid who isn't playing up to his potential, a kid with academic troubles, and a kid with personal problems. That's why it bothers me when Jerry is criticized for working with certain kids. Jerry is successful with these kids because Jerry himself has suffered. I think that's the key to working with kids who have had it rough. The kids look at Jerry and they see the suffering. They know he has been where they are, and they know he cares.

"Then there is one other thing that has made Jerry a great coach and a great motivator: the truth. That's right, the truth. It sounds simple, but how many people tell it anymore? The truth is so bold and spoken so little that when it is heard, people are astounded. That is why he has been in trouble with the NCAA. He told the truth, and they went at him. In the past, they have used Gestapo tactics and selective prosecution and Jerry has suffered from that."

Those who have watched and played for Tarkanian insist that practices are why he has won so often.

Former UNLV assistant and now New Jersey Nets player personnel director Al Menendez speaks from experience.

Al Menendez: "The impression of Tarkanian is that he is this super recruiter who is on the road all the time seeing these great players. That's not the case. Now, there are times when Tark is just blinded by talent. That's why he takes a chance on a kid like Lloyd Daniels. He really believes that if a kid is a great basketball player, down deep he also must be a good kid. In other words, he sometimes equates talent with character, and that's not always the case. If he does make a mistake in recruiting, that's it—thinking that a good player automatically must be a good kid. But he doesn't spend that much time on recruiting. When I worked for Tark, I had to beg him to let me go out and recruit. He likes all of his assistants in practice every day, because he thinks that practice is the most important thing we do, and he wants everyone's input. And he never wants to skip a practice to recruit himself. A lot of coaches do that. They go out recruiting and let their assistants run practice, but not Tark. I've been in the NBA for the last ten years, and I've seen all the so-called great coaches, both pro and college, in action during practice, and very few of them can compare to Tark in terms of his basketball mind or his work ethic in practice."

Pete Newell: "I can tell you that Tark stresses that his kids play hard, but all coaches talk about playing hard. Tark is a very physical coach. By that I mean he doesn't spend a lot of time putting X's and O's on the blackboard. He doesn't tell his kids to keep their knees flexed and to get down in a good defensive position. He puts them in drills where the kids have to flex their knees and they have to play good defense. And he drills and drills them over and over. He creates a physical habit, and the only way to do that is through physical repetition.

"That's why he can press like he does for 40 minutes. They play some of the best man-to-man, baseline-to-baseline pressing defense, and his teams can do that because they are superbly conditioned. Tark makes those kids believe in that press, and when they believe in it, they work at it even harder. To play a pressing defense, you have to put forth twice the effort of a normal basketball team. A lot of teams prefer to play a real soft man-to-man—by that I mean they play nothing more than a token defense. Then the kids drop back into a zone, and they just stand there, waiting to get the rebound so they can go on offense. But Tark makes his kids get in your face. Their feet never stop moving. If a ball is loose, they hit the floor and go after it. I don't care what anyone says; defense is the trademark of Tark's teams at Vegas, and his style of defense works because of his practices.

"Tark runs his own practices. He doesn't sit in a chair on the sidelines watching his assistants do all the work. He literally rolls up his sleeves and gets out there on the floor with the kids. He's intense. He's not just pushing them, he's pushing himself. He is all over the practice floor, talking to one kid after another. Like his players, he works at practice."

Reggie Theus has played in the NBA with Chicago and Sacramento and Atlanta, and he has never seen anything remotely like Tarkanian's practices as a pro.

Reggie Theus: "Tark said that no team in the country would be in better condition than us. He even used to make us run with weight jackets on. Late in the season, when other teams had stopped running sprints, we were still doing line drills. Tark had a way of making you extremely competitive in practice. I'm 6-foot-7, and he used to make me guard Robert Smith, who is 5-foot-10 and really quick. Tark wanted me to learn how to guard a guy handling the ball. I chased Robert Smith up and down the court, day after day. When Robert would beat me, Tark would yell.

"One of the funny things about Tark is that he would rant and rave so hard and for so long that he would just run out of air. Then he'd try to talk, and he couldn't get the words out. He just wouldn't stop to take a breath; he was too excited. When he got like that, we'd crack up. I mean, his voice would get higher and higher so that you thought he'd choke to death. By doing things like that, he created this frenzy in practice. We could feel his intensity and his competitiveness, and it would rub off on us.

"He has an assistant coach named Ralph Readout, and this guy fit right in. Ralph is one of the few people I've ever met who would be talking to you and then just start sweating. The intensity would come right out of his pores. We used to call him 'the Gung-Ho White Boy.' He was one of those people who could inspire you to run right through a wall. And what made it work for Ralph was that it was genuine. He was a real item when he got worked up like that. So when things got going in practice, we had Tark talking until he was out of air, we had Ralph yelling and sweating, and the players were killing themselves to run all over the floor."

This is the irony: When fans hear Tarkanian's name, they think about offense; when coaches and other basketball people hear it, they talk about defense.

Basketball commentator Dick Vitale: "I have Tarkanian on my All-Hank Iba Team. To get on the Hank Iba team, you have to be a college coach who teaches defense. That's Tark, [Georgetown's] John Thompson, [Indiana's] Bob Knight, [Kentucky's] Eddie Sutton, and [Villanova's] Rollie Massimino. Those guys all get their kids out on the floor and playing defense every night."

San Diego State coach Jim Brandenburg: "Tark gets his kids to play as hard as anyone for a sustained period. When they get tired, they call time-out. A minute later, they're back out there, going at it harder than ever."

Playing hard. Pressure defense. That's what other coaches worry about when the subject is Tarkanian. And that is because most teams are not used to being pressed. They only prepare for it in practice the week before they are to play a team such as UNLV, Iowa, Georgetown, or Cleveland State.

And what are those practices like? They usually consist of the second string pressing the starters. What does that accomplish? Very little. That's because the starters are the best athletes, so they can just outrun and outjump the bench. Also, the second string has been pressing for exactly one week, so the press is crude and ineffective.

Compare that to a team such as UNLV, where the best athletes learn to pressure man-to-man the moment they first walk into the college gym. The value of pressure defense is that it is insidious. Often, its effect doesn't show up early in the game. In fact, most teams break the press with relative ease in the first half. But as the game wears on, the opposition wears down. That is especially true of the teams that play the Rebels in Las Vegas. The crowd usually senses when their team needs to turn the screws a little tighter, when that intensity level needs to be raised another notch. They start yelling, and the players move just a little faster and jump a little higher. It's not uncommon for a team to commit only five first-half turnovers against the Rebels, and then double that total in the second 20 minutes.

What happens?

You get sick and tired of that guy who has been guarding you all night. Everywhere you turn, he is there. Every dribble you take is contested. Every shot you take means that there is a hand in your face. And when you lose the ball, you have to chase the other guy down the floor because he runs even faster when he is on offense.

Tarkanian's teams press just as hard in the thirty-eighth minute of the game as they do in the eighth minute. And when a team facing a press gets tired, the mistakes happen. The passes are a little lazy, and they are stolen. A dribbler becomes disoriented by the press, picks up the ball, and the next thing he knows, he has been called for traveling.

There are several rules about fatigue and basketball:

1. Tired shooters tend to have shots that bang against the front of the rim.

2. Tired rebounders don't rebound.

3. Tired ball handlers throw the ball away.

4. Tired teams play poor defense.

To press as Tarkanian does in the games requires long, hard practice. Tarkanian's practices often last three and one-half hours, which is ninety minutes longer than most coaches work with their teams.

Former UNLV assistant Lynn Archibald: "Fear is part of it. Tark is always afraid that he didn't cover something in practice, or he'll worry that there is some drill or some aspect of the game that the kids aren't executing properly."

Yet Tarkanian gives his players more freedom than most coaches. A common complaint you hear from NBA scouts is that so many major programs have talented kids, "but the coaches don't let them play." That means the coach handcuffs the athletes by forcing them to walk the ball up the floor instead of looking for a fast break.

Tim Grgurich, Tarkanian's main assistant since 1980 and before that head coach at the University of Pittsburgh, says on the subject:

Tim Grgurich: "I grew up in the East and was trained in the eastern style of basketball. By that I mean that I grew up where a coach always wanted control of his players. I always wanted to know where all my players were on the floor at all times and what they were doing. A coach's natural instinct is to hold back his players, because you're always afraid that if your kids starts running up and down, they'll throw the ball all over the gym or start forcing up bad shots. But Coach [Grgurich always refers to Tarkanian as 'Coach'] doesn't seem to have those same worries. He tells the kids to run and to take 3-pointers. He accepts the mistakes they make because he knows that his kids also will make big plays. Most coaches talk about the running game and the pressing defense, but when they turn on the clock and the official throws up the ball, those same coaches usually revert back to their old, more conservative style of play. Our concept of basketball is based on pressure defense. Our upperclassmen talk about it to our new players. The coaches talk about it all the time. Our press is a reward system. Work hard on defense, steal the ball, and then you can run. Our defense sets up our fast-break offense, and it clicks because Coach isn't afraid to let the kids express themselves on the court.''

Don't misunderstand. Tarkanian doesn't let all of his players cut loose from the 3-point line. In 1987, it was Freddie Banks and Gerald Paddio who had the green light. Before that, it was Anthony Jones. On his number-one-ranked team in 1983, it was Larry Anderson.

Larry Anderson: ''When I first went to UNLV, I used to like to drive to the basket. I was into dunking, being Doctor J. and all of that. Tark took one look at me in practice and said, 'Larry, you're a shooter.' In one of my first practices, I went in for a drive and as I jumped to slam, a guy came over my back.

''Tark screamed at me, 'Larry, what the hell are you doing?'

''I couldn't figure out what I'd done wrong. I said, 'Coach, I had the wide-open lane.'

''Tark said, 'Didn't I tell you that you were the shooter?'

''I said, 'But I...'

''Tark said, 'Then just pull up and take the 10-foot jumper. I don't want you getting hurt. I want you shooting from the outside.'

''So I concentrated on my shot and usually took the jumper. That's how I became a shooter—he made me one. Tark needed someone to hit from the outside, and that someone was me. Tark would say, 'A shooter is a shooter.' Once he decided you were the shooter, he really never yelled at you for taking a bad shot. Instead, he'd jump on you for passing up a shot. If you miss four shots in a row and look over to the bench, Tark will say, 'Don't look at me, just relax.' He has more confidence in his shooters than the shooters do in themselves, and that confidence rubs off.''

Then there is the flip side of Tarkanian's practices, those that come after losses.

Reggie Theus: ''I just hated those. It was as if someone was beating on him all the time. He was miserable. Sometimes it only took a bad practice to put him in that mood. He would try to snap us out of it. He'd yell, 'Gosh darn it, you're all a bunch of jerks. What kind of defense are you playing? You're like a bunch of MP's out there directing traffic to the basket. Unbelievable. You don't want to work hard. You don't want to play. You don't even want to win. I mean, which of you guys wants to win? You're robbing the university, that's what you're doing. You guys should just go in there and turn in your scholarships. I mean, you guys should wear a mask, because you're nothing but robbers.' Tark would be very sincere when he was saying this. But of course, he would run out of air, and then we'd put our hands in front of our mouths because we didn't want him to see us cracking up. Other times, he'd throw chalk at the blackboard, or even try to punch the blackboard, but that usually didn't work because all he'd end up doing was hurting his hand. Tark would act like it didn't faze him and he wouldn't rub his hand, but you knew it hurt because his face turned a little bit redder.

"I'll tell you what did work: his face. He has the most expressive eyes. He would get rings around his eyes, and then his eyes would get big and droopy like a basset hound's. He would have that look of absolute agony when things weren't going well, as if someone were shoving bamboo under his fingernails. That look would somehow be projected onto you, and you'd feel his pain. It was purely psychological, and I've never had another coach who could do it. I don't think Tark does it on purpose. It's just him. When you play for Tark, you like him. If you like him, you don't want him to suffer."

Sidney Green: "I know exactly what that look is, because people told me that I was starting to look like Tark during my senior year. They said I was hanging around him too much. But he has that effect on you. You pick up on his emotions and you start to feel things the same way he does, start thinking about basketball the way he does. It is an amazing thing, and you don't even know that it is happening to you."

Just as there has always been a special relationship between Tarkanian and his players, a special relationship also exists between Tarkanian and his assistant coaches. In terms of major college coaches, no one has probably taken more JUCOs and transfers from other four-year schools than Tarkanian. And no one has probably hired more out-of-work coaches than Tarkanian.

A coach in a bit of trouble, a coach who has been pushed out the door often finds a welcome mat in front of Tarkanian's office.

Tarkanian: "That's because of what happened to me with the NCAA. When they tried to suspend me in 1977, I knew how it would feel to be out of the game, even though it didn't actually happen to me. I decided that I'd try to help people who have done a lot for basketball, who love the game as much as I do. And when these people are fired, I'll give them a second chance. Basketball coaches are a different breed. The game is infectious. It just crawls inside of you, becomes a part of your life. It's not 9-to-5; you think about it twenty-four hours a day, seven days a week. Usually, a coach's last thought at night before he goes to sleep is about his team, and his first thought when he wakes up in the morning is about basketball. When a coach loses his job, it is like someone tried to take away a part of his life. The guys I've hired are very good basketball people. They've made tremendous contributions to our program. They deserve to be in the game.''

Among those who have received a second coaching life from Tarkanian are Tates Locke, Dave Buss, Rex Hughes, Bob Kloppenburg, Al Menendez, Tim Grgurich, Bud Presley, and Ralph Readout.

Locke had been fired by Jacksonville.

Tarkanian: ''In fact, Tates was one of the guys who told me to take the Lakers job when I had trouble with the NCAA. He said that no one would stand by me because that was what had happened earlier in Tates's career at Clemson. I hardly knew Tates, but I knew he got a raw deal at Jacksonville. I knew that Tates was a good basketball man and a loyal person, so I hired him. Now Tates is working for Bobby Knight.''

Al Menendez was hired by Tarkanian in 1976 after serving as an assistant at the University of Hawaii. The head coach was fired, and Menendez and the others were advised to find jobs elsewhere.

Al Menendez: ''Jerry believes in loyalty, and the assistants he has had know what Jerry has done for them. He takes them when they have been fired, or when they retired and then wanted to get back into the game. The coaches know that he gave them a chance when no one else would. So loyalty works both ways, and that is why he has always had strong staffs.

''How he hires assistants is something else. When Jerry first interviewed me he said, 'Al, do you like to hunt?' I said, 'No, Jerry.' He said, 'Do you play golf?' I said, 'I've never played golf in my life.' He said, 'Do you own a camper?' I said, 'No.' He said, 'Do you fish?' I said, 'Jerry, I'm from Brooklyn. I've never known anyone from Brooklyn who likes to fish.' Jerry smiled and said, 'Good, that's just the way I like it.' Believe it or not, that was the crux of my job interview. I had known Jerry before and we had talked a lot of basketball. But still, you have to admit those were a lot of strange questions.''

Not to Tarkanian.

Tarkanian: ''I don't want a guy who fishes, plays golf, hunts, or owns a camper. Our assistants are here to work with the kids, to be available. I've never played golf and I won't hire a coach who does. If a guy is on the golf course or in the woods, he isn't helping the kids. A guy who has a camper won't be there when a player has a problem.

Our assistants work year-round. They're not interested in vacations and other frills."

Tarkanian has wonderful things to say about all the men who have worked for him. He is proud that his former assistants have gotten better jobs. Lynn Archibald is the head coach at Utah, George Mc-Quarn is the head coach at California-Fullerton, Bob Kloppenburg is an assistant with the Seattle Supersonics, and Al Menendez is director of player personnel for the Nets.

The assistant who perhaps best exemplifies Tarkanian's philosophy is Tim Grgurich, who has been with UNLV since 1980. Grgurich was an assistant at the University of Pittsburgh from 1964 to 1975, and then became the Panthers' head coach from 1975 to 1980. In those five years, Grgurich had a 71–70 record, and had two teams appear in the National Invitational Tournament. Pitt basketball in the 1970s barely resembled what it is today. During Grgurich's tenure, there was no Big East, very little national television exposure, and a budget that was a fraction of the current one. Pitt was not committed to spending money or supplying other resources needed to succeed on the major college level. After three years as a player, eleven years as an assistant, and five more as the head coach, Grgurich's nineteen-year association with Pitt ended in 1980 when he was released by the school.

"I was a guy who needed a job, and Coach Tarkanian gave me one," says Grgurich.

Tarkanian says, "That was the best decision I ever made. He has added ten years to my coaching career."

Both men talk about loyalty. Tarkanian predicts that Grgurich "will become a great head coach." Grgurich says, "Coach is the best guy in the country to work for."

There is substance behind the words. Tarkanian says that since coming to UNLV, Grgurich has turned down chances to be a head coach at San Diego State, the head coach at Providence, and an assistant with the New York Knicks.

"I'm not sure those were really offers," says Grgurich.

"Believe me, they were offers," says Tarkanian. "I didn't hold Tim back. He wanted to stay. That has amazed me."

Danny Tarkanian says that Grgurich made his life much easier. "He knew that playing for your father would be tough on any son," Danny explains. "He understood that I was under a lot of pressure and there were times when I needed someone to talk to. He was there, and I knew I could trust him."

Grgurich usually arrives at the office by 6 a.m. and leaves at 8:30

p.m. Of course, that's a better schedule than he had as a head coach at Pitt, when his average day was seventeen hours.

Tarkanian: "I have been around a lot of hardworking guys. But Grgurich is the best, the most dedicated. He doesn't care about anything but basketball. He doesn't give speeches. He doesn't go to banquets. He doesn't like any attention. He won't even give interviews to the press. I think he has absolutely no ego. Zero."

Grgurich is so publicity shy that he manages to be absent when most of the team pictures are taken and rarely gives interviews. An exception was with the Las Vegas *Sun* early in 1988. Lois was stunned to see that Grgurich had finally spoken to the press.

"Tim told me he really didn't know why he did it," says Lois. "He said that he saw this guy who had a hole in his coat, whose clothes weren't very good looking, and whose shoes were scuffed. He thought, 'This guy looks like I used to look when I was in school,' and he sort of identified with him. So he did it."

Tarkanian says, "I rely on Tim so much. He is tireless. He takes care of a lot of the little things and gives me time to just worry about coaching."

Part of the reason why Tarkanian has kept quality coaches such as Grgurich is that he gives them responsibility. He endlessly praises his assistants.

Tim Grgurich: "When you work for Coach, you know that you are an important part of the program. Most head coaches don't want their assistants to say too much. Or they make their assistants into specialists, one guy for the defense and one guy for the offense. But Coach tells the assistants to speak up at any time during practice, on any subject. Sometimes he jumps on us to talk more during practice. He wants his assistants to have a high profile, and most head coaches don't like that. But Coach is a secure person. He isn't worried about some assistant coming in and taking his job. All Coach cares about are the kids and winning. If [Villanova's] Rollie Massimino or someone like that suddenly needed a job, Coach would hire him in a second. He wouldn't worry that this guy might get his job. Instead, Coach would say that this guy will help the program, he knows the game, let's get him in here and put him to work with the kids. That's why Coach is ideal to work for. Sure, you put in long hours, but so does he. Anyone who watches the clock isn't cut out for coaching."

In some circles, Tarkanian has been portrayed as a dubious coach and recruiter. Pete Newell has heard the charges.

Pete Newell: "Those are the things people say. Usually, it comes from people who only know Tark through what they've read in the newspapers or heard on television. What we are talking about is an uneducated opinion. The image comes from Jerry's problems with the NCAA. Most people know that he has been investigated and that his program was put on probation. They might even know that he took the NCAA to court, but they don't know the details of the case that showed Jerry did very little—if anything—that was wrong. Certainly, it was very minor in comparison to what goes on in many programs that are never investigated.

"Then there are some coaches who say, 'Now don't use my name, but did you know that Jerry Tarkanian does this or he does that?...' This is envy, pure and simple. Tark has won so much and for so long that he is the winningest college coach ever, and an easy way to explain it is that Jerry cheats. Well, let me tell you that a lot of schools in the country are cheating, and they don't win. As for labeling Jerry as a bandit recruiter, I think it's ridiculous. It's so easy to do cheap shots on Jerry, because his school is in Las Vegas with all the glitter and the neon. But look at where Jerry's players have come from over the years. They're JUCOs, transfers from other four-year schools, and high school kids who were good, but not great players. You can count on one hand the blue-chip high school players he has had in his career at UNLV.

"I'm a West Coast guy. I coached at California and I've lived in the area for years. I've watched Jerry very closely and I feel I know him well. I think it really bothers a lot of coaches that Jerry wins so much, and he does it in ways that coaches say won't work—with transfers, with kids who have had some personal problems. Jerry is breaking some coaching commandments. I'm very close to Bobby Knight. I know that Coach Knight has a very high regard for Tark. No coach in America is more sensitive to the illegalities of the college game than Bobby Knight, and he has a lot of respect for Jerry. I put a lot more stock in Bobby Knight's opinion than I do in the opinions of a lot of other coaches who have axes to grind and who are trying to make themselves look better by tearing Jerry down. Because of where he coaches, and because Jerry is one of the least political people I've ever met, he is an easy target."

Al Menendez: "To me, it's very simple why people knock Tark: sour grapes. The last thing other coaches want to admit is that Tark and his staff outwork them, but that often is what happens."

Southern California coach George Raveling: "I've never seen any real proof that Tark did something unethical. But he has that reputa-

273

tion, and once you get a reputation it is very hard to shake it. The bottom line on Tark is that he is a much better coach than he'll ever get credit for.''

The obvious criterion for judging player talent is to look at high school All-Americans and NBA first-round draft choices. This tells you how highly the players were regarded before they went to college, and what the pros think of the players when they are ready to leave the university.

Tarkanian has had four McDonald's high school All-Americans: Sidney Green, Eldridge Hudson, Freddie Banks, and Anthony Jones— and Jones was a transfer from Georgetown. So he was able to recruit only three out of high school. Schools such as North Carolina and Louisville had more than four high school All-Americans on their 1986–87 roster.

As for NBA first-rounders, Tarkanian has had five: Ricky Sobers, Sidney Green, Anthony Jones, Reggie Theus, and Armon Gilliam. Since 1973, fifteen other universities have produced more first-rounders than Tarkanian. Also, in 1987 there were sixteen players in the NBA from the Pacific Coast Athletic Conference, but only three were from UNLV. That is despite the fact UNLV has won the PCAA title every year since 1982.

One factor is size. The NBA likes its players big; Tarkanian's usually are small: no 7-footers in the middle, guards in the 6-foot-2 range, or forwards who are 6-foot-6 and can leap. Among Tarkanian's five first-rounders, three are guards, while Green and Gilliam are power forwards.

Cleveland Cavaliers general manager Wayne Embry: ''What Tarkanian does is to get very good athletes and put them in a system where they can run and best show their skills. These kids usually aren't great basketball players. They have holes in their games. But in Tark's running system, he disguises those weaknesses and accents their strengths. But in the pro game, you can't compensate, and that's why his kids usually aren't drafted that high or don't play that well in the NBA. By pro standards, they usually aren't that good.''

An example was Richie Adams. At UNLV, he was a 6-foot-8 jumping-jack center. After he was drafted by the Washington Bullets, Adams was placed at small forward, because NBA small forwards are now in the 6-foot-7 to 6-foot-10 range. Centers are 7-foot. Adams couldn't handle the ball or shoot well enough from the outside to play forward, and was quickly cut by Washington. At UNLV, Adams could play inside and didn't have to worry about dribbling or hitting the 15-footer. But the NBA is another game.

Freddie Banks was the greatest basketball player ever to come out of the city of Las Vegas, but in the NBA drafts, Banks was a second-round pick. In the NBA, shooting guards are at least 6-foot-5. That meant Banks had to play point guard, which emphasizes ball handling first, shooting second. Detroit made Banks its second-round pick in 1987, and cut him at the end of training camp. Tarkanian says Banks still has the skills to play in the NBA, but he needs a team that will be patient with him as he makes the conversion from shooting guard to point guard. Detroit was not willing to wait.

"Tark seldom has a player who is the total package," says Al Menendez, now with the New York Nets. "Those kids are going to North Carolina, Louisville, and the other so-called elite schools. Tark makes his kids better players than they really are, and that's what you want from a coach. His lack of first-round picks is really a compliment to him. It shows he is getting the most out of his talent."

Another consideration is that Tarkanian has worked with troubled players.

Al Menendez: "He does have the reputation of taking kids other coaches wouldn't touch. That might scare off some pro people who figure that only he can handle them. But 90 percent of the kids he has had are good kids. Tark is known as a guy who has taken some 'head cases' players and straightened them out, and that shouldn't be held against him, because it shows that he is a great coach and a great communicator. He looks at the positive side. He sees a kid who has had some problems. Tark sits down with the kid and talks to him, and if Tark decides the kid is basically a decent person, he'll take the kid and work with him. Eventually, a mutual respect forms between Tark and the kid. Also, Tark has the reputation among the players as being their kind of coach. Kids hear, 'If you can't play for Tark, you can't play for anyone.' So they come to him with a positive attitude, thinking that he is the one guy who can help them become better players.

"One of Tark's greatest abilities is to talk to a group of kids. He talks to them for fifteen to twenty minutes after each practice, and he talks about anything—basketball, school, work ethic, you name it. But Tark is so sincere. He speaks from the heart and the kids know it. If most coaches tried this, the kids would tune them out. But with Tark, they usually listen. That's because they know he cares about them."

Loyalty is a word Tarkanian continually uses, and he stresses that it works both ways.

Tarkanian: "Coaches always demand respect and loyalty from their teams, but they sometimes fail to realize that what you expect from your players is exactly what they should be able to expect from you. Kids make mistakes. I made mistakes. That's why I don't like to run kids off unless it's an extreme case.''

In college basketball terms, ''running a kid off'' means taking away his scholarship, or making his life so miserable that he quits school or transfers. UNLV has a reputation as a place where players transfer to, not out of. You probably can count on one hand the players Tarkanian has asked to leave.

Tarkanian says, ''We build pride in our program from the kids knowing that once they come to UNLV, they don't have to worry about someone shoving them out the door because they had a bad year. Our players know that even after they have been in our program, they remain a part of the Rebel family. That's why if a former player comes to one of my games, I'll try to get him a seat on the bench. I also like to bring him into the dressing room to meet some of the current players. Sometimes I may ask a former player to talk to the team. The point is that these kids still have a place in the program.''

Tim Grgurich: ''If you want to look at a program, see how many of the ex-players are still hanging around. Do they come to the games? Do they talk to the current players? Is there a feeling of family? That's what Coach has created here. In the summer, a lot of our former players take part in pickup games with the current team. Suddenly, the younger kids get to meet Jeff Collins, Sidney Green, Reggie Theus, and some of the other guys they have heard about. Before every big game, we can count on getting a telephone call or a telegram from guys like Reggie Theus. That means a lot, and it's the same kind of thing that happens at North Carolina. Just like a lot of their players go back in the summer to Chapel Hill to work out, our kids come back to Vegas.''

Pete Newell: ''I know what Tark does with his kids. Some of them are mavericks, kids that some other coaches wouldn't take. Or if the coaches did take them, they wouldn't try to help the kids once their eligibility was up. But Tark doesn't just discard his players. He and Bobby Knight also have that in common. Even if a kid doesn't graduate, Tark and his wife push the kid to come back to school, or else they help the kid get a job in Vegas. That is why I respect his program, and that's why I'll speak out for Tark. He cares about his kids.''

For a coach to last as long at one university as Tarkanian has at UNLV, he must do more than win. As the saying goes in college basketball, he needs to ''take good care of his kids after they leave the program.''

"Even if you help a kid get a job, he still has to do it for himself," says Tarkanian. "It's the kid who does the job and builds the career. He does the work for himself." But, he adds, to get a true reading on a basketball program, "you should talk to some of the guys who have been out of school for five or ten years. They'll tell you the truth. There is no reason for them to lie; nothing can be gained from anything that might be said. They've also had time to put their college years in perspective."

What most UNLV players tell you is that Tarkanian is there when you need a job recommendation, or even an idea where to look for work.

Jackie Robinson: "He has incredible contacts. Everyone in town knows and respects him. If he picks up a telephone, someone listens on the other end. He can get you through the door."

Another factor is the visibility Rebel basketball players have in Las Vegas. There are a lot of jobs in Las Vegas, and there are thousands of people who love UNLV baskctball.

Noted UNLV booster Irwin Molasky: "This is a community that wants to help the players get established in business after they are done with their careers. Remember, the basketball program is a big fish in a small pond. In Vegas, we have nothing else. There are no pro teams except for a minor lcaguc baseball team. The UNLV football team has not been very good, so that leaves basketball. Jerry Tarkanian and his players are true heroes. They have given the community a lot to cheer about. The basketball team and its players make Las Vegas feel good about itself, so the people like to see if thcy can do something for the program in return."

Flintie Ray Williams, a floor manager at the Golden Nugget and former UNLV guard (1978–1980): "Being associated with the baskctball team and Tark gets you through the door. Then, you have to show what you can do. But the people who hire you want you to succeed."

Those people know that it helps their public relations if they have a former player in a supervisory category.

"If you work hard, you can really move up," says Williams.

Michael Lloyd was a marginal point guard for the Rebels in the late 1970s, but the fans saw enough of him to give Lloyd credibility within the community that was an asset when he set up a finance company. Another former Rebel, Richard Box, has his master's degree and works for the district attorney's office in Las Vegas.

In short, there are many job opportunities.

Larry Anderson: "When I come back to Vegas, I run into boosters who ask me how I'm doing. I tell them that I'm living in San Diego and still playing ball in Europe. They'll tell me that I should move to Vegas—if not now, when I retire from basketball. They say they can help get me a job, or they know someone who could use a guy like me. I've been out of the program for five years, and these people still care about me and still want to see if they can do something for me. Believe me, any guy who played for Tark can come back to Vegas, and he'll help the player find a decent job and live a normal life. I've never heard of him turning anyone down."

Irwin Molasky says, "Tark is relentless when it comes to finding jobs for his old players. He calls all of his friends. I know that there have been a few players for whom he's found several jobs. Tark goes to bat for them again because he never gives up on a kid. He says that the kid needs one more chance and he'll straighten out."

Sidney Green: "No player has any right to knock Coach Tark. I played at Vegas during the probation, and we had some guys who were very difficult to coach. They did nothing but make Coach Tark's life miserable. But when they got out of school, he found them jobs. Any player from UNLV who can't find a decent career after basketball has only one person to blame: himself. The opportunities are there, and people are willing to help."

Irwin Molasky: "A recent example of how Jerry and Lois feel about their players was the Glen Gondrezick case. Glen played for UNLV during the middle 1970s, and then was with the New York Knicks for a few years. Glen was living in Boulder, Colorado, and recently his wife filed for divorce. He got very depressed and tried to commit suicide [Gondrezick shot himself in the chest]. While he was still in the hospital, Lois was on the phone to Glen and his friends. She brought Glen to Vegas and had a little gathering of his closest friends, so that he knew people still cared about him. The Tarkanians wanted Glen to move to Vegas for a fresh start. They helped lay the foundation to get him back into school so he could finish up on his communications major. Glen has been out of school since 1977, and he didn't go to the Tarkanians for help—they heard he was in trouble and made the offer. That tells you how Jerry and Lois Tarkanian work."

16

Tark in the Trenches

The only way to know how basketball encompasses Tarkanian's life is to observe him in the gym and the dressing room as he does what he does best: coach.

This is a look at Tarkanian from February 7 to 14, 1988.

Up to this point, the 1987–88 season had been an incredible surprise for Tarkanian. He never would have believed that his team would be ranked as high as number two. UNLV wasn't among the Top Twenty in any major preseason poll. Furthermore, this was a totally different team from the one that had a 37–2 record and went to the NCAA Final Four in 1987. Gone to the Phoenix Suns was Armon Gilliam (23 points, 9 rebounds), the bullish 6-foot-9 power forward who was the second pick in the 1987 draft. Gone was guard Freddie Banks (19.4 points and a deadly 3-point shooter). Also gone were point guard Mark Wade, who set an NCAA single-season assist record; and veterans Eldridge Hudson and Gary Graham, who supplied stability and had a knack for making clutch plays.

When the 1987–88 season opened, the word was that the Rebels weren't the same. It was a rebuilding year, a year when national rankings would be just a rumor and when the Rebels were vulnerable in the Pacific Coast Athletic Association, which they had won in all five of the years they had belonged to the league. In 1986–87, UNLV went undefeated in the PCAA and its average margin of victory was 21 points.

The base of Tarkanian's team was 6-foot-8 power forward Jarvis Basnight, who averaged 9.2 points for the Final Four team. Also back was 6-foot-6 forward Gerald Paddio, a 13-point scorer but only a 42 percent shooter in 1986–87.

Paddio and Basnight were the two seniors, and they were expected to be the leaders. Tarkanian had high hopes for sophomore Stacey Cvijanovich, but the point guard broke his wrist early in the season.

In addition to Paddio and Basnight, the other important players were Stacey Augmon, Anthony Todd, Clint Rossum, Karl "Boobie" James, and Keith James. Todd was a transfer from Lamar; Rossum, a transfer from Dixie Junior College; Keith James, a transfer from South Carolina. Augmon and Boobie James had to sit out their first seasons because of the NCAA's Proposition 48 rule.

All this meant that Tarkanian began the year with no experienced center or point guard, and had little idea what to expect from his team. Boobie James was made the point guard, although he had the instincts of a shooting guard. The only highly recruited high school player on the team was Augmon, a lanky 6-foot-7 forward who is a tremendous athlete and defensive player but still searching for consistency on offense.

Make no mistake: Tarkanian had a fine team, a team capable of winning 20 games and earning a berth in the NCAA tournament. But in Las Vegas, the fans expect more.

Tarkanian: "Lots of people say that Vegas happens to be a great basketball town. Well, what Vegas happens to be is a great *winning* basketball town. If we lose, I could hold the team banquet in my office—we wouldn't need chefs or anybody. But that's true at most places. There is a lot of pressure on the players. Everywhere you go in this town, you hear about Rebel basketball. The kids have to give more of themselves playing here than they would at other places where the support isn't as rabid. With all the attention our kids get, they have to pay a high price."

The 1987–88 Rebels were doing just that.

They went into the February 6 game at California-Santa Barbara with a 20–1 record. They had won nine games in a row, including a 1-point victory over Temple in the Owls' first loss of the season. They were ranked second in the country. If they had won that February 6 game at Santa Barbara, they would have been ranked number one.

But Santa Barbara had been a tough team for Vegas. They had already given UNLV its only loss of the season by a 62–60 count, in

UNLV's own Thomas & Mack Center on January 7. Going into the Santa Barbara game, Tarkanian was overjoyed with his team. They weren't just winning; they were overachieving. The consensus of most coaches and NBA scouts was that Tarkanian was doing perhaps the best coaching job of his career. Santa Barbara plays in the Special Events Center, a 6,000-seat gym that was jammed when the Rebels took the floor. As is the case in every PCAA contest involving UNLV, it was the biggest game of the season for the opposition.

In the first half, things went pretty much as Tarkanian had hoped. The Rebels took a 9-point lead into the dressing room, and even had an 11-point lead early in the second half. Then it unraveled. Boobie James and Clint Rossum couldn't hit from the outside. Gerald Paddio had 24 points, but he fouled out with 5:20 left to play. Keith James injured his ankle late in the first half and wasn't a factor for the rest of the game. Injuries and foul trouble forced Tarkanian to play Basnight the entire second half, and fatigue took its toll; he wasn't productive down the stretch. Final score: Santa Barbara 71, UNLV 66.

The loss meant that the Rebels could forget about being number one in the country. That honor went to Temple. It also meant that they were tied for first place in the PCAA with Utah State, both teams at 9–2. Santa Barbara was right behind at 8–3.

That was the situation as Tarkanian and the Rebels entered the second week of February. They had two games coming up: a PCAA meeting with California-Fullerton on Thursday, and an independent game with Missouri on Saturday. Both would be at the Thomas & Mack Center.

Tarkanian would be in for a challenging week. He had to keep his players believing in themselves, because their confidence and the team's work ethic were compensating for their lack of natural talent. But he also had to continue to mold this collection of newcomers to his program into a team, in the truest sense of the word. It would be a week of highs and lows, of laughter and sorrow—in other words, a typical week in the life of a major college basketball coach.

Monday, February 8, 1988

It is 2:30 p.m. in an empty Thomas & Mack Center. Practice is about to begin, but before it does, Tarkanian talks to the players. In many ways, what he says will be more important than what the team does

281

on the court this day. His team is shaken by the loss at Santa Barbara, and Tarkanian knows it. Tarkanian tells the players:

"The first thing I want to say is that in the fifteen years I've been here we haven't had a ball club that has given us as much as you have. You have nothing to be ashamed of.

"Now, the loss to Santa Barbara hurt. It was a game we didn't have to lose. I honestly believe that we let the game get away from us. After the game, I was really hurt, because I thought we hadn't played as hard as we could have. But when I went home and watched the tape, I saw that overall, we played hard. You guys played very hard. We didn't do some things that well, but the overall effort was good.

"No one could have expected any more out of you guys, because you have worked your tails off for us to be successful. So far we've done a great job, but we have a long way to go.

"Right now, we have seven more league games to play, and that concerns me. Listen, just because we are playing at home doesn't mean everything is well. That's a big problem. People say you're at home and you can't lose at home. Well, that's a bunch of crap. We can lose anywhere. We lost at home to Santa Barbara and we won on the road. In the last two years, we've been 24–2 on the road. So 24–2 is our record playing in front of hostile fans and in hostile houses. No other team in the country has that kind of road record.

"But just because a team is playing at home doesn't necessarily mean it will win. I want you to be aware of it. It used to be that in the PCAA, no one lost at home. During the PCAA press day, I remember [Fullerton coach] George McQuarn saying that if you go undefeated at home and can go only 5–4 on the road, you'll win the league. He figured no one could go better than 5–4 on the road. Last year, we went undefeated on the road, and coaches said that would never happen again.

"But that has changed. Look at Santa Barbara. They have lost three league games this year, all at home. On the road they're 4–0, and they're 3–3 at home. Hey, we've lost at home. Playing at home is a helluva lot better than playing on the road, but it doesn't guarantee a win.

"Now that we're home, we have to work our butts off to become a good basketball team. You know that if we had won at Santa Barbara, we would have been the number-one team in the country. Who in the world would ever have dreamed that we'd be the number-one team in the country? Who at the start of the season would ever have given us a shot at being number two in the country for as long as we were?

"But the reason we have done so well is that we've practiced three to three and a half hours a day; because you guys have cooperated; because you guys have worked your butts off. That's why we got to that level. If we had taken shortcuts, we would not be a successful team.

"We now have to face the rest of the season. There are eight games left—seven league games and the Missouri game. We have to figure out what we need to do to make us a better team. The coaches and I have been meeting about that.

"Number one, I don't want us to panic because we got beat by Santa Barbara. We lost there because Boobie [James] and Clint [Rossum] couldn't hit some wide-open shots. They've been hitting them all year long. That's going to happen. Every guy won't shoot well in every game. In other games when we haven't shot well, our defense carried us. But at Santa Barbara, Keith [James] was hurt and he couldn't play. Boobie [James] got his fourth foul early in the second half, and that meant I had to play Stacey [Augman] at point guard, where he hadn't played for two months. That also meant I couldn't rest Jarvis [Basnight] in the second half. Jarvis has played as well as any Rebel has ever played for us, but in the second half, Jarvis wasn't there. Physically, he was tired and he just couldn't play as he can. Gerald [Paddio] was carrying us. It was a great effort on his part, but...I just wish I could have rested Jarvis for five minutes; then he would have responded. I probably should have rested him anyway. That was an error on my part. Look, you guys worked hard, and what I want to do is build from that game.

"The last time we lost to Santa Barbara, we worked our butts off and won nine straight. They were celebrating, and Santa Barbara lost its next two games. I want us to work hard and get better again.

"This is the time of the year when teams start separating themselves. Those teams who aren't tough mentally are going to bail out about now. Practice gets boring. You come out every day and the coaches are on you. We're yelling at you, trying to get you to play defense and to execute. We are putting pressure on you. This has been going on for a long time. There are a lot of teams right now who are ready to throw the towel in. They are bored and tired of practice. They want to get away from basketball. They just don't have the drive, the competitiveness, and the willpower to try to get better. Those are the teams that will struggle, and I hope we won't be like that. I hope that we'll play through boredom. I hope we'll play through fatigue.

"It's a normal thing for you to be tired right now. If you're not sore someplace, it would be abnormal. If your legs aren't sore, if your body doesn't hurt someplace, it means that you haven't been working hard. All of you will be tired, all of you will be sore, and all of you will be bored...you hear, 'Square up, read the defense, pass the ball'... Coach Grgurich is yelling at you; Coach Readout is yelling at you; I'm yelling at you. But the tough teams who go at it hard and work through this will become better teams.

"I have some things that will make us a better team. Now, I can talk about it, but only you guys can do it. I want you to totally take off on the boards, rebounding. I want us to dominate both boards. If you want to make a quick improvement in a ball club, that's an area where teams are vulnerable. If you pound the boards, then there will be no wing man as quick as Stacey going to the ball and there will be no forward as quick as Jarvis going to the ball. I want to stress the boards. Every time a shot is taken, I want to see four guys on the boards. If we can do that, we'll improve our game 6 to 8 points. Stacey, you've got to be on the boards. Gerald, you've got to be on the boards. Everybody, on the boards. Pound the offensive boards, dominate the defensive boards.

"Another area is our passing. Early in the year, we did a lot of passing drills, and we've gotten away from that. We have to work on passing again. This will help us to pass the ball, to catch the ball under pressure. We need to concentrate. Teams are causing us to turn the ball over, and we're doing it on our own. At Santa Barbara, we just threw the damn ball away. Unbelievable, crazy passes. Just plain crazy passes.

"As long as we work hard, all the pieces will fall together. Fellows, if we all pull together we've got a chance to win. Not just the league, but we have a chance to go a long way. You watch those other teams play. There isn't anyone in the country we can't beat when we have our heads in the game. But by the same token, there isn't anyone on our schedule who can't beat us when we're not ready to play.

"We have one advantage that most teams don't have. We have the work ethic. We have worked so hard, given so much to be a good team. As long as we don't let up in that area, then we'll be all right. We're coming to the end of the regular season. Then comes the PCAA tournament, and after that, hopefully we'll go to the NCAA tournament. This is the time for everyone to reach inside and give a little more. This is the time for each one of you to try to get better individually; and it is our job as coaches to get us to play better as a team. As long as we concentrate, there is no limit to what we can do.

"Temple is number one in the country. Think about that. Temple is number one, and we beat Temple. If we had beaten Santa Barbara, we would have been number one. But the point is that we beat the number-one team in the country. What does that tell us? It says we have a chance, a legitimate chance. It's here for us if we all want to work for it. You can't just come out here and put in a couple of hours of practice and go through the motions. You have to make every minute of practice count. You have to get stronger and stronger as a team. All right, now everybody go to work."

Practice begins with drills, and sounds echo throughout the empty arena.

Tennis shoes squeaking.

The basketball pounding against the floor.

Coaches yelling.

Players huffing and puffing.

Tarkanian is all over the court, screaming, "Let's be sharp." "Rebound...Ricky Rob [Richard Robinson], rebound already." "Let's go, good passes....I said good passes."

The team breaks down to do some half-court five-on-five work. This is where the coaching staff works like an orchestra. Assistant Tim Grgurich is under the basket. Assistant Ralph Readout is on the sideline near the start of the 3-point arch. Tarkanian is at the top of the key. They have the team surrounded. They yell, berate, encourage, demand, plead, praise, and teach the players constantly. These men have worked together since 1980, and it shows. When one drops off, another steps in, and remarkably, they seldom interrupt each other:

Grgurich: "Don't reach in."

Tarkanian: "Rebound, Stacey."

Readout: "Work...WORK...*WORK!*"

Tarkanian: "Rebound."

Readout: "Catch the ball with two hands."

Grgurich: "Keep your hands up."

Tarkanian: "Rebound...REBOUND...*REBOUND!*" He yells "rebound" with the same desperation as you'd scream, "Get the children out *of the burning building!*"

The players always seem to be moving, sweating, running, working. It is exactly what basketball guru Pete Newell means when he says, "If I want my kids to get in a good defensive stance, I don't tell them how to do it. I put them in a drill, I get their butts low to the floor and their hands up, and I make them do it. You don't tell players, you make players do it."

It's repetition. Drill, drill, drill...work, work, work.

285

And please, *rebound!*

For Tarkanian, basketball is a physical game, a game of both instincts and desire. It's a game of quick feet and strong hearts. It's a game where the team that gets tired, the team that quits first, loses.

When Boobie James drives down the middle for an uncontested lay-up, Readout yells, "No free cuts...beat people up...put a body on them...let them know you're there. No one drives down the middle."

The theme of the pregame talk was confidence, hard work, defense, and rebounding. By the end of practice, the rebounding has started to suffer.

Tarkanian: "Stay on the boards."

Readout: "Be awake. Anticipate."

Tarkanian: "As soon as he shoots, get on the boards. Don't be a spectator."

Grgurich: "Work."

Tarkanian: "Rebound...REBOUND...*REBOUND*...Ah, Stacey, that's beautiful. That's it, that's exactly what we want."

Some head coaches like to sit back and watch their assistants run practice. Occasionally, they venture onto the court to say something, almost as if they think they are delivering a message from on high.

But Tarkanian is out there in the middle of his players. He sweats, they sweat, the assistant coaches sweat. By the end of the nearly three-hour practice, the players can barely walk and the coaches can barely talk. And that's how it is.

Tennis shoes squeak, coaches yell, players work. There is the pounding of the basketball filling the eerie, empty arena. There is the thud of bodies hitting the floor for a loose ball. There is the shrill, desperate voice of Tarkanian imploring his players to rebound...RE-BOUND.,.*REBOUND!*

Tuesday, February 9, 1988

Tuesday's practice is hampered because it is team photo day, and not as much is accomplished as Tarkanian would have liked.

On this day, Tarkanian is the speaker at the Rebel boosters' luncheon. His message here is much like the message he gave the team on Monday during the question-and-answer period after his remarks. Here is where Tarkanian is at his best, impressive both in his honesty and in his wit. He makes the boosters feel that they are an integral part of the program, that they really know what is going on, because he does far more than speak in the meaningless clichés that are the norm in these events.

Tarkanian's Remarks

I want to talk about the California-Irvine game first, because it was the start of our two-game trip to California. As a whole, I was worried about the trip because I thought our kids might look ahead to Santa Barbara and forget about Irvine. Also, Irvine has been a strange team. Their record isn't that good, but they have knocked off some very good teams, especially when they play at home.

Our kids shot the ball very, very well. We put in a half-court zone press early in the game when we had only a 1-point lead, and we had a 14-point lead at the half because the press really hurt Irvine.

The thing that bothered me was that we made too many turnovers. But there was one good thing about our turnovers: they couldn't convert them into points, because when our kids threw the ball away, they threw it right into the bleachers. I mean, they didn't even steal the ball from us; we just threw it into the stands. Overall, we played a very good game.

Our next game was at Santa Barbara, and I want to say something up front: if we played Santa Barbara ten games in a row at Santa Barbara, those would be ten even games, because they would be played on their floor with the crowd and the atmosphere at their place. Their crowd was up for us, and they get more fired up for us than anyone else because they really want to knock us off. I knew it would be a game that would go down to the wire, but I was hoping that we would be on top at the end. Santa Barbara has a very fine team. They're 16–4 and have beaten North Carolina State, Oregon State, and Pepperdine. I didn't consider losing to them at Santa Barbara an upset. The upset was earlier in the season, when they beat us at our place. We should not have let them beat us at home.

We played hard against Santa Barbara, and I liked our man-to-man defense early in the game, and we had a 9-point lead at the half. In the second half, we shot the ball very poorly. We didn't play defense as well, but our defense still wasn't that bad. They just got hot and were 6 for 8 from the 3-point range in the second half.

For the first time all year, we didn't get a good effort out of Jarvis Basnight. He just got tired. I should have rested him. If I had let him sit for five minutes, he probably could have gone back in there and been fine. He just was fatigued.

You know, you can play a good game on defense and you can make good passes, but if the ball doesn't go into the hole, you don't score. Guys such as Boobie James and Clint Rossum who shot well all year just weren't hitting. Also, Keith James got hurt.... Listen, when you lose a game, you can have all kinds of excuses. Injuries, illness, officials...none of that matters. It was a great win for them, and we didn't play real well. We just didn't have enough in us to hold on in the second half.

Look, you either won or you lost. Excuses don't count for anything.

We have two tough games this week. On Thursday, we play Fullerton. George McQuarn is a very good coach, one of the top coaches in the West. He has two of the best players in the West in Richard Morton and Henry Turner. Morton is as good as any player in the conference. The problem with Fullerton is that George McQuarn had two or three red-shirts who he thought would play well for him, and they haven't yet. But they are capable of turning it on at any time, and that scares me. It always takes red-shirts a little longer to get started. We had a tough game with them at Fullerton. With 20 seconds left, we had a 1-point lead, and they had the ball. We made a couple of good defensive plays, made some foul shots and a 3-pointer, and won by 6 points, but it was really like a 1-point game.

On Saturday, we play Missouri, and they are a mystery team this year. They will have better players than any team we have seen, and that includes Temple, who is number one in the country. Let me tell you about Missouri. They have all five starters back from a team that won the Big Eight championship last year. People don't realize that, because Kansas and Oklahoma got all the publicity, but Missouri won the Big Eight regular season and the conference tournament. They got knocked out of the NCAA tournament in the first round by Xavier and everyone forgot about them. They have great personnel. Before the season started, it was either Dick Vitale or Billy Packer who told me to watch Missouri because they could be a sleeper to win the national title. They struggled early in the year, then played well. They lost at Oklahoma last week, but I was talking to Oklahoma coach Billy Tubbs, and he said he didn't know if his team could beat Missouri at Missouri.

As for our ball club, we took Sunday off. Monday, we sent Jarvis Basnight and Gerald Paddio to the doctors to get vitamin B-12 shots. They have been run-down and need some energy. We let Jarvis sit out practice Monday, and that was good so he could rest his legs.

The kids are working hard and I'm very proud of this team. What they have accomplished this year is more meaningful than a lot of teams we've had here. Coach Ralph Readout told me that he can't remember a Rebel team that has given us more than this team has given us. We just need to keep a positive attitude and finish the season as strong as we can.

Are there any questions?

QUESTION: The officials really hurt us in the Santa Barbara game.

TARKANIAN: There were some calls that bothered me. I was upset when Gerald Paddio got called for his fourth foul. On one play near the end of the game, Jarvis got totally hammered and they called a jump ball.

QUESTION: I know that you and the players look at the tape of the game to see how well you played. Do the officials ever look at tape to see if they blew some calls?

TARKANIAN: I doubt it. Those guys have immunity. That's what bothers me. Those guys can walk into a gym, stick it in your ear, and walk right out. If you say anything about it, you're a crybaby. Jim Killingsworth said, "One or two officials should be hung and shot at the coaches' convention, and all the other coaches and officials have to watch." It's like [North Carolina State coach] Jimmy Valvano said, "Those officials come up to you and say, 'Relax, Coach, it's just a game.' But wait a minute—a coach's whole future is based on the game. Your job, your recruiting, everything is based on winning, and the officials tell you to relax, it's only a game." I've been here for fifteen years and I've never criticized an official after a game. When I was a student teacher, a coach told me that you never criticize an official after you lose. After you win, you can tell an official that he did a lousy job, but not after you lose. If you talk after you lose, it sounds like sour grapes. But the more you're in the game and the more you see, it bothers me. Officials should be more accountable.... They should have to do something to suffer after all the suffering they've caused the coaches. But we can sit here and pinpoint the calls made against us and [Santa Barbara coach] Jerry Pimm can do the same about the calls made against Santa Barbara. It's over and that's it. Still, officials weren't why we lost to Santa Barbara.

QUESTION: How is the recruiting going with Don MacLean?

TARKANIAN: I think we have a great shot at MacLean [a 6-foot-10 forward from Simi Valley, California, and a B-plus student], and it probably will come down to us and Georgia Tech for him.

Some people say UCLA is in the picture, but I think it's us and Georgia Tech. I'll be very disappointed if we don't get him. We talk regularly. I talk to him every Sunday and Coach Grgurich talks to him every Tuesday. We're in constant touch. He likes us and our players. His mother liked Duke because that is a great, great academic school, but Don eliminated Duke. She also liked Georgia Tech. During our home visit, his mother said that Don would make up his own mind, but she liked Georgia Tech and Duke. She told me that every kid on the Duke team scored over 900 on their college boards. The bottom line is that I really believe that Don will make up his own mind. Don is good friends with Trevor Wilson, who plays for UCLA, and Trevor is in constant touch with Mac-Lean, trying to hang around with Don....I just think we have a great shot at Don. Don is good enough to come in here and play right away because he can shoot. We have a lot of great athletes, but we need a shooter, especially since we lose Paddio next year. So we tell MacLean that he can come in and be our shooter, and he gets a big smile on his face....He likes that.

QUESTION: Will Keith James play against Fullerton?

TARKANIAN: I think he will. Keith wanted to play in Santa Barbara, but he was limping and he couldn't guard anybody. Even when he doesn't limp, Keith sometimes has a hard time guarding people. But Keith is a great kid, a tough kid, and he is feeling better.

QUESTION: How did you vote in the coach's poll?

TARKANIAN: I voted for Temple as number one, Purdue at number two, and Arizona at number three. I put us number eight. I tell you, I watch Purdue and Michigan play on television and they look so good to me. That's always the case. Whenever I watch somebody else, they look good to me. That's true with most coaches. All of us coaches watch each other play and we all think that the other guy is so good. The team you coach doesn't look as good as the other team. With your own team, you know your own weaknesses, and when you look at the other teams, you just see their talent and their great players.

QUESTION: How is the mood of the team?

TARKANIAN: The kids are working hard. Their attitude was good going into the Santa Barbara game. We didn't lose because we had a big head or anything. Jarvis Basnight has played great for us all year. The kid is going to end up a hunchback from carrying this team as he has all year. Part of Jarvis's problem in getting tired is that he hardly sleeps the night before a game and he barely eats on the day of the game. We have to figure something out so he won't get worn down.

QUESTION: What about recruiting Matt Othick [a 6-foot guard from Bishop Gorman High in Las Vegas who signed with New Mexico]?

TARKANIAN: Matt and his dad both love our program, and they're great people. We could have had Matt Othick, but his father wanted a promise that if Matt went to UNLV, he would start as a sophomore. I told his dad that I couldn't make him that promise. Matt is going to go to New Mexico and will play very well. But we have Greg Anthony sitting out as a red-shirt, and I think Matt knew that he couldn't beat out Greg right away. I feel bad. But Boobie James and Greg Anthony will be sophomores next year. Anderson Hunt is a freshman, and those three kids are guards. I couldn't promise the father that Matt could start. I think that we may end up two or three years down the line kicking ourselves in the pants for not taking him. If you recruit a local kid, you have to play him. You can't make promises and not keep them. For example, when we signed Freddie Banks, we told him that he would start by the time he was a sophomore, and he did. We told Clint Rossum that he might not be able to start, but he decided to come anyway and he has helped us off the bench. I don't believe that you can tell a kid he'll start if there are some doubts. I couldn't go in and tell Matt Othick that he would beat out Greg Anthony.

A lot of boosters tell you to sign local kids. What if you sign all local kids and start the season at 6–4? Those boosters stop showing up. In this town, if we start 8–2 they don't show up.

The kids were really hurt after losing in Santa Barbara. Not one word was said on the bus after the game. You know, we never talk about the number-one ranking or even winning the game or winning the conference championship, because that just adds to the pressure. You don't have control over those things. There is so much pressure on these kids just by playing in Las Vegas.

There are a lot of people around the country who have a hard time accepting that there is a great team in Las Vegas. They also have a hard time believing that we have great fans in Las Vegas. That's why the Temple game and the other games on national television show the country how strong our fans are, and we've had tremendous followings from our fans on the road. This is a great town as long as we win. But when we lose, the Lone Ranger would be lonely traveling with us. I've already talked too long, so thank you very much.

Wednesday, February 10, 1988

It is 2:30 p.m. at the Thomas & Mack Center. Tarkanian opens practice by telling his players:

"I want to emphasize this—you know how tough Fullerton can be. With about 20 seconds to go, we could have lost the last time we played them. We had a 1-point lead and [Henry] Turner had a wide-open 20-footer and he missed it. If he'd made the shot, it'd have been a different game. I don't care about their record [6–14, 2–9 in the PCAA]; Fullerton scares the hell out of me. They have athletes and they are talented.

"The problem is that their red-shirts haven't done the job yet, but they are capable of doing it. It takes only one game for them to come through, and they could destroy us. We have to get our heads into the game. The thing you need to understand is the fact that being at home doesn't solve the problem. We've got six of the last eight games at home, and hell, we've already lost at home this year.

"Something that makes me very proud about the Rebels is that in our last three years, our record playing on visiting courts is 36–3. That's visiting floors, not counting neutral courts. I don't know of any college team in the country that has done as well as we have. So we know that a team can win on the road because we've done it; and that means that just because we are at home, we won't automatically have our problems solved. I know that Fullerton is going to come at us. They're going to play hard as hell. [Los Angeles Lakers broadcaster] Chick Hearn is coming up to do the game, and to the players from Fullerton, Chick Hearn really means something. Those kids grew up listening to him do the Lakers in L.A. They'll be jacked up to play well because Chick is there and the game is being televised in L.A. We can't stub our toes in this game. If we're prepared, we'll do the job. If we play as we have in practice this week, executing our offense and defense, we'll be all right. So let's play as smart as we can play. Let's cut down the passing lanes and pound the boards. I know that their coach has the stat sheet out, and those guys are talking about how they beat the hell out of us on the boards and how they are tougher than us. So let's get ready and let's kick their butts on the boards. Okay, that's it."

Watching practice today are former Rebel players Eldridge Hudson, Gary Graham, and Ricky Sobers. Also in the arena is Don Nelson, general manager of the Golden State Warriors and former coach of the Milwaukee Bucks. While with Milwaukee, Nelson earned a reputation as a man who could get the pros to play defense, and he also was known for his trapping defenses. He coached the Bucks for eleven years, winning NBA Coach of the Year honors in 1983 and 1985.

Tarkanian is happy when his former players attend practice. It's part of that family atmosphere he treasures. He also likes the NBA coaches and other coaches to stop by. First, Tarkanian is proud of how hard his players work. Second, another coach might have an idea that Tarkanian can use.

As the players start their drills, Tarkanian spots Mark Warkentien and immediately goes to talk with his former assistant. Warkentien was Tarkanian's chief recruiter from 1980 to 1987, and now is UNLV assistant athletic director. Basketball is not the subject.

"All Jerry wanted to talk about was my daughter," says Warkentien later. "That was it. Nothing about the Fullerton game, the season, or anything else."

Warkentien's 11-month-old daughter is hospitalized with cystic fibrosis. Tarkanian is obviously upset by the news, which isn't good. Warkentien's daughter is in serious condition and Warkentien is hurting. Tarkanian's ever-expressive face reflects that pain.

Practice is as always:
   Push yourself.
   Work.
   Rebound...REBOUND...*REBOUND!*
   Deny the ball.
   Get your nose on the ball.
   Don't get beat on the dribble.
   Smother 'em.
Tarkanian is happy. His team is working hard. He likes what he sees of Greg Anthony, a 6-foot-2 red-shirt point guard who transferred from the University of Portland.

During a brief break in practice, Tarkanian talks to Don Nelson, who asks about Anthony.

"That kid has a chance to be the best point guard I've ever had," says Tarkanian. "I don't know if teams will be able to get the ball up the court against him, he's that quick."

Nelson agrees. He has become an immediate Greg Anthony fan.

Turnovers start to pile up, and Ralph Readout is unhappy. He asks a player, "Hey honey, a basketball is of some value, about 60 dollars.

Why do you keep throwing it away?'' When Readout wants to get a player's attention, he calls him "honey," as in, "Hey honey, get on the boards."

Tarkanian also wants better execution.

"I don't understand this," he says. "If you see six guys on one side of the floor and two guys on the other side of the floor, why do you want to go where the six guys are? Go where there is more room, go where there's two guys. You don't have to be a magician to figure that out."

By the end of this speech, Tarkanian's voice is shrill and he is out of breath. His face looks as if his wife has just died, and he is so upset he is mixing up his words, which is why he said "magician" instead of "genius."

While Tarkanian is talking, center Anthony Todd says something to a player next to him. Readout approaches Todd and quietly chews him out. "I don't care what you're saying, no one talks when Coach talks." Todd stammers an excuse, but Readout cuts him off: "It doesn't matter what you have to say. Understand?" Readout walks away, shaking his head and mumbling, "He must have picked that up at Lamar."

Todd spent his first three years at Lamar before transferring to UNLV.

Tarkanian brings his five starters into a huddle at one end of the court. He is on one knee, drawing up a play. They look like six kids making plans on the playground. And it's the childlike qualities in Tarkanian that appeal to his players. Tarkanian delights in these moments of being close to his players, sharing the game he so loves with them. It could be a scene right out of "Our Gang" as Spanky tells his friends, "Okay, now here is what we're gonna do..."

Gerald Paddio proves that he isn't a magician. He dribbles the ball right to the area of the court where all the players are positioned, instead of going to the other side of the floor where he would have room to operate.

Tarkanian: "Gerald, didn't that part of the floor look congested?"

Paddio: "No."

Tarkanian, in disbelief: "No...no...well...I mean, then what are all those guys doing there?"

From the sidelines, Ricky Sobers sees Greg Anthony drive to the basket for an uncontested lay-up.

"Middle!" yells Sobers at the players. "Don't let a guy drive right down the middle!"

Readout: "Come on, Jarvis honey, get on the boards."

Tarkanian has developed a special relationship with Karl (Boobie) James, the 6-foot-3 freshman guard from Dunbar High in Baltimore. His older brother was Frank "Spoon" James, a former Rebel player. Another older brother is Keith James, a reserve Rebel forward.

Boobie James was an explosive scorer in high school, and is now being asked to play point guard with the Rebels. It's difficult enough for most players to adjust from high school to major college basketball, but switching to a new position creates an immense challenge.

"This isn't easy for Boobie," said Tarkanian. "His instincts are to shoot, and we're asking him to think about passing first. He will be a great two [shooting] guard for us."

But that won't be until the 1988–89 season, when Greg Anthony is eligible to assume the point guard duties. Until then, the ball is in Boobie's hands. In the loss to Santa Barbara, Boobie shot 2 for 13 and had a very tough day on the court.

Tarkanian senses that Boobie may still be suffering. Tarkanian touches Boobie often—a pat on the back, an arm around him. Tarkanian wants Boobie to know that he's there, that the team and the coaches are behind him. Boobie has very expressive brown eyes. He wants to please Tarkanian desperately. Theirs is almost a father-son relationship.

Tarkanian and his coaches like Boobie because he has guts.

"Boobie reminds me of me," says Ricky Sobers. "He's not afraid to take the big shot, to drive to the basket. He'll make mistakes, but he'll also make big plays."

As a freshman, he will make more mistakes than big plays. But in a few years, Tarkanian is convinced that the opposite will be true: Boobie has the makings of a clutch player.

When practice ends, Tarkanian talks to Nelson. The subject is defense: specifically, when to double-team the man who has the ball at the low post. In the NBA, that is the norm. When a guard passes the ball to a big man near the basket, the big man is double-teamed as the defensive guard leaves his man open to drop under the basket.

Tarkanian mentions that the college game is different because of the 19-foot, 9-inch 3-point line.

Tarkanian: "I hate to just have the big guy throw the ball back out to the guard and have him wide open to take the 3-pointer."

Nelson: "What do guards shoot from that range?"

Tarkanian: "About 40 percent."

Nelson: "That's a problem...then you have to rotate."

Tarkanian sends a manager to get a notepad and pen, and the two coaches sit down to talk serious X's and O's.

Afterward, Tarkanian asks Nelson if he will come back to Thursday morning's shootaround and talk to the players about some of his defensive concepts. Nelson agrees.

Nelson on Tarkanian: "This is the first time I've met Jerry. It was interesting to spend a couple of hours with him. If you just watch practice for a few minutes you can sense it: they like him—no, they love the guy. He made me feel the same way. There is something honest about him. I think what happens is that Jerry makes you feel that he likes you, that he trusts you. He opens himself up to you, and you want to do the same for him. I had no plans to stay around for another practice, but he asked me, and there was no way I could turn him down. It's strange...I came to see him, to talk to him about a few of his players, and in a few minutes, he had me doing all the talking. Then, he was asking me for help. His hunger for ideas and his lack of ego makes you want to do it for him, to make him happy. It's very disarming."

Thursday, February 11, 1988

The 2 p.m. shootaround is a light practice on the day of a game. The name describes the purpose of the workout—the players take the court and they shoot around. The idea is for them to get loose and to start thinking about the game.

The setting is informal. Several television crews are present, doing interviews to be used on that night's 6 o'clock news as a preview of the game. Tarkanian spends some time chatting with Fullerton coach George McQuarn, a former Tarkanian assistant. Don Nelson also is present.

Tarkanian is wearing a red shirt and a grey UNLV sweater. When he finishes with McQuarn, he walks out to half court and just stares. It seems as if he doesn't move for ten minutes; only his eyes dart from side to side. It is almost as if he is in a trance.

Tarkanian has done this before.

Former Long Beach sports information director Gary Wright: "I remember when Tark was coaching at Long Beach and we were in the California-Irvine tournament. We were playing a weak team, some-

296

one like Edinborough State, and it was a close game at the half. Their press was giving us problems. When the half ended, all the players went into the dressing room, but Jerry stood on the floor, right under the basket. He was just staring at the court, and he didn't move for a few minutes. I watched him, and you could almost see the X's and O's moving around inside his head. Then he went into the dressing room and drew up some plays on the blackboard. We demolished their press in the second half."

Finally, having seen enough, Tarkanian calls the players in. This is the final preparation for the Fullerton game. The players walk through UNLV's offense, and they also are reminded of Fullerton's offense and defensive strategy.

Tarkanian calls his players to mid-court and tells them: "Guys, pay attention—let's get our heads into tonight's game, because Fullerton has some great athletes. Their season has been in a shambles, but this is the one game that can salvage their year. If they can knock us off, they'll be heroes wherever they go, and they know it. It's not like they are coming in here with a bunch of dogs. They have the quickness we have and they can jump as high as we can.

"We've worked hard on our defense this week, and if you guys go out and do your job, we can defend them. If we don't do a good job on defense, they'll run 35 seconds off the [45-second shot] clock before they start to run their plays. They'll try to keep you on defense 40 seconds on each possession. In the first 35 seconds, they won't even be looking for a shot unless [Richard] Morton is wide open. We've got to make every one of their passes a potential turnover. That's the best way to get a team to speed up their style of play—and our plan is to do that, because Fullerton wants to keep you on defense as much as they can and for as long as they can.

"We have to understand that Morton is a big part of their offense. Whoever is on Morton has to play him tough. There isn't a better shooter in the conference than Morton. He's a scoring machine. He's had games where his team has had 46 points and he has scored 30 of them. The night we played Irvine and won [99–77], they lost to Santa Barbara by a point. Morton scored 31 against Santa Barbara. He's a helluva player, so let's not let him get started. I know I told you the same thing the first time we played them at Fullerton, and he had a cold night, but he's a pure shooter. He's a tremendous pure shooter, a 3-point shooter. He had 31 points at California last year in the NIT [National Invitational Tournament].

"Now [Henry] Turner is a great athlete. He will jump as high as or higher than anyone in our ball club. The point is that they're going to

297

come in here and try to beat our butts off. If we do our jobs and work on our defensive pressure, we can take them right out of the game. For years, Fullerton has feared our defensive pressure. And at their place, they beat us on the boards. They had 16 offensive rebounds to our 4. We can't let that happen again.''

Tarkanian's fears of any team he plays are legendary.

Former Tarkanian assistant Al Menendez: "One year we were playing Northern Arizona, and they just weren't a very good team. Before the game, Jerry was pacing back and forth in the hallway. I said, 'Jerry, what are you worried about; these guys aren't very good.' He turned grey. I thought he was going to pass out. He didn't say anything; he just looked sick. It turned out that Northern Arizona came up with a sleeper, some guy we didn't know about who had gotten out of the Marines. He was drilling all these outside shots, and we were losing when we went into the dressing room at the half. Jerry turned to me and said, 'See, Al? See what I mean? That's why I worry.'

"Then Tark started yelling at the team, 'You guys won't believe me. If you don't play hard, anyone can beat you...I mean, the way you guys are playing now, you aren't even good enough to play the YMCA in Pahrump.'

"We all looked at each other. Where was Pahrump? No one knew. It turned out to be a small town in Nevada. We ended up beating Northern Arizona easily, and the joke for the rest of the year was that you had better shape up or Tark would ship you to Pahrump.

"The point of this story is that Tark is convinced that anyone can beat him, and that's why he seldom loses a game his team should win. He worries so much that the players can't help but worry, too. It just rubs off. If he wasn't sincere, it wouldn't work. The kids would just tune him out. But he looks like he sees the end of the world when he talks about how they can lose if they don't play well, and the message gets across.''

After yet another of Tarkanian's warnings about Fullerton, Tarkanian brings Don Nelson on the floor. Nelson talks about his ideas of playing defense. Then some players go out on the floor and work a little bit on Nelson's concepts. This is not something that Tarkanian will use this night or even this season, but it is an idea he might incorporate for next year, and he wants to watch Nelson explain it on the court with the players.

*   *   *

At 6:30 p.m., Tarkanian gives his team the first of two pregame talks:

"The key to winning this game is defense. I want pressure on the ball. When a guard brings the ball up the court, I want us to pick him up at half court. Put your nose on the ball. Use quick hands. I don't want you to get beat on the dribble [a Fullerton player dribbling past a UNLV defender]."

Tarkanian then goes into great detail about how to handle the various Fullerton offenses, when to switch on defense, when to double-team, and when to sag back on defense. He also reviews the Rebels' offense, reminding the players to reverse or swing the ball, which means to pass it from one side of the court to another. All week, Tarkanian has worked his team on the concept of swinging the ball; without ball movement, a team is easy to defend. This is Tarkanian's most technical talk of the week to the team, and he makes extensive use of the blackboard. It is X's and O's basketball talk.

"I want to stress that this is a one-game shot. What has happened before to them doesn't matter. We've got to play pressure defense and we've got to rebound hard. They kicked your butts on the boards at their place. They're planning on that again. We have depth; we can run guys into the game. So bust your butts. We have more depth than they do and we can use it. Stacey, let me see you climb all over the boards. Let me see all of you pound the boards. All right, let's go."

The players take the floor to shoot around. They return to the dressing room about half an hour before the game, and Tarkanian talks to them again:

"We have to go out and play hard right from the beginning. These guys stayed in the game with us at their place. They felt when the game was over that they should have won. They're coming in here with a lot of confidence. They think they can beat you. They're going to come at us. If we play hard right from the beginning, we can show them what we can do. But if we're lackadaisical, if we're careless, then they'll be able to stay in the game and they'll get more and more momentum, and we'll be in for a tough night. So let's concentrate, let's execute, let's do the things we have to do to be a great ball club, and let's do it from the beginning.

"This week, we also said that we're going to concentrate hard on rebounding. So when we shoot, I want four guys on the offensive boards, with Boobie back guarding against the fast break. So pound the offensive boards. Gerald, that means you and Stacey are on the offensive boards.

"And pressure the ball. That means good defense; no fouling. I don't want to put them on the foul line. All right?

299

"Okay Jarvis, go ahead."

Jarvis Basnight leads the team in the Lord's Prayer. After the amens, the players chant: "Go to work!"

Before the game begins, Tarkanian sees an official he just doesn't like. He tells Readout, "We won't get a call from that SOB tonight, you can bet your life on that."

The game begins and the teams trade baskets early. At one point, Boobie James goes for a loose ball and falls out of bounds, where he is caught by Tarkanian and pushed back on the floor. Tarkanian smiles. He likes Boobie, and he likes his players throwing their bodies after the ball.

Early in the game, it is apparent that UNLV just isn't executing its offense. They bring the ball up one side of the floor and keep it there. The key to getting an open shot is ball movement, inside to outside, left side of the floor to right.

"Throw the extra pass" is one of Grgurich's favorite phrases. It means always to be looking for the open man and not automatically thinking shoot once you get the ball. The extra pass often is the difference between a 20-footer and a lay-up.

But on this night, there are few extra passes and very little ball movement.

"Reverse the damn ball!" screeches Tarkanian. "Swing it!"

The Rebels' performance on another of the week's themes—rebounding—also leaves something to be desired.

"Rebound...REBOUND...*REBOUND!*" screams Tarkanian.

With 8 minutes left in the first half, Tarkanian calls time-out. As he goes to kneel down in the huddle, the public-address announcer tells the crowd, "A final score: Utah State 82, Santa Barbara 65."

Tarkanian had been right. He had predicted that Santa Barbara would lose after its victory over UNLV, and the Gauchos did.

In the huddle, Tarkanian has to scream over the crowd and the music.

"Get on the offensive boards!"

"Reverse the ball, already!"

"Get the ball inside to Jarvis!"

With 6 minutes left in the first half, UNLV has pushed its lead to 32–15 and seems to have the game under control. But then the Rebels' offense breaks down.

No extra passes.

No swinging the ball.

No one on the boards.

Tarkanian is sucking on the towel, expecting the worst.

Right before the half, Keith James loses the ball when he steps on the out-of-bounds line. It is the second time in the game that James has stepped over the line.

Tarkanian can't believe it. He kicks the chair, curses, and heads into the dressing room for halftime.

In the dressing room, Tarkanian is livid.

"How can you stand out of bounds? They have boundaries on the damn floor. Once in a season is all right, but two in a half—what the hell are you doing?" Tarkanian's voice is shrill; he is almost out of breath. He stops for a moment.

"Damn...

"You guys bust your ass defensively, and the only thing that keeps you in the game is defense.... You know what? You're the worst offensive team in America. You know why? Because you're selfish. You're not playing intelligently. I'm embarrassed to watch you. I'd think you'd be embarrassed. For crying out loud...

"There's no execution whatsoever to anything. We call time-out to tell you to reverse the ball. Do you reverse it? No, you don't reverse it. You don't even listen to us. I MEAN, YOU DON'T EVEN LISTEN TO US!

"It's a damn horror film watching you guys execute an offense. In practice, you do it really well. You get in a game, and you're so damn selfish all you care about is your own well-being.

"Someone comes out and plays you tight, and it's one pass, maybe two passes, and then someone has to shoot. You're not going to reverse the ball. You're not going to execute anything.

"I'm telling you right now: you're in great trouble in this ball game. We had a 9-point lead at the half in Santa Barbara, too. The way you execute your offense, hell, I don't know how you beat anybody. Don't you have any pride? Aren't you embarrassed to look like damn jackasses?"

Once again, his voice is shrill and he's almost out of breath. Tarkanian pauses, then tells Tim Grgurich to speak. But before Grgurich begins, Tarkanian yells, "That's the worst offensive execution we've ever had at UNLV. Ever!" Now Grgurich takes over and does some X and O work on the blackboard, the theme being to reverse the ball. Tarkanian breaks in, screaming: "Every day we tell you the same thing. Every time out we tell you the same thing. All the time, we tell you the same thing. But pretty soon, you just stop listening to us....You just stop listening to us. You ought to think that maybe we might be right once in a while.''

Tarkanian is silent. Grgurich goes back to the blackboard and shows the players how to get open on offense. The theme is the same: *swing the basketball*. Then Grgurich makes a different point: ''That's the bad thing about the damn 3-point shot. That's all you care about; that's all all our guards care about. If it doesn't go in, then what? Play the game, don't just shoot!''

Tarkanian speaks again:

''I don't understand why you guys won't execute the offense. I don't understand what goes through your mind. I wish the hell that medical science could find out what goes on in your mind during the game. It would startle mankind. We can call time-out and tell you exactly what to do, and by the time you get back out on the court you don't know what the hell we said. That's absolutely amazing! Then you go out and make jackasses of yourselves and you don't even feel bad. Don't you have any pride?''

There is a long silence, then Tarkanian speaks again.

''The only reason you're in the game is that you've busted your asses defensively. You can't go on like this, or it's going to be a short season. You've got to make up your mind whether you want to be a basketball team or a bunch of clowns.

''You can't beat teams without an offense. You have no offense—absolutely no offense!''

Tarkanian is silent. Assistant Ralph Readout talks about the Rebels' offense. At one point he says, ''Listen, look at Basnight. If he gets the ball and he's double-teamed, he does what he's supposed to do—he passes the ball back out. If I'm captain of this team and I'm Jarvis, I'm so pissed right now, I can't believe it. But he won't say anything.''

Tarkanian continues:

''If they put a little defensive pressure on us, we go totally haywire. You figure that you've got to shoot the ball if they put any pressure on you at all. You can't pass the damn thing. You can't even make a simple pass. You can't pass it to the first guy who is open. We'll come out to practice tomorrow and we'll run it through. Everybody at practice says, 'Hey, nice pass. Good job. Way to go.' Then the game starts and everybody says, 'The hell with it; I'm not gonna run it anymore.' This is the damndest thing I've ever seen.

''All right, on offense, let's pay attention to what we're going to do in the second half. We're going to SWING THE BASKETBALL

...I mean, SWING THE BASKETBALL...Catch the ball, square up, and pass it. And come to meet the pass.

"Listen, let's play with some kind of intelligence, some kind of teamwork. Let's swing the ball. If you swing the ball, you'll get wide-open outside shots. You won't have to take a shot with a hand in your face.

"They've already shot sixteen free throws and it's only the first half! Go out there and play good defense without putting them on the free-throw line. Okay, we have a 10-point lead, and keep in mind that we had a 9-point lead last week at Santa Barbara. We better come out and play hard and play as a team. Go to the offensive boards, execute the offense! We have twelve turnovers this half, and it's because we don't play as a team. We try to force situations. Don't force situations; let things develop. All right, let's go."

The half-time speech serves it purpose. The Rebels start the second 20 minutes playing harder, but more importantly, smarter than they did in the first half. The passing is not ideal, but the ball is starting to move, and UNLV has a 49–33 lead with 16 minutes left in the game.

UNLV continues to dominate the backboards and to use its pressure defense to force Fullerton into turnovers. With 12 minutes left, the lead is 56–37.

Then it happens.

For whatever reason, the Rebels let down, and Fullerton comes back behind the shooting of the man Tarkanian feared—Richard Morton. And then there is someone else Tarkanian feared: the mystery player, as if this were the Northern Arizona game all over. Morton does most of the damage from the outside, but a kid with no name on the back of his jersey comes off the bench to drill two quick jumpers.

"Who is that guy?" asks Tarkanian.

His name is Benson Williams, which means nothing to Tarkanian or his coaches. Williams is a 6-foot-7 walk-on who has played only two minutes all season.

With 6:12 left, the Rebels are clinging to a 63–56 lead. Tarkanian calls time-out and goes into a box-and-one defense. That means Stacey Augman chases Morton everywhere on the court while the other four Rebels play a zone defense. If you were to look at the game from the ceiling, the four Rebel defenders would be in a square, a "box," while Augman followed Morton.

Going to the box-and-one is an unorthodox move for Tarkanian, who usually lives and dies with the pressure man-to-man defense. If he does play zone, it's his old 1-2-2. But Tarkanian knows he has to do something to stop Morton, that this is a night that calls for invention and imagination.

In the next five minutes, Fullerton does not score a point. In that span, Fullerton tries six field goals and two free throws and misses them all. The Titans also turn the ball over twice. Meanwhile, the Rebels are on the boards and have their fast break in high gear.

With 1:20 left in the game, UNLV has a 20-point lead and Tarkanian clears his bench.

Final score: UNLV 77, Fullerton 61.

In the dressing room, Tarkanian goes up to each player and individually congratulates him. Then he says, "Practice tomorrow at 2:30," and walks out of the dressing room.

Tarkanian's next job is to deal with the media. Here are his basic remarks to the reporters:

"I thought we played very hard."

"Our defense was excellent, especially in the first half."

"This Rebel team has been the most pleasant surprise of any team we've had here. On a given day, we can beat anyone. Of course, on a given day anyone can beat us. We do have a lot of shortcomings, but our kids also have a lot of heart."

"Jarvis Basnight is having a great year. He has absolutely no ego. All he wants to do is win."

"Boobie James will be a great shooting guard for us. We are asking him to do a lot as a point guard, and he's coming through. Remember, he's just a freshman. We have to be patient with him."

Friday, February 12, 1988

It's 2 p.m. Friday. Another way to look at it is that Tarkanian has his team on the floor only sixteen hours after the Fullerton victory, and in less then twenty-four hours UNLV will be playing on this same floor against a very fine Missouri team, ranked fifteenth in the country.

There are several spectators at practice, including such NBA people as Lakers general manager Jerry West and New Jersey Nets player personnel director Al Menendez. Also watching are CBS commentator Billy Packer and former Rebel players Eldridge Hudson and Danny Tarkanian.

Tarkanian and his coaches know that their players are mentally fatigued. There is a natural letdown the day after a game, and the Fullerton win was rather emotional, given the Rebels' flat first half, Tarkanian's rip-roaring halftime speech, and then their strong finish.

During some practices, the players can pretty much motivate each other. On this day, the coaches know that this responsibility falls to them, and they are louder than at any time during the week.

"Work hard."

"Intensity."

"Push yourself."

The coaches want almost a frenzied atmosphere. That's the reason for the yelling and the body-banging drills. That is why the arena, whose official name is the Thomas & Mack Center, is also known as Tark's Shark Tank. And what is the trademark of sharks? They swarm; they fight; they are in a frenzy. A team with a great pressing defense is like a school of sharks.

And the games themselves are so noisy a player can barely hear the guy screaming at him from five feet away. During a game, the senses are heightened, and emotions are raw and out in the open.

So from the moment that practice begins, with a two-on-one fast-break drill, the coaches are yelling.

Readout: "Work, Chris, honey."

Grgurich: "Good passes."

Readout: "He wasn't picked once out there. Get a piece of meat, will ya?"

Tarkanian: "I tell you what to do and you just don't do it. Didn't you learn anything last night?"

Once the fast-break drill is over, the team works on its defense in a half-court setting. The object of the defense is to stop Missouri's big men, especially 6-foot-7 Derrick Chievous, a 23-point scorer destined to be a first-round NBA draft choice. Tarkanian assigns 6-foot-8 freshman Stacey Augman to guard Chievous. All three UNLV coaches talk to Augman.

"Cut him off, Stace."

"Stacey, talk on defense."

"Way to go, Stace."

"Oh no, Stacey, you can't let him do that."

Tarkanian stops practice and tells Augman, "You can't let Chievous post you up like that. If you do, you'll foul out. You won't last ten minutes in the game."

Practice resumes.

"Stacey, hit the boards."

"Stacey, good switch, yes!"

"Stacey, play him tough."

Tarkanian stops practice again and says:

"You can't let their big men post us up like that. When the ball goes down low, you've got to get it. You've got to be desperate down there—do something. You've got to get the ball. Fight for it, tickle 'em, do something."

Did he really say "tickle 'em?"

Indeed Tarkanian did, and though there wasn't a smile from the players on the floor, muffled laughter could be heard from those watching on the sidelines.

While Tarkanian is talking, Jarvis Basnight walks to the sideline and gets a cup of water. Grgurich approaches Basnight and tells him not to walk about when Tarkanian is talking. "That's what we talked about last night. You have to show better leadership than this."

Basnight apologizes.

Grgurich is especially effective when he works one-on-one with the players, giving Basnight a quick word of advice on the side or helping other players to improve their games. He also is very strong in the X's and O's department; and he has a knack for taking all those marks on the blackboard and making them mean something to the players.

The last segment of practice is devoted to the offense. This is a clear statement of Tarkanian's priorities. He believes in defense first, offense second—the lion's share of practice time is spent on defense. The themes are very familiar:

"Swing the ball."

"Extra pass."

"Good shots."

"Extra pass...extra pass...SWING THE BALL, ALREADY!"

"Rebound...REBOUND...*REBOUND!*"

During a brief break, Ralph Readout tells Basnight, "You have the best left-handed hook shot in America, but you never use it."

Eldridge Hudson also has a few words about playing the low post for Anthony Todd.

Practice is over and the players gather at half court in a circle. Tarkanian tells them:

"Get your rest. Tonight, make sure that the lights are out and you're well rested. There's no gimmicks, no tricks to the game. We have to come out and play harder than hell. We've got to climb right in their jocks. Missouri is a helluva team. They have better players than Temple does. Man for man, they're a better team than Temple is. We have to come out and go after them.

"We're going to try and do something that most teams won't even try: we're going to pressure their guards. They have good guards, but we're going to do it. That's why we need to be prepared mentally. Breakfast tomorrow morning at nine. All right, that's it. Let's go."

The players raise their hands and chant: "Go to work!"

Saturday, February 13, 1988

The Rebels—Tarkanian included—spend the night before their games at the Tropicana Hotel. Lights are out by 11:30 p.m.

It is now 9 a.m., four hours before the game with Missouri. Players are arriving in the hotel's Tradewinds Banquet Room number two for the team breakfast. The meal is a buffet of scrambled eggs, hash brown potatoes, toast, pancakes, sausage, orange juice, and grape juice. There is no coffee or tea.

At 9:02, Tarkanian walks in and says to Grgurich, "Jarvis's mother called last night."

Grgurich just nods.

There is an immediate pall in the room. Basnight has a stomach virus. He has been vomiting and hasn't been able to eat or sleep. The prospect of facing Missouri without his best player is weighing heavily on Tarkanian.

After helping himself to toast and eggs, Tarkanian sits down and says to Grgurich, "We didn't work on [defensive] switches."

Tarkanian eats his eggs as a sandwich. Since he has been in the room, no one else has spoken. Tarkanian returns to the buffet for another helping, and then another.

Tarkanian is finished, and as he leaves, he asks Chris Jeter to step outside. Jeter is a 6-foot-9 sophomore who seldom plays. What Tarkanian wants to do is to explain to Jeter why David Willard had gotten into the Fullerton game before Jeter did. Willard had left the team early in the season and since returned.

After Tarkanian leaves the room, one of the student managers says that he has to be on guard because lately people have been trying to steal Tarkanian's towels from the bench. When a towel disappears, Tarkanian starts screaming for another one. The manager has started to prepare two towels for each game, so Tark will always have one in reserve.

For obvious reasons, the players aren't wild about the team meals. No one speaks, all you hear is the clinking of the silverware against the plates, and Tarkanian just looks worried.

According to the waiter, many of the players prefer to eat elsewhere, at places such as Wendy's. Freddie Banks liked to stop at the Taco Bell before games, while Armon Gilliam usually had a healthy appetite and ate with the team. Tarkanian's hunger on this day is somewhat out of character. He usually eats very little, and when he does eat something, it's not meat. If there is a night game, the meal is at 4 p.m. and the choices are usually spaghetti, chicken, and lasagna.

Tarkanian gives his first pregame talk to the team:

"The first thing I want us to do is to deny every single pass. Every time they get the ball, I want a hand in their face. Their offense is based on timing and spacing. As I've been telling you all year, when you face that kind of offense you can disrupt it by getting a hand in their face and preventing them from throwing the pass where they want to.

"Defensively, I don't want anyone playing behind the post and letting them just throw the ball down low. Especially you, Stacey—if you do that you won't last five minutes. They'll shoot ten free throws and you'll be watching the rest of the game. You have to fight him [Chievous] and you have to be in front of him."

The talk turns to defensive X's and O's, with Tarkanian at the blackboard.

"We will fight through the screens. Do you hear me? We're going to fight through the screens. I don't want anyone telling me, 'I got screened.' Well, you're gonna get screened, and you'll get screened all game long. You have a choice to make: either you're going to get screened and surrender, or you'll slash through the screen. But you are going to get screened, so getting screened is no excuse. Slash through it; you know the technique used to do that.

"I want your hands up. What good is it to swarm a guy if your hands are by your sides? So battle them, battle them all over the court and go get the ball. Got it?

"I want to tell you once again, if you don't pressure the ball, our whole game plan backfires. There are different ways of playing them. Kansas played them by playing soft. They didn't pressure anyone; they just sat back in a zone.

"But I want to play them hard. But if four of us play them hard and one guy doesn't, that sonofabitch is a traitor, because he destroys what everyone else is doing. So our plan is to play them hard and press them, and everybody has to do that. Everybody! So everyone get your head into it and carry out your responsibility. Every pass within 25 feet of the basket is to be challenged. If your man catches the ball, smother him. Every post-up is to be fronted. Every screen...on every screen, you're to slash through it. Play aggressive and play hard. That's the way the Rebels play when we're at our best.''

Tarkanian now does X's and O's for his offensive. The theme is to swing the ball.

"Missouri is a great running team. They'll run like hell. They scored 111 points against Iowa State and 101 against Oklahoma. They're a good shooting team, too. So play good sound defense, rebound, and execute the offense. Most of all, let's play together and let's play as hard as we can play. We need a great effort from everybody.''

As the team leaves the dressing room for pregame warm-ups, Tarkanian says that Basnight wants to play, but is very sick, and Tarkanian doesn't know how long or how well he can play.

The second pregame talk by Tarkanian begins with a review of the UNLV out-of-bounds plays. Then he talks about Missouri's out-of-bounds plays:

"We have to get back defensively and go to the boards hard. GO TO THE BOARDS HARD. We have to hit the defensive boards hard, too. Their coach has been making a big thing all week about rebounding, so they're going to be jacked-up to hit the boards, too. Defensively, we're in tremendous defensive pressure.

"Fellows, I'm going to say this again: if you don't play the defense the way we tell you to play it, you'll get embarrassed, because it's all going to backfire on us. We can't get down 16–4 to start the game and have some guy say, 'It's all my fault.' God darn it, you know how we want to play. Everyone is in denial and everyone is in pressure defense. We have no one playing soft. Pressure the ball so they can't throw good passes. Offensively, we'll move the ball and get good shots. All right, Jarvis.''

Basnight leads the team in the Lord's Prayer, and the players conclude with the chant, "Play hard!...Go to work.''

As the team takes the floor, the arena is jammed and the fans are chanting "REB-ELS...REB-ELS.''

As if Basnight didn't have enough problems, he has a heating pad placed on his left leg, which has bothered him periodically during the season. But he does start.

UNLV gets the opening tip and throws the ball away. On their next possession, Anthony Todd blows a wide-open lay-up. Tarkanian is worried.

The first half is a disaster. Chievous posts Augmon down low, scores a couple of quick baskets, and Augmon draws two fouls. The Rebels aren't giving Augmon any help. They are putting no pressure on the Missouri guards, who are having an easy time of getting the ball to Chievous near the basket. Basnight looks like the sick guy he is, dragging up and down the floor and not his usual self on the boards. Tarkanian calls several time-outs, urging his team to play hard, to pressure Missouri. Offensively, UNLV can't hit an open shot.

In the middle of the first half, UNLV is behind 26–16, and Tarkanian goes to the towel. A minute later, Missouri scores on a 3-pointer, making it 29–16, and Tarkanian puts the towel on top of his head. With seven minutes left in the first half, Tarkanian disgustedly junks his man-to-man defensive in favor of a 1-2-2 zone. This goes against his instincts, because he is convinced that the way to beat Missouri is with a pressure man-to-man—not with a zone, in which the defensive team has the danger of becoming "soft" (passive). Besides, Rebel teams play pressure defense; they don't sit back. That's the tradition. Nonetheless, he has to try something.

"You're doing nothing on defense," he tells the team in the huddle. "So work on the 1-2-2 zone. Bust your ass. Hit the boards. Play hard, for cryin' out loud."

But nothing helps. With three minutes left in the half, Missouri is in front 37–24 and Tarkanian calls time-out.

"You guys aren't even playing the damn zone right....You're not even playing the zone right....Do you want to play at all?" Ralph Readout starts to make a suggestion; Tarkanian quietly but firmly cuts him off with one word: "No." Then Tarkanian continues.

"Get in the game, will ya? Play hard defensively. On offense, the shots will start falling. We'll be all right. But defense will get us back into the game."

Not much changes, and at the half, Missouri has a 44–32 lead.

In the dressing room, Tarkanian begins talking in a quiet, calm voice.

"Defensively, you guys did nothing. You're playing on national television, a big game, and we're getting nothing defensively. We're getting no effort, no concentration...there's no effort whatsoever."

310

He raises his voice.

"It's like you're on a damn picnic. No effort at all defensively!"

Tarkanian is calm again.

"Offensively, the ball will fall. Just keep taking those shots; we'll be all right. The shots are there. If you're shooting a decent percentage, we're right in the game. BUT DEFENSIVELY, WE STINK!"

There is a long silence.

"We take pride in our defense, but we have no damn defense. We take pride in our effort, but we have no effort."

Tarkanian's voice is high, almost cracking. You can feel his pain by just listening to him.

"Why would you play a nationally televised game on your home court and not play hard? Why would you play a team this big and not even play hard? They're kicking your ass on the boards, they're getting all the loose balls. They're totally out-hustling you. AND IT'S HAPPENING IN YOUR OWN GYM!

"Our effort is a damn disgrace.

"Offensively, you're trying to do a good job. You're playing intelligently. You're trying to move the ball. The shots will fall.

"But defensively, just play hard. The whole country is watching you. At least play hard. Then when the game is over you can hold up your head. I told you guys before the game that if we don't go out and play hard, it will all backfire on us. Well, nobody played hard. We had no pressure on anybody. Everything I told you guys before the game you totally ignored. Okay, Tim, go ahead."

Grgurich then talks offensive strategy, the theme being, "Everything we worked on in practice, we're doing. Just take your time and shoot the ball; it will go in."

Tarkanian differs on this.

"I think we're trying to be too patient on offense. If you're open, don't think; just shoot the ball. We're using too many pump fakes. Just shoot it, we'll be all right. The shots will go. Our problem is defense and rebounding. Ralph, go ahead."

Before Readout can start, Tarkanian adds, "Our real problem is effort. If you don't play hard, you'll have problems against anybody."

Readout starts to say something, but Tarkanian isn't finished.

"We worked so hard on pressure and everything in practice, and we did a great job. Why won't you do it today, when there are millions of people watching? Why do it yesterday and not today? That doesn't make any damn sense to me."

Finally, Readout gets into his defensive chalk talk, his theme being, "We can still win this game; it's the damndest thing I've ever seen. All we have to do is play defense like Rebels do."

Tarkanian goes on.

"Early in the game, Stacey was trying to do a job on Chievous, but you guys sold Stacey out. He was busting his ass, but we had no pressure on the ball [the players passing the ball to Chievous], so they got two or three easy buckets on us, and Stacey got two quick fouls on him. Then I went to the zone, and we didn't even play the zone right.

"But it's like I told you before: if you don't all do this together, it will backfire. And that's what happened. We weren't all in this together.

"All right, here's what we will do to start the second half: we're going to come out and pressure them. We will play the way I wanted to play to start the game. Everybody get out and pressure them. There's 20 minutes left. If you can't do it, I'll take you out. Jarvis, if you can't do it, I'll play you for three minutes, then take you out. So go hard for three minutes, then come out. Everyone go hard. You have to play with some organization. At one point, we had four guys in a half-court trap and one guy in a full-court trap. How the hell can that happen?

"Offensively, move the ball, and when you're open, shoot the ball. Boobie, if you're open, shoot. Clint [Rossum], if you're open, shoot.

"Fellows, we haven't had a good effort from you guys. We told you all along that we never ask you to win a game, just play hard. All we ask is that you prepare yourself physically, emotionally, and mentally to play as hard as you can. That's our only goal for the year, and we didn't get that today. THE SAD THING IS THAT WE'RE NOT GETTING IT AT HOME!

"We need 20 minutes of an all-out effort. Twenty minutes of an all-out effort. They haven't seen it yet. The way we played the first half, they're very confident. They're not even concerned. You have to come out and bust your butts. Stacey can't guard Chievous unless everybody does their jobs. Work hard. Don't surrender. I want everyone to hold their head up after this game. Now, let's go."

In the huddle to start the second half, Tarkanian once again reminds his players, "Don't surrender...play hard."

Ralph Readout says, "Play like Rebels."

And they do.

UNLV makes two steals in the first 30 seconds that become 4

points. Two minutes into the second half, the Rebels have cut the Missouri lead to 44–40, and it's a ball game.

What happened?

Intensity. Pressure defense. Hard work. Pride.

All the virtues Tarkanian talked about in the dressing room are seen on the court. And with 10:30 in the half, the Rebels take their first lead at 61–60. That means they have outscored Missouri 29–16 in the second half.

The game remains close hereafter. Missouri appears somewhat tired under the Rebels' relentless pressure, but Tarkanian has a problem in that his team still isn't shooting very well. Also, Basnight is dragging. Tarkanian basically sticks with his plan of playing Basnight for three minutes, then resting him for one. Tarkanian is milking everything he can out of his 6-foot-8 senior, but Basnight has only so much to give.

A game such as this is often decided by a point guard. That is especially true now, since the Rebels' captain is not his usual self. The Rebels' point guard is freshman Boobie James. With 52 seconds left in the game and Missouri leading 80–79, Boobie drives the lane and goes down under two players. His shot is an air ball that ends up in the hands of a Missouri player. James waits for the foul and the whistle, and so does Tarkanian, but none is heard.

"I thought Boobie got hammered on that play," Tarkanian would say later. "I think he lost both his arms. He must have got them amputated."

The Rebels have one more chance. Boobie James brings the ball up the court with 36 seconds left and Missouri in front 81–79. James looks inside to Basnight, who is covered. He throws a pass to Clint Rossum on the wing, who is open for a 3-pointer. But Rossum passes the ball back to James. Then Boobie passes to Gerald Paddio on the other wing. Paddio's covered, but he might have a chance to drive. Paddio decides it's best not to force the action, and he passes back to James. So with 14 seconds left, James has the ball again. He is beyond the key, about 23 feet from the basket in 3-point range. It suddenly dawns on Boobie that someone has to take the shot, and he is that someone. He unleashes a jumper that looks good—fine arch and rotation—but it rims in and out and is hauled in by a Missouri player.

That's it. Final score: Missouri 81, UNLV 79.

Tarkanian stares at the floor for a moment and says to no one in particular, "That was a real kick in the gut."

He is silent for a moment and then says, "But weren't those kids something?"

Then he picks up his coat and slings it over his shoulder. Wearing a slight, very distant smile, Tarkanian walks over to Missouri coach Norm Stewart and shakes his hand and congratulates a few Missouri players. Then he slowly heads to the dressing room, still staring at the court as he goes.

Meanwhile, Danny Tarkanian has come out of the stands to comfort Boobie James, embracing him. Danny knows what it is like for a point guard in that position, to have the ball in your hands and the game riding on your decision. In the dressing room, Grgurich puts his arm around Boobie and talks to him quietly. Boobie nods, but he is on the verge of tears. The immediate instinct of the Tarkanians and the coaching staff is to close ranks around Boobie. They may have lost the game, but they don't want to lose him. At least he had the courage to take the shot.

That's what Tarkanian likes: heart, guts, pride. Those things count even more than winning.

To prove it, in the dressing room, he tells the players, "You worked hard. Practice Monday at 10 a.m. You guys gave a great effort in the second half. You can be proud."

Tarkanian is hurt by the loss, but he hides it well. He tells reporters that his team worked hard in the second half. He defends Boobie's shot. He credits Missouri coach Norm Stewart for doing a good job, and he praises the Missouri players. He does not mention Basnight's illness. He offers no excuses and doesn't knock the officials. He says the game was great for college basketball and leaves it at that.

Sunday, February 14, 1988

Last night was a long night for Tarkanian. He replayed the game over and over in his mind. Lois has said, "I won't even sleep with Jerry after we get beat. He just sits up all night, moaning. It is like someone is stabbing him over and over with daggers, and it goes on for hours. Nothing you can do will make him feel better. He doesn't completely snap out of it until we play and win another game."

After the Missouri game, the Tarkanian family knows that their father is suffering. Daughter Pamela is having pregnancy problems, yet she comes to the house to see her father early in the morning. Daughter Jodie is a nurse in Seattle, and she calls Sunday to ask Lois, "How is he doing? I feel so bad for Dad." Danny had come from law school in San Diego for the weekend. Son George, an assistant coach at Pamona-Pitzer College in California, left immediately after his own basketball practice to be with his father on the weekend.

As for their activities on Sunday, Lois and Jerry stop at the hospital to see Mark Warkentien and his wife, who are at the bedside of their gravely ill daughter. Tarkanian spends quite a bit of time comforting his former assistant coach. Later, Tarkanian does his coach's television show, *The Jerry Tarkanian Show*. He praises his team's effort, and for the first time reveals that Basnight had been very sick. He also defends Boobie James's shot:

"You have to keep shooters in the right frame of mind, and keep up their confidence, so they don't have to stop and think if they should shoot the ball. If you get them thinking too much, it can really screw them up. Ever watch them when they are missing? They go around with funny looks on their faces. They shake their heads. They keep grabbing the ball and looking at it as if it is crooked and that's the problem. They stare at the rim, thinking maybe the rim is too high. They start thinking of all the reasons that they are missing, and it makes them worse."

Tarkanian wants to head that problem off at the pass. This is a day for comforting Boobie through the media.

What does this week say about Tarkanian?

There is his passion for loyalty—perhaps both his greatest strength and his greatest weakness. Why do his players practice longer and harder than almost any team in the country, and not complain? Why are his current and former players his best recruiting tools? Why did Jarvis Basnight drag himself out of a sick bed to play when he could barely stand up?

Loyalty. He shows it to the players, and they return it to him.

Tarkanian never rips a player to the press. In fact, he seldom does it within the confines of the team. Think about his paint-peeling speech at halftime of the Fullerton game: "You're the worst offensive team in America....You're not playing intelligently....Don't you have any pride?"

Harsh words? Of course. But notice that they are addressed to the team as a whole, and names are seldom mentioned. His attacks are general, although his point may be aimed at only one player in the room. In the case of the Fullerton game, he may have been trying to placate the big men, who were pounding the boards and shutting down the lane on defense, yet had been left completely out of the offensive scheme by the quick shooting guards.

Yes, Keith James did receive about ten seconds of criticism from

315

Tarkanian. But Keith James also stepped out of bounds twice in a half, which is remarkable and probably unprecedented. It also is something that would have had most coaches ranting for ten minutes. In fact, once the words were out of Tarkanian's mouth, he nearly choked trying to stop them, not wanting to berate James.

Occasionally, his loyalty perhaps extends too far.

Consider the case of Richard Robinson, the 6-foot-11 senior center on the 1987–88 team. Tarkanian thought that he may have hurt Robinson's development by playing him so little during his freshman season. But four years later, all that could be said about Robinson was that he was tall and had some potential. He never averaged more than 5 points a game and was a study in inconsistency. Yet Tarkanian continued to start Robinson throughout his senior season. He just believed in Robinson. At banquets, Tarkanian would say, "Ricky Rob has his best days ahead of him"—a very curious comment to make about a senior. For better or worse, Tarkanian believed it and played Robinson.

Another example was Michael "Spider Man" Burns, who played for the Rebels from 1978 to 1982. During Burns's senior season, he was converted from a wing player to a point guard. Regardless of where Burns played that season, he struggled. Nonetheless, Tarkanian stuck with him, for better or worse. Later, Tarkanian would remain at Burns's side when he had problems in school. Tarkanian found him about a dozen jobs, and Burns lost them all. He'd call and ask for help, and Tarkanian would say, "You've embarrassed me, you've embarrassed our program, and you've embarrassed the university.... All right, Mike, one more chance. Just one more." It turned out that Burns's real troubles were drug-related, and he is now working with counselors at a rehabilitation center.

Lloyd Daniels is yet another example of Tarkanian's faith in kids. Of course, Daniels never played for Tarkanian. He also was the source of negative publicity for the coach and his program after he was arrested attempting to purchase cocaine. But Tarkanian still insists that Daniels is a "good kid."

When 6-foot-10 center David Willard left the team because of personal problems, the Rebels were in desperate need of size, and it was a setback for the program. But when Willard asked to return, Tarkanian took him back. He told the other players, "David needs our help. He is starting to put his life back together. We can help David, or we can leave him out in the cold. If you have any problems with David coming back, talk to me. I'm the coach, and I have to make the decision, but I want you to know that if David were any one of you, I'd take you back."

To the outside world, Tarkanian's loyalty might seem blind. But those who come in regular contact with him know they have a foxhole friend for life. So when Boobie James misses the shot at the end of the Missouri game, Tarkanian circles the wagons and protects his freshman guard, and Boobie James responds as most people would—he works harder, plays better, and does more, because he respects his coach.

Loyalty also is the reason why UNLV has been able to develop an emotional bonding between its players and fans that only the traditional powers such as Kentucky, North Carolina, Notre Dame, and Indiana can match. Former players stay in Las Vegas, and attend the games and practices. There is a strong feeling among nearly all those who ever wore a UNLV uniform. Remember, UNLV is only twenty years from it first four-year graduation class. When Tarkanian arrived at the school in 1973, it had never had a national ranking, or made an NCAA tournament appearance. It had virtually no basketball reputation outside of its immediate area. And certainly, there was no such thing as Rebel pride.

But if you listen to the coaches and the players now, all you hear about is what it means to be a Rebel. "Play like Rebels," assistant Ralph Readout had told the players as they started the second half of the Missouri game. "You have given me as much as any Rebel team ever has," Tarkanian had said at the start of the week, and the players knew that was a supreme compliment.

At the halftime of the UNLV–Soviet Union game in 1987, Tarkanian's theme was that they were special; they were representing not just their school, but the entire country. It's always pride he emphasizes—in themselves, in the school, in being a Rebel.

Tarkanian preaches the old-fashioned virtues: hard work, discipline, endurance. A lot of other coaches do, too, and there are coaches who have come from even more deprived backgrounds than Tarkanian. But with Tarkanian, the kids believe and accept these values. There is something in Tarkanian that legitimizes what he says.

Perhaps it can be traced back to his Armenian roots. His ancestors were massacred, and his family was forced to roam halfway around the world to find a safe harbor. His people were storytellers; they gathered around the fireplace to tell tales of the clan, how it was persecuted and how it survived. Tarkanian comes from a people who were often afraid, and who overcame that fear with hard work, loyalty, and courage.

Tarkanian tells his players:

"Don't surrender."

"Don't be humiliated."

"Play desperate."

"Have pride, play hard."

Underneath it all, there seems to be a current of fear and insecurity in Tarkanian. It is constantly revealed in his vocabulary and in his strange face, with its luminous, dark, wet eyes. He seems to worry that everything he has built at Las Vegas can just disappear. After all, his people are accustomed to disaster and they almost expect it.

Irrational? Naturally.

In terms of the coaching profession, Tarkanian's is a Horatio Alger story. He came from nothing and seemingly has everything—a wonderful family, a major college basketball program, a job he loves. He is genuinely amazed when celebrities such as CBS's Billy Packer or even Golden State general manager Don Nelson want to talk to him. His hunger for basketball knowledge prompts him to get Don Nelson on the floor to work with his players.

Unlike many coaches who came up the hard way, Tarkanian doesn't remind us of this fact. He knows that he does not have all the answers. Unlike many successful men, he has not bought his own legend. Could this be because he knows that as he had nothing before, so could he lose it all now?

His answer to this insecurity is to work harder, to push himself even more. That is all he knows and all he believes. This is the truth that LSU coach Dale Brown refers to when he discusses Tarkanian.

A misconception about Tarkanian is that he has tunnel vision, and all that can be found in the tunnel is basketball. Rather, as North Carolina State coach Jim Valvano says, "Tark is focused." And the focal point isn't just basketball; it's also his kids. If all he cared for were the game and winning, he would not have taken the time at the Saturday morning breakfast to console the twelfth man, Chris Jeter, about playing behind David Willard in the Fullerton game. Jeter's happiness would not matter against Missouri. It would not cure Jarvis Basnight's virus. He would not be a factor, but Tarkanian was worried about him and wanted to assure him that he was remembered, that he might just be a practice player now, but he counted and his feelings counted.

Former Bradley coach Dick Versace describes how he knew it was time to leave college coaching for an assistant's job with the Detroit Pistons. "It was when I realized that my family got too big—by that, I mean my basketball family. I was getting calls from kids I coached in high school fifteen years ago who wanted me to help them find a job. There just were too many people."

Tarkanian still revels in the fact that his family or clan is large and

318

needs him. It's tiresome and worrisome. It keeps Tarkanian and Lois up at night trying to figure out how they can help their former players. But Tarkanian needs this as much as he needs the practices, the victories, the X's and O's on the blackboard. That's why he fought so hard when the NCAA wanted to suspend him from college coaching for two years. That's also why he turned down the offers to coach the Los Angeles Lakers. He needs the kids, needs to feel that they are somehow dependent upon him.

Valvano also says that Tarkanian "moves through the world away from the gym in a state of bewilderment." But that's never the case when he is dealing with basketball or the kids.

University of Nevada regent Chris Karamanous, who has spent a lot of time watching Tarkanian interact with the players, says that Jerry has a special gift for reaching kids on various levels. He touches them with both his words and his hands.

Think back to his talks during the week. On Monday, it was time to lick the wounds after the Santa Barbara loss. He told the team how proud they made him, how they had overachieved. And, naturally, he talked about the need to keep working hard. Wednesday was spent warning about Fullerton, an erratic team with a losing record that nonetheless totally frightened Tarkanian. Over and over, he told the players how they could be upset. At the half of the Fullerton game, that fear produced perhaps his strongest chewing-out of the season.

Interestingly, Tarkanian said little to his players about Missouri's talent, despite the fact that Missouri had better overall athletes than UNLV. He didn't want to damage that fragile ingredient which is the team's confidence. And the halftime of the Missouri game was generally calm. He knew that this was a time for soothing, not screaming. With two widely different halftime talks, Tarkanian received exactly what he wanted: a tremendous effort in the second half.

Tarkanian doesn't spend a great deal of time planning what he will say. He is not a master psychologist in the classroom sense. He just has a feel for what the kids need to hear, and says it.

"That's because he is a great instructor, a teacher," says Karamanous. "He continually tells the kids, 'If you don't understand, tell me.' He makes it easy to ask questions. Just as he makes adjustments in his basketball strategies, he makes them with his kids."

To Tarkanian, basketball equals the kids. He calls them by their first names. He worries about them ten years after they are gone. The bottom line on Jerry Tarkanian is that he needs the kids as much as he needs the game.

17

Academics

One of the most demanding aspects of a coach's job is the classroom. Coaches are expected not only to win, but to make sure their players are educated. Here is UNLV's approach to academics.

Tarkanian: "Whenever I recruit a player, one of the first things he says is that he wants a degree. The kid is sincere. He really wants to go to college, to graduate, and he believes he can do it. Most players come to us with the academic focus and discipline necessary to graduate, but when a kid comes from the inner city and has a limited academic and socioeconomic background, that dream of a diploma often dies after his first few weeks on a college campus.

"The majority of kids recruited to play Division I basketball have the right intentions, but many have no idea how to balance obtaining a degree with the demands of major college athletics. During the first few weeks of class, these kids begin to have doubts. The professors are different from any teachers they had in high school. There's less personal attention given and more responsibility expected. The kid may never have been faced with a teacher demanding so much of him—extensive reading assignments, term papers, and essay exams—and the students are much different from the kids he went to school with. Most of the other students seem to be staying with the teacher, but the kid feels himself falling behind. He starts to get embarrassed when he's called upon. He feels he can't keep up his image. On the court, he's a big star and he can feel good about himself; but in the classroom, he can't keep up with the others and he begins to develop negative feelings of self-worth.

"Making matters worse is that occasionally there are professors who just don't like athletes. These professors feel that sports get too much attention, and they have preconceived ideas that athletes are poor students. Lois tells about a time when Danny was playing at UNLV and the team had a game in Reno on a Friday, the same day as a scheduled exam. Danny, who was an honor student and never had difficulties in his classes, went to this particular professor, explained the circumstances, and asked to take the test either before or after the game. The professor replied, "That's tough luck," and left it at that, even though the school guide states that students should be given excused absences when participating in university sponsored activities.

"Lois believes that the more secure and confident a professor is of his own abilities, the less resentful and more understanding he is towards athletes. She cites Georgetown University, with some of the best professors in the country, as an example. In 1984, the Georgetown basketball team was sent to the western regional for tournament play. They spent several weeks in the West and won all their games. Everyone on the Georgetown campus helped make special arrangements for the players so they could keep up with their classes while they were on the road or make up work when they returned, whether they were honor students or not.

"We've had to change kids' attitudes, and we don't do it by just talking about it. Most athletes know what it's like to be a big star on Thursday night and then go to class Friday morning and not know the answer. Good athletes usually have big egos. The confidence that they will succeed is what often carries them through when the clock is ticking down, the ball is in their hands, and the score is tied. But that confidence just isn't there when they face a midterm exam. On the court, the player remembers the time when he got a big shot or a key rebound to win a big game. In the classroom, he often remembers messing up on a test or having nothing to say when a teacher called on him. There is no confidence, just bad memories.

"So some basketball players learn that college is far more difficult than high school, and they didn't enjoy their high school classes that much. Instead of going to the professor or a tutor and asking for help, some kids try to deny the problem by just not going to class. They find excuses to do other things when they are supposed to be in the classroom.

"I have strong opinions about academics. My family is strong academically. Lois has a Ph.D. and has been both a teacher and a school administrator. I have a master's degree. My daughter Pamela has a master's degree and teaches emotionally disturbed children. My other daughter, Jodie, is a registered nurse in the critical care unit at UCLA Medical Center. Danny is a law school graduate, and my youngest son, George, is working towards his doctorate in political science. This does not make any of us experts at everything, but it does show we know what it takes to get through college.

"We often seem to spend more time at UNLV talking about how kids are doing in the classroom than how they're playing on the court. In 1987, Dr. Richard Lapchick, director of the Center for the Study of Sport in Society at Northeastern University, visited one of our booster gatherings after a basketball game. He and several members of his group were surprised that far more comments from the boosters related to pride in what the players were doing academically than to the game just won. I feel that attitude exists because of the great emphasis our basketball program has been placing on our players' academic growth.

"In 1987, we had two big stories connected with our team. We went to the Final Four for the first time in ten years, and five of our six seniors would obtain their degrees [Armon Gilliam, Freddie Banks, Leon Symanski, Gary Graham, and Eldridge Hudson].

"The reason why five of our six seniors graduated is that we changed our approach to working with inner-city students. It used to be crisis prevention. If something went wrong in one area with an athlete, we'd rush in to give all the help we could, but then another problem would occur someplace else. We began to realize that we could not effectively meet the needs of these athletes with the resources then at our disposal.

"It was not that these players lacked the inherent ability to complete college, or that they did not meet entrance qualifications. They did. But they lacked the proper foundation to complete college work without a strong academic support program.

"You have to make a choice. The easiest thing is to say that the elementary schools didn't do the job, or that the high schools didn't do it, so how can you expect the college to help them earn a degree? I feel that any kid who meets legitimate entrance requirements deserves a legitimate chance in college. If extra tutoring and guidance is needed, it should be given."

Lois: "Schools are continually asked about the graduation rates of their players. We always try to provide whatever data is requested, but we have found that much of the information printed about our graduation rate was inaccurate. Now, we ask those who want the information to set specific parameters for the comparisons they are making. We found that some schools were giving data based only on student athletes who had played four full years at their institutions. Many schools did not include junior college players or transfers. Some schools did not include anyone who left the team, even if it was after three years of playing. Some schools did not count all the years involved. The statistics being compared were like apples and oranges—similar, but not alike, and certainly not accurate.

"The most stringent means of accounting is to include data on every athlete who has played even one minute of ball at your school. The least stringent means is to count only those who have played four full years. There is a big difference in statistics along that continuum, and yet the media lumps all the figures together, often giving significant misimpressions of what exists. To show the difference, our graduation rate for student athletes enrolling at UNLV since 1980, who have played their entire major collegiate career with us, is 100 percent. Our graduation rate since 1973 for all athletes who even spent a minute on the court is approximately 50 percent. That's quite a difference. Most schools don't count individuals who played less than a semester. Yet even the lower figure is almost double the national average.

"To understand academics in major college basketball, you need to know these numbers: 27 percent, 60 percent, and 5½ years.

"Twenty-seven percent is how many Division I college basketball players eventually receive their degrees, according to a survey in *USA Today*. The 60 percent figure is the average national graduation rate for all students entering college. And five and one-half, not four, is the number of years it takes the average student to earn a degree. This includes not only athletes or only major colleges, but all students.

"So there are widespread misconceptions—the first being that the normal student gets a degree in four years. Maybe that was the case a number of years ago, but it isn't now. So if the average student needs five and one-half years to get a degree, why would an athlete be expected to do it in less? The players at North Carolina, Indiana, and Notre Dame usually get their degrees in four years. All of those schools have tremendous graduation rates. They also have over 100 years of tradition and experience behind them. I came to UNLV only nine years after its first four-year graduation class, and we had a lot of learning to do.

"Those numbers also are deceiving, because the kind of kid who goes to one of those elite schools already is academically inclined. He is motivated not just on the court, but also in the classroom. I know about that kind of kid, because Danny was one. He was a two-time Academic All-American who set an NCAA assist record. I didn't have to worry about Danny, or Richard Box, or Paul Brozovich, or players like that getting up in the morning to go to class or handing in papers on time. We have our share of players like that, but the average state university is not North Carolina, Indiana, or Notre Dame. The average major college player is not like Steve Alford or Danny Tarkanian.

"I wish reporters and the public would take the time to fully understand the facts when the subject is academics in basketball. Most people don't know.

"Just about every player we've had on our team had the ability to do college work. That didn't mean he was able to do it when he entered UNLV. In many cases, he had no idea how to apply himself, but the raw material was there. So the kid has a lot of gaps; do you just write him off, or do you work with him? The answer to that question will express your view of education. Do you believe college is only for those whose family and socioeconomic background prepare them well for the college experience, or do you think a public, state-supported institution is also for those who meet entrance requirements, but who need extra tutoring and counseling to succeed? I believe college is for both types of students, and we have had a mixture of both on our UNLV teams.

"Sometimes, I am absolutely amazed at a professor's attitude towards giving extra help to a student, an act that is second nature to teachers on the high school and elementary school levels. In the February 24, 1988, edition of *The Chronicles of Higher Education,* an assistant professor of English at Colorado State commented on their athletic department's academic counselor sending midterm progress questionnaires to every teacher of varsity athletes. He stated that the procedure amounts to 'preferential treatment' that it requires teachers to take time from other teaching duties to fill out and return the forms for the athletes, and that no other students get such progress reports.

"First, these types of forms usually take less than five minutes to complete. That doesn't seem like too much extra time for any student in the class. Second, a subject currently in the news is the large drop in black and Hispanic college enrollment. The athletes' problems often are the same as the typical inner-city students. Many of these kids need the same help as our players, and no one gives it to them. Instead of moaning about 'preferential treatment,' faculties should try to make the same treatment and quality support system available to other minority students. Athletes or not, they need time, patience, and strong academic support programs if they hope to graduate. It can be done, and the value of offering such assistance is immeasurable in terms of enrichment to the communities in which these students live, and cutting the welfare rolls and gang memberships.

"UNLV was only twelve years old when I became its basketball coach in 1973. We had no system of academic support at that time for our players. My wife did almost all the tutoring, as she had done at junior college and Long Beach, but it was obvious that we needed additional assistance.

"In 1977, we requested through board of regents member Chris Karamanous that part of the monies received by the school from that year's Final Four appearance be set aside for academics. This was done, but the academic adviser hired was put in charge of the entire athletic department, and most of her time was used guiding students in what courses to take for graduation. It was not enough. We were working hard and some of our players were graduating, but it was evident that for all the time and effort we put into the academic progress of our players, there was no strong consistency in their finishing requirements for graduation.

"As a coach, I stress academics. I talk to the kids regularly about their responsibility to get to class, meet with tutors, and keep their attention focused not just on basketball, but also on school. If we find that a player is skipping classes or assignments, we deal with him on an individual basis. It might mean only a good heart-to-heart talk, or it might mean that he will have to get up early in the morning to do some extra running so he knows he is accountable for missing class. It depends on the circumstances. The administration of the day-to-day functioning is left to the academic support staff, but they keep me informed by a weekly memo.

"My assistant coaches, Tim Grgurich and Mark Warkentien, and academics assistant Cleveland Edwards also devote a lot of their time to what the players are doing in school. There have been several years when my assistants stayed on campus all summer to work with the kids in school rather than go to the NIKE basketball camp at Princeton, which is where you can see the best high school talent in the country. Our first responsibility is to the kids we have recruited, both as players and as students. Our next responsibility is to recruit new players. The ones we already have come first, and when we've skipped the NIKE camp it's been due to the fact that we had several kids in summer school who needed extra attention. I've been told that we were the only major university not represented at the camp.

"At UNLV, we've worked with several players who did not have strong academic skills in high school. They had the grades to get into a state university, but when classes started, they were obviously far behind. You have to work hard to give those players the academic foundation they're missing and get them on track to graduate."

Lois: "I used to ask myself why certain players we had in the 1970s, like Eddie Owens, obtained their degree while others didn't. Eddie came to us from Wheatley High in Houston. His chances of getting a degree would have been considered slim by most people. He had difficulties in class his first semester and became so discouraged that he talked about quitting UNLV and going to junior college. I started helping Eddie that second semester. I began by having him take aptitude and academic evaluations from specialists working within the Las Vegas community. The results showed that Eddie had the ability to complete college work, but was extremely low in certain grade placement scores.

"I worked out a program for him, and he never let me down on following through on his work. One summer he had an English literature class at 9:20 each morning. He would come to my house at 8 a.m. We worked together on his class assignment for an hour, and then he would leave for class. After class, he would return to my home and for almost another hour we would review the material presented that day. Eddie did this without fail for the entire six-week summer session. Some of the material in the class readings was quite new to Eddie—certain poems, the symbolism of *Animal Farm,* and material such as that—but somehow motivation took hold.

"At the end of his four years, Eddie left UNLV as the school's all-time leading scorer, and was two courses short of a degree. He was drafted by the NBA, but that didn't work out. He played several years in Europe. We didn't hear from him for three or four years. I guess he was despondent about not making the NBA, and that was understandable. It's still a mystery to our coaching staff why he didn't play in the NBA, because all of them thought he was good enough. He was a tremendous shooter.

"We finally heard from Eddie, and Jerry was able to help him get a good-paying job at Caesar's Palace. Lonnie Wright, then president of our basketball alumni association, encouraged Eddie to finish those last two courses, and Eddie did. I believe Eddie was able to get his degree because we helped him change his attitude about education. Once he saw he had the capabilities to do it, he bore down and, with a large amount of one-on-one tutoring assistance, he completed the work.

"In contrast to Eddie, we had another player, a graduate of a highly respected California high school, who came to UNLV well prepared for college work. He began his college years with far more capability to graduate than Eddie. I also started working with him early in his freshman year, and remember quite clearly his English IA class. He was a creative young man and selected original ideas for his essays, most of which were quite good. However, his papers would be returned covered with red marks and cryptic comments from graduate assistants. I was told that in most universities it is graduate assistants, not professors, who grade most of the freshman-level English course work. I do not agree with that policy, because of the great needs of young people in the area of English, and because it is the early college years, when students are most impressionable, that expert guidance is needed.

"It seemed to me that this particular class was a catalyst for negative feelings the player began to have about himself. There was no personal follow-up from a professor or even a graduate assistant on the red marks and comments. I tried to work with the player, and he did eventually obtain a B in the class. But he had felt very capable as a student when he started that class, and very unsure of himself when he finished.

"The result was that he began to lose his desire to learn. He was an extremely sensitive, and, I felt, gifted young man, but after we lost in the Final Four of 1977, he dropped his classes and left school without completing his final twelve units. We communicate regularly and remain good friends, but I have not yet been able to convince him to return, either to UNLV or to a college closer to where he now lives.

"I spent the same amount of time with both these student athletes, yet the one with lesser potential graduated, while the other did not. I could not find a consistency in what we were doing as far as the end product, graduation, was concerned. What I did learn was how important attitude was, and that it was possible to develop, within young players who had not done well previously, a pride, a desire to achieve in the classroom as well as on the court. I realized that first we must change attitudes, and second, we need to provide large amounts of individual tutoring tailored specifically to meet each individual athlete's needs.

"In 1981, the team began making regular NCAA play-off appearances. Jerry requested that the university put some of the money earned by the team into the academic support program. Dr. Brad Rothermel, UNLV athletic director, gave his full support, and Nancy Hunterton was assigned half-time as an academic adviser to the basketball program.

"As Nancy Hunterton began to organize a network of tutors for our players, she ran into difficulties. She found that the university's tutoring center closed at five each evening. Many of our players needed tutoring after practice, which usually ended about 6 p.m. Several months later, through Hunterton's efforts, the tutoring office hours were extended. Then she found that most of the available tutors were upper-division or graduate-level students at the university. They had little experience or expertise in working with inner-city students. It was not until the end of that first year that we enlisted sufficient financial assistance from within the community to increase hourly payments to a level where we were able to hire the best tutors available. We had top teachers from the Clark County School District, counselors, and businessmen included in our group of tutors. The basketball academic adviser's position became full-time the following year.

"When I reflect on where we began and how much we had to do on our own, statements made by individuals such as Notre Dame coach Digger Phelps seem all the more ludicrous. Phelps became coach at an institution that was 118 years old before UNLV held its first class. He joined a university of high academic standing that already was attracting students from among the most capable in the country. The school's president, Father Theodore Hessburg, was among the most highly regarded academic leaders in the world. By the time Digger Phelps set foot on the Notre Dame campus, all the academic components were in place, and additional needs could be met with an expansion here or there. Yet he claims full credit for the high graduation rate of his basketball players. In that situation, I feel the credit goes far more to the institution than to Phelps. It would be interesting to see how well he would have done if he had had to do everything from scratch.

"All schools must begin somewhere, however; and since its inception, UNLV has grown in student enrollment and competency as fast as any university in the country. Our academic support system has grown faster in quality and comprehensiveness than any other of which I'm aware.

"In early 1984, we again evaluated our basketball academic support program. To help us make this evaluation, we invited to our campus the man regarded by many as the most vocal critic of education of student athletes, Dr. Harry Edwards of the University of California at Berkeley [no relation to Cleveland Edwards]. Dr. Edwards is a former Olympic track star and well-known sociology professor whose main field of study is the exploitation of black athletes in society. He was hired recently by major league baseball commissioner Peter Ueberroth to help that sport integrate its front-office management.

"Edwards spent several days on our campus evaluating the breadth and depth of support services provided by the university as a whole, as well as specifically by the athletic department. He provided us with a lengthy written report covering all areas of his investigation. He complimented us on our program functioning 'equitably and ethically ...particularly with regard to recruitment and postenrollment care of black scholarship athletes.' He also stated that 'the UNLV basketball program is vastly superior to the "dumb jock dumping ground" image portrayed in some of the media....'

"During the 1987 Final Four, Dr. Edwards was quoted in the *Washington Post* as saying, 'I was ready to write a blistering report about UNLV, but I came out with a completely different perspective. You have to use a different yardstick. UNLV [sometimes] takes athletes...with difficulties. And he [Tarkanian] does as well as anyone given the fact that he has to evolve out of this problem. He falls in love with his players....'

"Edwards gave us numerous suggestions for our program, almost all of which we have been able to put into practice. The class of 1987 was the first class to represent our renovated program after Dr. Edwards' visit. I think the fact that five of six seniors graduated shows we are now on the right track. We believe we have a solid academic support program which compares favorably with the best in the country.

"The UNLV academic support program for men's basketball consists of the following components:

Summer and Early Fall
Academic assessment testing for all freshmen and transfers (Entrance and yearly monitoring, including Brigance Secondary Level Development Inventory and selected reading tests)
Study skills/social issues workshop (yearly)
Classroom social interaction skills presentation by UNLV faculty (Entrance and as needed)
Fall, Spring, Summer Sessions
Academic advising
Academic progress monitoring
Career testing and counseling
Tutoring

Remedial skill building (Selected classes freshman year and individual tutoring as needed)
Communication skills training
Personal counseling
Computer-assisted learning/resources data

"The program staff consists of two full-time academic advisers, a part-time learning specialist, a pool of fifteen tutors trained in specialized areas and used as needed, and the services of a community psychologist. In 1986 we began taking tutors on team road trips. This year, we are initiating a program of coordinated academic home visits on a semester-by-semester basis, where assistant coach Mark Warkentien will visit homes of parents to personally explain their son's progress and be available to answer questions they might have. This will be in addition to our regular telephone and letter contacts.

"A fifth-year scholarship has been available from the university since 1973 for all players who have not finished their degree in four years and who wish to continue immediately following their final season of play. Since 1978, the Basketball Alumni Association has provided funds to cover books and tuition costs for any returning player who wishes to complete his degree. In 1987, the Artie Newman Scholarship was established by local businessman Jim Newman. Proceeds from his $410,000 donation were placed in the UNLV Foundation account. Interest is used each semester to cover tuition, books, and living expenses for any former basketball player who wishes to complete requirements for a degree at UNLV or any other institution. The funds also can be used for advanced degree work. Some of our former players have moved to the master's and doctoral level of study, and we expect more to do so in the future. The Artie Newman Fund is available to help cover expenses for these students.

"Lonnie Wright, a former UNLV player, founded the UNLV Basketball Alumni Association, which was the first in the nation to sponsor intersectional alumni games with profits going to help returning athletes complete degrees. The association now also contributes to local charities. Jackie Robinson helped form the Lettermen's Club, which may be the first organization to establish career links with local businesses for student athletes when they are juniors and seniors. The focus of the group is to assist players when they leave athletics and take their places within the business community.

"I believe that kids can make far more progress than most people realize. I've seen it happen here and I know it can be done. We've had a few players most people thought would not graduate, but they earned a degree because they learned what it takes to get through college and they became motivated to apply themselves. We've designed special meetings and workshops for them that cover classroom demeanor, listening skills, note taking, and study skills. We tutor them on a one-to-one basis or in small groups. Tutors are available when the players need them, and we currently are putting in a strong computer program to keep track of the students' progress, previous class papers, and other academic records. Most of all, we try to reward good schoolwork as well as good play on the court. Our academic awards are as big as or bigger than any athletic award or trophy. Our city is behind us, so that helps with placing attention on education. The town is proud of our players when they graduate.

"I remember when we recruited Eldridge Hudson. He had enough academic credentials to attend a state university, but he was not known for hitting the books anymore than was necessary. When our academic adviser, Dr. Ann Mayo, talked with him about his college plans, Eldridge told her that he wanted to major in 'eligibility.' He was convinced that he was going to be the next Magic Johnson. His goal wasn't to get a degree; it was to get into the NBA. There were times when even we had some doubts about his making it. There were certainly times when he gave us all a few heartaches. Eldridge severely injured his knee during his freshman season. In his situation, a lot of kids would have quit. But Eldridge worked hard to rehabilitate his knee, and it was amazing that he came back and played—that he didn't just give up on both basketball and school. He had reason to be moody, but he came through for us and himself in the end.

"It puzzles me when people do not want to accept the fact that these young men have pulled themselves up and are making it. Sometimes, you just have to hold tight to the knowledge of what you are doing. That's what keeps me going—not the games, the rankings, or the newspaper stories. I'm not naive. I know about education, and I know when something really helps a kid and when it doesn't. I can accept failure and learn from it. I work with the handicapped, and have learned to accept that certain things won't work. We have made tremendous strides with our players. Some people will say, 'Sure, you help them out, because they are 6-foot-10 and can dunk.' Yes, we've helped kids who were 6-10, but we've also helped kids who were only marginal players at best, and we've worked with some who weren't even in the basketball program.

"Too many players entering college have three priorities: get a pro contract, get a job that makes a lot of money, and stay eligible. The mothers and fathers often tell us that they want their son to graduate, and the kids say the same thing. But in many cases, the kid has been able to slide through high school, skipping classes and getting minimal grades, because that was all that was expected of him. The main thing was basketball—was he scoring, was the team winning? As long as the answer was yes, he didn't have to worry about school. Believe me, the majority of coaches do not support this attitude. It is our society as a whole that puts a greater emphasis on athletics than on academics. That's why almost every newspaper in the country has a separate sports section and not a separate education section.

"Of course, different families have different economic levels. Some of the players we get are the big hope of their relatives. They are the ones who are supposed to make it in basketball. They are supposed to make the big money, buy the family a new house, and take care of everything that went wrong. In many families, however, it's not like that. All the parents of 1987's Final Four seniors had good jobs. None of those players had to become a pro to feed his family.

"Freddie Banks has always been the Golden Boy in Las Vegas. He was a star from junior high on up; thousands of kids in Las Vegas idolize him. You can go to almost any local playground and find a couple of little kids shooting around pretending they are Freddie Banks. Freddie is a good hero for them because not only was he a great player, he also obtained his degree.

"We can tell youngsters that their chances of being a doctor are better than their chances of being a pro basketball player, or that they would be better off spending more time in the library than in the gym. But most won't believe it. By the time they get to college, they've been living the basketball dream since they could walk. I don't think you can just destroy a kid's dream. You can't tell him, 'Forget it; you have no chance at the pros.' That would be totally demoralizing to him if he believed it, and he probably wouldn't believe it, because no matter how many statistics you show him or personal cases you discuss with him, each player feels he's the one-in-a-million shot that will make it, and his parents and friends think so, too.

"At UNLV, we tie into the basketball dream. We mention that a player could get hurt, just like Eldridge Hudson did; or that the average NBA career is less than five years, and they'll have to learn to do something else. We emphasize that schooling gives them a supplement to a possible basketball career. We stress that getting an education gives you alternatives in life, and having alternatives gives you strength, gives you power."

*   *   *

332

Tarkanian: "We begin by talking about the basics—getting up early and getting to class on time. But the kids also need to know how to act *in* class. This is something that should have been learned years ago, but it some cases, it wasn't. And even if the kids do know, it never hurts to remind them. Early in the school year Lois brings the freshmen and new transfers over to our home, where a professor from the university talks to them about college classroom demeanor. I don't want the kids to think that they can show up for class and then sneak out after ten minutes. When you're 6-foot-10 and everyone else in the room is a foot shorter, you can't sneak anywhere."

UNLV academic adviser Ann Mayo: "I remember when I first started working with Eldridge Hudson. He'd sit in the back of the classroom wearing sunglasses, and sometimes he dozed off. That isn't exactly the way to impress a professor. I don't mean to pick on Eldridge. In fact, he is a tremendous example of how far a student can progress if he works at it. It would be great if kids all got up early and always went to class, and it would be even better if they knew exactly what they were supposed to do once they got into the classroom. But certain kids just don't have that background. We don't want a professor to look at one of our players and say, 'Look at him, he's acting like a basketball player.' We tell the players to sit near the front of class. We tell them not to sit together and to ask questions to make the professor notice that they're paying attention. It's difficult for a professor to fail you if the professor sees you at the front of the class every day, is getting your assignments on time, and has gotten to know you because you ask questions in class. That's our message. But you can't just say, 'We're going to change behavior; we're going to make the kids straighten up and act right in class.' That doesn't happen just because you tell them what to do."

Tarkanian: "My assistant Mark Warkentien has gone to class with players. Lois has gone to class with players, and so has Ann Mayo. I've never heard of this being done anywhere else in the country. I suppose an academic adviser might have taken a few classes with the players—but the coach's wife? An assistant coach? What other school has a coach's wife or assistants willing to go that extra mile? In fact, this is another area where I wasn't sure that Lois was right. I kept thinking, 'No one else does it, why should we?' But Lois insisted that it was the best way for us to help the kids."

Lois: "None of us believe in going to every class with every player. I want to stress that. The idea isn't to hold a player's hand for four years, but to get him off to the right start, to show him what needs to be done to succeed in college, to model for him. And then the kid can go off on his own. Our attending classes with players is just a transition step, taking him from where he was when he came to college to where he can be, showing him how to become a successful, independent student.

"A couple of years ago, I took a sociology class with one of our point guards, Gary Graham. I audited it, and auditing is good because you find out a lot about a kid, such as:

1. Is he going to class?

2. Is he arriving late?

3. Is he leaving early?

4. Is he taking notes and are they good notes?

5. Is he listening attentively?

6. Is he asking questions?

7. How much of what he hears does he really understand?

"For the most part, Gary was a good student, but he had a streak where he missed several classes. So I wrote Gary's mother a very strong letter and told her what was happening. After I did it, I thought that maybe I shouldn't have. I saw Gary and told him, 'Gary, what do I need to go to a sociology class for? I have a Ph.D. I'd like to be at home reading a book just for pure enjoyment. Or maybe I'd like time to do nothing but take a long hot bath. But I care about you. That's why I'm in this class with you. When you don't show up, you're telling me that you don't care about my efforts.'

"I also worried that Gary's mother might get upset with me and that perhaps I had gone too far, because it was a very strong letter, but it seemed that incident turned the key. I'm sure his mother talked to him and Gary knew that I was going to be there in class every day. Suddenly, his work made a tremendous leap forward. I didn't need to attend the class anymore and Gary did get his degree in 1987."

Ann Mayo recalls the first time she took a class with our players.

Ann Mayo: "I was in a sociology class with several players who were new to UNLV. I sat there and discovered that they had no idea what was appropriate behavior in a college classroom. They were still doing a lot of high school things—talking in the corner, dozing, all that. College professors weren't going to put up with that high school stuff. The guys weren't taking notes; they had no idea how to take notes. So that was our first lesson—does he know how to act like a student?

Does he know how to take notes? If the guys made a good effort to take notes, then I'd show them my notes. If not, they were on their own. Most of them straightened out, because they knew my notes were better and they wanted to use them. As the class went on, their note-taking style started to resemble mine, and they developed appropriate classroom behavior."

Assistant coach Mark Warkentien: "I've taken about a dozen classes with kids, and I take each one for a grade. We started in 1982, and it was my idea for me to go with the kids. Tim Grgurich and I work as a team with a few players. Tim beats on the doors about an hour before class, and he doesn't settle for the 'Yeah, yeah, I'm up' routine. Tim tells the kid, 'Come out here and see me.' Only when the kid opens the door and steps outside does Tim leave. Then, an hour later, the kid walks into class and sees me sitting there. That's a pretty strong message about how important we think academics is.

"In the summers of 1985 and 1986, I never took a vacation and never left the campus, because I was going to school with the kids. I've been at UNLV since 1980, and our biggest obstacle was academics. We had been ripped so much on that. But now, it's the area of our biggest gain, and I'll match what we do for the kids against any program in the country. At first it sounds strange—coaches going to class with the players. But think about it for a moment. Instead of running all those periodic checks and all the other bull we supposedly do to supervise the kids, we're right there, on the front line. Study halls? Forget that. If the kid isn't in class, he sure as hell isn't going to study. By going to class with the kids, you eliminate the cops-and-robbers routine. In high school, a kid would cut a class and he'd tell his teacher that the guidance counselor wanted to see him, and he'd tell the counselor that the coach wanted to talk to him, and he'd tell the coach something else. The school would figure out that the kid was up to something, but then it would take a couple of days to get in touch with the kid's parents to tell them what was going on. Finally, a meeting would be set up with the kid, his parents, the teacher, and the guidance counselor. By then, days had passed, and everything would be so muddled that no one knew exactly what happened.

"There was a Monday night ethnic studies class that I took with a player a couple of years ago. It started at 7 p.m. and ended at 10 p.m. One night the kid didn't show up. So after class, I called his mother. Now, the family lived on the East Coast, so it was 1 a.m. when the mother's phone rang with me telling her that her son skipped class. I told her, 'Listen, you want your son to graduate and so do I. I'm taking the class with him so that as soon as there is a problem, I know about it. I just got out of class and he wasn't there. So now you know about the problem, too. And I want you to know that I'm mad and I'm sick of this crap. Will you help me with your son?'

"The parents are pretty embarrassed, and they come down on their kid as hard as they can. You don't need too many 1 a.m. phone calls to take care of that. I've been recruiting for UNLV since 1980, and when I go into the homes, I talk a lot about academics. I'm sincere when I tell the parents that I want their kids to graduate and that we're going to do everything in our power to make that happen. The parents all say that they are interested in their son getting a degree. Well, calling them gives them a chance to prove it, and they almost always come through for you. The kid can't come up with some bull like, 'I was there but the teacher didn't see me' or 'The teacher doesn't like me.' None of that stuff will wash if the coach is in the classroom, too.

"What also happens is that the kid can take a little tougher course, or a course he doesn't like, because I'll work with him. If a player knows I'm going to be sitting there at 8 a.m., he'll have perfect attendance because he knows that if I'm there, he'd better show up. If he's in class every day, he'll pay attention and learn.

"I'm taking notes, reading the assignments, and doing the papers. Remember, I'm taking the course for a grade, so I know what is going on.

"If there is a problem or if the kid needs to study, he can come to my house *that night* and we'll work on it instead of waiting a couple of days to get a tutor or go to study hall. I'll tell him, 'Come over to my house; I'll order a pizza or my wife will make dinner. Then we'll study and we'll get this done.' I can take a book, throw it at a kid, and say, 'I've read it, have you?'

"I've taken theater arts a couple of times because most of these kids aren't into the arts. They like to watch boxing, but a play is something else. Shakespeare is not real big in the inner city. By taking the class with them, I can help them understand what college is all about.

"Another good thing that comes out of all this is that the professors can see what is happening. At first, they are wary. What is a coach doing in my class? Coaches aren't supposed to give a damn about academics. We're supposed to be the problem, remember? But here's a coach, taking their class for a grade. They see the coach going about it the right way and they see the kids acting like students. Everyone is trying. Now, the professors are ready to do their part. They really want to teach, and they become sold on it. I've had professors volunteer to get the basketball players together for special sessions, because they see the kids making an effort. This is especially helpful after road trips.

People say that the job of a coach is to motivate an athlete. How much more of a commitment can we make?''

Despite the time, effort, and money, some kids don't graduate.

Tarkanian: ''Why don't some kids make it in the classroom? That question is asked of all college basketball coaches. Sometimes a kid is recruited who just can't cut it. It has happened to almost every coach in the country. Despite all the tutoring, all the attention, and all the understanding a coach has to give, the kid just can't handle college. In high school, he was the star and he got decent grades because he was an athlete. He just never figures out what college is all about, or his academic and/or personal background doesn't allow him a chance. Usually, this kid is gone after a year, if not sooner. But in most cases, the kids have a good shot at getting a degree if they are able to get through the first two years of school. By then, they have a good idea of what it takes to pass most courses. They have learned about taking notes, writing papers, and being tested. The initial shock of switching from high school to college is over and they know that they won't get A's and B's just because they can dunk a basketball. Still, some of these kids don't graduate, despite going to school for four years.

''What happens?

''The semester that kills a lot of kids is the spring of their senior year. That's what is so frustrating for us. We will have worked with a kid for nearly four years and helped him get into position where a degree isn't just a dream, but a reality, and then the whole thing just falls apart. It often happens right after the basketball season. Remember how college basketball works. Assuming you make the NCAA tournament, you play until you either win a national championship or get beat. In other words, almost everyone ends the season with a loss, so you may have had a great year but you still lost at the end. For the coaches, there's always next year. For everyone on the team but the seniors, there is next year. You can talk about what you need to improve, think about what you'll practice in the off-season.

''But for the seniors, that's it. The team lost, and he's done. There's nothing gradual about it. One minute, you're up there high, name in the newspaper, 20,000 people cheering for you, and the next, you're finished. For the first time in your life, you don't know if there will be a next game. There's nothing gradual, nothing that can prepare you for it. I'm talking about this in very realistic terms because only about thirty-five kids go from college to the NBA each season. Maybe another seventy play in Europe or the Continental Basketball Association. So you're looking at about one hundred kids who can keep playing basketball at the pro level, and only about twenty of those—the higher first-round picks—are assured of a job. The kids are very aware of these statistics. They know how hard it is to play pro ball. They've seen guys who were stars in their neighborhoods come back after playing in college, and it's over—they never made it as a pro. Yet, almost all these kids think that they're the one who is going to beat the odds. That's what makes them good athletes: they don't think that any deficit is too big, and they believe they can overcome anything.

"For an underclassman, you can convince him to study hard during that spring quarter so he can keep his grades up and be eligible for next season. He has something to look forward to.

"The senior who is a legitimate pro prospect is thinking about the NBA. The scouts want him to play in a number of all-star games—in Hawaii, Portsmouth, and Chicago—and that takes him away from school for weeks at a time. A first-round draft pick will be interviewed by six to ten teams, and that also takes him away from school. One of the last things a kid in this situation is thinking about is his degree. He is being courted by agents, who are talking big money. He is meeting coaches and general managers. One day he flies to Boston to meet Red Auerbach. The next, he goes to Cleveland to meet Lenny Wilkens and Wayne Embry. Then maybe he's off to Los Angeles to meet Pat Riley and Jerry West. The player starts thinking about million-dollar contracts and making the all-star team. He has moved into the world of pro basketball, at least in his head, and he often forgets about school.

"That's why so many kids are ten to twenty hours short of their degree."

Sidney Green, who was a star for UNLV and a number-one pick by the Chicago Bulls, is an example of what happens.

Sidney Green: "During my senior year, we lost to North Carolina State in the NCAA tournament. Suddenly, it hit me that I'd never play again for UNLV. I knew I'd make it in the NBA, but I was still so depressed after that game that I hid in my room for a week. I just disappeared. I wouldn't see anybody and I wouldn't let anyone see me. I was doing all right in school, and I was in position to graduate. I had come so far in terms of the books from when I left Brooklyn and came to Vegas, that all I had to do was stick with the program and I'd have gotten my degree. But I just quit going to class. After I got over the depression of getting beat in the NCAA tournament, all I was thinking was NBA, NBA, NBA. I was, I think, five courses short of a degree, and it took me three summers of going back after I turned pro to get it. Now when I look back, I see that I really was dumb to blow off school that spring semester. But that's what I did, because my priorities changed. In fact, Lois told me that they wouldn't retire my number until I went back and got my degree, so I kept going to school in the summers so I could keep my promise to her and graduate."

Tarkanian: "When a kid like Sidney quits in the spring semester, it upsets me. But at least we knew that he was going to make a lot of money and be a high draft choice. We also believed that Sidney would eventually come back to school and finish up. He made that promise to us, and he came through. Most kids don't have a clear pro future. They will be a low-round pick, if they get drafted at all. A fact of life in the NBA is if you don't go in the first twenty-five picks, it gets very tough to make a team. There are only a couple of kids each year taken after the second round who make it, yet almost all the players still think they'll be a pro. They aren't being interviewed by pro teams, but they are going to one tryout camp after another. They become almost desperate as they try to extend their careers, because basketball is all they've ever known. It would be like a kid who has spent his entire life studying the violin. When he's about to leave college or the music institute, all he can think about is getting a job with a professional orchestra.

"That's why we consider that spring semester of the senior year a danger zone. What the academic staff does is to show the kid on paper how close he is to graduating. We talk about all the work he's put in during his four years, and how he shouldn't throw it away with one bad quarter. Sometimes it works, and sometimes it doesn't. With the class of 1987, who were some of the greatest kids with the greatest parents any coach has ever had, the guys made it. Freddie Banks and Armon Gilliam, who were legitimate pro prospects, missed some classes during the spring, but they came back in the summer to finish up. Eldridge Hudson also had to pick up his last seven hours, and he made it. Gary Graham and Leon Symanski already had enough credits before summer school.

"A lot of our kids have gone on to play in Europe. The money is pretty good—$30,000 to $200,000 a year—and it can be a great experience. It also lets the guys keep playing. I can't tell a kid, 'Hey, skip the money. Stay in school another couple of semesters and get a degree.' That would be a stupid thing to say to a kid who finally has a chance to make a good living playing the game he loves. It takes the average student over five years to get a degree, so when most players have used up their four years of eligibility, it should come as no surprise that they need another semester or two to finish. Playing major college basketball is just like working your way through school, be-

cause of the demands on your time. Very few students have to physically extend themselves or travel as much as basketball players.

"We like to get the kids up early and in class by 8:30, so that they
can be finished with their class work by noon or 1 p.m. The tutors can
work with them and then they can go to practice late in the afternoon.
At night, they work on their studies alone or with tutors. When you
put all that together, the school and basketball, the players work as
hard as or harder than most students.

"They always are driven by basketball. For example, my son
Danny was a late-round pick by San Antonio in 1984. His academic
credentials were so strong that he had been a candidate for a Rhodes
Scholarship, but he wanted to play pro ball. Danny told me it really
hurt to get cut by the Spurs. Then he went to Portland and was one of
the last cuts at that training camp. While in law school, he sometimes
wished he had tried to play longer. He had chances to go to Europe,
but he went to law school instead. Sometimes he thinks he should have
gone overseas. As he says, 'You can always go to law school, but you
only have a few years to play ball.'

"The dreams die hard. But what we're really concentrating on is
getting the kids to come back to school after they have dropped out to
play ball or get a job. Interest from our $410,000 grant, known as the
Artie Newman Fund, is used to pay for athletes who wish to finish
their education. I think we're the only school in the nation with this
kind of scholarship program that is so well funded. A lot of guys—
from Eddie Owens, to Sidney Green, to Jeff Collins, to Ricky Sobers—
have come back and finished their degrees. Often these guys are the
best students, because they have seen the real world. They've had to
earn a living and they've grown up. They tend to be more serious because they realize how valuable that degree can be.

"People don't want to hear this, and it certainly is not a part of the
usual academic thinking, but I'll always believe that college is a good
thing for a kid even if he doesn't get a degree. Not every kid who goes
to college has to graduate for it to have been a good experience for
him. I can hear the critics right now. They'll say that a kid spends
four years on a campus, and if he doesn't get a degree, he comes away
with nothing. Basically, they say the kid wasted those four years.

"Well, I just don't buy it. I want my players to get a degree, and
it should be obvious that we go to great lengths to make sure that the
kids have every opportunity to graduate. But just because a kid doesn't
graduate doesn't mean he failed. Take your average kid from the
ghetto, a kid such as Richie Adams, who grew up in the Bronx. In
that environment, he is always walking a fine line between getting in

trouble and trying to stay away from it. In the ghetto, life is a minute-to-minute proposition. Crime is the rule, not the exception. You hear more stories about a guy being in the wrong place at the wrong time and getting shot by someone who didn't even know him. There is too much crime, too many drug addicts, too many guys out of work, and too little hope. If that's all you ever see, that's all you'll ever live.

"Take that kid out of the inner city and put him on a college campus, and he sees the other side of life. He can walk around without fear. That may not sound like much, unless you grew up like a Richie Adams. Then the idea of being safe, of not having to look over your shoulder every time you hear footsteps behind you becomes very important.

"College teaches kids the basics that they need to know in order to get a job. For example:

"We make our kids get up early in the morning so they have to be on time for classes and practices. That's the same kind of discipline a boss wants in the work place. He wants to know if the guy will show up for work on time. We teach our players that kind of discipline.

"Big-time college basketball pushes kids very hard. They learn to take orders and they learn how to handle pressure and stress.

"Our kids have to take communications courses, and we work with them on their public speaking. Communication is very important on the job.

"Playing basketball at UNLV means a lot of publicity for the kid. About everyone in town knows the names of the players, even the guys on the bench. They are often interviewed by the papers, radio, and television. This helps the player make connections to get a job. When a former UNLV player goes in for a job interview, he may not know the boss, but the boss probably will feel that he knows the kid just because he watched him play. Also, there are certain people in town who like to hire former basketball players because they have credibility with the community. When a kid is in the ghetto, it's so hard to make himself known to people who do the hiring. That's not a problem for a college basketball player. If you're a boss, are you going to hold it against a kid because he is a couple of courses short of a degree? What you really want to know is whether the kid is a good person and can do the job. Just because you're a college graduate and got all A's and B's doesn't necessarily mean that you're a good person.''

Another view of academics is offered by Dr. Jerry L. Crawford of the department of theater arts, who has been with UNLV since 1962. He has had several plays produced off-Broadway and regionally, and is a Barrick Distinguished Scholar as well as a noted critic and director on the West Coast. Dr. Crawford was UNLV's dean of faculty from 1965 to 1968, and in 1987 he was among the top three finalists for the distinguished professor award, which honored the best professor in the history of the university.

Dr. Jerry Crawford: ''When I came to UNLV, no one knew what it would become. It was just blooming in the desert. We had only 500 full-time students, and they came here for only three semesters. Then they had to go up to Nevada-Reno to finish their degrees. In 1965, I was on a committee that set out to get the university some recognition. We wanted to make this a real university; but to do that, we had to let people know that it existed. We picked four areas where we thought we could grow and gain some national exposure: desert biology, hotel management, performing arts, and basketball. We picked basketball over football because it is too hot here to play football on Saturday afternoons. We play football at night, but to be traditional and have a strong following, I think you need to play those afternoon games. Basketball is played inside and in the winter; it's a fast-paced sport, and that seemed to appeal to the personality of the town.

''It isn't easy to build a quality university in the middle of a place like Las Vegas, with its hotel and 'gaming industry,' as it's euphemistically called. I've heard all the jokes. People hear that I'm a professor at Las Vegas and they ask, 'What do you teach? Roulette?' They've called us Tumbleweed Tech and Casino Gulch. Well, we now have almost 14,000 students. While most colleges are losing enrollment, we've been increasing almost 1,000 per year this decade. I think it's safe to say that we've become a very legitimate university. But I'm well aware, probably more aware than a number of my colleagues, that we aren't like Stanford, Yale, Harvard, or Oberlin. Some of our programs are better than theirs, but we are a state institution with a different mission. We are here to educate the masses, not the elite.

''Basketball has been critical to us. People around the country know UNLV because of the basketball team. If we didn't have a strong team, we'd be just another state school with a hyphen in its name—a Texas-Arlington or something. There are some academics who are convinced that the tail is wagging the dog because of all the attention and the money the basketball program produces, but basketball is a tremendous fund-raiser for the university. I'm not just talking about the fact that it clears $3 million a year and carries the football program, the women's sports, and the rest of the athletic department. The high visibility that the basketball program has given the school makes it easier for us to raise money for all areas, not just athletics. Every time the basketball team is on national television, we get one of those five-minute blurbs at halftime that shows the school and talks about its academics—hotel management, desert biology, theater arts, and the rest. No school has enough money to buy that kind of positive publicity.

"I know that the basketball program has been controversial. I think that they went too far when they tried to help Lloyd Daniels. I understand that he is an engaging young man and has had a very tough life, but a closer look at his background would have shown that he was just a bad risk and the odds were astronomical against his working out. That incident didn't help the basketball program or the university, and it could have been avoided, because there were several warning signs. Once in a while the program carries its Father Flanagan image—something that is positive and deserved—to an extreme. We blew it on Daniels; there's no other way to put it. But I've seen nothing but an honest effort from the basketball program to educate the players, to help them get a degree, or at least protect them by finding them a good job after college. I also like the fact that the program doesn't forget its ex-players. It tries to bring them back to school for undergraduate or graduate work, or to find them a job if they're down on their luck.

"I'm not snobbish about education. I think there is some truth to the argument that a kid can become a better person even if he doesn't get a degree. We get a lot of that in theater. A kid comes in and says he wants to be an actor. So he takes all of our acting courses, a couple of playwriting and scenic designing courses. He is out to enhance himself in his field, not to get a degree. I don't think every theater student or basketball player should take this approach, but when I look out at the court and I see some of the players from Brooklyn, the Bronx, or Watts, it doesn't bother me. They were admitted as regular students to the university. I've been to Brooklyn, the Bronx, and Watts and I'd rather see those kids walking from our Judy Bayley Theatre to the Thomas & Mack Center than down the streets of those places. At least at UNLV, they have a chance to make something of themselves, and it is especially gratifying that they are starting to graduate regularly.

"Getting those kids through school takes a lot of work. I was shocked and amazed to learn that coaches, coaches' wives, and academic advisers were going to class with the players. Some of my colleagues have been outraged by it. They see it as the worst form of baby-sitting. They ask, where is the line? How far do you go to help the players? In my own field, I don't think we'd take those extreme measures to help a good actor stay eligible. At least, we never have. I suppose I'm saying that I'm almost overwhelmed by the dedication of the basketball program. Okay, you can ask, why aren't the players self-reliant enough to make it on their own like the rest of the students? Why is all this money being spent on the academic end of the program? Shouldn't that money go into the general fund?

"But you're talking about a program that makes $3 million a year, and you're investing about $100,000 of it for education; that's a drop in the bucket. Those kids deserve to be educated. They are not like the rest of the student body; their lifestyles are different by virtue of the fact that they play big-time basketball. Look, either you spend the money and take the time to tutor these kids, or you say forget major college ball and play Division III. I don't mind coaches calling me two or three times a week to check on a student, as Mark Warkentien has done with several players. If Mark Warkentien or anyone else wants to sit in my class, he is welcome to so long as he does the work like the rest of the students and doesn't do the work for the basketball player.

"I admit that I'm a believer in the basketball program. Not in everything they do, such as the Lloyd Daniels case. But I think their heart is in the right place. I've had probably a dozen basketball players in class over the years. Most have been quiet. They come to take their courses and pass, and that's what most of them have done. They show up, they hand in their assignments, and they usually make a decent effort. That's all I ask."

Tarkanian: "In my twenty-six years of coaching, what makes me proudest is that our players have been good kids. Only two have gotten into trouble. Lawrence West was arrested on a shoplifting charge that was later dropped, and Richie Adams was involved in a strange case having to do with a misunderstanding and a car that may or may not have been stolen. Adams's problem with the car came after he left school and went home to New York. We begged him to stay in Las Vegas and had a job available for him with the recreation department, but he went home, fell in with the wrong guys, and got in a scrape. If you count the Lloyd Daniels problem even though he was not a team member, that makes three guys out of twenty-six years of coaching. Three guys out of maybe 250 players I've coached. I'll match that record against about any major college program in the country. We have good kids and a solid academic program. Any one who takes the time to check, as Dr. Edwards did, will back us up.''

18
Getting to Know Tark

You know Las Vegas is Tarkanian's town. For clues, you can see the following:

Jerry Tarkanian T-shirts

Jerry Tarkanian towels

Jerry Tarkanian posters

Jerry Tarkanian basketballs—regular and miniature-sized

Jerry Tarkanian masks

Jerry Tarkanian stuffed sharks

Shark candy, cookies, and drinks

Shark earrings

Shark hats

Shark decals running along the side of cars sold as shark automobiles in the school's scarlet and grey colors

"Sharks," the hottest disco in town

A religious music group called "911" put out a record and video called "Walk Like a Tarkanian," which was adapted from the Bangles' hit "Walk Like an Egyptian" and starred you-know-who sucking on a towel. On a cold February night in Logan, Utah, 2,000 local fans showed up at the Utah State–UNLV game holding cardboard Tarkanian masks in front of their faces while watching the Rebels run to a 113–78 victory. UNLV fans liked the mask idea so much that a few games later, 6,000 similar masks were distributed at a UNLV home game.

If you watch a basketball game in Vegas, there is a sign stretched across one side of the arena which proclaims: WELCOME TO TARK'S SHARK TANK. A huge shark mascot stands with the cheerleaders. Fans open and close their arms to imitate a shark's mouth as the pep band plays the theme from *Jaws*. A giant stuffed shark with a towel draped through its teeth hangs from the arena ceiling amid the basketball team's championship flags. When basketball season is over, the shark is hung in a large alcove of the arena's foyer above a bronze bust of Tarkanian donated by the Art Thomas family, prominent Las Vegans.

Tarkanian: "People in town went crazy for us in 1987. The whole state was just nuts about the Rebels. Before an NCAA play-off game, we got a telegram with 1,400 signatures. It came from about everyone in Ely, Nevada. It was amazing. But you have to understand Nevada, particularly Las Vegas. There are such good people in this state and this city, and so often others have the wrong perception of them. They want to be identified as the kind of people they truly are, and that 1987 team gave these people a reason to feel good about themselves."

In a town of big wheels, Tarkanian may be one of the biggest wheels of all. He is known by Frank Sinatra, Sammy Davis, Jr., Don Rickles, Lola Falana, Wayne Newton, and the other celebrities who regularly appear in Las Vegas. And when they aren't on stage, they sometimes like to stop at the Thomas & Mack Center, where the pregame light show may be the best in town. Where else but at the Thomas & Mack can you find fireworks inside a building? And if that isn't the best show, the basketball team is. At the Thomas & Mack Center, there are eighty floor seats that sell for $1,500 each. They are known as Gucci Row.

"People call me all the time about those seats," says Tarkanian. "You can't get one. There's a waiting list."

The Rebels sell about 16,000 season tickets and quickly sell the remaining 3,000 well before game time. The basketball program usually clears about $3 million annually and ranks among the top five schools nationally in attendance.

"For every dollar the basketball team spends, it brings in four," says prominent UNLV booster Irwin Molasky. "The basketball program carries the entire athletic department."

At the center of it all is Tarkanian.

"Sometimes I read where people say that I'm a celebrity," says Tarkanian. "I don't even know what it means to be a celebrity, and I don't think I am one. I really don't think about it at all. I still talk to the same people I first talked with when I came to town. I do the same things I always did. I think if you start thinking of yourself as a person who has reached a certain level, if you think of yourself as special, you start treating people differently than you did in the past, and suddenly you'll find out that those people won't like you any more."

That's the key to Tarkanian's success in Vegas: he is a winner who acts like just another guy. His coaching makes him unique, but his personality is appealing.

"I like to go out with the boosters," says Tarkanian. "It's good to get close to the people who like the basketball team. I did the same thing at Long Beach State. I go to every function and I know many of the fans by name. To me, a big part of coaching is going out with the guys, drinking a few beers, and talking about the game. I know a lot of coaches don't like to do it, but I get a kick out of it."

And Tarkanian works cheap.

"I've never charged anyone in Vegas for a personal appearance or a speaking engagement," says Tarkanian. "A lot of coaches I've known, such as Al McGuire and Jim Valvano, tell me, 'Tark, you can't do that. You're a professional and you speak for nothing. That doesn't make any sense.' But these people don't know what Vegas is like. I never charge people for appearances, and they don't charge me. It's just how the town works—everybody comps everybody else. Maybe I'm a bad businessman, but I never cared much about marketing myself or doing promotions."

Certainly Tarkanian's wardrobe is not one of his top priorities.

Lois: "If Jerry had his way, he'd always wear his Nike tennis shoes and his warm-up suit. If he has to go somewhere nice, he'll ask our daughter Jodie what he should wear. He knows his taste in clothes is not the best, and hers is. He just has no interest whatsoever in what he wears, and it's only because members of the family nag him that he makes any attempt to look better. There are periods where he tries to dress better for things like speaking engagements. He'll take the time and go to a great store and buy more expensive clothes. But then he'll read again in the newspapers that his clothes look as if they just came off a rack. We've come to the conclusion that it isn't the clothes, it's just Jerry.

"What does he look good in? At games, he'll start out in a really nice looking suit. Then he'll get so nervous during the game that soon the tie is askew and the shirt is wrinkled, and he takes his jacket off. I don't really know what to do, and Jerry really doesn't care. But our kids do. Any criticism of him hurts them, so they work hard in any area where they think they can help. They beg him to dress better, and for a while he will pay attention to his clothes, but then he'll slip back.''

What's Tarkanian like at home?

Lois says, "Jerry puts on his warm-up suit, sits on the sofa with a bowl of popcorn, and watches the tape of a basketball game. Or else he'll shut off the television and talk to the kids.''

As for anything else, Tarkanian usually ignores it. That's why so much of the Tarkanian paraphernalia in Las Vegas is bootleg, items from which Tarkanian derives no revenue.

"Lois and my attorney, Chuck Thompson, have been on me to do something about all the Tark the Shark stuff around, but I never seem to get around to much of it,'' he said.

Why not?

"I've got a one-track mind,'' said Tarkanian. "I'd rather talk about basketball.''

And he'd rather think about nothing but basketball, even when he's driving.

"All those stories about my driving are overrated,'' said Tarkanian.

"Those stories are true,'' said Lois.

Example, please.

Lois: "One day we were in the car and writers from *USA Today* and the *Los Angeles Times* were in the backseat. Jerry was feeling very euphoric because we had won a big game. He was talking to the reporters, and he kept turning around and looking right at the guys. He was so excited about what he was talking about that he almost forgot he was driving. I reached over to get my hands on the wheel because I was afraid something might happen. The next day in the story in *USA Today,* the writer wrote, 'His wife reached out and took the steering wheel from Tarkanian.' I did try to do that. I tell him, 'Jerry, please be more careful; you've got to watch where you're going.' He says, 'Lois, I am. I am.' But he's not. He makes me nervous when he's driving, but he also insists on driving.

"One time in junior college, Vicki Trapp [mother of George and John Trapp] was getting a ride to the airport from Jerry. She is a very religious woman. When Jerry started making the turns on the old Pasadena Freeway, Mrs. Trapp closed her eyes and started saying, 'Oh, Lord,' over and over. She had her prayer book in her purse, and she took it out and clung to it all the way to the airport. Throughout that entire trip I kept telling Jerry, 'Slow down, be careful,' and he kept saying, 'I am, I am,' and Vicki kept praying.

"Here's another example. My father served in the Navy during two wars. He was on a submarine in a Japanese harbor in World War II when the Japanese dropped depth charges on them. But when Jerry drove my father from Riverside to Los Angeles, my father said he was more afraid riding in the car with Jerry driving than he was during the wars."

For Tarkanian, the games seem easier than driving—so long as UNLV wins.

Lois describes her husband as "effervescent" after a victory. "He is so ecstatic," she says. "His face beams. He talks and talks, especially if the team has played well. He could go straight through the night talking, and that's when he's the wittiest. He has everyone laughing.

"After a loss, it's agony. I've been in bed with him after we get beat and he starts to moan, 'No, no, oh no!' It's like someone is stabbing him over and over. When you care about someone and he is suffering so much, it's hard to take. That's why I've started sleeping on the sofa when we get beat. I just can't stand hearing him moan over and over. As I've gotten older, I've started to realize that I'm not a bottomless pit. Sometimes, the best thing to do with Jerry is to just leave him alone. No one can comfort him. He doesn't get better until we play again and win. When we get beat, I think, 'Thank God we've got a game in two days.' I want us to get out there and win so that Jerry will feel better."

More than anyone else, Lois is aware of her husband's moods and eccentricities.

"He is so superstitious. One time we were in the bathroom and I reached for a tube of toothpaste. Jerry grabbed my hand and pulled it away from the toothpaste. I thought, 'What the heck is this?' Then Jerry said, 'Here, use this one,' and he handed me another tube. I didn't have to ask; I knew that Jerry had decided that this particular toothpaste tube was lucky and we were going to have to make it last through the season.

"Another time, our daughter Pamela gave us a nice electric blanket for Christmas. But it was during one of our worst seasons, and Jerry stopped using it after a short while. The next winter, I went to put the blanket on the bed and Jerry said, 'No, no, I don't want that.' I said, 'But Jerry...,' and he said, 'I don't like that blanket.' He never would tell me why. It finally clicked in my mind that he had used that blanket during the worst season in his life, so it didn't matter that it was a perfectly good electric blanket—he was never going to use it again. And he never has. I finally gave it back to Pam. When I explained why, she understood. All the family understands his superstitions."

Another adjustment those around Tarkanian must make is to tread softly on game days.

"Jerry doesn't talk on the way to the games," says Lois. "If you're in the car with him and jabbering away, he'll cut you off sharply and he'll get angry if you continue."

Tarkanian's players have their own stories about Tarkanian's code of silence.

Reggie Theus: "The pregame meals when I played were the worst. There was no talking. I mean *silence*. You just could not talk. Not a word. We ate steak and potatoes for every pregame meal, and you better believe that those meals went pretty fast, because no one was allowed to talk. There was nothing else to do but eat."

Sidney Green: "When we were freshmen, Larry Anderson and I made the mistake of laughing during the pregame meal. I don't remember why it happened, but Tark went crazy. He cussed us out so bad, I couldn't believe it. I don't think he ever came down on me as hard in my four years as he did when I laughed during dinner. He even had the waiters sneaking in and out."

Former UNLV assistant Al Menendez: "You can't imagine how much noise knives and forks make when no one is allowed to talk. There is no other sound in the room. And if you want the catsup or the salt, you can't ask for it. You just point and hope that someone notices you. Jerry likes the silence because he thinks that it builds up the players' concentration. I'll say this much: those were the worst meals of my life, and everyone got tense all right. It would have been great if you were going out to play the game right after that, but you still had to wait about four hours."

The pregame silences were only part of Tarkanian's superstitions, as former UNLV coaches and players attest.

Sidney Green: "Once at the pregame meal, someone had put the silverware down differently from usual. I think the spoon was in the wrong place or something. At first, Tark didn't even want to touch the silverware. Finally, he started fiddling with it, moving a fork here, a knife there. We could tell that something was wrong and no one would touch their silverware until Tark got done with his. So we waited a few minutes and watched him. When he ate, then we finally did."

Menendez on towels: "Tark says that he has the towels to keep moisture in his mouth, but does anyone really believe that? He is convinced that the towel has brought him luck, and the team manager has to fold it a certain way before each game. When one manager graduates, the first thing he does is to teach the new manager how to fold the towel. Watching it, you'd think the kid was a Marine corporal folding an American flag. He almost went crazy when he lost Gil Castillo, who was the best manager at folding his towel.''

Menendez on hotels: ''If we went to a city and lost, you can bet we would stay at a different hotel the next time we went back to play a game there.''

Menendez on the ghost chair: ''That is the chair on the bench next to Tark's chair. No one is supposed to sit in it. Once, I sat in it by mistake, and Tark stared at me as if he were going to kill me. His eyes were on fire. [UNLV assistant coach] Ralph Readout grabbed me and pulled me out of the chair. When Lewis Brown played for Tark, he intentionally sat in that chair just to drive Jerry insane.''

Reggie Theus on the ghost chair: ''Lewis Brown was a guy that Tark never could reach. He tried and he tried, but Lewis was just too different. Tark is a very patient man, but he just went off when Lewis sat in the ghost chair. Tark pointed at Lewis sitting there and screamed, 'Holy cow, look at that guy. Jeez, he's done it on purpose. He's just sitting there, trying to sabotage the whole damn basketball program.'''

Former UNLV assistant Lynn Archibald on Tark's wardrobe: ''He would never wear brown to the games. Once, a long time ago, he had lost a big game while wearing brown, and that was it. If he wore a certain coat or tie and lost, he wouldn't wear it again.''

Archibald on Tark's recruiting: ''He had a thing about players from certain areas of the country. For example, he always said that he had good teams when he had a kid from New York.''

Menendez on music in the dressing room: ''Tark also wanted the players quiet in the dressing room before games. Some coaches let their players play music, but not Tark. But when we were recruiting Albert King out of New York, I told Tark that Albert loved his radio. He carried that ghetto blaster with him everywhere. Tark said to me, 'Well, Al, maybe we can tell Albert that a little music before the game won't be too bad.' That was the answer I expected. Tark could be so blinded by talent that he'd even change one of his superstitions, but since we couldn't sign Albert, that was never put to the test.''

Another of Tarkanian's eccentricities is that before he leaves his office, he makes sure that everything on his desk is squared evenly. Before he leaves home to coach a game, he does the same thing by the sink and by his bed. If he sees a piece of lint, he'll pick it up and throw it away. It's the same at the arena. Nothing can be out of place. If there's even a shred of paper or thread on the floor, he'll spot it and pick it up. That's why before games Tarkanian can be seen prowling the sidelines, picking things off the floor.

Finally, Tarkanian has a thing for telephones.

Menendez: "The best way to get Jerry's attention is to call him. There were several times when George McQuarn and I went into his office to tell him about a recruit, but he'd be far more interested in what someone else was telling him on the telephone. It was as though he put more credence in what he heard on the phone than what people were telling him in his office. It got to the point that George and I would just call him when we wanted Jerry to listen. One day I was telling him about a recruit, and Jerry stopped me and said, 'Where are you?' I said I was in my office. 'Right next door?' he asked, amazed by that. I said I was. 'What the hell are you doing calling me when you can take ten steps and tell me in my office.' I told him he listened better when he was on the phone."

Tarkanian has little to say about the superstitions. He says he doesn't remember where or when most of them began. Some are long-standing, such as the ghost chair. Others come and go with the season, such as the toothpaste tube. For a time, he didn't let anyone eat catsup at a pregame meal. Steak sauce was fine, but no catsup. Did it remind Tarkanian of his days at Fresno State, when he would order a bowl of hot water and then pour catsup into it to make tomato soup? Or had he once had catsup on something and lost a game? No one knows, and Tarkanian won't—or can't—say.

Tarkanian always insists that he cares only about two things: his family and basketball.

Lois: "Jerry deeply loves his children and has been a great father in many ways. He helped me with their diapers when they were small. He took the kids places even when we didn't have the money to afford it. He'd just find a few extra dollars. When we were younger, I used to work in the summer because I could earn more money than he. So when the school year ended, I went to work and Jerry stayed home with the children. When we lived in Riverside, he made them a sandbox. And he wanted to get the best, smoothest sand he could find, so he drove all the way out to the desert at Palm Springs, about a seventy-mile round trip, and brought back a pickup truck full of sand. Jerry was not a great builder, and I remember that the sandbox ended up looking sort of crooked, but it had the greatest sand in Riverside.

"Jerry liked to get the kids involved in whatever he had to do. For example, collecting the trash and driving it to the dump was a big deal at our house. The kids got a big kick out of riding in our pickup truck with their father. He liked to take the kids with him when he went to the gym. Sometimes, they just played in his office while he sat there making phone calls. When we moved to Hunington Beach, he'd take them to the ocean and they'd swim and play in the sand together. For years, every morning the children would run into our bed and spend ten to fifteen minutes wrestling with Jerry. Jerry would pin Danny, and Danny would yell, 'Help me, my brother, help!' and little George would come running into the bed and jump on Jerry's shoulders.

"Jerry likes family traditions, and another one was that no one got out of bed on Christmas morning until Jerry had put on a Christmas record. That was a sign for the kids to rush to the tree. Since Jerry didn't play golf or have any other hobbies, his family became his hobby. If he wasn't working, he was home with the kids. I think that's why the children have turned out so well. They always meant so much to him."

The four Tarkanian children are four different combinations of the personalities of their parents. Lois tutors children who are hearing-impaired. She has always been involved in special education. So it should be no surprise that Pamela became a teacher for children with learning disabilities. She earned a master's degree from Nevada-Las Vegas and works in a counseling-based program for children with emotional problems.

Jodie is a registered nurse specializing in intensive care, working with critical cases. "Of all our children, the one most like Jerry is Jodie," says Lois. "She is not as serious as our other children. She has had an active social life, and it took her longer to get through school. She was one of our middle children, and the middle children usually have it the toughest. Jodie has done exceptionally well in nursing."

Danny graduated near the top of his law school class at San Diego University. While he is the son who played for Jerry, it is youngest child George who wants to be a coach. An Achilles heel injury prevented George from playing extensively in college. He is now an honors student studying for his Ph.D. in political science at Claremont College in California. He also serves as a part-time assistant basketball coach at Pomona-Pitzer College.

Lois: "When I think about the fact that our kids grew up in very troubled times—the 1960s and 1970s—and that their father was a very visible public figure, I am very proud of what they've accomplished.

In school, the other kids would tease them about their father. Or they would end up in situations where people didn't know that they were Jerry Tarkanian's children, and people would start criticizing him. They endured the NCAA investigation with us, when we were subjected to a lot of bad publicity, and when Jerry and I were so busy with the NCAA that we didn't give them all the attention they deserved.

"Some of our friends have had children who developed troubles with alcohol or drugs. It's not the parents' fault, but it happens. We are thankful that our kids have been good kids and I know that we've been very fortunate."

One of Tarkanian's child-rearing theories is that kids should have a dog.

"We once had a dog that was a tremendous watchdog, so Jerry thinks we always need a watchdog," says Lois. "He's traveling so much now that he doesn't have time for a dog, but Jerry likes Shepherds so he keeps bringing them home. At one time, we had four dogs. Two of them belonged to Pamela. It was crazy. When Pamela married, she took her two dogs with her. I gave away one dog to a family who had lost their dog, so now we are down to one dog. I really don't want a dog, but Jerry insists that we keep one."

Lois and Jodie love cats; Jerry can't stand them.

Lois: "Jodie wanted a cat very much. One day she and I went to buy some plants for the house. At the garden shop was a box with some kittens. The store owner was giving them away. Jodie saw a kitten she really liked, and we took it home. We named the cat Wilma. For the longest time, we didn't tell Jerry that she was ours. We'd say that she just hung around the house. When Jerry would go out the front door, Wilma would try to come in the house. Jerry kept saying, 'Why is that cat always hanging around here?' When he left, we'd let Wilma in the house. If he saw her when he came home, he'd just throw her outside. After a while, I got tired of the farce and told Jerry that Jodie and I liked cats and wanted to have some. He complained about it, and he still doesn't like cats, but we now have three of them. The cats are in the house and Jerry's dog is in the yard. It's still a running battle. Jerry comes home, lets the dog in the house, and the dog scares the cats. He leaves, we put the dog back outside, and the cats rule again.

"Jerry is a very tolerant person. He likes to complain about the cats or the other pets we've had, but we've kept them. I think that is why we have stayed together all these years—we give each other a lot of freedom."

*   *   *

The Tarkanians have been married for thirty-two years. In that span, Tarkanian has had seven different coaching jobs. They have been under extreme pressure: pressure to win, pressure from the NCAA, and pressure to do the best they can with their players and to help them academically and socially.

Tarkanian: "Coaching is unlike any other job. That's why Lois is such a great person. She has had to cope with things other wives and mothers never have to face. No coach's wife has ever worked harder with the players, and no coach has ever had a wife who has helped him more than Lois helped me."

While Tarkanian coaches, Lois helps to organize her husband and assists him with much of the peripheral work that is a part of big-time coaching. She also helps supervise the academic program for the UNLV basketball players, tutors hearing-impaired children in her home, and writes a column for the Las Vegas *Sun*.

Lois: "A lot of people have asked me how Jerry and I have stayed married for so long, because they say we are so different. But we have a lot of common ground. Jerry is family-oriented and so am I. Jerry is a loyal person, and I put a high value on loyalty. Neither one of us is pretentious, or worries about wearing the latest styles and that sort of thing. We both are religious people. Jerry grew up as an Armenian-Orthodox; I'm Roman Catholic. When we were married, I said I would move wherever he wanted to live, as long as he went to church with me. That lasted throughout our early marriage until we went to Riverside, where there was a priest who always yelled at the people who came to Mass about those who weren't going to Mass. That really turned Jerry off. It's sort of an interesting facet of his personality that he'll go a long way with people or situations that bother him and show incredible patience. I've seen certain people treat him badly time after time and he just takes it. Then one day that's it. It's as if someone turned off a faucet—that's it, no more, not a drop of patience left. That's what happened with Jerry and the priest. Jerry didn't want to hear it any more and he stopped going to church, except for significant holy days such as Christmas and Easter. Ever since we've been married, I've never seen him miss his morning or evening prayers, so I may be going to church and he may be staying home, but we both believe in the same thing.

"When we first got married, neither one of us had any thought that we would someday end up in big-time sports. I'm not really a big fan of big-time sports, and that sometimes causes problems. There were times, especially when the NCAA investigation was going on, when I'd wonder, 'Why am I in the middle of all this?' I don't even believe that much in competitive sports. There are so many more important things to do. Jerry likes to compete and he likes to win. I prefer not to get involved in competition and will not seek it out, but when I'm put in a competitive situation, then I become very competitive myself. Jerry cares a great deal about doing well, and I care a great deal about Jerry. I care very much about all our players, and I want them to succeed because it means a lot to them. Pretty soon I get caught up in it all. It can be a terrible strain on us both. I really don't enjoy the basketball season.

"For example, the 1986–87 season was tremendous. We were 37–2 and went to the Final Four. I'm sure I enjoyed it less than anyone involved. When the games are going on, I'm afraid that we're going to lose or that someone will get hurt. I can hardly watch. People in the media sometimes make a lot about my praying at games. I wish they wouldn't, but they do. I don't pray necessarily to win. I pray that no one gets hurt and that we play well and that if I have to, I'll be a gracious loser. Sometimes I pray because praying is the one thing that can calm me. I just wish the media would not make a big thing about this personal part of me.

"When we come from behind to beat a team such as Iowa in the NCAA tournament, how do I feel? Not happy. Not overjoyed. Just relieved that we didn't lose. Relieved that no one was injured. Relieved that the people I care about are happy.

"What it comes down to is the fact that I love Jerry, and loving Jerry means that basketball has to be a big part of my life. We had our children early in our marriage. By the time I was 29, I was the mother of four. I was working part-time and Jerry was coaching. I've mentioned that Jerry grew up in a very conservative family where the women stayed at home and cooked. You can't imagine what a wonderful cook Jerry's mother was. Well, I had a career. I'm not a very good cook, but Jerry has never complained about it in all the years we've been married, and he has had plenty of opportunities. When I had to work, Jerry helped with the children. So when I think about our marriage and sometimes get upset at the heartache big-time college athletics has caused us, I think about how patient Jerry has been with me, how good he was with our children. It really doesn't matter to me that Jerry is a great coach; he has been a great father and a loyal husband.

"Once, when we were going through some trying times, I said to Jerry, 'Please get out of the profession. It's no good. It's full of hypocrites and phonies.' He just said to me softly, 'Lois, don't ever say anything bad about basketball. It's been good to me my whole life.'

"It's not Jerry's fault, of course, that being a coach has changed so much in the last fifteen years. I can remember when it was one of the most secure professions, and when the marriages of coaches were among the most steady. Now, since the great involvement of television and big money, the profession has changed. I talk with younger wives whose husbands earn more than Jerry and who seem to have so much security, and it puzzles me some that they don't seem happier. Then I realize, it's the pressure, pressure all the time.

"If your husband's team wins most of the time, there are always some people who complain when they lose. Al McGuire says it's like creating your own monster that then devours you.

"Sometimes people will ask me what it's like to be a coach's wife—how I feel about his being gone so much. Many young wives of coaches have told me that they are concerned by the long separations. People have said, 'Your husband is away so much. Don't you worry about him?' I can honestly say that I've never been concerned about what Jerry is doing on the road. As Vicki Trapp once said to me, 'You'll never have to worry about another woman. It will always be another basketball.' I've never questioned Jerry about where he went. He calls me every day and tells me where he is and what he's doing. He's done that every day of our marriage. Some nights he may be out late with other coaches talking basketball, but it comes down to this: At some point in your relationship, you decide if you will trust your husband or not. If anyone breaks that trust, it's over. I trust Jerry and he has never given me reason to doubt him.

"Not that I agree with him all the time. There are many times we disagree. I did not think he should recruit Lloyd Daniels, and I attempted to dissuade him. After a few minutes of heated discussion he calmly asked me if I would say Lloyd didn't deserve a chance if he were not a ball player. He had me there, because in all my own professional work I'm one who believes that we can achieve what others may consider impossible.

"There are times when Jerry's intense interest in basketball precludes interest in some of the activities I feel are important. I used to ask him to accompany me to plays or ballets I enjoy. He'd go with me, but he really wasn't there. I'd want to exchange a thought about something and he'd be thinking about basketball. I found myself feeling lonely even though his body was sitting in the chair next to me. So I've mostly given that up and go with my children or friends.

"When Jerry is focused on a person or situation, however, he is one of the kindest, most perceptive human beings I've ever known. His eyes seem to melt, and his voice softens, and you can see caring in every part of his body.

"I remember a time in Long Beach when Jerry gave a talk at a junior high school. The teachers there were having quite a bit of trouble with one student who greatly admired the Long Beach State basketball team. So they asked Jerry to work with the boy and see if he could help. Soon Donald Mitchell became a part of our life. Jerry had him over to the house or would buy him things. One day, Jerry received a letter at his UNLV office from Donald. Donald was in prison, and would be for several years, but he asked Jerry for help with a few things and Jerry helped him. Jerry also sent him some tennis shoes and socks.

"I can recall many such incidents where you couldn't find a more empathetic person than Jerry.

"In addition to our family and our trusting each other, we've stayed together because we put Jerry's job first. There has never been a time when Jerry's job didn't come first. There were years in my career when I was extremely lucky to be in special education, because that was the golden age of special education. I was elected to a position in my field where I'd have to travel between California and Washington, D.C., quite a bit. I turned it down because I couldn't be away from Jerry and the children. I know that I have kept my hand in special education through tutoring, but I also know that I haven't achieved what I would have if we had stayed in California and I had continued to pursue my career. So the move from California to Las Vegas was the toughest I had to make, but I did it for Jerry. He wanted the UNLV job and he wanted me to help him, and that's what I've done, and that's why we've stayed together all these years.

"It's the same with all of us in the family. We all care about Jerry, so we all care about basketball."

19

First Person: Reforming the NCAA

Considering the differences I've had with the NCAA, you might be surprised that I think there should be such an organization as the NCAA. But I believe in a strong NCAA because the organization provides structure and support for numerous activities that are of extreme importance to the student athlete. I also believe that the NCAA should have a strong enforcement staff, because cheating is a problem. My concern is that safeguards should be placed within the enforcement program to ensure that selective enforcement does not occur, because the enforcement staff has the most power within the NCAA. Entire university athletic programs and the lives of coaches and players can be destroyed by unfair enforcement decisions.

There is a general feeling among major college basketball coaches that some players are receiving thousands of dollars to attend some schools in the South. I had one NCAA investigator tell me that a certain southern school, a major power, supposedly paid $70,000 for a kid—and that school is not on probation. I have no idea what kids are getting paid by some schools. I do know that when coaches get together, you'll hear them joke that if some southern schools were in the NBA, they'd be over the salary cap.

As for cars, you hear stories about All-Americans driving BMWs. One Southwestern Conference football coach told me that you can tell who is winning and losing in their league by walking through the parking lot near the athletic dorm. If a team is on top, you see BMWs; if it is losing, you see Fords. I've heard the same stories about the Southeastern Conference.

There is so much cheating—and I'm talking about big-time cheating by big-time schools—that the NCAA should have plenty to do just finding out who is buying players. The cheating is being done by major universities.

There are two kinds of probation. The first is very soft; maybe the school loses a couple of scholarships. The second is probation with sanctions, where the school is barred from the NCAA tournament for two or three years and from appearances on national television. That second category is an effective means of enforcement because it kills your recruiting. But it almost never happens to a big school. Usually, it's places such as Marist and Bridgeport where the NCAA lowers the boom. One time it was Hayward State and Cornell. When was the last time Marist or Bridgeport or Hayward or Cornell, was involved in a big game? Why hit the little guys all the time?

A major problem has been the relationship between the NCAA's elected officials and the enforcement staff. The elected NCAA officials are the representatives from colleges and universities, and they sit on the NCAA's infractions committee and council. The enforcement staff consists of paid individuals hired by the NCAA to investigate schools. The infractions committee determines the validity of charges brought against schools by the enforcement staff, and the committee is supposed to control the enforcement process. The members of the infractions committee and council usually are full-time employees at their respective colleges. Most of their time is spent on their jobs at their universities.

In reality, it is the full-time staff hired and employed by the NCAA in Shawnee Mission, Kansas, that controls the process. I don't believe that the infractions committee intentionally allows the enforcement staff to run the process. Rather, it is a practice that has evolved over the years. The enforcement director and his assistants work full-time at the NCAA headquarters, where all official actions are conducted. It is natural for NCAA representatives, who are fully employed elsewhere, to depend heavily if not entirely upon information and opinions supplied by the enforcement staff.

In the enforcement process, the people supposedly in charge [elected university representatives] meet occasionally. Congressional hearings and court cases showed that the NCAA's hired staff determined what schools to investigate, drew up charges against those schools, conducted the investigation, and controlled all correspondence and information given to the schools being investigated. The enforcement staff also prepared memorandums and explanations for the infractions committee and council. The enforcement staff put together the actual findings of the committee and council, prepared press releases about those findings, and sometimes actually wrote the letters and memos that were attributed to the infractions committee. In other words, the hand of the enforcement staff could be felt throughout the entire process.

A former infractions committee chairman, Dean Arthur Reynolds, has said, "I think it is a practical matter. My colleagues and I are not employees of the NCAA. We are not primarily working in the matter of serving on the Committee on Infractions, because we are busy men."

The relationship between the enforcement staff and the infractions committee is so close that it almost is incestuous. It is very hard for the two groups to have an objective relationship. It is just natural that the infractions committee will believe what it is told by the enforcement staff. These people have worked together before on other cases. Sometimes, they go to dinner and form personal friendships. When a school appears before the infractions committee to state its case, sometimes this is the first time that the committee members have seen representatives from the school under investigation. That's why it's no surprise that when decisions are made about conflicting testimony, infractions committee members consistently choose to believe members of the enforcement staff. Even when the choice is between the non-documented recollections of the investigators and several pieces of documented evidence supplied by the school, the infractions committee still may "choose to believe" the investigators' recollections.

That is a serious problem. This has happened often to many schools, and it happened to us at UNLV.

What about the quality of the investigators who receive such respect from the infractions committee?

Certain of these investigators made an official charge against UNLV for putting up a recruit at a motel in a southeastern city. When UNLV representatives tried to find the motel, they learned that the place didn't exist. With a simple phone call, the enforcement staff could have found out the same thing, and there would have been no need to make the charge. There are many examples of this kind of investigative problem.

When questions were asked in the UNLV case about the misconduct of the enforcement staff, no objective outside sources were brought in to evaluate the charges, either before or after the infractions committee meeting concerning UNLV. The investigators in question were simply asked if the improprieties had occurred, and they said no. That was it—end of the internal review. Written records of the infractions committee and council meetings reveal that no further investigation was held.

In 1978, the United States House of Representatives Subcommittee on Oversight and Investigations conducted a yearlong investigation into the NCAA's enforcement practices. Those hearings documented the inequities of the NCAA's enforcement process. For example, it was revealed that the infractions committee never refused a case that was brought to it by the enforcement staff, and in each case some violations were found. What happens is that the enforcement staff almost acts as prosecutor, judge, and jury.

Nothing better shows the control the enforcement staff has over the infractions committee than this fact: by his own account, former NCAA president Neils Thompson was unaware of the enforcement staff's practice of including allegations not based on fact in official inquiries into schools.

The facts show that once the enforcement staff formed an allegation in the UNLV case, they worked consistently to support it and ignored and failed to report refuting information, even when the information was offered and documented by individuals being questioned. Enforcement staff did not reveal refuting information to infractions committee members even when the information was contained within their files.

Recommendations

I am not an expert on management, but here are some of my thoughts about what needs to be done to correct the situation:

In seeking fair and impartial hearings, my first recommendation to the NCAA would be similar to that put forth by the congressional subcommittee: Create a new collegiate body within the NCAA which would be responsible for supervision of enforcement staff, for setting and administering policy guidelines for enforcement staff, and for being responsible for authorization of official inquiries. All other functions would remain with the Committee on Infractions, which would otherwise have no regular contact with NCAA investigators. The new committee could consist of three individuals.

If NCAA membership felt that forming such a new body would take too much from the infractions committee, then an objective, impartial group distant from NCAA staff activities should be formed to evaluate questions of impropriety involving the enforcement staff. This seems little to ask when so many lives and careers are at stake. You can give a school or a coach a hundred hearings lasting a thousand hours, and it will make no difference if the information provided by the enforcement staff is inaccurate and if NCAA officials "choose to believe" the recollections of investigators rather than documentation presented by others. How fair is it that enforcement staff were allowed to meet with infractions committee members outside formal hearings to provide information supporting their claims, when the accused are not included in the conversations, and thus not provided an opportunity to refute what the investigators say?

It's not just myself and others who have been through the process who share this concern of how the enforcement staff and the infractions committee work together. This came out at the congressional hearings.

Former NCAA president John Fuzak is certainly no detractor of the association. In the 1978 Congressional hearings on the NCAA, he testified as follows:

> Looking at the Infractions Committee, I believe, and have believed, that there is an inescapable relationship between the Infractions Committee and the investigative staff. There must be communication between the two. There must be decisions made by the Infractions Committee after a preliminary inquiry to decide whether there is enough substance to proceed with an official inquiry. I believe at that point decisions are made which have some effect of making the Infractions Committee become involved in the matter itself. Further than that, over a period of time, they come to know members of that staff. They come to respect them. They tend to accept their evidence less critically than the evidence put forth by an institution or by individuals in their own defense.

Another staunch supporter of the NCAA echoed his views. Mickey Holmes, then Missouri Valley conference commissioner, said:

> Because of this close working relationship between the enforcement staff and the Committee on Infractions, it is not difficult for an institution to conclude that its case has already been weighed and judged before even receiving the official inquiry containing the allegations. Because of this close working relationship, I feel the enforcement staff and the Committee on Infractions communicates freely before, during, and after a hearing and before adjudication.

First Person: Reforming the NCAA

Brent Clark, a former NCAA investigator, told the congressional subcommittee:

> The real deception, however, comes after the evidence is received, and it is time for the Committee on Infractions to retire to deliberate the fate of the institution or individual who stands so much to lose. It is not, as schools are led to believe, a matter of the five distinguished gentlemen on the committee dismissing the staff and the institution, going behind closed doors, and thereafter deliberating in a dispassionate atmosphere. On the contrary, after the school is dismissed, NCAA staff and committee members commonly adjourn to a hotel room, open a richly deserved store of liquor, and begin to discuss the case in earnest. It is at this point that the staff makes its hard pitch to the committee members in a convivial and totally ex parte session.

Big Eight Conference commissioner Charles Neinas, a former NCAA employee, was asked by Congress what happens when the infractions committee has questions about a case after it has supposedly dismissed representatives of the NCAA enforcement staff and the accused institution. Neinas stated that he thought the practice was "to call back, if they had a question of the staff, they call back the staff." When asked if that was without the institution present, Holmes replied, "That is correct."

These three witnesses before the committee, all staunch NCAA supporters, endorsed some sort of structural divorce of the staff from the infractions committee. "I think the members of the infractions committee are outstanding individuals," said Fuzak. "Yet they must practice a full-time profession. They must depend upon staff work and that work involving the investigative staff puts them too close to being both investigator, judge, and jury."

My second recommendation for reforming the NCAA would be to give to the infractions committee any additional but independent staff it would need. This could be, as suggested by congressional members, a full-time clerk, preferably a lawyer, responsible only to the infractions committee. Then, as former commissioner Neinas suggested, "...the accused institution would not find the enforcement staff serving in the dual capacity of prosecutor as well as assisting those who are to judge the case."

The sole record for an appeal to the NCAA council consists of one item, the "expanded confidential report," which was prepared not, as would be expected, by the Committee on Infractions, but instead by the enforcement staff. When infractions committee member Charles Wright was asked if the final report was read verbatim to the committee members, he replied, "No." A clerk working only for the infractions committee could in a more unbiased manner prepare the committee's final report. Considering the institutional and individual reputations at stake, it would not seem to be asking too much to have each infractions committee member read the report, make suggestions for changes or additions, and sign the copy.

My third recommendation is that the NCAA should send guidelines and procedures on how to conduct an investigation along with the official inquiry. UNLV representatives tried continually throughout the investigation to obtain such assistance, and received none. The congressional hearing indicated that other schools had met with the same problem. If these guidelines were given, I'm sure there would be fewer problems, and that is certainly the least that should be done for something that is called a "cooperative" venture.

My fourth and final recommendation for reforming the NCAA is to throw out the multitude of rules and regulations that currently exist. As it now stands, almost all of the NCAA manual's 430 pages are related to rules, regulations, and interpretations of rules and regulations. There are so many rules and regulations that no one—not even the NCAA investigators—understands them all. In fact, when you call the NCAA office in Kansas for an explanation of a certain rule, the answers you receive will vary from official to official. The NCAA could make life easier for universities, coaches, and its own investigators if there were only about a dozen hard-and-fast rules, clearly spelled out— such as no cars, no cash, and no phony entrance exams—and with the penalties clearly spelled out and applied consistently for all institutions. As I understand, such a revision may now be in progress.

For years, I had little hope that these types of recommendations would be adopted by the NCAA. Little progress was made after the congressional hearings, although the NCAA now requires its investigators to take a copy of their notes back to the person they interviewed, so that person may make any corrections and then sign the notes. The importance of what is being signed, however, must be impressed upon the individual so that he doesn't just browse through the material.

That was a positive move, but what really has caused me to become optimistic is that Dick Schultz is the new NCAA executive director. He was both a coach and an athletic director, so he came up through the ranks and understands our problems. He seems to be a caring, humanistic person. If he doesn't get swallowed up by the NCAA bureaucracy, the organization can really move forward.

Proposition 48

Cars and cash payments have been a problem for a long time, but a new area of cheating is entrance exams. One night, I got an anonymous call. It was a guy offering to make sure that one of our recruits who didn't meet the NCAA requirements on the ACT test the first time would pass the test the next time. He said he had done it for kids going to several different major schools. He said that it would cost $2,500 to fix the test. I said, "No," and he was very polite. He said he understood, and that was that; I never heard from him again. I do know that other coaches have been getting these kinds of calls, and that worries everyone.

I am in favor of the concept of Proposition 48, which says that an incoming freshman must have at least a C or 2.0 grade point average in his core courses, along with either a 15 on the ACT test or a total score of 700 on the SAT test to be eligible for athletics. I like the idea that kids are told early in school that they have to buckle down and get good grades if they want to play college basketball. I'd make the grade requirement tougher, though—maybe make a kid have a 2.4 grade point average, which is a C+. This is a truer indication that the student has been going to class, handing in his assignments, and has solid academic skills.

I am completely opposed to the standardized test requirement. In the first place, many studies have shown that the tests are culturally biased against minorities. Also, I think a look at a kid's transcript, which shows his entire high school career, tells you far more about him than how he scored on one test. Another reason I don't like the tests is because that's where you'll find the next-biggest scandal in college sports.

I've heard too many stories about a kid taking the ACT and getting something like a 6 or 8 the first time. Then on his second try, he gets an 18. I don't care if the kid had Einstein tutoring him, he won't go from a 6 or 8 to an 18. It just can't happen, unless the kid had a brain transplant or someone else took the test. I've read that 91 percent of all football players and 83 percent of all basketball players have met the requirements on the standardized tests; this is a large increase over previous results. I just can't accept the fact that about 90 percent of these athletes really passed the test. I've worked with too many good kids, kids with decent academic backgrounds, who tried very hard. Yet they kept missing the requirement by a few points. If these kids came up short, so should a lot of others. Something is up with these tests, and that something will hurt the college game.

If the NCAA would drop the test requirement and raise the grade point average, it would still send a strong message that the kids have to study, and it also would eliminate one area of cheating. There is enough for the NCAA to enforce when it comes to recruiting.

Recruiting is a lot of hard work, and it can be very frustrating. Every coach has had a kid he's lost at the last minute, a kid who talked to him for two years and promised him that he was coming to his school. At the last minute, the kid turned around and signed with a school that came in really late and contacted him only once or twice. That's when a coach begins to get suspicious.

I've been recruiting long enough to know that:

1. Some schools have almost complete immunity from the NCAA. They can buy players, give away cars, and fix tests, but they either are never investigated or are given a cursory investigation with no serious sanctions resulting.

2. Not everyone is buying players, giving away cars, and fixing tests. Some schools don't have to do anything. They barely recruit. My former assistant, Mark Warkentien, says, "At North Carolina, they don't recruit; they draft. Being a recruiter for North Carolina is like being born a Kennedy."

3. Some schools always seem to have the NCAA looking over their shoulders. I remember when Idaho State was put on probation. Idaho State? Boy, it makes you wonder. As former Idaho State coach Jim Killingsworth once said, "You can shake down every booster in Pocatello and not find as much as you would on one booster in the state of Kentucky."

4. Often, it's not the kid but one of his relatives or friends who has a hand out. That's just as bad as the kid asking for something, and when that happens I tell our assistant coaches to back off from the kid.

All I'm saying is that the NCAA needs to crack down on the cash and the cars, and to watch those entrance exams.

Also, the NCAA needs to be fair. It is common knowledge that there are a few schools in the country where they are buying players, but the NCAA tells you that they can't prove it. That's always the NCAA's answer: "We know they are up to something, but we can't prove it."

Well, the NCAA can find something on any school in the country, so I don't accept that. Because there are so many rules and because the extra benefit rule can be interpreted to the point where a coachcan't do anything for a kid, the NCAA can walk onto any campus in the country and within a week find some violations.

Because of the extra benefit rule, coaches aren't the only people watched; the boosters are watched, too. The NCAA can define almost anyone as a booster, or a representative of the athletic department's interest. For example, anyone who has a season ticket could be considered a representative of the school's athletic interest. In every college community, you can find someone who has given a kid a ride home or given him dinner.

My main concern is fairness and equality. The NCAA is far too political. Coaches joke that the NCAA will never do anything to certain schools, or that some schools must have life insurance policies from the NCAA because they never get hurt. That's what I'm against— the selective prosecution. I want hard-and-fast penalties against schools that are guilty, and those schools should be penalized the same, based on their violations. Too often, major schools are given slaps on the wrists, while lesser or newer programs are clobbered with sanctions.

As a coach, you know the power of the NCAA. You are scared to death of them because they can ruin your life. This fear pervades the coaching profession; it was expressed during the congressional hearings. The NCAA can intimidate you. They can come after you as an act of revenge for something you said once that maybe they didn't like, or a stance you took against them. You can be unfairly destroyed by the NCAA, and that's terribly wrong.

How to Stop Violations

The reason for the cheating is that a winning college basketball team can make so much money. If you are nationally ranked, on national television, and in the NCAA play-offs, you are talking about at least $1 million. When we went to the Final Four in 1987, it was worth almost $2 million to UNLV.

I'd like to revamp that system. The play-off money should be divided equally among all the NCAA members. A team that gets to the Final Four deserves a bigger share than some other schools, but it shouldn't come away with a million dollars. The money should be passed around to all the NCAA members.

I'm just talking about fairness.

Also, if the money weren't so big, there would be less of a temptation to cheat.

When you can make $1 million for the Final Four, imagine how important the superstar becomes—not just to the team, but to the entire university. Some coaches become desperate. When they recruit a kid, they promise him anything and everything to get him to sign. When the kid gets to the school, he finds out that he has been lied to. This happens quite a bit, and that's why some kids transfer.

The penalties for buying kids should be severe—both for the coach and for the player. I find it hard to believe that the kid who takes the money isn't as guilty as the coach who provides it.

In the recruiting process, you run into players on early visits who aren't asking for anything. They seem happy to meet you and talk about your school. But then there's someone in the family, a counselor from school, or some guy from the playgrounds who says, "Hey man, look at all those big arenas and all the people in those arenas; you should get a piece of that, too." Suddenly, the kid is asking for money.

In the South and Southeast, some high school coaches want money just so a college coach can talk to their kid. You have to pay a coach just for a recruiting visit, and if the kid signs with you, the coaches want even more money. That's why we don't recruit in the South. That doesn't happen out West.

So coaches who pay kids ought to be suspended, and kids who take the money ought to lose their eligibility. Enforce that kind of penalty and you'll cut the cheating.

Limiting Recruiting Contacts

The NCAA has a number of rules about how often you can see a kid, when you can talk to him, and so on. Right now, you can only talk to a kid a total of five times, on and off campus.

There are a couple of reasons why I don't like the rule.

First, it gets in the way of the kid and the coach getting to know each other. They just aren't allowed to talk to each other enough. Suppose you fly to L.A. to watch a kid play a high school game. After the game, you can't even tell the kid that he played well. That's ridiculous.

Second, the contact rule really hurts the hardworking coaches at the smaller schools. We never could have won so many games at Long Beach State if the contact rule had been in existence back then. We got kids by showing them more attention, talking to them and getting to know them. We spent far more time with them than the bigger schools. The contact rule hurts the aggressive coach who can outwork everyone.

For us at UNLV, the contact rule is good. We are established and have become known on a national scale. The rule helps us and the other traditional powers. But I still don't like it because I don't think it's fair. It works against the little guy.

Signings and Transfers

One of the best things the NCAA has done was to establish the early signing period, where a player can sign with a college in November. This is good because the kid knows where he will be going to school next year. It takes the pressure off both the player and the coach who is recruiting him. Also, a player who isn't a blue-chipper should take a scholarship when it is offered. Maybe he'll get hurt or not have a great senior year. The early signing period can serve as protection, because he knows he has a scholarship lined up.

I agree with Dick Vitale when he says that a player should be released from his scholarship agreement if the coach he signs with is fired or leaves that school. Often, a kid picks a college based on the coach. If that coach leaves, it isn't fair to make the kid still go to that original college. Basketball is a significant part of that player's life, and who coaches the team is critical to deciding where he will attend school.

As for junior college transfers, the NCAA did the right thing when it required JUCO kids to have a degree in order to be eligible when they transfer to a four-year school. This makes players in junior colleges aware that they have to buckle down and hit the books. If they want to play basketball, they know they have to study.

That also is the good aspect of Proposition 48. It gets the message to the kids in high school. They know that they have to get decent grades if they want to play ball in college. They also know that they can't wait until their senior year to try to do something about their grades. It makes kids get their priorities in order.

Freshman Eligibility

One of the best things the NCAA can do for the athletes is to return to the days when freshmen were ineligible to play varsity basketball.

Kids often are in for such a shock during their first year. That goes not just for basketball players, but for all students. For our players, basketball is just a small part of the adjustment. I'm also talking about what they experience academically and socially. Of the three areas—basketball, academics, and social life—basketball often comes the most easily.

A number of freshmen players have been ruined because they are under so much pressure to produce immediately. If they don't play well right away, they start to lose their confidence. If they are on the bench, they sometimes become disgruntled, their grades go down, and they are just miserable.

I say don't let the freshmen play, but I also don't think they should lose a year of eligibility. Let the kid spend that first year learning how to handle his college studies. Let him find a girlfriend and join a fraternity. Let him feel a part of the college community. In other words, give him time to grow up.

If a kid has that first year to adjust to college, he will have something to fall back on if he does not play well on the varsity level. Anyone who is sincere about the student athlete as a total person should believe that we need to keep freshmen out of varsity athletics.

Drug Testing

Drugs really scare me, and that's why I like drug testing. At UNLV we were two years ahead of the NCAA in terms of drug testing. Testing has helped us keep our program clean. That's because the kids know that we're serious about drugs and that we are going to test them. We usually test about six times a year.

When a player has a problem, you need proof because he'll look you right in the eye and say, "No, not me. I don't do that stuff." If you have drug testing, you can pull out the report and say, "I don't want any more bull from you. Here it is."

If a kid tests positive for the first time, we bring him in and talk to him. It's just me, my assistant coach, and the trainer. We don't tell anyone; we just talk to the kid.

Our rules are like this:

1. The first time we give the kid a stern warning. This clears up the problem in 90 percent of the cases.

2. The second time, we talk to his parents and set up counseling.

3. If the player tests positive a third time, he is suspended from the team for a year. But we don't get to the third level. Usually, we don't even reach the second level.

Most of the time, when kids do test positive, it is right after they come back to school. They say, "Coach, I was at a friend's house this summer and we smoked some grass."

On campus we don't have a problem, because our kids are working hard in school and basketball, they know the penalties for using drugs, and they are surrounded by good people.

What's Best for the Kids?

Everyone in college sports needs to keep in mind that the kids playing basketball are just that—kids. They are 18 years old. Think back to when you were 18. How mature were most of us? What needs did we have?

Throughout this book, I've made my thoughts known about the extra benefit rule. It's too vague, and it makes every school in America guilty of some violations. Any rule like that isn't worth keeping.

Let's define what is considered a benefit. That would make it easier on everyone.

I don't agree with some people who say, "Let's just pay the players." That's opening a can of worms that probably wouldn't stop cheating.

When my son Danny went to college, he had a basketball scholarship, but he got spending money from me. That was fine; I could afford it. But a lot of parents can't.

I like the Pell Grant system, which gives money to kids who show financial need. As the rule stood in 1987, nonathletes could receive $2,000 a year from a Pell Grant, but athletes could only be paid $900. I felt this was unfair. If a kid deserves financial aid because his family is poor, he should get it. Being an athlete has nothing to do with it.

Now the rules allow the student athlete to receive up to $1,700 a year, which is better. The kid can buy himself a shirt or take his girlfriend to the movies. It will give him some pride. He can do what the rest of the students are doing, the students who are getting money from mom and dad. I say, if a kid shows need, let him receive a full Pell Grant. That's only fair.

What can kids receive?

For example, if the Los Angeles Lakers were to play an exhibition game on your campus, it would seem that your players should be given tickets to see the game. But the NCAA says no way; they have to buy the tickets. I don't think that's right.

Most of the rules governing NCAA basketball were conceived in a period when the players were upper- or middle-class kids who were naturally expected to go to college. Their parents usually could afford to give them whatever spending money they needed. The reality of the situation is that basketball has become an inner-city game. Most of the kids playing today cannot get financial help from home. The NCAA must recognize this and establish regulations that are more fair.

An athlete is someone special to the school. That doesn't mean he should be paid or given cars and clothes, but what's wrong with giving him a ticket to a Lakers game or other athletic functions at the school?

Let's keep the human element in coaching. When you coach a major college basketball team, you work the kids so hard and demand so much. A kid has to give you at least four hours a day of total physical and emotional effort. He watches films, goes to practice, does individual work with coaches, listens to scouting reports, and practices on his own. That easily consumes four hours a day.

Then you take the kid on the road and put him in a gym where 18,000 people are screaming at him. That's not easy.

A coach and his players need to be close to one another. If a coach doesn't care about his players as kids, he's not a good coach, and I don't care how much he knows about the X's and O's. And if a coach is close to his players, how can he tell them that they can't call their parents in case of an emergency? How can he not give them a ride home when he is driving right by their place? What's wrong with these things? Who is getting hurt?

A player should be able to go to his coach's house for dinner, and after dinner they should be able to call the kid's mother to say hello and tell everyone that the kid is all right. That's just human decency.

If a kid joins your program and if he works hard, he has made a commitment to you and your university. The NCAA should remember that commitment works both ways. A coach should be allowed to treat his players like human beings. He owes them at least that much.